"In *The Color of Social Security*, Jon Dubin offers a powerful reexamination of one of America's most revered social welfare programs, revealing how race, disability, criminalization, and colonialism have shaped both its design and its outcomes. Through meticulous legal, historical, and policy analysis, the book exposes enduring structural inequities while making a compelling case for strengthening Social Security by confronting its racialized foundations and current disparities."

– Deborah N. Archer, President of the ACLU and Margaret B. Hoppin Professor of Law, New York University School of Law

"At a time when we are repeatedly whitewashing history, this trenchant analysis of racial exclusion and racialized disparate impacts in our quintessential, ninety-year-old, American social safety net – Social Security retirement and disability benefits – shows us how history can pave a road to real, practical, and equitable solutions."

– Nancy Cantor, President and Professor of Psychology, Hunter College, CUNY

"In this meticulously researched and important book, Jon Dubin confronts the inequities built into the structure and policies of our nation's most important public benefit program. Dubin traces the role of race in the design and implementation of Social Security, and the failure of the program's benefits to inure equally to Black recipients and those from other marginalized groups. It is a stunning blueprint for reform of a program whose fate is much in the news, but whose origins, design, and effectiveness are rarely analyzed through the lens of the history of racial discrimination and white supremacy."

– Sherrilyn A. Ifill, Vernon E. Jordan Jr. Esq. Endowed Chair in Civil Rights, Howard Law School

"Jon C. Dubin confronts the racial history and policy choices that have shaped Social Security from its inception to the present. With legal precision and historical depth, *The Color of Social Security* shows how legislative design and administrative practices – shaped by racialized political choices – produced unequal outcomes, and how reform can advance fairness and equal protection under the law."

– Maya Rockeymoore Cummings, founder and CEO of Global Policy Solutions

"Breathtaking in its command and nuanced interpretation of the Social Security Act, this book is indispensable for all concerned with social and racial justice, disability rights, and administrative law. It supplements the work of Dorothy Brown, Dorothy Roberts, Mel Oliver, Thomas Shapiro, Richard Rothstein, Jill Quadagno, and Mehrsa Baradaran."

– Florence Wagman Roisman, William F. Harvey Professor of Law and Chancellor's Professor, Indiana University Robert H. McKinney School of Law

"Professor Dubin's compelling and invaluable analyses of institutional racism baked into the Social Security Act's law, administration, and outcomes within our nation's largest safety-net and adjudication system, illuminate hidden social welfare failings while mapping out reform measures for equitable economic support for all Americans."

– Jonathan M. Stein, former Executive Director and General Counsel at Community Legal Services, Philadelphia

"In *The Color of Social Security*, Jon Dubin delivers a rigorous and unflinching examination of how racial inequities have been embedded within the design, implementation, and administration of Social Security across generations. Through careful legal and historical analysis, he traces the structural decisions that have shaped disparities in retirement and disability benefits alike. Now, ninety years after the New Deal, and at a critical moment for Social Security, Dubin calls us to a necessary reckoning – challenging us not only to acknowledge this uncomfortable history, but to take responsibility for shaping the program's future. When Franklin D. Roosevelt described Social Security as 'a cornerstone in a structure that is by no means complete,' he recognized that the system would require continued building and reform. *The Color of Social Security* offers a vital blueprint for that unfinished work – strengthening Social Security so that it more fully serves the dignity and economic security of all Americans."

– Rebecca Vallas, CEO, National Academy of Social Insurance

"As the federal government continues to ratchet up its assault on the social safety net in this country, and administration officials, courts, and political pundits try desperately to erase the sordid history of racism in the United States, *The Color of Social Security* serves as a powerful and much needed reminder of just how deeply our institutions have been permeated by the legacy of white supremacy."

– Jason D. Williamson, Executive Director, National Center for Law and Economic Justice

THE COLOR OF SOCIAL SECURITY

The Color of Social Security traces the myriad ways and interconnected social systems in which racism has been embedded into American social security programs. Drawing on American history, Jon C. Dubin exposes institutionalized processes undermining racially equitable receipt of retirement and disability benefits. Examples include the 1935 Social Security Act, which excluded Black agricultural and domestic workers in order to protect the postbellum Southern racial economic and political order; the 1972 Supplemental Security Income program's exclusion of persons of color in the US territories, with genesis in 125 years of racialized colonial domination; 1980s criminal justice system restrictions; systemic racial bias in disability decisions in the 1990s; disability eligibility obstacles from "race-norming" in the 2000s; and the misevaluation of Black claimants with sickle cell disease under Social Security Administration regulations since 2015. While exploring these histories, Dubin offers concrete solutions to address racial inequity and create a more equitable future.

Jon C. Dubin is the award-winning author of multiple books and articles on social security law and policy and an elected member of the National Academy of Social Insurance. As a law professor, he has created and/or taught courses on poverty, race and economic justice, social security law, civil rights law, administrative law, constitutional law, and the Economic Justice Clinic. As a lawyer and clinical supervisor, he has worked on several precedent-setting cases in social security and civil rights law and his writings have been cited by the US Supreme Court.

The Color of Social Security

RACE, RETIREMENT, DISABILITY, AND DISPARITY

JON C. DUBIN
Rutgers University

CAMBRIDGE
UNIVERSITY PRESS

CAMBRIDGE
UNIVERSITY PRESS

Shaftesbury Road, Cambridge CB2 8EA, United Kingdom

One Liberty Plaza, 20th Floor, New York, NY 10006, USA

477 Williamstown Road, Port Melbourne, VIC 3207, Australia

314–321, 3rd Floor, Plot 3, Splendor Forum, Jasola District Centre, New Delhi – 110025, India

Cambridge University Press is part of Cambridge University Press & Assessment, a department of the University of Cambridge.

We share the University's mission to contribute to society through the pursuit of education, learning and research at the highest international levels of excellence.

www.cambridge.org
Information on this title: www.cambridge.org/9781009858991
DOI: 10.1017/9781009859004

When citing this work, please include a reference to the DOI 10.1017/9781009859004

First published 2026

Cover image: richcano / E+ / Getty Images

A catalogue record for this publication is available from the British Library

Library of Congress Cataloging-in-Publication Data
NAMES: Dubin, Jon C. author
TITLE: The color of social security : race, retirement, disability, and disparity / Jon C. Dubin, Rutgers University.
DESCRIPTION: New York : Cambridge University Press, 2026. | Includes bibliographical references and index.
IDENTIFIERS: LCCN 2026015477 | ISBN 9781009858991 hardback | ISBN 9781009859004 ebook
SUBJECTS: LCSH: Race discrimination – Law and legislation – United States | Equality before the law – United States | Social security – Law and legislation – United States
CLASSIFICATION: LCC KF4755 .D83 2026
LC record available at https://lccn.loc.gov/2026015477

ISBN 978-1-009-85899-1 Hardback
ISBN 978-1-009-85902-8 Paperback

Contents

Figures

Acknowledgments

I am fortunate to have had a career as a lawyer, teacher, and scholar working on, writing, and teaching about race, poverty, injustice, and inequality from a variety of vantage points. This has included teaching classes in social security law; poverty, race, and economic justice; civil rights law; and welfare law; and running a law school free clinic supervising and teaching clinical law students representing low-income, mostly Black or Brown social security claimants in Newark and northern New Jersey at Rutgers Law School and earlier in San Antonio and south Texas while I was at St. Mary's Law School. I have also worked as a staff attorney in the public benefits unit and later as Litigation Director at a neighborhood legal aid office in Harlem in New York City, and as a staff attorney for the NAACP Legal Defense and Educational Fund, Inc., and the American Civil Liberties Union, working on civil rights cases around the United States.

This book is the culmination of several decades of these experiences and the intersection of insights from immersion in the law and policy of the social security system, including the struggles of real people seeking sustenance through it, and exploration of and confrontation with racial injustice working in low-income Black and Brown communities seeking justice and dignity across multiple systems. The book, and more specifically Chapters 1 and 4, build on writings I first introduced two years ago in the article *The Color of Social Security: Race and Unequal Protection in the Crown Jewel of the American Welfare State*, 35 Stan. L. & Pol'y Rev. 104 (2024). I thank my partner, Vivienne Unsoon Kahng, for her careful review of the entirety of that article, her ideas and perspective as an administrative adjudicative decisionmaker, and her support and encouragement throughout the writing of this book. I am also grateful to my many current and former colleagues at Rutgers who have reviewed parts of the book in draft (or reviewed the earlier law review article) and who helped shape the book's content and structure, including Professors Bernard Bell, Laura Cohen, Rachel Godsil, Carlos Gonzalez, Tanya Hernandez (now at Fordham University), Alexis Karteron (now at New York University), David Lopez (now at Arizona State University), Randi Mandelbaum, David Noll, David Troutt, and Rose Cuison-Villazor.

This book benefited significantly from the comments and suggestions of the anonymous peer reviewers selected by Cambridge University Press. Rutgers law students Barbara Ferreira Gomes Cabral (2024–26) and Saturday Zammit (2023–25) provided excellent, tireless, and essential research assistance over a three-year period on the book. I am particularly grateful to University of North Carolina Law School Dean and Professor Emeritus, and Poverty and Race Research Action Council co-founder and long-time board member, Jack Boger and Penn State-Dickinson Law School Professor Emeritus Bob Rains for their careful reviews of the book in draft and their many comments and suggestions. I also thank a series of nationally renowned SSI and social security disability program litigators and legal experts from the nonprofit legal services and public benefits advocacy community, especially the former Executive Director and General Counsel of Community Legal Services (CLS) of Philadelphia, Jonathan Stein, and, in addition, CLS Supervising Attorneys Richard Weishaupt and Chi-Ser Tran, Urban Justice Center of New York City Litigation Supervisor Ann Biddle, and Empire Justice Center of New York State Managing Attorney Emilia Sicilia, for their reviews of sections of the book and many helpful suggestions and provision of materials. This group of disability program experts from the legal services community who contributed to the disability program chapters in this book also, of course, includes Legal Services of New Jersey Chief Section Counsel for Disability Rights Kevin Liebkemann both for several suggestions and provision of materials for the book and for filling in for me and serving as Acting Director of the Rutgers Economic Justice and Public Benefits Clinic during a period of significant writing and finalization of the book in the fall semester of 2025. This book was supported by research grants from the Rutgers Summer Research Fund.

Finally, I am especially thankful for the guidance, research suggestions, hours of discussions, and comments from review of portions of the book in draft by Dr. Leslie Dubin Kerr from Mount Sinai Hospital in East Harlem in New York City. She led me to the issues of race-norming and race-correction in clinical care support tools and algorithms in Chapter 6 and several issues in Chapter 5, including reinforcement of the persistence of erroneous and damaging concepts of "biological race" in present medical practice and medical school teaching and the misevaluation of sickle cell disease, and their potential racially adverse impact on social security disability benefits eligibility. Dr. Kerr is not only a brilliant physician, clinician, and medical school professor but a lifelong inspiration and role model and the most generous sibling one could hope for in life.

Introduction

The year of this book's writing marks the ninetieth anniversary of the Social Security Act of 1935. The Act created America's largest social welfare cash benefit income security programs, eventually affecting over 96 percent of all Americans.[1] They provide a lifeline for many, taking more Americans out of poverty than any other programs.[2] These programs were the "cornerstone" or "crown jewel" of President Franklin Delano Roosevelt's (FDR's) New Deal; they were intended to provide a foundation for a baseline of economic rights and income security commencing at a time when material human suffering was at its zenith during the country's greatest depression.[3]

FDR addressed Congress on the proposed Social Security Act of 1935 in the winter of that year. He described the bill's "main objectives" as protecting "the security of the men, women, and children of the Nation against certain hazards and vicissitudes of life" and providing a "more equitable … means" for addressing "the consequence of economic insecurity."[4]

This book analyzes and examines myriad ways in which the Act and its cash assistance programs have fallen short in delivering on this promise of equitable economic security for African Americans and other historically subordinated and underserved communities of color.[5]

Among the various forms of government social welfare benefit programs established by the Social Security Act and its amendments and administered by the Social Security Administration (SSA), Social Security is a social insurance program. It is also known as Old Age, Survivors, and Disability Insurance (OASDI). It is financed from separate trust funds for the Disability Insurance (DI) and the Old Age and Survivors' Insurance (OASI) programs and supported by payroll taxes on the earnings of insured workers. Premiums in the form of Federal Insurance Contribution Act (FICA) taxes are automatically withheld from most workers' paychecks, enabling workers and certain family members to receive monthly benefits if the worker retires, dies, or becomes disabled.[6]

Both employees and employers pay FICA taxes of 6.2 percent on earnings up to a cap of $184,500 in 2026.[7] FDR is reputed to have characterized the social security program as politically untouchable because of its contributory nature based on taxes from earnings; he famously declared: "with those taxes in there, no damn politician can ever scrap my social security program."[8] SSA also operates a means-tested income support program for low-income disabled and elderly persons titled the Supplemental Security Income (SSI) program, which is funded from general revenue and provides benefits mostly for those lacking insurance coverage for significant OASDI entitlement.[9]

The Social Security Act's history reflects an initial reluctance to address the needs of persons with disabilities. Although FDR sought to address many of the significant contributors to unemployment and poverty during the Great Depression through the original Social Security Act of 1935, that initial enactment included only the old age provisions of the current OASDI program. The survivors' benefits program for dependents of deceased insured workers was added shortly thereafter in 1939.[10] No benefits based on disability were included in the New Deal-era legislation.

The obvious omission of the disability category from the initial Act was due in part to Congress and the administration's "inability to determine whether disability benefits should be distributed in the form of 'welfare' – that is, as means-tested public assistance, as social insurance benefits, or as both."[11] The omission was also due to a second concern that the definition of "disability" would be too subjective and malleable and could not be sufficiently circumscribed to restrain program costs within predictable and manageable limits.[12]

In the 1950s, Congress addressed the first concern by adding disability categories to both the joint federal–state public assistance (or "welfare") program, and then, a few years later, to the federal social insurance program.[13] Congress accomplished the former through amendments to the Social Security Act in 1950, which added the joint federal–state Aid to the Permanently and Totally Disabled (APTD) welfare program.[14] Congress then replaced the APTD program with the Supplemental Security Income (SSI) program through the Social Security Amendments of 1972, providing means-tested benefits for adults and children with disabilities and for the elderly. Next, Congress transferred the responsibility for welfare benefits for aged, blind, and disabled persons from a joint state-federal, locally controlled, scheme consolidating APTD with programs from Titles I (Old Age) and X (Blindness) of the original Social Security Act of 1935 to a nationally uniform program administered by the federal Social Security Administration. Congress had added the disability insurance, social insurance program – the DI in OASDI – in 1956.[15]

This book's focus is on the role of race in the design, application, and impact of certain provisions of the ongoing cash benefit programs, OASDI and SSI, under the Social Security Act. It examines the law and judicial interpretations of these provisions, their policy implications and soundness, and the impact of the SSA's adjudicative system in creating and perpetuating racial inequity. These programs utilize the same SSA adjudication system for resolving claims and the same statutory definition of disability in their respective disability components and are frequently analyzed together.[16] Chapter 1 includes a secondary and much shorter examination of the role of race in the origins of the 1935 Act's means-tested cash benefits public assistance benefits programs to inform the Act's broader racialized context. The book does not include analysis of racial disparities in the design or application of the Act's health benefit (Medicaid and Medicare) programs or the temporary benefits for unemployed, "ready, willing, and able" workers through the Act's Unemployment Insurance Compensation Program.

As is common in many areas of administrative law and policy as well as the study of government bureaucracy, scholars who focus on Social Security law and administration and the Social Security benefit programs often examine process, procedure and the "technocratic language of government agency action."[17] They also explore bureaucratic functioning or competing theories and explanations for agency dysfunction,[18] or the balancing of efficiency, consistency, and process fairness in agency administration.[19] Substantive Social Security law is sometimes perceived as tedious or impenetrable in interpretation, and wonky in policy, leading courts to observe that "[t]he Social Security Act is among the most intricate ever drafted by Congress [with a] Byzantine construction [which] makes the Act 'almost unintelligible to the uninitiated.'"[20]

In addition to these features, this book argues that despite detached, technocratic overtones, basic features of the Social Security program, its history, distributional outcomes, and operational reality cannot be properly understood without examining the history of racism, white supremacy and systemic discrimination in the US. To illustrate this point, this book deconstructs the Act's principal cash benefits programs' history, scope, law, policy, and adjudicative system through the lens of race. Admittedly, this writing comes at a time when racially distributional deficiencies of the Social Security programs can easily be overshadowed by unprecedented existential threats to both the social security programs and to the pursuit of racial justice more broadly through the Make America Great Again (MAGA) agenda of the second Trump administration and MAGA-leaning Republican majorities in both houses of Congress.

During this book's writing, the administration's makeshift Department of Government Efficiency (DOGE) fired or pressured out thousands of SSA staffers and 140 senior SSA executives.[21] It has also substantially diminished SSA services to the public (by, for example, discontinuing phone service) and placed all putative social security beneficiaries in jeopardy by providing DOGE's staff with access to Social Security cardholders' available private and personal work, medical, and other information.[22] A member of the bipartisan Social Security Advisory Board and President of Social Security Works, Nancy Altman, has described the Trump administration and DOGE's actions as "*The Greatest Threat to Social Security in Its 90-Year History*."[23] By the end of 2025, the *Washington Post* characterized the Trump administration's actions on the SSA – "the sprawling federal agency that delivers retirement, disability and survivor benefits to 74 million Americans" – as a "hostile takeover" which concluded the 2025 calendar year "in turmoil."[24] The *Washington Post*'s examination revealed that the SSA's "diminished workforce has struggled to respond to up to 6 million pending cases in its processing centers and 12 million transactions in its field offices – record backlogs that have delayed basic services to millions of customers, according to internal agency documents and dozens of interviews."[25]

The Trump administration and DOGE have also made the Social Security Insurance program more politically vulnerable to assaults on its integrity or significant cut backs by labelling it a "ponzi scheme" and a program riddled with "massive fraud," alleging at various times that "as high as 40%" of all callers to social security phone lines have been placed by alleged "scammers."[26] The president has amplified the social security fraud narrative with the assertion of "shocking levels of incompetence and probable fraud in the Social Security program" and the false claim that "millions of senior citizens over age 100 – including some he maintained were older than 160 – were collecting Social Security checks."[27] In addition, the administration's new signature legislation, through the absurdly named One Big Beautiful Bill Act (OBBBA) of 2025,[28] provided enormous tax cuts for the wealthy and massive reductions in funding to essential Medicaid, Affordable Care Act, Supplemental Nutrition Assistance (SNAP, formerly food stamps), and other social welfare-based programs. These cuts place further direct and indirect pressure on the social security insurance programs at a time when further supports are needed to avert impending trust fund insolvency and the inability to pay full benefits perhaps as early as 2032.[29]

At the same time, the administration has launched a war on programs designed to address and ameliorate the country's legacy of structural racial discrimination stemming from slavery, Jim Crow exclusion, racialized economic exploitation and segregation, redlining, and from pervasive racial discrimination in housing, employment, voting, education, and credit, with resulting generational disparities in wealth, income, and opportunity. The administration has issued a series of Executive Orders prohibiting all efforts at racial diversity, equity, and inclusion (DEI) by programs and entities supported by federal funds and taking "all appropriate actions" to achieve the same result in the private sector.[30] It has also directed the Department of Justice (DOJ) to pursue anti-DEI legal and law enforcement actions more broadly.[31] The DOJ has since abandoned efforts at traditional civil rights enforcement actions on behalf of Black and historically subordinated groups and communities and has instead focused its resources on protecting and advancing the position of historically dominant white Americans.[32]

The administration has also issued an Executive Order calling for removing accounts of historical events that might cast the country's "founding principles and historical milestones in a negative light," such as by portraying historical circumstances as "inherently racist, sexist, oppressive, or otherwise irredeemably flawed."[33] This action has even led to the modification and sanitizing of Black history and the histories of other marginalized groups as well as the removal of books describing Black achievements from federal and military libraries and references in federal agency websites detailing the accomplishments of various leaders and historical figures from African American and other communities of color.[34]

This follows recent similar actions in Republican-led states.[35] The administration's actions have also extended to the removal of various monuments, mementos, and photographs and renaming of federal buildings, military bases, and naval ships previously celebrating nonwhite persons and accomplishments, and the restoration of the names of military bases previously named after confederate soldiers and of related confederate monuments.[36] In late 2025, the National Park Service canceled free national park admission on the holidays of Martin Luther King Jr.'s birthday and Juneteenth, and extended free admission instead on President Trump's birthday, "as part of a broader effort by the White House to erase or play down Black history at government sites."[37]

Notwithstanding the regressive currents of this temporal moment, American democracy ultimately requires a deeper understanding both of our racialized history and its ongoing, adverse distributional legacies embodied in law and policy and engrained in American life. Along those lines, efforts to chill or even erase African American history, including legal history, remain a serious impediment to progress toward a true multiracial democracy.[38] While numerous aspects of this country's social and legal history of race have been carefully explored in other areas, such as housing, education, criminal justice, employment, voting, health care, banking, infrastructure, child protective and foster care system, and even the tax system, this book seeks to supply a similar focus on the legal and social history of the social security cash benefit programs and their present operation and impacts.[39] To do so requires exploration of the distributional inequities within the enormous social security benefit programs even as these programs face unprecedented challenges. Indeed, awareness of inequities may be most important in devising ways to strengthen and protect social security program systems to vindicate the programs' goals of enhancing economic security for all in times of the greatest threats to program sustainability and integrity.

This book's principal demographic focus is the Black or African American community, acknowledging that this nation in the main singled out Blacks/African Americans for enslavement and entrenched racial subordination and segregation by law and practice with profound and lingering consequences and through structural discrimination which persists through the present.[40] I use the terms Black and African American interchangeably and quote historical material referencing the terms "negro" or "colored" in historical context. The book also explores programmatic impacts in similarly historically subordinated and disproportionately impoverished communities of color where applicable and where research and/or empirical material support comparable analysis.[41] For example, the analysis in Chapter 4 focuses on the role of race in a major Social Security Act benefits program for persons with disabilities and the elderly – the SSI program – and equal protection issues in excluding certain groups from SSI coverage, residents of Puerto Rico, Virgin Islands, Guam and American Samoa who are part of more varied, census self-identified largely non-white communities – that is, Latino/a/Hispanic/Brown; Black/African American; mixed-race; Asian American; Native Hawaiian; and other Pacific Islander – in those island territories.

This writing expressly acknowledges and celebrates the Social Security benefit programs and their particular importance to African American and other historically subordinated and disproportionately impoverished communities of color. Social security programs are essential in such communities owing to several factors: well-documented substantial disparities in generational wealth and savings;[42] lesser access to jobs generating pension and retirement income; the consequences of historic and systemic discrimination in the health care system; lesser access to quality health care and health insurance coverage; lower income levels; the consequences of racialized mass incarceration; lesser formal educational attainment; greater dependence on employment involving arduous physical labor and unskilled low wage work; and systemic discrimination in the labor market including in the lower wage, lower skill job market applicable for most social security disability claimants and a disproportionate share of other social security beneficiaries of color.[43] These programs have taken countless families of color out of poverty and helped lessen the toll of financial suffering and hardship of many through its provisions.

This writing acknowledges the views of some longtime progressive scholars and advocates of the Social Security programs who have helped safeguard the programs from evisceration over the years but have also discouraged social security advocates who are also race and gender justice advocates or scholars from turning a critical race or gender lens on social security for fear of fueling conservative and present-day Trumpian program-eviscerating tendencies.[44] It is this book's position that the critically important and societally transformative social security programs discussed herein should be continued and bolstered. But, as with many of society's important institutions, they can be strengthened and further solidified and supported with greater acknowledgment of the ways in which they may underserve historically subordinated segments of the population. Such acknowledgment can foster greater resolve and focus to address and mitigate identified inequities.

Indeed, the SSA's own issuance of its 2022 Equity Action Plan and 2023 Update to its Equity Action Plan reflect the agency's acknowledgment of the same.[45] More specifically, in soliciting further stakeholder engagement and feedback on the SSA's 2022 Equity Action Plan, the SSA's then Acting Commissioner, Kilolo Kijakazi, declared: "My leadership team and I will discuss our comprehensive approach to advancing equity for people who have been historically underserved, marginalized, and adversely affected by persistent poverty and inequality," and "[d]iscussion topics will include: *Identifying inequities in our programs and services*."[46] This book is predicated upon the assumption of an eventual return to a political climate in which the SSA's quite recent Equity Action plans can be pursued and implemented, and in which it endeavors to identify specific areas for action consistent with the spirit of those general plans and the SSA Acting Commissioner's stated focus and requested engagement.

This book explores through historical inquiry, policy, legislative and legal analysis, and interdisciplinary examination of medical and scientific literature the manner in which the Social Security programs' origins, evolution, scope, adjudicative system, operations, interactions with other social systems, and potential future plans produce or portend significant racially disparate impacts. It assesses how these developments limit attainment of the Act's lofty objectives and undermine equitable or equal economic protection against financial hardship and insecurity extended to white Americans.

Whereas other social security program-centered books and writings usually focus on either the retirement/old age programs or the disability programs, this book endeavors to be one of the first to examine both and include extended analysis of the disability programs and race. Disability program usage steadily increased and crested owing to the recession in 2008 and demographic factors such as the aging of the baby boom generation, which resulted in people from this age group attaining advantaged positions for disability eligibility under a statutory standard that includes age as a factor.[47] While the same demographic factors have also expanded usage of the social security old age programs, their eligibility standards and processes are largely fixed and far less subject to legal dispute and contention beyond recurrent policy suggestions to continue to add years to the retirement age category to limit benefit outlays.

Moreover, while not nearly as large in scope as the social security old age/retirement programs, the social security disability programs provide benefits to over 13 million persons at present.[48] Because disability applications, as opposed to those seeking old age/retirement or survivors benefits, are usually carefully examined and contested, an enormous federal bureaucracy has been created to address disability claims, and a significant portion of the federal courts' docket is attributable to disability program appeals.[49] The SSA's adjudication system for evaluating disability claims has been touted as the "Mount Everest of bureaucratic structures,"[50] stemming from the "largest adjudicative agency in the western world."[51] Indeed, "there are more SSA Administrative Law Judges (ALJs) adjudicating Social Security Disability Insurance (SSDI) and SSI disability administrative hearings and more such cases than there are judges deciding and presiding over the smaller quantum of all civil and criminal cases and trials in all of the federal courts of the United States."[52]

The SSA system contains a four-stage adjudication process, with three stages in addition to an evidentiary hearing stage; it processes over 2 million new claims and issues over 3.4 million decisions at the various stages each year.[53] Congress has devoted increasing attention to the complex and often misunderstood disability eligibility standards and disability programs' elaborate adjudicative processes, and on proposals for social security disability reform.[54] The disability benefit programs have also received significant public media attention and often largely negative scrutiny in relatively recent years with extended series and chronicles in National Public Radio, the *Wall Street Journal*, and the *Washington Post*.[55]

As the total reserves in social security trust funds have declined and are fast approaching a level of insufficiency incapable of supporting full scheduled benefits payments (now predicted in 2033 and perhaps as early as 2032),[56] proposals to strengthen short term and longer term trust fund solvency are sometimes coupled with calls for restricting the disability standard and process, and cutting disability benefits.[57] Congress has intermittently and more broadly labelled impending "entitlement reform," especially reductions in public benefits for working class and lower-income Americans, including social security reform through benefit cuts,[58] as an even greater priority after budgetary pressures generated from the passage of the large tax cuts and attendant substantially expanded budget deficits. This has included the fallout from the Tax Cuts and Jobs Act of 2017 and undoubtedly what can be anticipated from the even more drastic tax cuts adopted and the resulting deficit impacts created by the second Trump administration's signature 2025 OBBBA legislation. Indeed, at the tail end of this book's writing, news accounts referenced the administration's not yet publicly disclosed initial, albeit subsequently suspended, plans to issue regulations that would substantially restrict disability eligibility requirements and reduce the number of SSA disability program recipients by 20 percent.[59]

As a roadmap for the book: The initial chapter illustrates the importance of race in examining the Act's structure and New Deal origins. Both Chapters 1 and 4 deconstruct the Act's benefits programs' history through the lens of race and equal protection doctrine as applied to two major legislative provisions in the Act's benefit programs, disproportionately excluding persons of color from program coverage. These statutory exclusions largely involve different Social Security cash-benefit programs, enacted in different time periods, involving different exclusionary bases, and affecting different communities of color. Yet they arise from a common thread of the American experience emanating from racism and white supremacy and abetted through political disenfranchisement of the excluded communities of color.

Chapter 1 specifically examines racial inequity in the Social Security Old Age/Retirement Insurance program and focuses largely on the original 1935 SSA's exclusion of disproportionately Black agricultural and domestic workers from coverage. It directly challenges and critiques the conclusion reached relatively recently by the SSA public historian, Larry DeWitt, that race played no meaningful role in the social insurance program exclusion's adoption and resulting impacts on African Americans and similarly situated persons of color. It also explores, in less depth, discrimination facilitated through local administration of the means-tested welfare programs, and contemporaneous and intertwined racially infused legislative history of the respective means-tested and social insurance old age programs enacted in Titles I and II of the 1935 Act. It includes analysis of the influence of southern legislators' efforts to preserve the postbellum plantation and sharecropping system's exploitation of Black farmworkers on each program's design.

It also seeks to reconcile conflicting scholarly positions on the presence and decisiveness of racial and nonracial justifications for the statutory exclusions by examining the Act's history through the lens of equal protection doctrine to inform further the inquiry into the salience of race in the exclusion's enactment in situations where multiple legislative motives are present.

Chapter 2 explores contemporary racial inequity facing elderly Social Security beneficiaries. It includes examination of structural discrimination in the labor market and in many other core aspects of American life (i.e., housing, education, credit/banking, health care) contributing to disparately lower levels of social security-based earnings upon which benefit levels are based, and to greater financial precarity in retirement. It concludes by providing recommendations of potential remedies and mitigations for the disproportionately significantly lower and often below-poverty-line benefit levels received by elderly Black and Brown social security program beneficiaries and the major threats of additional inequities from regressive benefit cuts owing to impending social security trust fund insolvency in 2032–33.

Chapter 3 analyzes Social Security legislation from the 1980s through 2009, adding various criminal justice system-involved restrictions on benefit receipt in both the Social Security old age/retirement insurance and disability insurance programs. It examines the phenomena of American mass incarceration and the collateral consequences of system involvement on social security benefit receipt. This includes the damaging and socially counterproductive impacts on Black and Latino/a individuals, families and communities from these benefit restrictions owing to the racially disparate consequences of overcriminalization and mass incarceration policies from the 1980s through the 2000s. It explores the policy justifications for these restrictions, initially adopted hastily in 1980 based on the serial killer "Son of Sam's" receipt of benefits while in prison, including the public policy rationales for a law suspending OASDI benefits to most incarcerated beneficiaries and the consistency of those rationales with core principles of social insurance benefits under the Act (as opposed to the Act's means-tested subsistence benefit programs).

It further examines the consistency of these restrictions in the old age/retirement insurance program, with modern social conceptions of retirement benefits as a resource or catalyst for facilitating a transition into a new phase of life and not exclusively as bare subsistence for persons too old to function in the workplace in the years shortly before death (which was perhaps the original conception of the retirement program's goals at the Act's passage ninety years ago). This chapter also includes analysis of another Social Security Act provision, permanently excluding consideration of impairments arising in connection with commission of a felony in the disability evaluation process in SSDI cases. It explores arbitrary, vague, and overbroad aspects of this law as well as its particularly racially disparate potential application to Black and Brown SSDI claimants not only owing to racialized policing and mass incarceration but likely also to racially disproportionate imposition of disabling impairment-producing injuries from police misconduct and brutality. The chapter concludes by offering arguments for repeal, or alternatively reform, of each of these two criminal justice systems-based social security benefit-restricting statutory provisions.

Chapter 4 is the only chapter focused principally on inequity in the SSA's means-tested SSI program, providing cash benefits for low-income adults and children with disabilities and low-income elderly persons. It explores the statutory exclusion from the SSI program of residents from the principal US territories (i.e., Puerto Rico, Virgin Islands, Guam, and American Samoa) who are overwhelmingly Latino/a/Brown, Black, mixed-race, and/or Asian American, Native Hawaiian, and other Pacific Islander. This chapter includes a critical evaluation of the application of equal protection doctrine in the US Supreme Court's 2022 decision in *U.S. v. Vaello Madero*.[60] It also examines the lingering shadow of the overtly racist yet still operative (not yet overruled) *Insular Cases* decided in the early twentieth century hovering over this controversy. This was a series of cases launching and reinforcing a separate and unequal regime of rights and benefits for territory residents through the construct of indefinite "unincorporated" territory status based on assumptions even conservative Justice Neil Gorsuch has characterized as grounded in "ugly racial stereotypes," "bigotry," and the "theories of social Darwinists."[61] The chapter concludes by arguing for congressional reversal of the SSI territorial exclusion and chronicles a recent, albeit narrowly unsuccessful, legislative attempt after *Vaello-Madero* to do so.

Chapters 5 and 6 focus on the SSDI and SSI disability programs, apart from their respective old age components. Chapter 5 first contextualizes these Social Security Act disability programs (SSDI and SSID) and their statutory elements and processes, and then explores the social construction of disability thereunder. It also examines the socially constructed, nonbiological concept of race, as differentiated from class, and also the intersectionality of race and disability, to provide a theoretical and substantive framework for Chapter 5's examination of bias in pain and symptomology assessments in social security disability adjudication. It also examines the relevance of racial inequity in the health care system on social security disability assessments, medical evidence and decision-making, including from explicit and implicit bias in medical care, treatment and assessments, and from the impact of racially disparate access to quality health care, health insurance, treating physicians, and specialist care.

Chapter 5 commences with examination of racial disparities in SSA disability determinations underscored by a much-discussed, extensive 1992 US General Accounting Office (GAO) study of the topic documenting unexplained racial disparities, followed by other GAO reports and other studies revealing additional racial disparities in aspects of SSA disability adjudication. It explores possible causes of these disparities, starting with the systematic misevaluation, mistreatment, and undertreatment of Black patients' pain and subjective symptomology, including psychiatric conditions, by doctors, therapists, and other treatment professionals in health care. It also examines the racial impact of misevaluation of claimants with sickle cell disease (SCD), a unique, pain-producing condition disproportionately afflicting African Americans. The SCD section recommends that the SSA adopt

SCD criteria for automatic medical disability supported by medical science and the expert hematological and SCD treatment specialist community, and replace its present medically unsupported and racially disadvantaging regulatory criteria.

This chapter then delves more broadly into issues of racially disparate decision-making in all disability adjudication by the SSA's ALJs, including through biased assessments of pain and symptomology. This includes analysis of the compounded impact or "double whammy" of explicit and implicit bias by medical and health care professionals followed by comparable bias by adjudicators in the social security system. It includes analysis of all of the significant judicial decisions addressing ALJ bias in disability adjudications and the shortcomings of SSA administrative processes for policing bias. The chapter concludes with a series of remedial recommendations for monitoring and ameliorating racial bias and racially disparate decision-making in disability adjudications.

Chapter 6 continues the analysis of racial inequity in health care assessments and treatment leading to further inequity in SSA disability decision-making, by examining the practice by medical and health care professionals of "race-norming" or "race correction." Race-norming or correction involves the insertion of race into medical clinical decision support tools and diagnostic algorithms that "adjust or correct their outputs on the basis of a patient's race or ethnicity" predicated on fallacious principles of "biological race." Race-normed or "corrected" outputs often understate the severity of Black and other minority patients' conditions or require greater demonstration of illness to receive treatment for a range of severe and sometimes life-threatening conditions. As a result, they also inequitably, illegally, and unconstitutionally raise the bar on demonstration of disabling impairment severity for Black claimants and other claimants of color subject to race-norming. This chapter ends with recommendations for eradicating race-norming in SSA adjudication including strengthening a recent, albeit insufficient, 2022 internal SSA guideline precluding use of a race-normed kidney function clinical decision support tool in disability adjudications and expanding that guideline to commonly race-normed tools in other areas such as pulmonary function tests, and all other race-normed tools and algorithms.

1

The Social Security Act in Racial and Historical Context

The Agricultural and Domestic Worker Exclusion in the Old Age/Retirement Program

The allegations of racial bias in the founding of the Social Security program, based on the coverage exclusions, do not hold up under detailed scrutiny.[1]

— Larry DeWitt, Social Security Administration (SSA) Public Historian, SSA Office of Publications and Logistics Management, 2010

This chapter presents an alternative viewpoint from that prominently displayed on the website of the SSA since 2010 and expressed in the quotation from DeWitt.

1.1 THE ROLE OF RACE IN NEW DEAL REMEDIAL LEGISLATION

From its inception in 1935, the Social Security Act's social insurance program – the centerpiece of President Franklin D. Roosevelt's "New Deal" – embedded racial inequity in the Act. The Act excluded agricultural and domestic workers from coverage which served on the surface as a "race-neutral proxy"[2] for the preclusion of 65 percent of America's Black worker population from coverage under the Social Security old age social insurance benefits program.[3]

The reasons for this exclusion and the resulting disparate racial impact were numerous and are vigorously debated to this day.[4] Scholars who reject the significance of racial considerations principally point to factors such as the exclusion provision's origin as an amendment from Treasury Secretary Tom Morgenthau, his articulation of administrative and functional concerns with collecting Social Security taxes in these occupational categories, and the experience in some countries that included these occupational categories in their social security or contributory social insurance systems but did so in phases. They also point to the existence of other exclusions in the 1935 Act lacking disparate impacts on African Americans. They further note that Southern legislators devoted their most racist rhetoric in debates on the Social Security Act to the Act's old age public assistance program (Title I) and not its old age social insurance program (Title II) and the exclusions therein. They also claim a diversity of opinion within the Southern congressional caucus on racial considerations and the importance of limiting benefit receipt to Black workers under the Act.[5] Some also suggest that the passage of inclusion amendments to the Act in the 1950s, reversing those occupational exclusions in Title II in a period of comparable continuing overt and pervasive racial discrimination in American society as in 1935, further supports the absence of meaningful racialized considerations behind the 1935 exclusions.[6]

Scholars who emphasize the primacy of racial considerations highlight factors such as the blatantly racialized and exploitative rhetoric of Southern legislators in debates on the Act and their candid expression of a need to protect the postbellum Southern plantation agricultural economy and labor availability by withholding old age pensions and financial support from Black sharecroppers and farmworkers at least in the Act's Title I welfare provisions. They also point to Congress's unquestioned knowledge and awareness of the substantial disparate impact on Black workers of the exclusion amendment as well as its disregard of Black community leaders' advocacy against exclusion in congressional testimony. Other scholars point to the judgment of the Act's principal drafters in FDR's Committee on Economic Security who initially underscored the importance of including agricultural and domestic workers in the social insurance program's provisions and therefore their deliberate decision to include these occupational categories in the legislation's initial version. Some also de-emphasize or challenge the seriousness or presumed unmanageability of administrative obstacles to coverage of these worker categories. They reference other countries' experiences in surmounting the suggested occupational category obstacles in comparable social insurance legislation prior to the Social Security Act and the ability of Congress and the FDR's administration to do so as well through the Act's inclusion amendments in the 1950s.[7] Some also point to racially tinged rhetoric in opposition to the 1954 inclusion amendment providing the broadest reversals of the occupational exclusions to Title II of the 1935 Act, from members of the same Southern legislative block who had offered racialized opposition to antidiscrimination provisions in Title I of the 1935 Act and who supported the original 1935 occupational exclusions in Title II, and then later vigorously opposed the landmark civil rights legislation of the 1960s.

This chapter asserts that the presence of motives and considerations identified by each camp are not necessarily inaccurate, contradictory, or mutually exclusive. It analyzes these Social Security Act exclusions through the body of jurisprudence developed over forty-five years ago on "mixed" or "multiple motive" equal protection analysis of governmental legislation or action. This body of equal protection doctrine stresses that the presence of racial considerations or motives has special burden-shifting salience and that the identification of other, legitimate, nonracial considerations behind the same legislation or action is not dispositive on an Act's "intent." In this context, the presence of some legitimate, nonracial considerations does not demonstrably vitiate the Act's racially discriminatory taint. It also concludes that, regardless of ultimate potential equal protection liability, the clearly foreseen and regrettably experienced racially disparate impact of the Social Security Act exclusions is manifest and has produced generationally deleterious consequences for African Americans.

Viewed in broader context with much of the New Deal's otherwise progressive, remedial social welfare legislation, these exclusions were consistent with FDR's general strategy of appeasement. FDR viewed compromise as the price of passage.[8] He feared that opposition by powerful Southern legislators would jeopardize these programs' valuable attributes if he was to address racial inequity in the proposed programs or otherwise attempt to pursue progress on the American "race problem."[9] At the time, in the 1930s, the majority of African Americans lived in the South and in rural impoverished areas and worked mostly in unskilled agricultural or domestic employment.[10] The Southern antebellum mode of production, which depended heavily on coerced labor under slavery, was reestablished postbellum "under a system of sharecropping, which guaranteed planters great control of a subservient, primarily Black labor force."[11] The sharecropping system operated pervasively through the 1940s.[12]

At the same time, representatives from the Jim Crow South dominated Congress and held a majority of committee chairmanships and other leadership positions in every New Deal Congress.[13] In attempting to justify his nonsupport of anti-lynching legislation in the 1930s, FDR explained to National Association for the Advancement of Colored People (NAACP) Executive Secretary Walter White:

> I've got to get legislation passed by Congress to save America. The Southerners by reason of the seniority rule in Congress are chairmen or occupy strategic places on most of the Senate and House committees. If I come out for the anti-lynching bill now, they will block every bill I ask Congress to pass to keep America from collapsing. I just can't take that risk.[14]

At the time, lynchings were not only used to instill terror but also often conducted near the time for elections in order to suppress the Black vote.[15] FDR also backed off support of legislation to abolish the poll tax which had been used as a device to further disenfranchise Black voters.[16]

Accordingly, in much of the remedial social welfare legislation that followed, efforts to overcome racial discrimination in the emerging programs were rejected, and racial inequity was reinforced in the legislation ultimately enacted. For example, in the housing area, the National Housing Act of 1934 created the Federal Housing Administration to supply mortgage insurance to enable working-class and low-, moderate-, and middle-income families to access low- or no-down-payment mortgages.[17] However, in so doing, the Federal Housing Administration (along with the Veterans Administration, in its comparable program for veterans) reinforced racial residential segregation and substantially restricted Black homeownership through an underwriting manual that expressly warned banks and other lenders against integration through "the infiltration of inharmonious racial ...

groups" or "incompatible racial elements" and through redlining policies that denied mortgage insurance to communities with Black residents.[18] The impact on Black homeownership and accumulation and appreciation of housing and property wealth has had generational impacts on Black families persisting through the present.

The 1937 National Housing Act established the public housing program to supply affordable housing for low income families but, from the program's inception, public housing authorities assigned tenants on a segregated basis and largely located Black-occupied housing in spatially underserved areas.[19] When production goals were significantly expanded a few years later, Congress essentially ensured new public housing would continue to be constructed on a segregated and discriminatory basis by expressly rejecting anti-discrimination amendments to the Act.[20]

In the labor protection and employment area, Congress, after expressly debating adoption of a separate and lesser minimum wage for Black workers in the National Industrial Recovery Act (NIRA) of 1933 initial legislation, ultimately settled on the use of agricultural and domestic occupational and geographic classifications and codes which produced known disparate racial impacts in labor protection. The NIRA's use of these occupational and geographic classification and code provisions had the effect of establishing lower minimum wages for most Black workers.[21] Indeed, Congress had heard testimony in the debates on the legislation from a Southern employer that "a negro makes a much better workman and a much better citizen, insofar as the South is concerned, when he is not paid the highest wage."[22] Professor Juan Perea has pointed out that overtly racist testimony in support of a separate and lower Black wage scale, including reference to "the superior white race" and the subnormal intelligence of "the colored race," "was accepted without challenge or rebuttal at th[e] [congressional] hearing."[23] While a proposed differential minimum wage for Black workers was not ultimately adopted, significant discrimination in wage minimums was accomplished through less crude and explicit means facilitated by the codes, classifications, and occupational exclusions.[24]

Next, in the National Labor Relations Act (NLRA) of 1936, also known as the Wagner Act, the New Deal Congress protected the rights of low wage and other workers to unionize but rejected measures to prevent unions from excluding Blacks from membership.[25] "The final legislation permitted labor organizations to exclude African Americans, denied the status of 'employee' to Black workers engaged in strike breaking, and permitted the establishment of separate, racially segregated unions."[26] The National Labor Relations Act also excluded agricultural and domestic workers and rejected proposed anti-discrimination amendments to its provisions.[27]

The Fair Labor Standards Act of 1938, designed to establish minimum wages and maximum hour protections, also expressly excluded agricultural workers and, implicitly, domestic workers.[28] Several representatives also supplied overtly racist statements against utilizing the same wage protections for Black workers as extended to whites and underscored their potential disruption to the Southern economy.[29] Florida Representative J. Mark Wilcox's statement typified this position:

> There has always been a difference in the wage scale of white and colored labor … You cannot put the Negro and the white man on the same basis and get away with it. Not only would such a situation result in grave social and racial conflicts but it would also result in throwing the Negro out of employment and in making him a public charge. There just is not any sense in intensifying this racial problem in the South, and this bill cannot help but produce such a result.[30]

By ultimately denying wage and hours protections to agricultural and domestic workers, Congress assured that over 60 percent of Black workers would receive woeful, subminimum wages and often work long hours. An editorial in the *Baltimore Afro American*, pointing to the domestic maids at the spa FDR frequented for polio treatments and relief, asked rhetorically: "If he believes in a ceiling for hours and a floor for wages, why does he permit the Georgia Warm Springs … [to] pay colored women workers $4.50 a week for long hours?"[31]

1.2 RACE AND THE SOCIAL SECURITY ACT OF 1935

The racialized history behind these labor and housing enactments supplies insight into the New Deal legislative climate animating development and enactment of the Social Security Act.[32] In debates over the Act's means-tested welfare benefits program legislation (Title I) with benefits for elderly persons (Old Age Assistance), Southern congressmen blocked efforts to bar discrimination in the program or to federalize the program in a manner that would reduce the states' ability to discriminate and exercise discretion in adjusting benefit levels and selecting among recipients. They even defeated an amendment that would have required that Title I benefits be set at a level providing "a reasonable subsistence compatible with decency and health."[33] Senator Harry Byrd of Virginia expressed a common position of the Southern congressional delegation that this amendment "might serve as an entering wedge for federal interference with the handling of the Negro question."[34] Edwin Witte, the Executive Director of the Council on Economic Security, which drafted much of the Act, testified before committees in both Houses and attended their executive sessions; he related that Senator Byrd's position was "supported by nearly all of the southern members of both committees."[35]

Byrd's fellow Virginian, Congressman Howard Smith, an avowed white supremacist,[36] explained the economic motives behind denying or limiting life-support benefits under the Act, and thereby keeping Black sharecroppers and domestic workers vulnerable and dependent on farm owners and other employers. At the hearings on the Title I old age provisions (in reasoning with comparable applicability to the old age social insurance provisions in Title II), Congressman Smith stated:

> It seems to me that it should allow the States to differentiate between persons in this way: As we all know, $30 a month to one individual would be perhaps a mere pittance. To another individual who has lived in comparatively moderate circumstances, as they do in the rural districts, all his life, for 65 years, $30 a month would be affluence. You take the average laborer on the farm, let us say, all through the country districts, and his earning capacity on an average over the past times has been from $20 to $30 a month. To put him on a pension at 65 of $30 a month is not only going to take care of him, but a great many of his dependents, relatives, and so on, who could much better be employed working on a farm.[37]

If there were any question about what "farm laborers" Smith was referencing, later in this same testimony he had the following exchange with Representative Thomas Jenkins from Ohio:

MR. JENKINS: I was interested in the statement the gentleman made that practically 25 percent of the people over 65 in his State would be within one class. Would the gentleman state what class he means by that?
MR. SMITH: Of course in the South we have a great many colored people and they are largely of the laboring class.[38]

Around the same time, Southern commentators amplified Congressman Smith's concerns about the Social Security legislation. An editorial in the *Jackson Daily News*, "the great champion of" Mississippi Senator Pat Harrison, chairman of the powerful Senate Finance Committee overseeing the then pending social security legislation,[39] stated:

> The average Mississippian ... can't imagine himself chipping in to pay pensions for able-bodied Negroes to sit around in idleness on front galleries, supporting all their kinfolks on pensions, while cotton and corn crops are crying for workers to get them out of the grass.[40]

This is not to suggest that all Southern legislators, including those from less agriculturally significant Southern states, shared the same views – a point stressed by DeWitt.[41] The point is that these overtly racialized sentiments by some were a factor in the Act's shape and enactment. Indeed, no one in Congress from within the Southern delegation came forward during the congressional debates to challenge, disassociate from, or disavow these statements and sentiments.[42]

Moreover, in support of the assertion that some influential Southern legislators did not share the same highly racialized sentiments expressed on the Act, DeWitt offered the example gleaned from Senator Harrison's biographer of a belief that Harrison had disclaimed possessing the same racial concerns over the Social Security legislation voiced by some of the other Southern legislators.[43] However, regardless of the asserted ways Senator Harrison's views on race may have deviated from those of his fellow Southern legislators and committee chairpersons, historical accounts reflect Harrison's support for steering the Social Security legislation in a manner that would preserve racial hierarchies in the Southern agricultural economy and its reliance on cheap Black labor.[44] Professor Mary Poole noted that Senator Harrison "strongly opposed political and economic autonomy for African Americans and worked to keep them in the rural south, where their labor could be easily exploited."[45] She recounted Senator Harrison's statement: "The negra is one of the largest and most important factors in our [Southern] labor supply. By training and tradition, the negra is better adapted to the Southern type of agriculture … With respect to his working ability, his goodness and his trustworthiness, the negra can't be beat."[46]

Regarding Senator Harrison's views on the desirability of Black political participation, status quo disenfranchisement, and political subordination in Mississippi at the time, Nobel Prize-winning diplomat and political scientist Ralph Bunche, in his 1940 book on Black political status during FDR's presidency, quoted another statement by Harrison: "The nigra is satisfied down there from a political standpoint. In my state, the nigra has played no part in politics for forty years and has no desire to do so. We are all content to leave the situation alone as it is."[47]

Finally, apart from the statements of Southern legislators and their constituent commentators about the racial demographics of farm laborers (and the desirability, in their view, that Black sharecroppers and their families remain dependent on white farm owners and prevailing meager wages and working conditions for their survival, even in old age), Congress was well aware of the disparate racial impact of the agricultural and domestic exclusions from testimony on the Act. Legendary NAACP Director and Howard Law School Dean Charles Hamilton Houston, who devised the litigation strategy to dismantle the Jim Crow system of racial subordination and segregation commanded by law, leading to the *Brown v. Board of Education* decision,[48] also testified on the social security bill. Houston argued that the legislation was inadequate, in part, because it excluded domestic and agricultural worker categories where the majority of Black workers ("3 out of 5") were employed. In Houston's words, this bill "looks like a sieve with the holes just big enough for the majority of Negroes to fall through."[49]

DeWitt also argued that Houston's opposition to the agricultural and domestic exemptions should be viewed as tempered by his overall opposition to the Social Security Act and its social insurance program.[50] However, Houston's expressed concerns with both the Social Security Act's old age assistance and old age insurance proposals, and his advocacy for social welfare program options with potentially greater meaningful benefits to the Black community, were understandable. Houston viewed the proposed old age assistance program run by the states without anti-discrimination protections as wholly inadequate for Blacks in the South; he suggested it would be "political suicide" for politicians in such states "to advocate for a State old age assistance program in which Negroes would benefit in any way."[51]

He also viewed the old age insurance or annuity program as excluding most Blacks from the outset and, in any event, using average wage formulas which would yield benefit levels so low for many low wage and itinerant workers ("$4.50 per month or $54 per year") as not to replicate a "working wage."[52]

As alternatives, under those circumstance, Houston at one point suggested a program covering all elderly persons and elderly workers in all categories which would be "a strictly Federal old age assistance program either with direct benefits or with federal grants in aid to the States with guarantees against discrimination which will insure every American citizen shall receive his fair and equal share of the benefits according to his individual need."[53] At another point he described a recommendation that the "old age system and old age annuity be merged," so that if you had federal grants in aid to the states, "the worker should not get any less than what he has actually paid in – that should be the minimum," or if benefits were paid directly by the federal government, there would be a federal minimum which the state could then supplement.[54] In any event, Houston and the NAACP's advocacy for a better deal or more inclusive option for African Americans at the time appears motivated, at least in part, by Houston's expressed concerns over the exclusion of nearly two-thirds of the Black community from old age insurance owing to the agricultural and domestic exclusions in the proposed legislation and not because of indifference to them.

The National Urban League also advocated for "an alternative bill proposed by Congressman Ernest Lundeen" because it included "farmers and domestic workers and personal service workers" and also contained an anti-discrimination provision.[55] The Lundeen bill, along with the Social Security Bill and the Townsend Plan Bill – calling for more generous $200 per month pensions for all persons over sixty-five and initiated by a California physician, Dr. Frances Townsend – were the three major social welfare proposals submitted to Congress between 1934 to 1935.[56] Of these proposals, the Lundeen bill "was the only one of the three to create a system that unambiguously protected against racial discrimination."[57]

After Houston's testimony, the NAACP's periodical magazine, *The Crisis*, included an editorial titled "Social Security – for White Folk" that described FDR and his advisors as "preparing to dump overboard the majority of Negro workers in this security legislation program by exempting from pensions and job insurance *all farmers, domestics and casual labor*."[58] Other testimony before various congressional committees on aspects of the social security legislation reinforced Black community opposition to these exclusions, such as pointing out that "practically eighty-five percent of [African Americans] in the South are agricultural workers … [and] the large majority of domestic and personal workers in the United States are [African American] women."[59] Congress also excluded agricultural and domestic workers from the Unemployment Insurance program in the Social Security Act.[60]

Indeed, the agricultural and domestic exclusions in Title II of the Social Security Act were part of "a common pattern" of exclusion of these known, disproportionately

Black occupational groups that was instituted through a range of New Deal legislation rendering Black workers more vulnerable to economic hardship and exploitation and often employing expressly racialized rhetoric in debates over those laws. This patten included the same or similar exemptions from the Fair Labor Standards Act's wage and hours protections, the National Labor Relations Act's protections of the rights of low wage workers and other workers to unionize, and from the unemployment insurance program. This broader New Deal pattern of exclusions supplies further contextual background for situating the potential salience of race in the application of these same racially disparate exclusions in the social security old age insurance program.[61]

George Edmund Haynes, one of the National Urban League's cofounders,[62] also testified on the proposed legislation and urged inclusion of a nondiscrimination clause in the Social Security Act. He noted: "[T]here have been repeated, widespread, and continued discrimination on account of race or color as a result of which Negro men, women, and children did not share equitably and fairly in the distribution of the benefits accruing from the expenditure of such Federal funds" (presumably subsistence relief funds under the Emergency Relief Act of 1933 administered by the Federal Emergency Relief Administration [FERA]).[63]

As Professor Daiquiri Steele explained: "[U]ltimately, Congress passed the SSA without an anti-discrimination prohibition but with the agricultural and domestic worker exemption, leaving two-thirds of Black workers uncovered."[64] Moreover, the decision to allow local administration in the Social Security Act's Title I (and other Titles establishing the Social Security Act's public assistance programs), without nondiscrimination protection, enabled discrimination against even those persons of color who were included in the legislation, as Congressman Smith had impliedly urged and George Haynes feared. Political science and sociology scholar Professor Frances Fox Piven has described the resulting rampant racial discrimination in the locally administered Social Security Act's welfare programs:

> Southern congressmen had pressed hard and successfully for the elimination from the Social Security Act of any wording that might have been construed as constraining the states from racial discrimination in the administration of welfare. And they used the latitude they had won to run the welfare program in ways consistent with the racial order of their region … This meant that southern welfare laws and practices were designed to shore up a rigid caste labor system. Blacks were less likely to get aid, and when they did, their benefits were lower than whites so that the welfare check would compare unfavorably with even the miserable earnings of field hands. The average relief payment per person in the southern region was about half the average elsewhere, and black families received less than white families. In rural areas they received much less. And while welfare benefits might be used to sustain some black families at bare subsistence levels when they were not needed in the fields, they were either cut off when seasonal employment became available, or their benefits were reduced.[65]

Although Congress finally added coverage for domestic and agricultural workers to the Title II social insurance provisions in amendments to the Act in 1950 and 1954,[66] apparently recognizing that perceived administrative obstacles to tax collection and assessment were manageable,[67] Representative Smith still opposed adding these disproportionately Black workers to the Act through these amendments, as did several other Southern members of Congress.[68] Of the eight representatives who voted against the inclusionary amendments, six were Southern Democrats.[69] In the Senate, Mississippi Senator John Stennis also opposed the amendments and was joined by Virginia Senator Harry Byrd and others.[70] These same Southern legislators later opposed the landmark civil rights legislation of the 1960s, which provided tools to chip away at some of the underlying racialized structural and systemic political and social conditions undermining congressional respect for or solicitude to concerns for racial equity in otherwise remedial legislation such as in the 1935 Social Security Act and other New Deal enactments.[71]

In summarizing some of the significant changes in historical and political circumstances in the years between the 1935 Act and the most sweeping Social Security inclusion amendment adding agricultural and domestic workers in 1954 (and the lingering, sometimes racially tinged, opposition of some Southern legislators to inclusion),[72] political science scholar Professor Robert Lieberman explained:

> The amendments of 1954 finally brought agricultural and domestic workers, except those most irregularly employed, into the OAI [old age insurance] system. The partial inclusion of the 1950 legislation undoubtedly paved the way for full inclusion four years later … The newfound Republican support for OAI, combined with the newfound minority status of Southern democrats, meant that full inclusion was all but inevitable. The last gasp of Southern resistance, however, was heard in Congress. In the House, Howard Smith of Virginia, who had raised the race issue in 1935, tried to block the rule providing for consideration of amendments on the House floor, a tactic he would use with great skill in later years to obstruct civil rights legislation … In the Senate, John Stennis of Mississippi dredged up, for the last time in the fight over this issue, the racist language and traditions of the old South. He offered an amendment to drop the farm workers provision of the bill leaving the 1950 restrictions … [H]e addressed his central objection to the new [inclusion amendment]: "Under the bill, we are to bring in all the groups of migrant and reckless and irresponsible workers, who will pay virtually nothing, and the entire burden will fall on the employer, and those workers will get a vested right in the fund to which they will contribute very little." Stennis's speech evoked the traditional racial imagery of American political and social discourse; he might as well have added "lazy and shiftless" to "reckless and irresponsible." In the midst of the uproar over *Brown v. Board of Education*, which had been decided three months earlier, his message hardly could have been clearer.[73]

Notwithstanding this history, the SSA presently displays a 2010 article on its website by its public historian, DeWitt, from the SSA's Office of Publications and

Logistics Management, concluding, as referenced in the epigraph to this chapter, that the allegations "do not hold up under detailed scrutiny."[74] This conclusion rested on a review of the literature and the history of the Act focusing largely on the exclusion amendment's origination from Treasury Secretary Morgenthau (and not Southern legislators) and concern over administrative and functional obstacles in covering employees in these categories and collecting the required taxes from employers and employees.[75]

While there were undoubtedly identifiable, legitimate, nonracial, administrative burden and functional implementation factors supporting the 1935 exclusions,[76] DeWitt's conclusion offers a cramped view of the meaning of racial bias and the resulting implication that race played no meaningful role in the exclusions' enactment. It also supplies a narrow and compartmentalized view of the underlying racial climate and history animating the Act's passage by isolating the history of the Title II's Old Age Insurance program from that of the Act's more overtly racialized Title I Old Age Assistance welfare program.[77]

It assumes that legislators' voiced concerns about undermining the southern farm economy by diminishing Black workers' dependence on farm work and sharecropping owing to receipt of Title I old age welfare assistance benefits would not carry over to these same workers' receipt of Title II old age insurance benefits. Indeed, one would anticipate greater concerns about the latter. Title I old age welfare benefits would be subject to local administration, discretion, and control, and with neither anti-discrimination protections nor guaranty of benefit levels even supplying minimally "reasonable subsistence compatible with decency and health." The southern congressional delegation blocked efforts to include those latter two protections in Title I on expressly asserted racialized grounds and due to the fear of federal intervention on issues of race through control of these benefits. On the other hand, Title II old age insurance benefits would be based on a federally uniform formula and entirely nationally administered. In short, the suggestion that the expressly racialized positions of legislators seeking to perpetuate a racially exploitative southern agricultural economy could be isolated and confined to concerns regarding disruptive impacts from Title I of the Act but were deemed entirely irrelevant to the impacts from Title II, strains credulity. DeWitt's conclusion and the "Title I – racial economic subordination-exceptionalism" suggestion also fail to acknowledge the relevance of other racially inequitable restrictions in New Deal programs in labor protection (also excluding agricultural and domestic workers) and housing, expressly reinforcing racial exclusion, racial subordination, and racial segregation, emanating largely contemporaneously from these same lawmakers.

Moreover, that the exclusion amendment originated from Secretary Morganthau, who stressed administrative justifications for this provision, does not answer the question of whether race played a significant role in its ultimate adoption. In a report focusing on the domestic worker exclusion's history for the International Labour

Organization, cultural anthropologist Harmony Goldberg explained Morganthau's involvement and the "racial politics" surrounding this provision:

> At Roosevelt's urging, the original Act that was presented to Congress did, in fact, include domestic workers and farm workers in UI and OAI [Title II Old Age Insurance], but the administration made it clear to its congressional allies that inclusion of these two populations should be considered expendable bargaining chips in the legislative process. The Act made it through the Senate with the inclusion of farm workers and domestic workers intact, but when it came before the House Ways and Means committee – which was predominantly composed of Southern New Deal Democrats – these workers came to be excluded. The lobbying of Secretary of the Treasury, Henry Morgenthau, was decisive in advancing these exclusions. Morgenthau – himself the owner of a farm in New York State – argued that it was administratively impracticable to include these workers in the Act, given their low wages relative to the administrative costs of collecting their payments to these contributory insurance programs. This pragmatic argument was adopted by the Southern leaders of the Ways and Means committee members in defending the exclusion on the House floor … [W]hile these policymakers' advocacy for exclusion was not based on explicitly racist political arguments but on pragmatic ones – that pragmatism was based on an assessment and acceptance of the state of racial politics in Congress and of the low wages earned by workers in these racially degraded industries.[78]

Indeed, history and political science scholars and professors Gareth Davies and Martha Derthick, who reached a similar conclusion as DeWitt (and on whose analysis DeWitt relied), acknowledged that the support of Southerners, necessary for the exclusion amendment's approval and bill's passage, "*no doubt reflected racial factors*," but noted that the initial suggestion for the exclusion amendment to the initial inclusive draft was not based on race and originated from Treasury Secretary Morgenthau.[79] In short, race was a significant factor in the most dominant congressional block's support of the exclusions, although not the only factor involved in the exclusions' adoption and history. The Act's history suggests multiple or mixed motives or considerations in its passage. However, the presence of mixed or multiple motives behind the Act's racially disparate exclusions does not *alone* counterbalance or negate the presence or salience of "racial bias," or remove the racial taint.

1.3 THE 1935 SOCIAL SECURITY ACT THROUGH THE LENS OF EQUAL PROTECTION PRINCIPLES

Even formal, usually stringent in application, and regularly diminishing equal protection doctrine supports a more expansive approach to the assessment of racial taint or bias or even actionable, unconstitutional race discrimination, than is suggested in Dewitt's analysis.[80] For example, while unconstitutional race discrimination requires proof of discriminatory intent, the presence of multiple reasons or mixed motives for governmental action does not undermine the determination that race played an improper and ultimately unconstitutional role.[81] Rather, in *Village of Arlington Heights v. Metropolitan Housing Development Corp*,[82] the Supreme Court held that intentional discrimination can be established even where race is only one of several factors motivating a defendant's conduct. Recognizing that governmental entities rarely render decisions motivated by a single concern, or even a "'dominant' or 'primary' one," the Court found that "racial discrimination is not just another competing consideration."[83] Evidence that race played any part in motivating the challenged governmental conduct terminates the justification for judicial deference,[84] and shifts the burden of proof to the government to establish that "the same decision would have resulted even had the impermissible purpose not been considered."[85]

Decisions by courts applying this standard have also demonstrated that proof of racial animosity, "ill will," or "evil motive," on behalf of public officials is also not necessary to support a finding of discriminatory intent.[86] Nor is it necessary to produce a "smoking gun" or even direct evidence since the Court in *Arlington Heights* held that discriminatory intent may be predicated entirely on circumstantial evidence.[87] Accordingly, this section does not seek to excavate or deconstruct the ultimate conclusion of the spate of recent articles asserting that the Social Security Act and, indeed, the New Deal as a whole, were "not racist"[88] or "not intrinsically racist."[89] Demonstration of "racism," often connoting overt racial hostility or expression of racial inferiority in popular or colloquial discourse,[90] is unnecessary in equal protection race discrimination doctrine and analysis.[91]

In *Arlington Heights*, the Court articulated six categories of circumstantial evidence probative of discriminatory intent: first, the discriminatory impact of the defendant's decision; second, the historical background of the decision; third, the sequence of events leading up to the decision; fourth, departures from normal procedural processes; fifth, departures from normal substantive criteria; and sixth, the legislative and administrative history of discrimination, including "contemporary statements by members of the decision-making body."[92] The Supreme Court has also explained the circumstantial evidentiary salience of actions pursued with knowing or foreseeable racially disparate impacts:

> [A]ctions having foreseeable and anticipated disparate impact are relevant evidence to prove the ultimate fact, forbidden purpose … [T]he foreseeable effects standard [may be] utilized as one of the several kinds of proofs from which an inference of segregative intent may be properly drawn … Adherence to a particular policy or practice, with full knowledge of the predictable effects of such adherence … is one factor among many others which may be considered by a court in determining whether an inference of segregative intent should be drawn.[93]

The Court has further reasoned that circumstantial evidence of discrimination in a governmental-defendant's other distinct practices or as applied to other programs and agencies is relevant, probative evidence of discriminatory intent. For example, it has found that evidence of a government entity's discrimination in employment, education, and grand jury selection was circumstantially probative of intentional voting discrimination in a Georgia county.[94]

Applying these principles to the circumstances of the 1935 exclusions and their history should have unquestionably shifted the burden to the government to establish that the exclusions would have been adopted in the absence of the racial considerations which at least played a part in the enactment, as shown earlier. In this context, an appropriate rebuttal inquiry might ask whether this legislation would have transformed from a bill initially lauding the need to include all categories of workers and specifically referencing the importance of including agricultural and domestic workers to one containing these two large categorical exclusions, if the known putatively excluded and foreseeably harmed workers had been disproportionately white.[95] It is not demonstrably apparent, and at least highly questionable, whether the government could have met this rebuttal burden to overcome the taint of the Act's racial considerations and context, and no court has yet applied these equal protection principles and holistic contextual analysis from *Arlington Heights* and its progeny to this issue.[96]

The few courts that have passed on the constitutionality of these exclusions in New Deal enactments have ultimately rejected the challenges, but in doing so failed to apply these equal protection principles and burden-shifting formulation.[97] Instead, these courts have either determined that the unquestioned disparate racial impact of the agricultural and domestic exclusions in this and/or in other New Deal legislation was not enough, standing alone, to establish discriminatory intent under the Supreme Court's decision in *Jefferson v. Hackney*;[98] or, alternatively, that discriminatory intent was not even properly alleged in the lower court.

However, the contrast in results and findings between the courts in *Jefferson v. Hackney* and those in another case, *Whitfield v. Oliver* (essentially involving the same issues but reaching a different result), are instructive in evaluating the potential presence of an unconstitutional racial taint in Social Security Act benefit programs. The Supreme Court in *Jefferson* held that the mere disparate impact of lower benefit levels in the disproportionately Black and Chicano Texas Aid to Families with Dependent Children (AFDC) welfare program, compared with the higher benefit levels in the state's demographically whiter Old Age, Aid to the Permanently and Totally Disabled, and Aid to the Blind welfare programs (parts of Titles I, IV, X and XIV of the Social Security Act of 1935 and a later amendment), did not amount to unconstitutional racial discrimination since there was no evidence that the state was even aware of these disparities and no other evidence of intentional discrimination.[99] By contrast, in finding a violation of the Equal Protection Clause through intentional discrimination in the provision of welfare benefits under Titles I, IV, X, and XIV of the Social Security Act, as amended, and as implemented in Alabama, a three-judge district court in *Whitfield v. Oliver* distinguished *Jefferson* and explained: "throughout the history of the programs in Alabama, state officials have been aware of their racial composition … This kind of information, available to legislators and administrators for use in decision making, was not shown to be available to the Texas officials in *Jefferson*."[100]

The circumstances surrounding the Social Security Act's agricultural and domestic exclusions appear closer to *Whitfield* than *Jefferson*. Congress was, at all times, well aware of the agricultural and domestic exclusions' disparate and adverse impact on Black workers, as described earlier. Indeed, the legislative history also reveals the expressed desire of some southern legislators to tether Black farm laborers to agricultural work under then-prevailing wages and conditions by removing access to alternative sources of basic income security from Social Security Act benefits through various means, and the opposition of prominent spokespersons for the Black community to the exclusions based on the obvious harms to disproportionately Black workers in those occupational categories. Moreover, the acknowledged and largely undisputed evidence of racial discrimination in the design of the Act's Title I benefits provisions, combined with the comparable contemporaneous occupational exclusions exempting wage and hour protections in New Deal Labor Law – each adopted with legislative expressions of a need to protect the southern plantation and farming economy – supplies circumstantial evidence of the inclusion of a similar design and animating considerations behind Title II of the Act pursuant to equal protection doctrine. Analogously, the court in *Whitfield v. Oliver* also found that evidence of racial discrimination in other areas and programs such as public employment, voting, jury selection, and education supplied additional circumstantial evidence of intentional discrimination in the provision of welfare benefits under Titles I, IV, X and XIV of the Social Security Act, as amended, in Alabama.[101]

Finally, as described earlier, DeWitt's analysis, concluding that race played no meaningful role in the exclusions, relied on a similar nonracially influenced conclusion reached by Professors Gareth Davies and Martha Derthick.[102] However, Davies and Derthick also provide a disclaimer, acknowledging that if the groups most disadvantaged by the exclusions were not socially and politically subordinated to the degree of Black southerners at the time in the 1930s, and essentially powerless in this process, the fairness issues "might have surfaced [more] explicitly, producing at least a clearer revelation of [the] motives [of Congress] *if not substantively different policy choices [and] [m]ore pressure would have existed to include agricultural workers and domestics, no matter what the administrative difficulties*."[103] That Congress could knowingly disregard or effectively ignore the interests of millions of Black workers without electoral consequence, owing to systemic racial and political subordination, disenfranchisement and structural discrimination, is not a nonracially infused or nonracially biased justification for the resulting foreseeable and foreseen racially disparate and disadvantaging congressional action. Professor Lieberman explained:

> Southern society combined labor-repressive agriculture with racial disenfranchisement and segregation to subdue African Americans both economically and

politically. The hegemony of the Democratic Party in the South – built on these twin pillars of planter dominance and racial disenfranchisement – and the institutional structure of Congress combined to give white southerners both a strong interest in directing new social benefits away from African Americans and power beyond their numbers in the federal government, power they used to protect their racial and economic dominance of southern society.[104]

Finally, even assuming for the sake of argument that any significant palpable racial taint permeating passage of the 1935 Social Security Act's agricultural and domestic exclusions could be perceived as overwhelmingly or substantially vitiated by nonracial considerations, the foreseen and actually experienced racially deleterious impacts remain. As Kilolo Kijakazi, who served as Acting SSA Commissioner from 2021 to 2023 (writing with Karen Smith and Charmaine Runes), has acknowledged: "[i]rrespective of whether the decision to exclude domestic workers and farmworkers from coverage was racially based, this decision created a structural barrier that resulted in a disproportionate share of Black workers being excluded from coverage, compared with white workers."[105] Thus, the overall Social Security Act and its resulting social insurance benefits program disproportionately disadvantaged African Americans and other persons of color from its inception.[106] Although Congress eventually reversed these exclusions, their impacts on Black income insecurity, material deprivation, and intergenerational wealth generation have been significant. Social welfare policy scholar and Professor David Stoesz explained:

> While the exclusion of these low-wage workers can be quantified, the monetization of their loss of benefits does not address what this income might have purchased for them individually or contributed to these regions economically. While workers in other parts of America were enjoying the benefits of running water, flush toilets, electric refrigerators, automobile travel, plummeting disease rates, and increasing longevity, those in the South and Southwest continued to rely on hauling water from the pump, using the privy, an unhealthy diet due to absence of refrigeration, travel by foot or wagon, high rates of disease, and significantly shorter longevity … For a withholding tax of as little as $5.00 a year, individual workers could have been provided an annual pension of $240, which would have afforded them a modicum of comfort, security, and dignity. In aggregate, the amount would have been comparable to a domestic Marshall Plan, jump-starting the economy of a poverty belt that spanned the South and Southwest. The order of magnitude represented by these benefits – $618.24 billion in 2016 dollars between the inception of Social Security in 1935 and the amendments of the early 1950s – approximates for the South and Southwest what Congress appropriated as a stimulus to the *entire* nation to address the Great Recession, the 2009 American Recovery Act projected to expend $787 billion over a decade.[107]

The long-term consequences and present-day effects from the loss of such a large portion of income and the opportunity costs, human suffering, trauma, stress, and perils from the further deprivation of basic income security to a disproportionately Black worker population and the Black community (and to similarly situated persons and communities of color) is manifest. On a more structural and existential level, "the exclusion of agricultural and domestic workers from Social Security is but another event in an American tableau of second-class citizenship for minorities of color."[108]

2

Contemporary Racial Inequity for Beneficiaries of the Social Security Old Age/Retirement Program

Causes, Remedies, and Impending Challenges

Beyond the Social Security Act's racially disparate origins reflected in the 1935 statutory exclusions, the social security benefit structure and formula has further reinforced racial disadvantage and disparities in social security benefit levels, economic security, and retirement wealth through to the present. The social security benefit computation formula is somewhat complex and progressive – lower wage workers receive a benefit that is a higher percentage of their preretirement wages than higher wage workers – but it is still based, to a significant extent, on a worker's lifetime earnings. The amount of monthly social security benefits is based on the relevant wage earner's Primary Insurance Amount (PIA), which in turn is based on the earner's Average Indexed Monthly Earnings (AIME) over a worker's highest paying thirty-five years of earnings,[1] albeit with certain individual and family benefit maximum levels.[2] In short, lower and less consistent lifetime earnings usually lead to lower monthly benefit levels. In that sense, the social security benefit calculation formula locks a certain degree of labor market income and wage inequity into benefit levels,[3] and ultimately into retirement income and retirement wealth.

Factors such as structural racism and discrimination from a legacy of slavery, Jim Crow separation and subordination, occupational segregation, systemic employment discrimination in hiring, promotion, wages and benefits (both before and after the 1964 Civil Rights Act outlawed overt employment discrimination),[4] and through myriad practices which continue through the present as evidenced in modern employment discrimination testing,[5] all contribute to lower and less consistent wages and resulting lower social security benefit levels among Black and Brown workers.[6] Retirement policy journalist Mark Miller, quoting former Acting SSA Commissioner Kilolo Kijakazi, explained:

> Two-thirds of single Black retirees – and three-quarters of single Latinos – have incomes below the Elder Index, a data set from the University of Massachusetts Boston that aims to measure the capacity of older people to cover basic living expenses. By contrast, half of white seniors have resources below the index. The disparities stem from racism in the labor market, says Kilolo Kijakazi, a fellow at the Urban Institute [who also served as Acting SSA Commissioner from 2021–23 and]

who has written extensively on income, wealth and race: "We have a history of discrimination in hiring, pay, promotions and benefits. Discrimination in hiring also contributes to occupational segregation," she said. Labor inequities began with the enslavement of Black people, she adds. "White people dealt in human trafficking of people of African descent in order to create wealth for white people, but Black people did not benefit from the wealth of their labor. After Emancipation, we had laws and regulations designed to maintain that effect and even strip Black people of wealth they were able to create for themselves in the face of these odds." Policies served as barriers to wealth accumulation by Black people. The Jim Crow-era Black Codes restricted opportunity in many Southern states; racially restrictive covenants barred them from buying homes in white neighborhoods; and redlining practices made mortgages hard or impossible to obtain. The inequities have compounded over time, as families were unable to transfer wealth to subsequent generations.[7]

Other conditions reducing earnings and/or benefit levels and total benefits received by Black and Latino/a beneficiaries relative to white beneficiaries include lesser education, health care inequity and higher mortality rates,[8] lesser marriage rates,[9] greater caregiving responsibilities,[10] and the substantial and disparate loss of earnings owing to racialized mass incarceration and involvement with the criminal justice system.[11] In addition, factors such as lesser generational wealth including considerably lesser housing wealth from lower home ownership rates owing to systemic and government-supported redlining and mortgage discrimination,[12] and lesser inheritances and other forms of wealth,[13] less pension, 401(k) and other retirement assets,[14] and higher poverty, indebtedness, and unemployment rates,[15] coupled with poor health, injury, and illness – often due to more arduous and dangerous employment,[16] combine to necessitate greater resort to earlier retirement and less financial ability to defer retirement beyond full retirement age.[17] Early retirement at age sixty-two reduces benefit levels to only 70 percent of the full retirement benefit level; delayed retirement beyond full retirement age enhances benefit levels 8 percent each year, culminating in 124 percent of the full retirement benefit level, if not taken until age seventy.[18]

To concretize the ongoing and future effects of these structural racially disparate circumstances,[19] the Center for Retirement Research Study projects that average lifetime Social Security benefits received by adults born between 2001 and 2010 will be 19 percent less for Black beneficiaries and 14 percent less for Latino/a beneficiaries than white beneficiaries[20] An Urban Institute Study focused on adults born between 1996 to 2005, projected the Black–White differential in lifetime social security benefits at 26 percent, with average Black beneficiaries receiving $406,700 and average white beneficiaries $546,500.[21] The lifetime difference in this latter study takes into account disparities in annual benefits, benefit commencement ages, and longevity.[22]

In its 2022 Equity Action Plan, the SSA summarized the causes and results of racially disparate social security benefit levels described here, explaining:

Structural barriers such as labor market discrimination result in higher levels of unemployment and lower wages for African American people and Latino people at

> every level of education. Since Social Security benefits are based on years worked and prior wages, labor market disparities drive differences in Social Security benefits. Data prior to 2010 show that the benefit levels for White men were considerably larger than the benefit levels for people of color and White women, on average. In addition, occupational segregation – the disproportionate representation of people of color and women in jobs that have lower pay levels and are less likely to provide benefits such as employer-sponsored retirement plans – leave people of color and women with less income and fewer retirement resources. Social Security benefits typically make up a larger share of total income for people of color and White women than White men.[23]

A Congressional Advisory Committee – the 1979 Advisory Committee on Social Security of the House Ways and Means Committee – has suggested that the disparate racial impact of lower Black retirement benefits levels and utilization duration is offset somewhat by greater proportionate usage of social security disability benefits by Black workers, and social security survivors' benefits for their spouses and dependents since Black workers become disabled and die at younger ages and with greater frequency than white workers and have shorter retirement benefit windows.[24] Undoubtedly, significantly greater Black mortality and disability are due to heath care inequities and a variety of social determinants of poor health stemming from poverty and the legacy of racial discrimination and subordination described earlier. However, because the disability and survivors' programs combined are still much smaller programs, only about one-fifth the size of the retirement program,[25] the greater proportionate usage of the former does not meaningfully offset the disparately lower aggregate lifetime social security benefits of Black and Brown workers.[26] Indeed, an Urban Institute Study has quantified the racial disparities in benefits through all three social security programs collectively reflected in OASDI by calculating that "white Americans in 2020 would, on average, receive $1.25 in benefits for every dollar they contributed in taxes under OASDI over the course of their lives, whereas blacks would receive only 94 cents."[27] As another recent Urban Institute Study described:

> The availability of Social Security disability insurance benefits adds progressivity to the system, as many disability beneficiaries have limited lifetime earnings and thus collect benefits that replace a relatively high share of their earnings. … That progressivity, however, does not fully compensate for the employment and earnings disadvantages and other costs associated with disability, and disability beneficiaries with lower earnings before disability onset receive lower annual benefits than their counterparts with higher earnings despite their higher replacement rates. These benefit shortfalls, combined with high out-of-pocket costs for the assistive technologies and health care that many people with disabilities need, often leave many disability insurance beneficiaries in economic precarity.[28]

Moreover, there are numerous other obvious deleterious consequences associated with significant health inequity and poorer health care treatment and overall health leading to disproportionate disability and death rates and at younger ages for Black and Brown social security beneficiaries. Finally, as shown in Chapters 5 and 6, there are several more adverse and inequitable factors leading to lesser and diminished receipt of disability benefits by Black social security claimants than their adverse medical-vocational profiles would suggest. These factors include bias in impairment and symptom assessment by medical treatment professionals and agency adjudicative personnel, other unexplained and documented adjudicative bias by Social Security Administrative Law judges, disparately inadequate medical treatment and impairment documentation, and improper "race-norming" and "race correction" in the use of clinical care support tools and algorithms. Indeed, in 2022, SSA quite candidly acknowledged that "[t]here is evidence that although African American people are more likely to have a disability, they are less likely to be approved for disability benefits than white people."[29]

Several years ago, Professor Phoebe Weaver Williams proposed, in response to the statutory exclusions described in Chapter 1 and racially disparate and lower benefits levels and their ongoing consequences described in this chapter, that Congress adopt a remedial actuarial alteration of the Social Security earnings formula and/or program changes permitting an earlier retirement age, for the benefit of African Americans.[30] The proposal would permit more advantaged benefit accrual conditions similar to that which Congress adopted for women to remedy systemic societal gender discrimination in employment and its impact on women's Social Security earnings calculations, and resulting social security benefit levels. Professor Williams noted that Congress attempted to address the gender disparity in social security earnings and benefit levels in an enactment in 1956 changing the earnings calculation formula, and timing for an earlier retirement date, under 42 U.S.C. § 415(b)(3) which remained in effect until a further amendment in 1972.[31] The Supreme Court acknowledged the impact of this statutory remedial formula change in effect from 1956 to 1972, in passing on and rejecting a reverse discrimination challenge by a man excluded from this more generous remedial social security earnings computation formula for women, stating:

> Under [Section] 215 of the Social Security Act … old-age insurance benefits are computed on the basis of the wage earner's "average monthly wage" earned during his "benefit computation years" which are the "elapsed years" (reduced by five) during which the wage earner's covered wages were highest. Until a 1972 amendment, "elapsed years" depended upon the sex of the wage earner. Section 215(b)(3) prescribed that the number of "elapsed years" for a male wage earner would be three higher than for an otherwise similarly situated female wage earner; for a male, the number of "elapsed years" equaled the number of years that elapsed after 1950 and before the year in which he attained age 65; for a female the number of "elapsed years" equaled the number of years that elapsed after 1950 and before the year in which she attained age 62. Thus, a male born in 1900 would have 14 "elapsed years" on retirement at age 65 but a female born in the same year would have only 11. Accordingly, a female wage earner could exclude from the

> computation of her "average monthly wage" three more lower earning years than a similarly situated male wage earner could exclude. This would result in a slightly higher "average monthly wage" and a correspondingly higher level of monthly old-age benefits for the retired female wage earner.[32]

The Court nonetheless accepted the remedial purpose of this provision of the Act, observing that "the challenged statute operated directly to compensate women for past economic discrimination [and] [r]etirement benefits under the Act are based on past earnings."[33] It reiterated that "[w]hether from over[t] discrimination or from the socialization process of a male-dominated culture, the job market is inhospitable to the woman seeking any but the lowest paid jobs."[34] Therefore, "allowing women, who as such have been unfairly hindered from earning as much as men, to eliminate additional low-earning years from the calculation of their retirement benefits works directly to remedy some part of the effect of past discrimination."[35]

In rejecting the reverse discrimination challenge to this statute, the Court reasoned that reducing the economic disparity between men and women caused by a long history of gender discrimination was substantially related to an important government interest and therefore satisfied the intermediate level of equal protection scrutiny employed by courts to assess the constitutionality of statutory gender classifications. On that basis, the Court upheld the differential and remedial Social Security earnings and benefit calculation formulas for women.[36] However, even assuming Congress could or would adopt such a measure to benefit retiring workers of color (also based on an indisputable history of employment discrimination, occupational segregation, and exclusion), a comparable race-based Social Security remedial provision would undoubtedly stand considerably lower chances of surviving a similar reverse discrimination challenge before the present Court. The present Court has applied increasingly stringent, strict scrutiny standards utilized for racial classifications in remedial provision cases such as in the 2023 higher education affirmative action cases.[37]

Notably, the 1979 Advisory Committee on Social Security of the House Ways and Means Committee considered but rejected calls for similar remedial action to mitigate and address the legacy of systemic racial discrimination and its impact on Social Security benefit levels for African Americans.[38] It stated:

> Any differences in treatment of minority and non-minority members do not flow from the deliberate design of the social security programs, because social security law is color blind. The law contains no mention of any racial or ethnic group … Rather the question of whether social security treats minorities fairly relates to the impact of a color blind law upon groups that have suffered, and though there have been improvements, continue to suffer from discrimination and that continue to earn less on the average than members of the majority. The consequences of such discrimination are deplorable and demand the continued priority attention

> of the nation. The ultimate remedies for such discrimination will come through Congress, the courts, the schools, the job market and the political forum. It would be neither appropriate nor desirable to try to use social security as a device for dealing with these problems.[39]

Despite impediments to race-specific remedial legal measures, the Social Security program's inequitable history stemming from the initial Act's agricultural and domestic workers' exclusions' racial impacts, and the influence of articulated, racially discriminatory reasons by legislators and others behind the exclusions, should not be erased or diminished. Nor should the lower accrued earnings and ultimately lower social security benefits levels predicated on the exclusions and on years of lower earnings in structurally and pervasively discriminatory job markets and the panoply of other structurally discriminatory institutions and phenomena discussed earlier. Recognition of the Social Security Act's racially deleterious origins and ongoing disparate impacts should be added to discussions of reparations and reconciliation for a legacy of myriad governmental policies producing or enhancing intergenerational injuries to, and substantial wealth and well-being disparities in, the Black community.[40]

As a modest first step, SSA should provide more fulsome and inclusive additional materials on the historical section of its website. Those materials could incorporate accessible writings on the disparate racial impact of the 1935 Social Security Act's exclusions and structure and the undisputed presence of repugnant racist sentiments and considerations supporting an ultimately racially disparate program design with both foreseen and foreseeable adverse consequences. It should also include discussion of the impacts of known pervasive structural racial discrimination in the job market and beyond on the social security earnings formula and benefits calculations – in the same or similar manner recognized and acted upon with respect to pervasive societal gender discrimination.

Professor Alfred Brophy has stressed the value of forward-looking reconciliation (as opposed to an exclusive focus on compensatory reparations), which includes the goals of changing public understanding about the present impact of past injustice, acknowledging past contributions and harms, and effecting justice and preventing future harms.[41] These goals are increasingly important in a political climate and moment when Black history is more broadly under major assault,[42] and when Congressional and regulatory proposals for Social Security reform are regularly emerging with potential additional racially disparate future consequences. For example, current racially disparate Social Security program proposals include recent reintroduction of an oft-discussed plan to raise the Social Security full retirement age to seventy to cut benefit outlays and address trust fund depletion, as opposed to revenue-side payroll tax wage-cap or payroll-tax formula adjustments and other less regressive reform alternatives.[43] The retirement age increase would have a foreseeable racially disparate impact on benefit receipt by Black workers owing to shorter Black life expectancy and resulting shorter temporal benefit-receipt windows.[44]

Indeed, the same 1979 Congressional Advisory Committee that rejected race-based remedies to address racial inequities in the social security programs also stated:

> Although we reject explicit differentiation on the basis of race or ethnic status, the council believes that one of the important factors to be considered in making any changes in the social security program is the effect the change will have on racial and ethnic minorities. The council notes further that many of the recommendations we are making will have a favorable impact on minorities.[45]

The actions the Council recommended included: (1) "Increasing benefits for workers who have spent a major part of their careers working at low wages"; and (2) "Increasing, gradually, the income level guaranteed under the SSI program and liberalizing the [SSI] resource test."[46]

Thus, while there is little that can realistically be done in the legal system to retroactively remedy the 1935 agricultural and domestic worker exclusions, nor to redress lower social security covered earnings in that period and thereafter through to the present owing to the myriad consequences of structural racism and discrimination already detailed, avenues in public policy, and legislative and administrative fora remain available to mitigate contemporary racially disparate effects.

The additional actions which can and should be pursued include:

2.1 IMPLEMENTING A MORE PROGRESSIVE SOCIAL SECURITY BENEFITS COMPUTATION FORMULA THAT WOULD RETURN A GREATER PERCENTAGE OF EARNINGS IN BENEFITS TO THE LOWEST EARNERS

As described earlier, the benefits formula is based on calculation of the PIA from the AIME. The formula can be modified in a more progressive fashion by altering the bend points used to calculate the AIME.[47] For example, in a recent study by Richard W. Johnson and Karen E. Smith for the Center for Retirement Research at Boston College, the authors have proposed, based on 2024 figures, to increase the first bend point of the AIME from $1,174 to $1,503, add a new AIME bend point at $5,018, and keep the last AIME bend point at $7,018.[48] The new replacement rates for determining the PIA would then become 95 percent before the first bend point (up from 90 percent), 32 percent between the first and second bend points, 15 percent between the second and third bend points, and 5 percent above the third bend point.[49] As a result, Johnson and Smith determined that among adults born between 2001 and 2010, this more progressive formula "would increase mean lifetime benefits $23,800 for Black beneficiaries and $20,500 for Hispanic Beneficiaries compared with $800 for white beneficiaries."[50] In relative terms, it would increase mean lifetime benefits 4.7 percent for Black beneficiaries, 3.8 percent for Hispanic beneficiaries and 0.1 percent for white beneficiaries.[51]

2.2 RAISING THE MINIMUM SOCIAL SECURITY BENEFIT TO A POINT ABOVE THE POVERTY LINE AND EXPANDING IT TO A WIDER RANGE OF LOW-EARNING PUTATIVE BENEFICIARIES. ALTERNATIVELY, MODERNIZING THE SSI PROGRAM

In 1972, Congressional amendments to the Social Security Act added a special minimum benefit (MB) designed to provide a minimum floor to increase the adequacy of benefits for long-term, low-earning covered workers and their dependents and survivors.[52] In contrast to the usual determination of Social Security benefit levels that computes the PIA based on a worker's career-average wages, the special minimum benefit is predicated on the number of years of work and of garnering earnings at or above a designated threshold.[53] An individual must have at least eleven years of earnings at or above the designated threshold to qualify for the MB and the MB increases with each year of eligible earnings up to thirty years.[54]

By 1973, more than 204,000 Social Security beneficiaries qualified for the MB. By the end of 2023, that number diminished to approximately 21,000.[55] As Professor Kathryn L. Moore recently explained:

> the number of beneficiaries has fallen dramatically for two reasons: (1) the special minimum benefit is only paid if it is larger than an individual's regular Social Security benefit; and (2) the special minimum benefit has grown slower than regular Social Security benefits because regular benefits are indexed to wages while the special minimum benefit is indexed to prices and wages have grown faster than prices.[56]

Thus, either owing to low regular benefit levels or low MB levels for the small number of persons who qualified, (in 2003) 21 percent of Social Security beneficiaries aged sixty-four to seventy-three still received social security benefits that fell below the federal poverty line, including 43 percent of Black beneficiaries.[57] Because poverty policy experts largely view the official federal poverty line – devised in the 1960s and not updated for twenty-first-century financial realities – as an outdated measure and significant undercount of true poverty, the cohort of social security beneficiaries living below the poverty line is experiencing significant deprivation of basic life necessities.[58]

Several proposals have been floated to address elderly poverty among social security beneficiaries by reforming the MB to reduce the poverty rate among beneficiaries and provide a financial floor below which many more beneficiaries cannot sink. The Johnson and Smith study on improving Black/Brown Social Security benefits equity for the Center for Retirement Research proposed three alternatives for raising the MB: (1) tying the MB to a percentage (such as 100 or 125 percent) of the federal poverty threshold as in Representative John Larson's (D-CT) oft-discussed Social Security 2100 Act bill;[59] or (2) setting the MB at 40 percent of the average wage index (AWI) for workers with over forty years of covered employment and prorating the MB for those with less employment; or (3) establishing the MB at 100 percent of the federal poverty line for all workers who completed ten years of covered employment or received DI benefits.[60]

The study reveals that all three options have pros and cons and blind spots for various low-earning workers based on their work records, but it labels the second option as the "most generous" because it raises lifetime earnings by 2.3 percent whereas the other two options raise earnings by less than 1 percent.[61] It concludes that this second MB enhancement option, which provides 40 percent of AWI after forty years of work, modestly reduces benefit inequity for Black beneficiaries by increasing mean lifetime Social Security benefits for Black adults by $17,900 (or 3.6 percent). "This is a bigger increase than for Hispanic (2.7 percent) and white (2.1 percent) adults because Black workers tend to work longer at lower wages than other workers, and they gain more from this reform than the other minimum benefit options."[62]

Alternatively, some policy analysts and scholars have argued that the most efficient, equitable, and properly targeted approach to addressing poverty in the low benefits/low earning social security beneficiary population would be through the means-tested SSI program rather than through MB fixes in OASDI. A Brookings Institution white paper by Jack Smalligan points out that MB enhancement proposals have significant shortcomings. For one, they only produce modest decreases in poverty among beneficiaries since SSA anticipates that only 3 percent of beneficiaries are projected to have worked the thirty–forty years required for the full MB under some of the proposals and "[w]orkers of color experience greater career disruptions and lower earnings due to longstanding inequities in the labor market and criminal justice system."[63] The MB also does nothing for the 3.5 percent of seniors (2.4 million people) who never receive any Social Security insurance benefits and whose "poverty rate was a staggering 54% in 2020" since a "substantial majority" are "late-arriving immigrants or infrequent workers, who don't have enough earnings years to qualify for benefits … and 60% are people of color."[64] In addition, because SSI rules only disregard $20 in Social Security benefits and then reduce the SSI benefit dollar for dollar for any additional Social Security benefits, a beneficiary concurrently receiving both Social Security and SSI will not receive any benefit from the enhanced MB benefit until the benefit is large enough to fully offset the lost SSI benefits.[65] Finally, the MB may render some concurrent social security and SSI recipients ineligible for SSI and thus also ineligible for automatic Medicaid,[66] a development of increasing significance with the substantial pending cuts to Medicaid enacted in the OBBBA of 2025.

On the other hand, SSI is a means-tested program targeted to persons in poverty. It is more efficient and equitable in reducing poverty since it considers all of an individual's major sources of income and assets in determining eligibility and focuses exclusively on those in need. However, to reduce poverty more meaningfully and forge appropriate and equitable interactions with social security receipt in concurrent eligibility cases, Congress should modernize SSI's provisions in a few basic ways through reforms which have been advocated for several years mostly from the (proposed) Supplemental Security Income Restoration Act of 2021.[67]

First, SSI benefit levels should be raised to 100 percent of the federal poverty line with cost-of living adjustments thereafter. Second, the asset limit of $2,000 should be updated for inflation since last adjusted in 1989, to $10,000 for individuals and $20,000 for married couples and also indexed annually for inflation as supported in the (proposed) SSI Savings Penalty Elimination Act of 2025.[68] Third, the marriage penalty reducing benefits for married couples each receiving SSI should be eliminated. Fourth, the one-third reduction in benefits for in-kind support and maintenance for the voluntary provision of food and housing to the beneficiary from friends or family should also be eliminated. Fifth, Congress should recognize past work of low-income earners and make return of lifetime social security tax contributions more equitable in concurrent Social Security/SSI cases by changing the Social Security disregard rule in SSI from a $20 general income (general income refers to nonwage income such as Social Security benefits, pensions, interest, and child support; earned income refers to income from wages) to $60, index the $60 to inflation, and add an additional 40 percent disregard to Social Security benefits when calculating the SSI benefit. Sixth, and finally, the earned income disregard should be increased from $65 to $200 and indexed to inflation since "under current rules, the SSI program begins reducing SSI benefits at a 50% rate even before a beneficiary has enough income from SSI and earnings to be above the poverty line."[69]

These changes, largely derived from the SSI Restoration Act of 2021 legislation, "would lift 3.3 million people above the poverty line and would cut poverty among SSI beneficiaries by more than half, from 36 to 16 percent,"[70] while also specifically targeting a wider range of low-earning, low-benefit level social security beneficiaries eligible for concurrent SSI benefits, to take more out of poverty. Moreover, SSI enhancement would have a positive impact in addressing racial inequity among the elderly poor since 8 percent of Black adults of at least sixty-five years old receive SSI – twice the rate of white older adults.[71]

The recent passage of the OBBBA of 2025, with substantial reductions in Medicaid, Supplemental Nutritional Assistance Program (SNAP) benefits and Affordable Care Act subsidies,[72] coupled with the most massive tax cuts in American history and burgeoning deficits in the trillions, suggest that passage of legislation expanding social legislation for persons in poverty and the working class is presently unlikely. Yet it is notable that a recent bipartisan poll reflects large majorities in support of reforming the SSI program along the lines outlined here. This includes 90 percent of Democrats and 70 percent of Republicans polled who want to see SSI benefits increased to at least the federal poverty level and 74 percent of voters, including 84 percent of Democrats and 61 percent of Republicans, who support raising the program's outdated asset limits from $2000 to $10,000 for an individual and from $3,000 to $20,000 for a couple.[73] It also includes 77 percent of voters who want updating of SSI's outdated income disregards for inflation, including 86 percent of Democrats and 69 percent of Republicans; 72 percent of voters who support eliminating in-kind support and maintenance penalties, including 83 percent of Democrats and 62 of Republicans; and 76 percent of voters who support eliminating SSI's marriage penalties, including 84 percent of Democrats and 69 percent of Republicans.[74] Perhaps in a different political climate when/if democracy reascends and legislation supported by significant majorities can be enacted again, these proposals can be re-introduced.

2.3 ADDING CAREGIVER CREDITS FOR SOME PORTION OF TIME WHEN AWAY FROM EARNING FOR CAREGIVING

Feminist critics of the social security system have long argued that uncompensated caregiving labor is work meriting credit and the failure to incorporate such caregiving credit into the social security formulation is a gendered system flaw.[75] As such, credit for unpaid caregiving is a superior mechanism for addressing social security benefit level inequities based on loss of earnings owing to caretaking than enhanced survivors or spousal contingent and secondary benefits tied to a spouse's earnings.[76] Indeed, the Johnson and Smith study pointed out that "[p]roviding help directly to caregivers, rather than helping them indirectly through spousal benefits would [particularly] benefit single [spouse-less] mothers, who are disproportionately women of color."[77]

Other reports and studies have further explained how caregiving credits reduce the racial gap in social security benefits and retirement wealth. A National Academy of Social Insurance report found that while "roughly the same proportion of White and Black Americans – approximately one-fifth of each demographic – are engaged in providing care for a family member, … people of color are disproportionately lower earners and less likely to have a total of 35 earnings years."[78] As a result, caregiving years are more likely to add zeros to Black workers' earnings records, lowering their Social Security benefits.[79] Moreover, while women disproportionately assume caregiving responsibilities and "spend more than twice as much time as men caring for household members … women of color are doubly burdened by the gender and racial gap in retirement wealth."[80] Accordingly, "[c]aregiver credits would therefore be particularly effective at reducing the retirement wealth gap experienced by one of society's economically most vulnerable subgroups."[81]

While most developed nations grant caregiving credits in some form,[82] there is great variation in program structure and goals.[83] As Professor Kathryn Moore has summarized:

> [Among Organization for Economic Cooperation and Development (OECD) countries], the period of eligibility ranges from one year per child to up to sixteen years per child. Reference wages can be a percentage of actual wages, average wages, or a minimum wage. Depending on the country, caregiver credits may enable individuals to establish eligibility for benefits, increase the amount of benefits, and/or accelerate the date on which they may be eligible for benefits. Alleviating

> poverty is a common goal; other goals include increasing women's participation in the paid workforce, increasing birth rates, and promoting gender equity.[84]

Professor Moore has also summarized the political and functional obstacles to the adoption of caregiving credits in the American social security system such as deviating from a contributory system based on earnings, and the additional administrative expense and difficulty of adjudicating the validity of caregiving claims – likely at the cost of utilizing the elaborate bureaucracy through which the SSA adjudicates disability claims.[85]

The Johnson and Smith study reviewed the racial impact of three proposed caregiver credit proposals all basing the credits on the AWI and not on a worker's own prior earnings, "so that the credit would have a larger relative impact for low[-]wage workers than high-wage workers."[86] One of the options, based largely on a 2020 election cycle proposal by Senator Elizabeth Warren, would provide a credit of 100 percent of AWI, credited each year a caregiver provides at least eighty hours per month of care to a child younger than six or to a disabled dependent.[87] The other two proposals would limit credits to one-half of the AWI in different ways,[88] as would the more recently proposed Social Security Caregiver Credit Act of 2023.[89] Johnson and Smith concluded that "creating caregiver credits and adding a new minimum benefit to Social Security would also help Black and Hispanic beneficiaries."[90] In particular, "Hispanic adults would especially benefit from caregiver credits because they generally have more children than Black and white adults."[91] In more concrete terms, "a caregiver credit equal to 100 percent of the AWI would increase mean lifetime Social Security benefits $33,800 (or 6.4 percent) for Hispanic adults, compared with $21,100 for Black adults and $16,100 for white adults."[92] The National Academy of Social Insurance (NASI) paper pointed out that "even a modest credit – at half the average wage – could help close the gaps that caregiving leaves in many workers' Social Security earnings records."[93]

As with the proposals for SSI modernization and restoration described here, there is strong public support for creating caregiving credits in the social security system, including 73 percent of those surveyed, and 70 percent of those self-identified as Republican in an Associated Press survey.[94] Accordingly, this measure may also be amenable to adoption in a different political climate.

2.4 CREATING A PROGRAM OF BRIDGE BENEFITS MITIGATING THE REDUCTION IN BENEFITS FOR EARLY RETIREMENT AT AGE SIXTY-TWO FOR OLDER WORKERS WITH A HISTORY OF PHYSICALLY DEMANDING WORK

The Older Workers' Retirement Security Task Force convened by the nonpartisan NASI studied the problems of diminished social security and retirement security for older workers in their fifties and sixties with physically arduous work and job histories.[95] These workers often experience health issues, not arising to the SSDI/ Supplemental Security Income Disability (SSID)-entitling medical-vocational profile levels or otherwise meeting the stringent disability program eligibility standards, but inducing early retirement owing to the strain of continued strenuous work and lack of education, training, and/or capacity for successful adjustment to less-demanding office work or similar work.[96] Those in that older worker, long-term arduous work profile also often lack sufficient retirement assets and income security from the modest wages associated with their prior work and lack of pensions or employer-sponsored retirement plans so that retiring early at age sixty-two with reduced benefits can present significant additional financial hardship to them and their families.[97]

Not surprisingly, the Task Force's 2023 report, issued after two years of study, found that "workers of color" are disproportionately represented in that older worker cohort.[98] The report found that since "particularly Black and Latino workers, have less formal education on average, they disproportionately work in physically challenging jobs."[99] It cited a 2014 study revealing that whereas approximately 40 percent of older white workers had physically demanding jobs, more than 50 percent of older Black and Asian workers and over 60 percent of Latino workers do.[100] The "disparities were even more striking" for older workers in work characterized as "highly physically demanding jobs" with one in ten older Latino workers, one in twenty older Black and Asian workers, and only one in forty older white workers in that category.[101] The report also cited a 2022 study finding that nearly half of Black and Latino older workers but fewer than 30 percent of older white workers labored in physically demanding jobs.[102] Finally, the Task Force observed that the disproportionately nonwhite and increasingly female population of older workers in physically challenging jobs are particularly vulnerable to intersectional age, race, and/or gender discrimination, and to surmounting the many obstacles to challenge such practices.[103] They are also "the least educated members of the labor force, in the lowest paying, most precarious jobs and are often the first to be let go during economic downturns."[104]

Among the Task's Force recommendations to address this older worker profile included the creation of a "bridge benefit" in the period between early retirement and full retirement age for workers who have performed physically challenging jobs to "provide added income for these workers and reduce the lasting penalty they currently incur."[105] The benefit "would pay half of the difference between the worker's full retirement benefit and the worker's early retirement benefit at each age prior to full retirement age starting at age 62 through 67."[106] Workers at age sixty-two or thereafter before sixty-seven could apply for the benefit based on a sufficient showing of having performed a history of physically demanding work.[107] The mechanics of the bridge benefit are explained as follows by the original proponents of the concept:

> Under current rules, when the full retirement age reaches 67 years, a worker who retires at age 62 will get benefits that are permanently 30% below their full

retirement benefit. If they retired at age 63, their benefit would be permanently lower by 25%, and if they retired at age 64, it would be 10% below their full retirement benefit. With our proposed benefit, a qualifying worker who retired at age 62 would receive a benefit that is 15% below their full retirement benefit for one year. At age 63, their benefit would increase, so that it is 12.5% below their full retirement benefit. And at age 64, it would be 10% below their full retirement benefit. At age 67, a qualifying worker would begin receiving their full retirement benefit that they would have received if they had waited until age 67 to collect Social Security benefits. Workers would then not experience the lifelong benefit cut they would see had they retired early without the bridge benefit.[108]

The task force also concluded that adopting such a bridge benefit program "would bring the US in line with other wealthy nations, including those in the OECD whose social insurance systems take into account the toll that a long history of arduous work takes on older workers" and including "work in industrial and manufacturing settings, frontline health care work, and other jobs sometimes referred to as 'blue collar,' which are especially likely to lead to deteriorating health when performed over many years."[109] It noted that in the 1980s, "many OECD countries introduced early retirement models with an emphasis on jobs that workers cannot realistically continue to do beyond their early 60s" and "some, including Austria, the Netherlands, and Poland, have special retirement policies for such workers, allowing them to claim early retirement with smaller or no benefit cuts."[110]

While the somewhat speculative proposed "general revenue transfer" financing for the bridge benefit-would have to be solidified,[111] the program would bring further racial and economic equity to the program. Moreover, recent (2025) bipartisan polling also reflects strong support for inclusion of a bridge benefit in social security reform legislation; it is favored by 68 percent of Democrats, 57 percent of Republicans, and 50 percent of Independents, with only 22 percent of Democrats, 28 percent of Independents, and 29 percent of Republicans opposed.[112]

2.5 NO NEW INEQUITY/DOING NO NEW RACIALLY DISPARATE HARM: PURSUING NON-REGRESSIVE APPROACHES TO ADDRESS IMPENDING SOCIAL SECURITY TRUST FUND INSOLVENCY

As noted in the Introduction, the social security trust fund is facing insolvency and the inability to pay full benefits in only six to seven years (in 2032–33). Congress must act or beneficiaries will face an automatic benefit reduction of approximately 20 percent, which will have the greatest impact on the poorest beneficiaries who rely to the greatest extent on social security to address basic life needs and necessities. As also shown earlier, Black and Latino/a beneficiaries are disproportionately represented among the most financially and economically challenged cohort of social security beneficiaries and most at risk from the specter of trust fund insolvency induced automatic, approximately 19 to 24 percent, benefit reductions.[113]

The prevention of reductions in critically needed benefits to those with the greatest financial precarity should be a top priority among actions to shore up the trust fund. Accordingly, Congress should approach trust fund solvency measures in the manner least likely to cause additional disparate harm to low-wage, low-benefit claimants such as by focusing principally on resource/revenue-side remedies and not through regressive, across-the-board benefits-reduction-side remedies. It should reject proposals by Congressional Republicans to seek a flat benefit reduction through raising the retirement age,[114] or as will occur automatically simply if Congress takes no meaningful action on the matter by 2032–33. It should also reject attempts to reintroduce ill-conceived and ill-fated previous proposals to privatize the Social Security program as such proposals will further disadvantage persons and communities of color.[115]

Since the Social Security Trust fund is based solely on payroll taxes, taxes on social security, and interest on the trust fund, the centerpiece of progressive revenue-side reform should include an increase in the wage tax base cap above the current level of $184,500 in 2026. In 1983, the last time Congress enacted major trust fund protective measures, 90 percent of covered wages were included in the Social Security payroll tax maximum or cap. Presently, the rate has diminished substantially and only approximately 82 percent of covered wages are included within the FICA tax cap because of growing income inequality – wages for higher earners (above the wage cap) have increased far more rapidly than average wages, and wages for low and middle income workers (below the wage cap) have stagnated.[116]

Whereas most workers pay taxes on all their earnings and do so throughout the year, those earning at levels above the cap only pay FICA taxes on a portion of their earnings and stop paying taxes often well before the year's end.[117] "The top 1 percent of earners have an estimated effective FICA contribution rate of 2 percent, compared to more than 10 percent for the middle 50 percent of earners."[118] Economists estimate that the "ongoing leakage out of Social Security's revenue has led to a Social Security Trust Fund holding 50% fewer reserves in 2022 ($1.4 trillion fewer) than it would have if inequality had not increased (even before accounting for the larger interest income that a higher level of reserves would have been generating over this entire period)."[119] Accordingly, if the rate of covered wages within the FICA cap had remained at 90 percent from 1983 through the present, the OASI Trust Fund would have more than $1.4 trillion in additional reserves, which alone would close more than 25 percent of the present long-term shortfall.[120]

Another trend in the substantial growth of income and wealth inequality with implications for Social Security's financing, is that an increasing portion of wealthy Americans' income now derives from sources other than wages, such as investment income and "pass-through" business income.[121] As with wages over the Social Security's payroll tax cap, wealthy recipients of these forms of income from capital do not pay FICA taxes on them.[122]

Other factors contributing to a faster than anticipated depletion of the trust fund include greater longevity of retirees and longer periods of benefits receipt – especially among higher earners with higher benefit levels and superior health care access – and declining birth rates over several decades leading to fewer workers paying into the trust fund.[123] The impact of the decline in workers entering the workforce and paying into the fund is compounded by record numbers of workers leaving the workforce and drawing social security benefits out of the fund owing to peak baby boom retirements (referenced as "Peak 65" – when 4.1 million baby boomers are projected to retire each year between 2024 and 2027).[124]

Several Congressional proposals have been introduced to fill the impending trust fund deficit through revenue enhancements by relying principally, but not exclusively, on modifications of the FICA payroll tax cap. Proposals ranged from lifting the cap entirely to raising the tax cap so that it covers 90 percent of all earnings and then pegging it to that level in the future.[125] Others have proposed what NASI CEO Rebecca Vallas has coined as a "donut hole" in the tax base, taxing workers up to the maximum in the cap, carving out or exempting from taxation a portion of earnings above the cap until reaching higher earning workers at a specified level, such as over $250,000 or $400,000, and taxing all earnings above that level.[126] Some proposals couple the donut hole tax cap modification with taxation of investment income and some form of a progressive tax rate increase.

For example, Senator Elizabeth Warren's (D-MA) 2020 presidential primary election cycle plan called for lifting the cap to include earnings above $250,000, increasing the tax rate from 12.4 percent (6.2 percent for both employer and employee) to 14.8 percent (7.4 percent each but only applying the enhanced tax rate to earnings over $250,000); taxing net investment income as well as earnings for persons earning more than $250,000, and declining to increase benefits based on the increased contributions of these higher earners.[127] Warren touted her plan as one that would restore solvency to the trust fund for at least two decades and also permit a variety of benefit enhancements mostly targeted to lower earners such as increasing the minimum benefit, adding child care credits and an across the board $200/month benefit level increase for all, among several others.[128]

A recently reintroduced bill by Senator Sheldon Whitehouse (D-RI) and Congressman Brendan Boyle (D-PA), the Medicare and Social Security Fair Share Act of 2025, proposes to solidify both the Social Security and Medicare trust funds through increased tax revenue for each fund.[129] On the Social Security provisions, the bill proposes to tax covered earning starting above $400,000 and also tax investment income and income from "pass through businesses" in the same manner as wages for those with incomes over $400,000.[130] SSA's Chief Actuary has determined that the identical bill when introduced in 2023 would have solidified the combined OASI and DI trust funds and pay social security benefits "in full and on time throughout a 75-year projection period."[131] A similar bill by Senator Bernie Sanders (D-VT), The Social Security Expansion Act of 2023, recently updated slightly and reintroduced in 2025 and joined by Senator Warren and Representatives Jan Schakowsky (D-Ill) and Val Hoyle (D-OR),[132] calls for: combining the OASI and

DI Trust Funds; taxing covered earnings starting over $250,000 from the combined trust fund; applying a separate tax on investment income as defined in the Affordable Care Act starting with single filers over $200,000 and joint filers over $250,000 and taxed for the combined trust fund at 12.4 percent; increasing the special minimum benefit; increasing the PIA bend points first factor from 90 to 95 percent to make the formula more progressive; increasing the annual COLA adjustments by using the Consumer Price Index for the Elderly instead of the Consumer Price Index (CPI) for all urban wage earners and clerical workers (which will increase benefits); and restoring benefits for children of a disabled or deceased wage earner who are between age eighteen and twenty-one and attending high school, college, or vocational school.[133] The SSA's Chief Actuary also estimated that this 2023 bill "would extend the ability of the OASDI program to pay scheduled benefits in full and on time throughout the 75-year projection period."[134]

The basic revenue raising approaches outlined in the Whitehouse/Boyle Fair Share Bill and the Sanders Social Security Enhancement Bill (along with Senator Warren's earlier proposal), which call for lifting the payroll tax cap, are also popular with large majorities of responders in polling, including those who identify as Republicans.[135] They also offer hope for a path forward in a different political moment (perhaps closer to the rapidly approaching (2032–33) date of fund insolvency).

In short, the adjustments to the Social Security program identified herein would make the program more equitable, reduce poverty, prevent further regressive distributive backsliding, and reduce the racial retirement wealth gap, albeit modestly.[136] However, as the Johnson and Smith study concluded, greater, more meaningful progress on social security racial equity will only be achieved with transformative changes in relative employment opportunity and earnings from the dismantling of structural obstacles and ongoing discriminatory injustice confronting Black and Brown workers.[137]

3

Mass Incarceration and the Racial Impact of Criminal Justice System-Involved Statutory Restrictions in Social Security Programs

As described in Chapters 1 and 2, a history of structural racism and discrimination has fueled significant racial disparities in social security earnings and benefit levels. In turn, these disparate social security benefit levels have extended further the even more substantial racial gaps in income, wealth, and retirement assets described in Chapter 2. Another structural component of racial inequity with corresponding adverse disparate consequences in the social security system is mass incarceration.

3.1 THE RACIAL IMPACT OF MASS INCARCERATION

The US has the highest incarceration rate of any independent democracy in the world.[1] Fueled by the "war on drugs" with felonization of drug possession, and various "tough on crime" enhanced-sentencing initiatives including those with mandatory minimum sentences, greater frequency of life sentences, and limited access to parole,[2] the US prison population has skyrocketed. It has grown nearly sevenfold from 1973 to the present, increasing from 360,000 to nearly 2 million persons in American prisons and jails. The *Mass Incarceration Trends Report* of the Sentencing Project explained mass incarceration trends in the US, noting:

> Sentences of all lengths have expanded during the era of mass incarceration. The infamous "Rockefeller Drug Laws" (1973), which mandated 15 years for possession of small amounts of marijuana and other drugs, was the first in a broad range of state-level mandatory sentencing schemes. In 1984, Washington state adopted the nation's first "truth-in-sentencing" law that required people to serve 85% of their sentences, and 27 states quickly adopted similar laws over the next 15 years. Fourteen states had eliminated parole altogether.[3]

A report of mass incarceration in the federal system explained:

> Incarceration rates increased due to the expansion of the "War on Drugs" campaign under President … Reagan. Congress passed legislation, such as the Anti-Drug Abuse Act of 1986 and its expansion in 1988, establishing mandatory minimum penalties for drug possession and trafficking, which included marijuana

> and crack cocaine (Public Law 99-570; Public Law 100-690). For the possession of five grams or more of crack cocaine, an individual could receive an indictment between a five-year mandatory minimum and a 20-year maximum sentence (Public Law 100-690). Marijuana and crack cocaine have long been associated with the Black community, along with stereotypes of "crack dealers" and "crack babies." Crack cocaine only began to spread through impoverished Black communities after Reagan's campaign. The increased negative publicity against the use of crack cocaine and marijuana led to the drastic increase in federal funding for the "War on Drugs" campaign and the policies that followed … By the 1990s, violent and property crime rates began declining; however, in 1994, Congress passed what historians regard as the most significant federal crime bill ever passed, The Violent Crime Control and Law Enforcement Act, also known as the 1994 Crime Bill, incentiviz[ing] states to build more prisons and promot[ing] harsher criminal sentences, including for terrorism, crimes against women, and certain felonies such as drug-trafficking and drunk driving. The bill, co-drafted and sponsored by then-Senator Joe Biden, included an $8.7 billion incentive for states to enact truth-in-sentencing laws, which require offenders to serve at least 85 percent of their sentence before becoming eligible for parole or early release. (Public Law 103–322)[4]

By 2017, 7.7 million persons had been incarcerated and another 12.1 million have been convicted of felonies without incarceration.[5]

The substantial upswing in the prison population, imprisonment rates, and ongoing government control of system-involved persons outside formal prison walls, has been characterized by the label "mass incarceration."[6] Blacks, Latinos/as, and Native Americans are widely overrepresented among those so incarcerated. Of the 7.7 million persons who had been incarcerated up to 2017, 5 million were Black (2.7 million) or Latino/a (2.3 million).[7] In 2021, African Americans were imprisoned at five times the rate of whites, while Native Americans and Latinos/as were imprisoned at 4.2 times and 2.4 times the white rate, respectively.[8] Although African Americans represent 14 percent of the total US population, they are significantly overrepresented at 33 percent of the total prison population, 46 percent of the prison population who had already served at least ten years, and 55 percent of those serving life without the possibility of parole, the most extreme life sentence.[9]

It is anticipated that one in three African American men born in 1981 will be incarcerated at some point in their lives.[10] While some more recent changes to sentencing and corrections policies over the past two decades have helped lessen incarceration rates,[11] it is still estimated that one in five Black men in the generation born in 2001 will be imprisoned.[12] In addition, after reaching the apogee in incarceration in 2009 with at least marginal decline thereafter up through 2021, incarceration rates increased by 2 percent in 2022.[13] The rate of incarceration in jails for Black men also increased by 8 percent from March 2020 to December 2022 compared with less than 1 percent for white men in the same period.[14]

There are many cited causes and contributing factors to the dramatic racial disparities in incarceration rates. Racially discriminatory policing undoubtedly plays a role. A series of studies has documented that African Americans, Black men in particular, are disproportionately surveilled and stopped by the police.[15] These studies also reveal "[e]xcessive and unnecessary traffic stops uniquely concentrated among African Americans" leading to a "maze of criminal justice procedures,"[16] and interactions including incarceration.

The racially focused stops often derive from a broader practice of racial profiling – the targeting of individuals for investigation and policing based on generalized assumptions about the criminal propensity of membership in particular racial or ethnic groups – extending well beyond driving or walking while Black. Racial profiling also extends to standing, idling, shopping, bus riding, or traveling while Black.[17] Racial profiling is one of the primary reasons for the grossly disproportionate arrest rates of Black and Brown persons, which, in turn, fuels mass incarceration.[18]

Once in the system, additional drivers of racially disparate incarceration include, among other factors: explicit and implicit racial bias in discretionary prosecutorial charging and sentencing recommendations; the decisions of judges and juries at every stage of a criminal case, from pretrial motions to trial verdicts and sentencing and conviction; as well as post-conviction decision-making by parole boards, probation officers, and parole officers.[19] The same racially disparate result is particularly evident with respect to discretion exercised in the plea bargaining process – the end product of approximately 98 percent of all criminal cases in a given year.[20] A survey study by the US Department of Justice, Bureau of Justice Assistance of numerous research studies concluded:

> Studies that assess the effects of race find that blacks are less likely to receive a reduced charge compared with whites. Additionally, one study found that blacks are also less likely to receive the benefits of shorter or reduced sentences as a result of the exercise of prosecutorial discretion during plea bargaining. Studies have generally found a relationship between race and whether or not a defendant receives a reduced charge[;] [t]he relationship found between race and receiving a reduced plea has been consistent ... The majority of research on race and sentencing outcomes shows that blacks are less likely than whites to receive reduced pleas.[21]

Other significant factors feeding racially disparate incarceration rates derive from financial obstacles disproportionately disadvantaging Black and Brown defendants. These obstacles include cash bail requirements to avert pretrial detention and incarceration; criminalization of poverty such as incarceration based on inability to pay various fees and fines, driving without an active license, and vagrancy or nuisance charges based on homelessness; inability to afford counsel in segments of the criminal justice process such as in various post-conviction proceedings where counsel might not be legally or constitutionally required; and limitations in defense lawyering owing to chronic underfunding of public defender and other indigent counsel mechanisms.[22] Racially selective enforcement of low-level crimes such as trespass, small dollar value theft or drug sale, prostitution, and irrationally long sentences for drug possession also contribute to Black and Brown mass incarceration.[23]

Obviously, the devastating impacts of criminal justice system involvement, conviction, and incarceration far transcend any ancillary impact on access to or levels of social security benefits (or other public benefits). Criminal justice system involvement often "comes with many negative, long-term consequences, including restrictions on employment, housing, and voting, as well as negative impacts on physical and mental health."[24] The consequences of conviction and incarceration in limiting social security access is just an additional potential collateral consequence, out of many, from system involvement disproportionately confronting African Americans and Latinos/as.

A substantial collateral injury from incarceration is loss of earnings. Formerly, incarcerated African Americans and Latinos/as suffer significantly disproportionate and "greater lifetime earnings losses – $358,900 and $511,500 respectively – than their white counterparts whose losses amount to $267,000."[25] This lifetime loss of earnings depresses social security benefit levels, as detailed in Chapter 2. In addition, many incarcerated persons work in prison, but their labor ordinarily does not qualify as employment for social security quarters of coverage purposes owing to the absence of a traditional employer–employee relationship as well as the meager subminimum wages provided.[26] As a result, they will experience gaps in social security quarters and years of covered earnings while incarcerated so that even if working their entire prison sentences, they may "on release discover that they no longer have sufficient years left in their working lives to earn the benefits for themselves or their dependents."[27]

Moreover, the impact of racialized mass incarceration on social security benefits receipt by Black and Brown individuals and their families, is exacerbated by a series of amendments to the Social Security Act adopted mostly between 1980 and 2009,[28] which further restrict access to benefits for incarcerated or criminal system-involved persons in a variety of ways. The principal statutory exclusion or limitation is a mandatory suspension of social security retirement or disability insurance benefits for the period of incarceration for persons incarcerated for more than thirty days (with various exceptions), in 42 U.S.C. § 402(x). Congress first applied this restriction to the disability insurance benefit program in 1980 and then extended it to the Old Age/Retirement and Survivors' programs in 1983, consolidating the same language applicable to each program in §402(x).[29]

Up until 1999, these laws only stripped benefits from incarcerated old age or disability insurance benefit recipients if convicted of felonies or crimes punishable by imprisonment of at least a year.[30] In 1999, the law was extended to beneficiaries who are incarcerated for more than thirty days for any crime, not just felonies or those carrying at least a one-year maximum potential sentence.[31] Thus, persons who are receiving any form of OASDI benefits will lose them for the period of incarceration (beyond thirty days) when convicted of any crime.[32]

An additional criminal justice system-involved social security benefits exclusion, arising in the same initial disability insurance benefit/inmate-stripping 1980 legislation,[33] is not temporary but permanent. It is a permanent lifetime prohibition on finding a claimant disabled based in whole or in part on "a physical or mental impairment which arises in connection with the commission by an individual (after October 19, 1980) of an offense which constitutes a felony under applicable law and for which such individual is subsequently convicted," in 42 U.S.C.§ 423(d)(6)(A).[34] The SSA's implementing regulation provides that in jurisdictions without "felony" classifications, the triggering offense is one "punishable by death or imprisonment for a term exceeding one year."[35]

A 1960 Supreme Court decision shed light on the legality of such targeted program benefit restrictions aided by the Court's construction of the nature and character of social security insurance benefits created under the Act. Despite the contributory earnings-based design of social security insurance programs, the Court in a 5–4 decision in *Flemming v. Nestor*,[36] at the height of the Cold War and the McCarthy era, upheld a 1954 provision of the Social Security Act, permitting the forfeiture of benefits owing to the wage-earner's deportation based on subversive activities. In the social security claimant Nestor's case, the offending activities were predicated upon his membership in the Communist Party.[37] The Court rejected claims that Nestor's benefits, based on his earnings and payroll tax contributions, amounted to the deprivation of an "accrued property right" without due process in violation of the Fifth Amendment. The Court reasoned that while social security benefits are "in one sense earned," the interests created under the Act are "noncontractual," and to treat them as "accrued rights" would deprive the program of "the flexibility and boldness in adjusting to everchanging conditions which it demands" and which was written into a provision of the original Act.[38] The Court concluded that the only due process limits on Congressional action restricting social security benefits as so constructed, is whether the statutory restriction is arbitrary or "utterly lacking in rational justification."[39]

The Court found that "the fact of a beneficiary's residence abroad – in the case of a deportee a presumably permanent residence – can be of obvious relevance to the question of eligibility.[40] That is because

> [o]ne benefit which may be thought to accrue to the economy from the Social Security system is the increased over-all national purchasing power resulting from taxation of productive elements of the economy to provide payments to the retired and disabled, who might otherwise be destitute or nearly so, and who would generally spend a comparatively large percentage of their benefit payments [and] [t]his advantage would be lost as to payments made to one residing abroad.[41]

Additionally, the Court rejected Nestor's claim that the law amounted to a legislative punishment without a judicial trial or due process and thus a "bill of attainder" prohibited under Article I, §9, cl.3. The Court explained that the success of such a contention "is the validity of characterizing as 'punishment' in the constitutional sense the termination of benefits under § 202(n)."[42] It concluded that the benefits termination based on Nestor's deportation was not "punitive" because the statute's language and structure did not evince a "punitive design"; the sanction is the "mere denial of a noncontractual governmental benefit" without imposition of "affirmative disability or restraint, and certainly nothing approaching the 'infamous punishment' of imprisonment"; and the provision's legislative history did not demonstrate that Congress was concerned with the grounds (i.e., Communist Party membership) as opposed to the fact of deportation.[43] But even if such a focus on grounds could be shown, that alone would not suffice to establish a punitive purpose unlike the Court's prior bill of attainder cases where legislation on its face was directed at "particular individuals."[44]

3.2 THE OASDI INCARCERATION BENEFITS SUSPENSION LAW: 42 U.S.C. § 402(x)

The *Flemming v. Nestor* decision provided the doctrinal and conceptual basis for other restrictions on social security benefits emerging from temporal populist currents in later years, beyond the red scare of the McCarthy era. Indeed, the criminal justice system-involved restrictions already referenced were hatched in the midst of the "tough on crime" "war on drugs" populist fervor described earlier,[45] and the particularly animating public revulsion over a single, high-profile, notorious serial killer's receipt of social security disability insurance benefits while in prison. To place the social security incarceration suspension provision in historical context, neither the original Social Security Act of 1935, nor the Disability Insurance amendments of the 1950s placed restrictions on benefits by incarcerated persons or those otherwise system-involved. Indeed, in 1980 the SSA's Associate Commissioner for Policy, Lawrence Thompson, testified in a hearing on the first proposed exclusion that "imprisonment has never been a basis for non-payment of social security benefits."[46] Thus, for nearly a half-century after enactment of the Social Security Act's old age/retirement program and a quarter-century after adoption of the SSDI program, incarcerated beneficiaries regularly received their benefits.

In the late 1970s, a serial killer named David Berkowitz terrorized the nation's largest city – New York City – killing six people and wounding seven others in a series of shootings, mostly targeting young couples in cars or young dark-haired women.[47] He became known as the Son of Sam killer after he referenced himself with that moniker in a handwritten note for the police and media at the site of one of his murders during his killing spree,[48] causing further notoriety and panic over his murderous reign. When finally apprehended and incarcerated in 1977, sensationalized media accounts emerged about the Son of Sam mass murderer's "abuse" of the social security system by receiving disability benefits in prison although documentation about the nature of the system-"abuse," beyond simply "receiving social security benefits while evil," was neither supplied nor specified.[49] Thereafter, media accounts, quoting prison guards, police, and correctional officials offered additional purported examples of prisoners "abusing the social security system" by faking or feigning their disabilities, or purchasing items of leisure and entertainment with their benefits such as televisions for their cells.[50]

Congress responded to these accounts and public revulsion over the notion that famous incarcerated serial killers could purchase non-necessity items or otherwise live more comfortably through their social security benefits by enacting a law in 1980 suspending receipt of disability benefits by incarcerated persons convicted of a felony for the period of incarceration. In 1983, Congress extended that provision to receipt of old age/retirement benefits. The public's revulsion at Son of Sam's and other notorious violent criminals' receipt of disability benefits and "abuses of the system," as quoted and echoed in the comments and testimony of members of Congress and others during the 1980 Congressional hearings on the proposed benefit-stripping legislation, also sometimes pointed to the windfall or absence of a subsistence need to extend benefits to incarcerated persons. The "windfall" or "double dipping" assertion was based on the assumption that housing, food, and other expenses were already fully provided through the publicly funded penal institutions. In addition, some pointed to the strain on the diminishing social security trust fund from these benefit outlays, while expressing concern whether the trust funds would be sufficiently solvent to pay all other social security benefits.

In the Congressional hearings, at least eleven different witnesses referenced Son of Sam, and the transcript included thirty-three references to him and his receipt of benefits to support the importance of and need for this legislation.[51] One Congressman identified Son of Sam as the "focal point of unhappiness" with the receipt of SSDI benefits by incarcerated persons.[52] Another witness, a "correction sergeant," spoke to a "moral obligation to pass the proposed legislation" after recounting an anecdote of a sex offender nicknamed "Satan," incarcerated after facing a third sentence for "brutally attacking a six year old girl," and who was receiving $354 per month in SSDI benefits.[53] This witness also discussed potential abuses in the system, describing one convict who indicated the ease of obtaining social security disability benefits simply by "act[ing] crazy," and then suggesting that with all basic needs met by the prison, incarcerated SSDI recipients could purchase "luxuries such as stereos, electronic games, color televisions, tape recorders and athletic equipment" and sometimes undermine prison discipline by expanding the "underground prison economy" in "drug trafficking, numbers running and illicit sex."[54]

Others relied more heavily on the "windfall" rationale, viewing SSDI benefits as directed to subsistence needs of recipients and asserting that SSDI receipt by incarcerated persons is a windfall or unjust enrichment since all subsistence needs are met by prison authorities. Congressman William Whitehurst (R-VA), after expressing outrage at Son of Sam's and other "mass murderers'" SSDI receipt,[55] also opined that:

> [T]he Social Security system can be viewed as resting on two supporting pillars – individual equity, based on the relationship between contributions and earning; and social adequacy, based on a need factor … Under the social-adequacy concept, it can be argued and rightly so, I believe, that prisoners do not need benefits because their basic needs, including food, clothing, medicine, and shelter, are already being borne at considerable expense by the State.[56]

A former deputy warden for custody and security at a Michigan correctional facility, James Trout, further explained in his testimony:

> Abuses of the benefits paid to incarcerated persons under current Social Security Law are rife … [S]ocial security benefits make life much more pleasant for incarcerated recipients. Already being fed, clothed, housed, and educated at public expense, the recipient most often uses his/her social security bonanza to purchase the allowed luxuries of prison life. These luxuries include Sony personal portable televisions, cassette tape players, personal clothing from mail order catalogs, and food items from the resident store. Many recipients [rarely eat in the prison dining facility and can] afford canned roast beef, chicken, turkey, spaghetti, tuna and other items paid for by taxpayer dollars provided by the Social Security Administration.[57]

Still others stressed financial and trust fund solvency concerns, albeit without identifying how those issues could be meaningfully addressed through suspension of SSDI benefits to incarcerated persons. Nor could they articulate the logical soundness or the relative equities behind a focus on this particular population to bear the brunt of benefit elimination for trust fund savings after a quarter-century of practice to the contrary (and when extended to the old-age retirement program, after nearly a half-century of contrary practice).[58] Congressman Robert Daniels noted:

> The impending bankruptcy of Social Security must be terrifying news to the Americans who rely on these checks for their very existence. I believe we should take every step to ensure that the Social Security Fund remains solvent, so that those who deserve benefits will continue to receive them. Therefore I was astounded by reports that criminals who reside in penal institutions are eligible to receive [SSDI]. Some inmates even managed to put away a nest egg [with the benefits]. Just as convicted felons lose the right to vote, so should they lose the right to receive [SSDI] … Instead of punishing him, we are paying him overtime.[59]

The impact of the social security incarceration benefit suspension law has been significant and grown substantially over time. In 1980, there were 1,214 persons receiving retirement benefits and 4,300 receiving disability benefits who would be subject to suspension under the laws enacted.[60] By 2020, those figures had mushroomed "fifteenfold" to 17,885 for incarcerated social security old age/retirement program beneficiaries and "tenfold" for incarcerated disability benefits recipients to 39,766 undoubtedly in significant part because of the mass incarceration trends underscored earlier,[61] and the 1983 statutory program expansion of this law to all OASDI programs and 1999 extension to all crimes. Data on the racial makeup of those subject to suspension are not available. However, because the mass incarceration trends have a significant disparate racial impact, in all likelihood the substantial mass suspension of social security benefits to this enhanced and growing population of incarcerated retirees and persons with disabilities has a comparable substantially racially disparate impact as well.

In 1980, opponents of this legislation offered cogent and essentially unrebutted reasons for why the legislation was unsound from a public policy standpoint and constitutionally questionable, although no one expressed concern about the bill's potential racially disparate impact.[62] The SSA's top policy official, Associate Commissioner for Policy Steven Thompson, expressed skepticism and numerous concerns about the bill's soundness; he advocated pumping the brakes and taking time for careful study of the bill's implications and scope.[63] Although being urged by Social Security Subcommittee ranking minority member, Representative Bill Archer (R-TX) multiple times during the hearing to evince support or take a position on the bill, Commissioner Thompson declined to do so and ultimately expressed the view that SSA could not determine whether it would ever support this legislation as consistent with the Act, SSA program goals, and legal principles.[64] Commissioner Thompson's concerns included fears of altering or diminishing the core contributory "earned rights" nature of the social security insurance programs. He stated:

> Imprisonment itself has never been a basis for nonpayment of social security benefits … With rare exception, a person's eligibility for social security is based upon work in employment covered by social security, and without regard to need or circumstance. One prominent argument for restricting social security benefits to prisoners is that prisoners do not need the benefits. However, such a restriction would represent a major departure in program philosophy. For this reason we believe that any proposal that might be seen as moving in the direction of establishing a means test in the social security program should be subject to the most careful consideration of both its immediate and longer range effects.[65]

Although not mentioned by Commissioner Thompson, his point is bolstered by recognition of the differences in treatment on this specific policy issue between the means-tested SSI program and the contributory social security insurance programs. In 1976, the Supreme Court had weighed in on the decisive constitutionally relevant difference between means-tested subsistence programs and the SSDI program in *Mathews v. Eldridge*; it found a different level of presumed material deprivation owing to benefit termination and lesser resultant pretermination due process protection for SSDI recipients, because SSDI is an insurance program based on earnings and not subsistence need.[66] More to the point, the Congressional staff report to the Social Security Subcommittee on the pending 1980 legislation explained that "the denial of benefits to welfare recipients in public institutions has always been a distinguishing aspect between the public assistance and the social security social 'insurance' program."[67] Accordingly, Congress immediately withdrew benefits to persons incarcerated or institutionalized at public expense and supported therein in creating SSA's true, means-tested, subsistence-based SSI program (for indigent elderly persons and indigent adults and children with disabilities) and did so at the inception of the program's enactment in 1972.[68] In sharp contrast, it took many decades after enactment of the social security insurance programs, (and a public frenzy over Son of Sam's receipt of SSDI), to consider engrafting prisoner benefit restrictions on a social security insurance benefits program, at least in part based on notions of a "windfall" or "double dipping."

Commissioner Thompson also expressed a series of other concerns about the bill: (1) despite the continuation of auxiliary benefits to dependents,[69] the bill's mandate to suspend the principal wage earner's larger primary benefits would deprive many children and families of needed support upon which they had relied; (2) it would arbitrarily discriminate against incarcerated beneficiaries since beneficiaries convicted of the same crimes who manage to avert incarceration would retain benefits; (3) it could eliminate benefits to persons never found guilty of any crime but in pretrial detention and since detention practices vary from state to state, would also produce an uneven patchwork of benefit suspension results, in an ostensibly uniform national, federal program; (4) it would also suspend benefits nonuniformly based on state-to-state variations in criminal justice practices and have an "uneven impact on disability beneficiaries convicted of a crime";[70] (5) it could be viewed as "purely punitive in intent" and not serving any identified purpose of the Social Security Act or programs and therefore constitutionally vulnerable; and (6) it is a publicity driven "quick fix" based on "dubious" information from the media about (a) the scope of SSDI inmate benefit receipt and (b) the ease of attaining disability benefits perhaps through fraud or faking.[71]

Although not as fully available in 1980, much has been written debunking the latter point of disability eligibility ease and faking. These writings and reports include a bipartisan position statement in a 2013 open letter by all of the former SSA Commissioners (Republican and Democrat alike) attesting to the standard's unusual stringency; OECD studies of the comparatively unusually stringent disability standard in the American social security disability programs vis-à-vis other OECD countries; high application rejection rates also relative to those in other OECD countries; statistics showing high unemployment rates of persons denied benefits and high death rates within two to seven years of persons approved; medical studies rebutting the suggestion of complete inability to assess faking and malingering in clinical examination and testing by treatment professionals; and government studies documenting the extremely low level of overall fraud in the program, quantified at less than 1 percent.[72] Even in 1980, Congressional Staff for the House Subcommittee on Social Security of the House Ways and Means Committee, issued a report to inform consideration of the pending legislation, finding from a review of data in New Jersey that its "study does not support the proposition that prisoners are 'ripping off' the system."[73] The report also noted that "the denial rate for disability claims of prisoners in New Jersey is higher than that for the state or for the nation as a whole."[74]

A group of nonprofit and civil rights legal organizations also testified and supplied statements more directly opposing enactment of the incarceration/benefits-suspension legislation, including the American Civil Liberties Union (ACLU), the Lawyers' Committee for Civil Rights and others. Stephen Ney, the Director of the ACLU's National Prison project offered the most detailed comments of this group opposing the bill.[75] In addition to reiterating most of Commissioner Thompson's concerns including the improper transformation of a contributory earnings-based social security system into one predicated on need, Mr. Ney pointed out the fallacies of the "windfall" (excess of needs) assumption and the many ways in which inmates' basic needs are not adequately met. He specified systemic inadequacies in healthcare and medical treatment, nutrition and food, and often overcrowded and unsanitary housing conditions as reflected in a GAO report on prison condition inadequacy and court decisions and class actions from thirty-one different states, plus DC, Puerto Rico, and the US Virgin Islands, challenging the constitutionality and legality of these conditions.[76] The Report of Congressional Staff to the Social Security Subcommittee also noted that some states have laws requiring that states collect maintenance expenses from inmates to pay or reimburse subsistence expenses while incarcerated, initially borne by the institutions.[77]

The inadequacy of needs provision through incarceration and penal authorities, documented by the ACLU in 1980, is a problem that has not meaningfully abated in the present. Professor Aaron Littman explained:

> Incarcerated people are generally excluded by statute from eligibility for a range of public-benefits payments like Social Security Disability Insurance (SSDI). Such exclusions are typically based on the understanding … that the expenses of an incarcerated person's "shelter, food, clothing, and medical care [are] … being provided for him free of charge by the prison authorities." This justification is questionable as applied to SSDI … (because these are earned entitlements, not need-based programs). Even the factual premise that a prisoner's "basic needs are being met" at government expense is a shaky one: prisoners can be charged room and board, must often purchase supplemental food to avoid going hungry, and are commonly charged copays for health care. In certain jurisdictions where providing detained people with undergarments is "not a minimum jail standard," they must buy their own underwear or go without.[78]

Stephen Ney in 1980 also identified obstacles to reentry upon release owing to the benefits suspensions since such prisoners are deprived of the ability to have helped the support of children and family or to build a reserve to pay for housing or even more than a few nights of temporary lodging, medical care, rehabilitation services, and other needs.[79] He also rebuffed the accuracy of additional "horror stories" of system abuse from the media including: 1) the unfounded assertion of widespread subsidies to "mass murderers,"[80] noting that (at least at the time in 1980), "most [presumably SSD-eligible] prisoners [we]re serving time for property crimes and not crimes of violence" and 2) the exaggerated accounts of so-called luxury item purchases by prisoners with their benefits since the federal system imposed limits on purchases of $75 per month and inmates qualifying for benefits under SSA's stringent disability eligibility requirements, cannot participate in prison work programs so their social security benefits "are their only income from which to purchase personal items such as newspapers, magazines, and toilet articles."[81]

Moreover, Ney explained that prison authority concerns reflected prison discipline matters and not issues of SSA and/or social security program policy, and a far less burdensome alternative is available to address those former concerns. Accordingly, rather than a blunderbuss and sweeping nationwide total suspension of SSDI to prisoners, Congress could amend the Act to require that incarcerated beneficiaries deposit all but $75 of their monthly Social Security funds into a trust account, and then appoint the department of corrections as a representative payee to manage the remaining funds on the inmate's behalf for the benefit of identified additional legitimate needs of the inmate and/or the needs of children and family members.[82] Ney also noted that the SSA itself does not generally regulate recipients' use of social security funds as "recipients on the outside can do whatever they want with their benefits, squander their money or spend them on necessities."[83] Accordingly, even this far less restrictive alterative would reflect a significant departure from decades of social security policy and practice, albeit to a lesser degree.

Finally, the Lawyers' Committee for Civil Rights, as well as the ACLU (via Ney) each argued that the arbitrariness and irrationality of the bill based on the concerns raised and the bill's disconnection from Social Security Act and Social Security program objectives posed serious questions about the bill's constitutionality under due process and equal protection principles.[84] The Lawyers' Committee also argued that the proposed legislation "was not a rational regulation under the social security program, but a penalty imposed on an identifiable group by legislative act [and] if passed, would be unconstitutional as a bill of attainder."[85]

Despite the cogent, well-developed arguments against the proposed benefits suspension legislation, the bill became law in late October 1980. Notwithstanding all of the identified inadequacies and deficiencies in rationales for this law articulated here, every court to examine claims of due process irrationality or punitive bill of attainder, or both, has rejected them.[86] The bar on these arguments has been set high by the Court's decision in *Flemming v. Nestor*, and several courts have expressly relied on that decision in rejecting one or both of these claims.[87]

In the past few years, a series of law review articles has expressed renewed interest in examining the public policy soundness of this law.[88] In these writings, legal scholars have advanced additional contemporary critiques building on the 1980 arguments of SSA Associate Commissioner Thomspon and the civil rights organizational entities that strongly critiqued the law when proposed. These writings incorporate contemporary considerations not in active public consciousness in the 1980s such as the crisis of mass incarceration and solicitude to the serious issue of offender reentry after incarceration. With respect to the suspension provision's application to the Social Security old age/retirement benefits, one paper emphasized the relevance of evolved, contemporary societal constructions of the function, purposes, and expectations around "retirement" beyond mere "subsistence."[89]

Each paper advocates for repeal of the law, and the analyses are sometimes joined with similar explication of the public policy unsoundness and suggested repeal of the incarceration restrictions on "earned benefits" receipt in other programs such as the Veterans Disability program and the Earned Income Tax Credit program.[90] None has urged continued litigation on these issues in light of the unanimous rulings of all the courts over many years and the absence of even a dissenting opinion, or trace of legal disapproval or skepticism in any court, even in *dicta*. Only Professor John Mitchell has reasserted the due process and bill of attainder arguments anew but has done so, in his view, only for the purpose of underscoring the poverty and perhaps duplicity of the asserted rationales supporting the law, and the law's social counterproductivity in application, in order to bolster a case for legislative repeal focused on the retirement program provision.[91] In so doing, Professor Mitchell has also developed a series of new arguments or new expansions or applications of prior ones, in support of repeal of the OASDI benefit suspension law for incarcerated persons.

First, Professor Mitchell has pointed out that the suggestion of universal subsistence provision as applied to the social security retirement program is no longer consistent with modern notions of retirement (if it ever was fully consistent with societal conceptions of retirement).[92] This is true, he argues, notwithstanding the reality that for many persons, especially Black and Brown beneficiaries, social security is often a major or principal form of retirement income support as described in Chapter 2 and in the Introduction. No longer tethered to the 1935 concept of retirement being the period where one is prevented from working owing to age and inevitable body breakdown at age sixty-five from a career of backbreaking arduous labor shortly before inevitable death and/or pervasive customary age limits and preclusive age discrimination in employment,[93] the modern, twenty-first-century conception of retirement is different. It is predicated on an anticipated passage to a new "phase of life" in pursuit of additional and different fulfillment as a reward for past work, supported by savings, pension, Social Security, Medicare/Medicaid, and retirement assets.

In short, modern retirement is not currently or predominantly visualized and experienced as merely the period of life reflecting a significantly heightened challenge of "subsistence" or for "protection against the poorhouse" and abject destitution for the "unable to work elderly," as perhaps it was perceived by many in 1935 when the Social Security Act was enacted.[94] Many persons work well beyond age sixty-five (including the last two American presidents elected to four-year terms extending into their eighties), and many average Americans may still work while collecting social security retirement/old age benefits well beyond age sixty-five or other full retirement age and/or pursue active lifestyles bolstered by social security receipt.[95]

Professor Mitchell has also expanded the 1980 arguments by the ACLU and others about the reliance on OASDI benefits by the families of the incarcerated wage earner beneficiaries, pointing to the substantial rise in multigenerational housing between 1970 and 2016 and issues with family housing debt from rent, mortgage, and/or property tax arrears and other individual or familial financial obligations (e.g., car payments, child or grandchild's tuition/other educational payments). These are all ongoing expenses in which the incarcerated wage earner's OASDI benefits may have been essential to averting default, often with deleterious consequences for the whole family.[96] The loss of housing, auto and means of transportation, and the undermining of credit and other consequences of default also produce significant additional obstacles to successful reentry upon release, even when benefits are restored.[97]

Moreover, the loss of the incarcerated wage earner's social security benefits creates myriad additional financial pressures on households by generating more pressure on their families that already bear the burdens of incarceration, such as the expenses of grandparents or other family members taking in children and the costs generated by maintaining contact with the inmate.[98] Professor Mariam Hinds has coined the term "shadow defendants" to describe the persons significantly burdened by the incarceration of a family member or loved one.[99] She has pointed out that this cohort is mostly women (and disproportionately Black women and other women of color), and she has also devised the phrase "secondary criminalization" to describe the panoply of damaging impacts on "shadow defendants" including the strain on their financial resources.[100] In addition to the costs of fines, fees, bail, and other criminal justice system expenses which can produce unpaid debts that undermine effective reentry and can lead to reincarceration, shadow defendants often bear ongoing incarceration expenses which are undoubtedly magnified by the incarcerated wage earner's loss of social security benefits. These expenses include "pay to stay charges, [in jurisdictions where costs of jail and prison stays are charged to inmates], medical co-payments, commissary deposits [typically used to pay for food, toiletries, clothing, stamps, and other basic necessities], telecommunications charges, and visitation costs and fees," among other ongoing expenses.[101]

Professor Mitchell has also pointed out the significant disparate racial impact of the social security incarceration benefit suspension provision in light of the effects of racialized mass incarceration discussed earlier along with the "dramatic economic disparit[ies]" confronting Black and Latino/a communities including disproportionate reliance on multigenerational housing.[102] Approximately 27 percent of Latino/a families and 26 percent of Black families live in multigenerational households compared with only 16 percent of white families.[103] Mitchell also noted greater Black grandchild caretaking incidence, and other familial and individual basic commodities and needs supported through Social Security and further undermined by this law.[104] (Most of these realities of disparate Black/Brown existence have been developed in Chapter 2 as drivers of lower social security benefit levels and diminished relative lifetime benefit receipt vis-à-vis white beneficiaries). Professor Mitchell concluded:

> A Ph.D. in economics is not required to conclude that 42 U.S.C. § 402(x) seriously harms many members of communities of color … So, what does our government gain from this economic and social devastation? Supposedly, the original intent was to save money in the Social Security Trust Fund from being wasted. It was peanuts in 1980 and 1983. How much are we talking about now? Compared to the $738 billion provided to 45.1 million retired workers, the amount saved by denying 17,885 seniors who are prisoners their earned retirement benefits is approximately 0.0004% of the funds actually paid out for retired workers. Compared to the $136 billion paid to 8.4 million disabled workers in 2019, the amount saved by denying 39,766 disabled workers their disability benefits that same year is approximately 0.004% of the funds actually paid out for disability. Small potatoes. Within the context of a national economy, equivalent to the change you take out of your pocket at the end of the day and lay down on your nightstand – a fraction of the private wealth of single individuals like Jeff Bezos and Bill Gates. That is the trivial reward our country gets for adding to the economic suffering which already clouds the daily lives of so many families of color.[105]

Finally, apart from the benefits suspension provision's disparate racial impact on incarcerated wage earners and their families and households, the cumulative impact from the loss of such a significant chunk of ongoing financial resources to so many inmates of color often damages their communities at large owing to the hyperconcentration of carceral control in Black and Brown communities.[106] Because mass incarceration is concentrated by race and poverty, and housing and residential patterns in the US remain segregated by the same factors, "Black people in certain neighborhoods [are] more likely to be subject to carceral control."[107] For example, Chicago has 851 single census blocks in some of its predominantly Black neighborhoods, referenced as "Million Dollar Blocks" because authorities are paying more than a million dollars annually (estimated at $22,000 per inmate annually in 2015) to incarcerate the residents of each block.[108] Since the average social security beneficiary in 2026 receives approximately $1,850 per month in benefits ($1,630 on average for disability benefits; $2,071 on average for retirement benefits),[109] the annual loss of benefits from incarceration is approximately $22,000 per year per inmate. If an incarceration-concentrated neighborhood has several "million dollar blocks" or similar numbers with fifty incarcerated persons from each such census block or extended neighborhood area (i.e., 50 x $22,000 = $1,100,000), and even a small percentage of them are or become eligible for social security benefits, the cumulative neighborhood losses of social security revenue could exceed millions of dollars annually, causing further economic hardship to the economy of these communities of color.

In short, the OASDI incarceration benefits suspension law (42 U.S.C. §402(x)) was rushed through to passage in a hasty, emotionally laden media frenzy without meaningful consideration of its purposes, scope, or impact beyond a retributive, punitive revulsion against the thought of the Son of Sam killer and similarly reviled felons (such as Satan, the violent pedophile) potentially receiving social security benefits while incarcerated. The law's only nonpunitive, non-bill of attainder-focused purposes were unusually weak in contrast to the familial and individual hardships created by the law (if not utterly irrational per the extremely deferential *Flemming v. Nestor* standard). The law's particularly disparate impacts in light of racialized mass incarceration since 1980, resultant impediments to reentry, and disparate hardships to families and entire communities of color further reinforce the law's manifest harms and unsoundness. It is overdue for repeal.[110]

Alternatively, as the ACLU persuasively explained and proposed as far back as 1980, Congress, in lieu of straight repeal, could replace the current law with a far less burdensome alternative to address the presumed misuse of social security funds by inmates or for receipt of "excessive windfalls" while incarcerated. It could substitute and enact a considerably narrower remedy than total benefit forfeiture during incarceration by amending the Act to require that incarcerated beneficiaries deposit all but a small portion of their monthly social security funds into a trust account, and then appoint the department of corrections or an inmate-wellbeing-focused nonprofit as a representative payee to manage the remaining funds on the inmate's behalf for the benefit of identified additional legitimate unmet needs of the inmate and/or the needs of children and family members, including the inmate. The trust account could be used for expenses such as maintaining payments on housing, car loans, tuition, medical, dental, and other necessary expenses or consumer debt payments, and to help remove unnecessary obstacles to reentry upon release.

3.3 THE FELONY-RELATED IMPAIRMENT SSDI EXCLUSION LAW: 42 U.S.C.§ 423(d)(6)(A)

Apart from the OASDI incarceration benefit suspension law, the 1980 Social Security amendments also added the SSDI felony-related impairment exclusion in 42 U.S.C.§ 423(d)(6)(A), permanently barring consideration of any impairments in the SSDI eligibility evaluation process, arising (or aggravated) "in connection with" a felony. For similar and related reasons, this law undoubtedly has a deleterious disparate racial impact, although precise data are unavailable. In addition, because the law is also arbitrary in numerous respects as well as vague, overbroad, and conceptually unmanageable, it should also be repealed.

There is a paucity of legislative history on this provision as the bulk of debate and testimony at the legislative hearing on these 1980 Social Security Amendments focused on the incarceration benefits suspension provision discussed earlier. Indeed, some nonprofit organizational advocates who offered arguments against hasty adoption of the incarceration benefits suspension law at least acquiesced in the passage of the felony-related impairment provision. For example, the American Association of Retired Persons (AARP) and National Retired Teachers' Association argued that the "windfall" rationale offered in support of the incarceration benefits provision does not "comport with basic principles of the social security system," would "weaken the system," and "set a dangerous precedent."[111] However, they urged instead that Congress focus on "apparent abuses" and "inequitable receipt" of benefits owing to "crime-related disabilities while leaving the basic system of distribution intact."[112]

The ostensible purpose of the felony-related impairment SSDI exclusion law (and what would avert the asserted "inequitable receipt of benefits" therefrom) would be to preclude persons from benefiting from their own felonious wrongs by receiving benefits based in part on their felonious actions. The common law has long recognized the Latin maxim *Nullus Commodum Capere Potest De Injuria Sua Propria or Commodum ex injuriâ suâ nemo habere debet* (No one should have an advantage from his own wrong).[113] This principle is grounded in public policy against unjust enrichment and in deincentivizing and deterring the wrongful action. Indeed, this maxim has found resonance in another provision in the social security system through a regulation, 20 C.F.R. § 404.344, preventing persons convicted of the felonious and intentional homicide of an insured wage-earner from receiving monthly survivors' benefits (or the lump-sum death payment) based on the earnings record of the deceased (killed) victim. Indeed, the 1980 Congressional Staffers report expressly made the connection between these two provisions, noting: "[T]he authority for this [§ 404.344] is common law doctrine that an individual should not profit from his own wrongdoing. Perhaps this doctrine could also support the denial of disability benefits for individuals whose onset of disability occurred during the commission of the crime – presumably a felony."[114]

From the outset of the consideration and adoption of this law, many questions were raised about its scope and application and whether the law's underlying purposes are met in many or most circumstances. Indeed, the 1980 Congressional Staff report referenced and attached a Congressional Research Service report "outlining possible administrative difficulties in defining and administering such an administrative concept."[115] Except in the most obvious of circumstances – such as in the exchange of gunshots with law enforcement seeking to prevent commission of a violent felony and applying necessary and reasonable force, where a defendant suffers an obviously disabling injury from return gunfire – it is hard to ascertain how the law's ostensible purposes are met, what public policy concerns are vindicated beyond additional punitive sanctions, and what other policy concerns may be undermined in a particular application of the rule for a number of reasons.

First, a seemingly arbitrary anomaly in the application of policy rationale underlying the SSDI felony-related impairment rule, is the exclusion of the rule from the SSID program. While SSDI and SSID have otherwise utilized the same definition of "disability" and the same SSA adjudicative system and processes to resolve disability claims for the past forty-five years, only SSDI program applicants and beneficiaries have been subject to this rule. Neither the legislative history nor any administrative or judicial guidance provides even the slightest patina of reasoning in support of this distinction in treatment of felony-related impairments in these two SSA disability programs. Indeed, at least one court has promptly reversed, without any extended reasoning, the application of the rule by an Administrative Law Judge (ALJ) to an SSI disability applicant, noting simply that the law and its implementing regulation "applies to an application for Title II social security disability benefits (SSDI) [and] … there is no SSI rule … corollary" to the felony-related impairment rule applicable to SSDI.[116]

Nor is there any apparent public policy or logical reason for excluding impairment consideration of certain impairments for disability evaluation purposes in a disability benefit program predicated on social insurance through earnings and past contributions (SSDI), while including consideration of such impairments in a means-tested disability program predicated on indigency and financial need (SSI). Indeed, Congress has seen fit to impose various crime-related restrictions on other need-based programs, not applied to social insurance programs, such as through the Personal Responsibility and Work Opportunity Reconciliation Act (PRWORA) of 1996's imposition of lifetime benefit bans under SNAP (formerly food stamps) and Temporary Assistance to Needy Families program (TANF, formerly Aid to Families with Dependent Children derived from Title IV of the original Social Security Act of 1935), for conviction of drug felonies, in the absence of subsequent state legislation affirmatively abrogating the bans.[117] This is *not* an argument to extend the SSDI felony-related impairment rule to SSI but rather to underscore the arbitrary, haphazard, under- and overinclusive application of this law, adopted with little thought or reasoning, in the course of the 1980 Son of Sam media frenzy as described earlier. Rather, that neither Congress nor the SSA has even intimated an extension of the rule to SSI in over forty-five years underscores the weakness of the law's policy justifications and provides further reasons for its repeal, rather than continuation of its irrational, arbitrary, and discriminatory application to SSDI applicants.

Second, while the law's limitation to persons convicted of "felonies" was obviously intended to preclude consideration of impairments only attributable to violent or highly dangerous or serious crimes, its application in furtherance of this rationale is often arbitrary. As the 1980 SSA Deputy Commissioner for Social Security Policy, Steven Thompson, pointed out in discussing the original felony restriction in the incarceration suspension provision of the 1980 legislation, the legislation suspends benefits nonuniformly based on state-to-state variations in criminal justice practices and can have an "uneven impact on disability beneficiaries convicted of a crime."[118] This includes significant state-to-state variation in crimes classified as "felonies" (or with maximum sentences for greater than a year) – a predicate for this law's application.

In suggesting that a veterans benefits law suspending benefits for veterans while they are incarcerated for felonies is arbitrary, overinclusive, and lacks even a rational basis, Professor Jennifer Oliva has pointed out that "the proliferation of crimes classified as felonies is so ubiquitous in the United States [that a book and various articles estimate] that the average American unintentionally commits *three felonies a day*."[119] Indeed, over four decades ago, the Supreme Court acknowledged "that distinctions between a 'felon' and a 'misdemeanant' are often arbitrary."[120] The Court explained:

> [W]hile in earlier times "the gulf between the felonies and the minor offences was broad and deep," today the distinction is minor and often arbitrary. Many crimes classified as misdemeanors, or nonexistent, at common law are now felonies. These changes have … made the assumption that a "felon" is more dangerous than a misdemeanant untenable. Indeed, numerous misdemeanors involve conduct more dangerous than many felonies.[121]

The problem of significant variation in already somewhat arbitrary felony definitions is compounded by property crime felonies and the substantial variations in the value of property stolen, embezzled, or destroyed that is needed to classify the crime as a felony. That issue has resonance for the application of these criminal justice system-involved social security benefit-restricting rules since, as the ACLU pointed out in 1980, most incarcerated social security beneficiaries are "serving time for property crimes, not crimes of violence."[122] The felony definition and variation problem for property crimes is further compounded by the failure of some states to adjust the predicate felony property value amounts for inflation over time.[123] For example, New Jersey's theft statute has not been updated since 1978, so a $200 dollar theft is still chargeable as a fourth-degree "indictable offense" – New Jersey's version of a felony.[124] Adjusted for inflation, the statute originally essentially felonized the equivalent of an approximately $1,000 theft today, five times the value felonized when last updated.[125] Moreover, the felony predicate amount in Wisconsin is $2,500, reflecting a substantial statewide variation from New Jersey (more than twelve times the predicate amount) in this ostensibly uniform federal, nationwide program justifying a lifetime disability impairment exclusion for SSDI evaluation purposes.[126]

The often amorphous and arbitrary distinctions between felonies and misdemeanors provide further opportunity for the application of discretion in criminal justice processes with racially disparate consequences. As already described, among other factors, explicit and implicit racial bias in discretionary prosecutorial charging, plea bargaining, and sentencing recommendations, as well as in the decisions of parole boards, probation and parole officers, juries and judges – including in sentencing – are in play, and regularly are disproportionately exercised to the detriment of Black and Brown defendants.[127] This includes situations where determinations are made on whether a defendant is charged, sentenced, or offered a plea to a misdemeanor or felony.[128]

A comparison of cases applying the SSDI felony-related impairment rule further illustrates its potential contextual arbitrariness. In *Satterwhite v. Astrue*, the district court reversed an SSA ALJ's decision that had applied the SSDI felony-related impairment rule to deny the claimant's SSDI application after excluding consideration of her disabling mental disorder which arose after (and presumably "in connection with") an accident in which she was charged with felony-aggravated vehicular homicide of the person killed. It did so because the claimant had *pled guilty only to misdemeanor* vehicular homicide.[129] However, in *Ramirez v. Commissioner of Social Security* – a case where no one was killed or injured – the district court and US Court of Appeals for the Ninth Circuit affirmed an ALJ's application of the SSDI felony impairment rule to deny the claimant's SSDI application after excluding consideration of her disabling mental disorder which arose after (and presumably "in connection with") her felony conviction for bringing drugs to her husband in a correctional facility. These courts affirmed the ALJ's decision despite the claimant's assertions of actual innocence of the offense, since she had *pled guilty to a felony* drug charge.[130]

Third, the law's linkage of the felonious crime to the impairment through the phrase "arises in connection with" as opposed to one connoting some concrete degree of causation is a vague, overbroad, and conceptually unmanageable standard promoting further arbitrariness. The SSA's explanatory social security ruling 83–21 makes clear that a "causative connection" between the felony and the impairment is not required and the impairment can merely be "associated with the commission of the offense" such as having "occurred at a time and location that is near (i.e. close in time and location) to the felony."[131] The ruling further provides:

> Ordinarily, the decision as to this issue will be obvious. Most impairments that can be identified as arising in connection with a felony will be of a traumatic nature, such as an impairment resulting from a gunshot wound. However, some nontraumatic impairments may arise in connection with the commission of a felony, since the law does not require that there must be a causative relationship between the commission of the felony and the impairment.[132]

The indeterminate malleability of this standard is manifest. Consider the example of a parent who shoplifts $200 worth of baby formula from a Walmart in New Jersey,[133] who is then run over by a drunken driver in the Walmart parking lot in a hit and run and paralyzed for life. After a conviction for the fourth-degree indictable theft offense (NJ's lowest level equivalent to a felony) for shoplifting the baby formula, this parent-shoplifter could apply for SSDI benefits, but the felony-related impairment law would preclude consideration of the paralyzing impairment. This impairment, although not caused by the shoplifting but rather by the wrongful and reckless act of a drunken driver, still arose "in connection with" the felonious theft/shoplifting and is both close in time and place to it. Yet one would be hard-pressed to identify what policy rationale is served and what just result would be accomplished by permanently denying perhaps critically needed social security disability insurance funds (including auxiliary benefits to dependent family members), predicated on years of earnings and contributions to the social security trust fund, to the paralyzed victim of this reckless driver solely because of proximity to the wage earner's baby formula shoplift.

If the rule's rationale is to prevent benefiting from one's wrong as indicated in the Congressional Staff report, the criminal and civil laws governing legal liability for wrongs (tort law on the civil side) provide at least some guidance through proximate cause doctrine. They generally absolve parties from responsibility for the consequences of wrongs that are attributable to independent intervening, superseding causes.[134] They distinguish between independent and dependent intervening causes and look to the reasonable foreseeability or abnormality of the intervening event to determine whether the causal chain is broken by the intervening event.[135] For a famous example from the seminal book on legal causation:

> A defendant who culpably pushes his victim to the ground is not liable for that victim's death when the victim is killed on the ground by a falling tree. The falling tree, in such a case, intervenes between defendant's push and the victim's death. By contrast, if the defendant's push caused the victim to stagger into a rotten tree, and the impact caused it to fall and kill the victim, the defendant is held to have caused the death. While the tree's falling was subsequent to the defendant's act of pushing, it was not causally independent of the push and so does not constitute an intervening cause.[136]

Even the much-maligned felony murder doctrine in criminal law, which permits imposition of murder liability for unintended deaths occurring in the course of felonies, usually has limits on the doctrine grounded in various culpability and/or causation requirements in many jurisdictions.[137] For example, some states require that the death was caused by the defendant or another participant in the felony and not by a third party.[138] Other jurisdictions require that a death occurred during the commission of inherently dangerous felonies, or with reasonable foreseeability of seriously injurious or fatal results, among other limitations.[139]

If causation principles were applied to the SSDI felony-related impairment law, results would likely be different in many cases. Apart from the Walmart baby formula-shoplifting/drunk driver hit and run example, the case law on the rule's application supplies some potential examples. In *Leach v. Saul*,[140] the clamant suffered serious impairments to his right shoulder and right foot from gunshot wounds from an unknown source which occurred while he was driving a car. He was subsequently arrested when authorities found crack cocaine in his car and pled guilty to a drug felony.[141] When he applied for SSDI benefits, the ALJ upheld the denial of his application and applied the felony-related impairment rule to exclude consideration of his impairments caused by the gunshot wounds.[142] The court ultimately remanded the ALJ's decision, noting that the case presented a "close call" but required clearer rationale on how the gunshot-produced impairments "factor into the overall disability determination" and whether the gunshot impairments were felony related.[143] It provided no guidance on the circumstances under which experiencing a shooting and gunshot impairments from an unknown assailant while possessing drugs, would be "deemed connected or not connected" to drug possession under the rule.

Similarly, in *Moore v. Sullivan*, the claimant, while simply standing in front of the residence of person A, was shot by person A with a "20-gauge shotgun," albeit for reasons which were unknown and "unclear"; – that is, there was no indication the claimant was unlawfully present on person A's property or threatening person A in any manner.[144] Thereafter, the clamant took out a gun and pointed it at a person B "standing 15–20 feet away."[145] The claimant was then arrested, charged, and pled guilty to aggravated assault presumably for raising a gun at person B.[146] When the claimant later applied for SSDI, the SSA Appeals Council, on its own motion, reopened and reversed an otherwise favorable ALJ decision and denied SSDI benefits after applying the felony-related impairment rule to exclude consideration of the claimant's gunshot-induced serious injuries to his leg which had been fractured and had contributed to bone weakness and other impairing fracture.[147] The court affirmed the agency's application of the rule and denial of benefits, finding the gunshot-induced impairments "arose in connection with the felony," without any analysis (or identification of any reasoning or analysis in the Appeals Council decision) on whether the claimant's impairments from the unexplained earlier shooting by person A were sufficiently connected to the claimant's subsequent aggravated assault of person B. Certainly, the later assault did not cause the earlier shooting in which the claimant was (or may have simply been) the victim.[148]

Another avenue for anomalous and potentially arbitrary application of this law and its "arising in connection with" language can occur in cases involving exacerbation of preexisting mental impairments. Attributing the disabling aggravation of mental impairments as closely connected with the stress and anxiety stemming from arrest, submission to the criminal justice process, indictment, trial, and/or plea bargaining on a felony charge – for the purpose of denying lifetime consideration of the mental impairment (to the extent aggravated) in the SSDI process under the law – will often be questionable from a psychiatric science perspective. Since neither causation nor traumatic injury is required under the law, ALJs and sometimes courts have determined that criminal process-induced mental impairment exacerbation can arise "in connection with" the felonious act, leading to the stress/anxiety-inducing prosecution and justifying application of the felony-related impairment rule.[149]

However, mental impairment symptomology and limitations are characteristically nonstatic, fluctuating, and cyclical, producing "waxing and waning" of symptoms often with good days and bad days over time.[150] To exclude consideration of the mental impairment from SSDI eligibility forever, as attributable to exacerbation from the criminal process resulting from a felony charge, would require decoupling that symptom enhancement from a series of other periodic symptom exacerbations arguably caused by stress or anxiety, chemical imbalances, or countless other events and circumstances not involving commission of a felony in a longitudinal assessment of a claimant's psychiatric condition and history over an extended period of time. This decoupling process, or lack thereof in the identified SSDI cases on this fact pattern,[151] for the purpose of application of the felony-related impairment rule in mental impairment cases, seems tenuous at best in many if not most cases.

Moreover, the lack of a causation requirement in the felony-related impairment law also produces another huge avenue for racially disparate application and benefit exclusion. In situations where a claimant's impairment arises after interactions with police, other law enforcement, school disciplinary, or prison/correctional authorities, the subsequent charging and either plea or conviction to a felony from the interaction could forever preclude consideration of very serious disabling impairments caused by police and official brutality and misconduct. This is true, whether or not the interaction was initiated by police authorities during or after commission of a felony (as opposed to a random "stop and frisk" or traffic stop). In 2022, African Americans (4 percent) were four times as likely than white persons (1 percent) to experience the threat or use of nonfatal force from police contact.[152] African Americans also "experience police misconduct at six times the rate of white people" and Latinos/as experience police misconduct at two times the rate of whites.[153] In terms of fatal police violence, by mid 2025 and in 2024, African Americans were 2.8 times more likely to be killed by police than whites.[154]

African Americans are not only nearly three times more likely than whites to be shot and killed, but they are also "five times more likely to have police intervention-related injury."[155] In addition, African Americans with disabilities also face an increased rate of police violence. Fifty percent of people killed by police have disabilities and "more than half of disabled African Americans have been arrested by the time they turn 28" which is twice the number for white disabled Americans.[156] Often the disability is portrayed as a threat to police, and owing to lack of police training on how to respond to crisis calls and persons with disabilities, the police respond with violence. Police often interpret the disability as "the person being difficult" or resisting arrest.[157]

While there appears to be no available specific data on the incidence and demographics of disabling impairment-producing illegal, unconstitutional, improper, or unnecessary encounters by police and other law enforcement personnel, the data and studies referred to here provide strong support for the assumption that the same disproportionalities hold for permanent and long-term-impairment-producing improper police encounters. However, if a felony conviction or plea is entered – even a low-level felony plea in response to charges of resisting arrest, or assault of a police officer based on the suspect's defensive actions in seeking to mitigate the consequences of a police beating in some manner – the resulting impairment will likely be permanently excluded from SSDI evaluation under the rule. Moreover, because in many jurisdictions a guilty plea would serve as a bar or significant impediment to a subsequent civil rights lawsuit for police brutality, prosecutorial authorities working regularly with police may aggressively pursue guilty pleas for aggravated resisting arrest or assault on a police officer-type charges for a victim of police brutality, with threats of considerably greater sanctions on the defendant for rejecting a plea in cases where the "resisting" evidence is weak and nonprosecution would be appropriate.[158] That guilty plea, by a putatively innocent defendant, could then also become the predicate for application of the felony-impairment rule to preclude SSDI consideration of the serious impairments caused by police misconduct.

Because of the rule's absence of a causation requirement, the possibility that such a police encounter-based serious impairment was caused or decisively exacerbated by police misconduct or brutality is not even considered or discussed in cases involving potential application of the SSDI felony-related impairment rule. This result can lead to further potentially arbitrary, inequitable, and ultimately discriminatory application of the rule and resulting SSDI benefits denials. For example, in *Hixson v. Colvin*,[159] the court remanded an agency decision to consider whether the SSDI benefit claimant's serious knee impairment occurred while he "vigorously struggled with the deputies while they attempted to place him into custody" and not earlier (thereby excluding consideration of the knee impairment under the felony impairment rule), without identifying any relevance to consideration whether the deputies' forceful and potentially injurious impairment-producing conduct was justified or appropriate.

Similarly, in *Finkbeiner v. Comm'r of Soc. Sec.*,[160] the court remanded an agency decision for further consideration of the question whether the claimant's shoulder impairment occurring while "fleeing from the police after shoplifting" and after being brought for emergency treatment to "the hospital in handcuffs" should be excluded from SSDI consideration under the felony-related impairment rule, without any mention of the relevance of the propriety of the police conduct potentially leading to or exacerbating the shoulder impairment. Yet excessive police force, police brutality, and official misconduct-induced impairments are usually not legally or otherwise attributable to the victims of such conduct (or deemed caused by the victims), and can even give rise to criminal and civil liability of the authorities committing the injurious acts (although there are many structural, doctrinal, functional, and political obstacles to overcome in such legal actions).[161]

Like the misguided OASDI incarceration benefits suspension law, the SSDI felony-related impairment law in 42 U.S.C. § 423(d)(6)(A) should be repealed for the reasons given here. Alternatively, and at a minimum, Congress or SSA, perhaps through a quick modification of Social Security Ruling 83–21 (providing SSA's extended guidance on the rule's application), should add a causation requirement between the felony and the impairment to cabin the "arising in connection with" language, in the guidance to this rule's implementation. On the question of rule abolition versus reform (and in a manner more consistent with contemporary norms and values of causation and/or culpability), the previously identified highly criticized felony murder doctrine might supply some guidance.[162]

Professor Guyora Binder has argued for reform of felony murder doctrine through a "dual culpability" principle, which "justifies imposing murder liability for killing negligently in the pursuit of an independent felonious purpose" and noting that "most jurisdictions" meet this standard and "condition the offense" at least on "negligence through a combination of culpability requirements, dangerous felony limits, foreseeable causation requirements, and complicity standards … and require felonious motive through a combination of enumerated felonies, causation standards, and merger limitations."[163] Others have advocated for full abolition, arguing that limits on the doctrine are insufficient to remedy injustice in its application.[164] Virtually all other common law countries have abandoned the felony murder doctrine, which originated as a common law doctrine, as have three states – Hawaii, Kentucky, and Michigan.[165]

One of the reasons asserted for abolition, as opposed to reform, is the doctrine's significant racially disparate application.[166] Even, Professor Guyora Binder, a leading reform advocate, has pointed out that the degree of racial disparity in felony murder convictions is considerably greater than the racially disparate level of convictions in all other second-degree murders – undoubtedly aided through discretion produced by the doctrine's legally and morally questionable dimensions and perhaps the inability to prescribe clear and consistent limits on its applications in particular cases.[167] The likely racially disparate application of the SSDI felony impairment rule similarly provides further support for rule abolition as opposed to the rule's reform with a causation requirement as alternatively suggested herein.

4

The Exclusion of the Supplemental Security Income Benefits Program from the Principal US Territories and the Racial Origins and Implications of American Colonialism in the Welfare State

4.1 THE SUPPLEMENTAL SECURITY INCOME PROGRAM AND ADVERSE RACIAL IMPACT OF EXCLUSION

The tortured and peculiar 125-plus-year history of the US's acquisition and colonial domination of the US territories also reveals racial inequity in access to a vital Social Security program. Although Congress eventually included the territories in the contributory Social Security insurance programs (OASDI) in amendments in 1950 and 1960,[1] at present, the Social Security Act excludes four of the five major territories, Puerto Rico, Virgin Islands, Guam, and American Samoa, from the critically important SSI program – the entirely federal, means-tested,[2] public assistance benefits program for adults and children with disabilities and for the elderly.[3] The Supplemental Security Income (SSI) program has been described by social welfare policy experts as "a core component of the nation's Social Security system" providing "nothing short of a lifeline for nearly 8 million of the nation's poorest seniors and disabled people, including more than one million disabled children."[4] Through SSI's enactment, Congress sought to assure "that the Nation's aged, blind, and disabled people would no longer have to subsist on below-poverty-level incomes."[5]

The 1972 Social Security Amendments that created the SSI program excluded the territories by confining eligibility to "resident[s] of the United States," which the statute further defined as those residing in "the 50 States and District of Columbia [hereafter DC]."[6] In later legislation, Congress only added residents of the territory of the Commonwealth of the Northern Mariana Islands (CNMI) to the program, leaving the remaining territories excluded.[7] The absence of SSI in the remaining major territories has a significant deleterious impact owing to their extreme levels of poverty,[8] material deprivation, and vulnerability to natural and man-made disasters.[9] Moreover, the deficient alternatives for subsistence aid in the otherwise scattershot patchwork of safety net public assistance programs fail to fill the void for vulnerable, impoverished, disabled, and elderly territorial residents. For example, Puerto Rico has a joint federal-local welfare program (Assistance to the Aged, Blind and Disabled; AABD) but maximum benefits are only $164 per month,[10] compared with $994 per month in SSI. "The Government Accountability Office estimated that in Puerto Rico alone, 2011 federal spending on AABD was less than 2 percent of what it would have been if Puerto Rico residents received full SSI benefits" and would extend to over 435,000 potentially eligible persons rather than only 37,000 persons who received AABD in an average month in 2015.[11] Accordingly, the loss of subsistence benefits from the absence of SSI in Puerto Rico is about $830 per month in cash income for each of the 37,000 persons receiving AABD and living in extreme poverty, and more – perhaps as much as $994 per month – for the other close-to-400,000 persons who do not currently qualify for AABD but would qualify for SSI.

Puerto Rico and American Samoa residents also lack the traditional SNAP/Food Stamps program and food relief at stateside levels,[12] and all four territories have only partial Medicaid with limited funding, causing denial of "coverage to specific groups, such as impoverished children and pregnant women, that would be mandatorily covered in the 50 states and the District of Columbia."[13] The impacts of SSI disability program exclusion are also greater because disability levels are significantly higher in regions with a confluence of high poverty, a lower-skilled, less educated workforce, and inconsistent health insurance and health care quality,[14] a situation present in all four SSI-excluded territories. None of the four territories has a program supplying additional means-tested benefits to children with disabilities, an important component of SSI; this is significant since, for example, Puerto Rico has a child poverty rate of 57 percent and children are ineligible for AABD.[15] Moreover, whereas SSI is a mandatory federal spending program extending benefits to all who demonstrate eligibility, benefits under AABD and the territorial adult assistance programs are not guaranteed; they are conditional and limited by a flat block grant appropriation and benefits are restricted to the amount appropriated, even if the number of those eligible exceeds the funds available under the block grant.[16]

The SSI territorial exclusions also have a significant racially disparate impact, as the overwhelming majority of residents in each excluded territory are persons of color. Puerto Rico is by far the most populous territory, with over 3.2 million residents, more than twenty states.[17] The 2020 census found that approximately 99 percent of its population identify ethnically as Latino/a or Hispanic and a substantial majority identify racially as either mixed-race, Black, or another nonwhite racial group, with only 17 percent designating one-race-white.[18] According to 2020 census figures for those other three territories, 71.4 percent of Virgin Island residents are Black/African American and only 13.3 percent are one-race-white;[19] in Guam,[20] 81.5 percent are AANHPI – Asian American (35.4 percent), Pacific Islander/Native Hawaiian (46.0 percent), with only 6.8 percent one-race-white; in American Samoa, 94.5 percent are AANHPI – Asian American (5.8 percent), Pacific Islander/Native Hawaiian (88.7 percent), with less than 1 percent one-race-white.[21]

4.2 THE OVERTLY RACIST CONSTITUTIONAL FOUNDATION FOR INFERIOR TERRITORIAL RESIDENTS' RIGHTS AND BENEFITS: THE INFAMOUS "*INSULAR CASES*"

The territories' history after US acquisition reveals the centrality of their racial character (and the role of American racism) in the creation and reinforcement of conditions of subordination under which separate and unequal systems of territorial rights and benefits emerged.[22] All of these US territories were acquired on or after 1898, with Puerto Rico, Guam, and the Philippines ceded by Spain following the Spanish-American War through the 1898 Treaty of Paris.[23] They have had somewhat amorphous status and correspondingly limited access for their residents to the rights and benefits of stateside Americans since acquisition. In describing the influence of American racism on law and policy in the territories at the turn of the century, historian and Professor Rubin Weston observed:

> Those who advocated overseas expansion faced this dilemma: What kind of relationship would the new peoples have to the body politic? Was it to be the relationship of the Reconstruction period, an attempt at political equality for dissimilar races, or was it to be the Southern "counterrevolutionary" point of view which denied the basic American constitutional rights to people of color? The actions of the federal government during the imperial period and the relation of the Negro to a status of second-class citizenship indicated that the Southern point of view would prevail. The racism which caused the relegation of the Negro to a status of inferiority was to be applied to the overseas possessions of the United States.[24]

The infamous *Insular Cases*,[25] a series of Supreme Court decisions from 1901 to 1922, solidified the subordinate, perpetually uncertain, and unresolved status of the territories and diminished treatment of their residents, and they employed overtly racist and white supremacist reasoning in doing so. These cases have been referenced as "the most racist Supreme Court cases you've probably never heard of,"[26] and about which it has been noted, "[t]oday, any judge or lawyer who used the same racist rhetoric … would face professional discipline."[27] Scholars and jurists often point out that these decisions and their novel racialized doctrines were initiated by the same Supreme Court that decided *Plessy v. Ferguson* and created the "separate but equal" doctrine that legitimized Jim Crow and facilitated American apartheid.[28] In those cases and in the Supreme Court's own words, the then-newly acquired territories were not governed by "Anglo-Saxon principles,"[29] and were "peopled with an uncivilized race,"[30] who would be "absolutely unfit" for citizenship,[31] on islands inhabited by "alien races,"[32] "savages,"[33] "uncivilized tribes," and "savage tribes."[34] As such, the residents could not be trusted with the rights and privileges of Americans or even self-government.[35]

Statements by Members of Congress expressed similar overtly racist sentiments about territorial natives, with particular animus directed against Filipinos. One senator referenced them as "physically weaklings of low stature, with black skin, closely curling hair, flat noses, thick lips, and large, clumsy feet," or "savages, cannibals, Malays, Mohammedans, head hunters, and polygamists," and urged fellow legislators to "beware of those mongrels ... with breath of pestilence and touch of leprosy ... [and] with their idolatry, polygamous creeds, and harem habits."[36] Another senator argued more broadly about the collective new territories that "the United States could not and would not 'incorporate the alien races, and ... semi-civilized, barbarous, and savage peoples of these islands into our body politic as States of our Union.'"[37]

Although some legislators distinguished Puerto Rico from the Philippines on racial grounds, identifying the former as closer to white, stateside Americans – referencing Puerto Ricans as "two-thirds ... white, of Spanish origin,"[38] other legislators contested this account and supplied racist rationales for opposing according Puerto Rico similar treatment to other incorporated territories that became states. For example, the former Speaker of the House, Representative Joseph G. Cannon of Illinois, opposed the 1917 legislation granting citizenship to Puerto Ricans and noted that "[t]he people of Porto Rico have not the slightest conception of self-government," and the island "is populated by a mixed race. About 30 percent are pure African ... [and fully] 75 to 80 percent of the population ... was pure African or had an African strain in their blood."[39] Representative Cannon concluded: "God forbid, that ... there should be statehood for Porto Rico as one of the United States."[40] The positions of both groups of legislators reveal the pervasive influence of overt racism and conceptions of white supremacy in the treatment of Puerto Rico, the Philippines, and their residents.

Accordingly, although owned, possessed, and governed by the US, these territories would be "foreign in a domestic sense,"[41] and their residents "nationals, but not citizens,"[42] with only those constitutional rights deemed "fundamental,"[43] and such other rights as provided by Congress. Indeed, although not yet deemed citizens by virtue of the Fourteenth Amendment's Citizenship Clause, it took an act of Congress to eventually extend birthright citizenship to persons born in Puerto Rico, Guam, and the Virgin Islands; American Samoans still have not been accorded birthright citizenship.[44]

Through these cases, the Supreme Court also "invented, out of whole cloth,"[45] the concept of "unincorporated" territories to define the new insular possessions. As distinguished from prior territories which were incorporated into the US upon annexation and deemed to be on the road to statehood (such as Alaska) and therefore with full constitutional coverage and protection, these alien race island territories were "annexed but not incorporated."[46] While "what it means to be 'unincorporated' remains contested to this day," there is little dispute that the *Insular Cases* established that "the federal government has the power to keep and govern territories indefinitely, without ever admitting them into statehood (or deannexing them [for independence], for that matter)."[47] The Court's interpretation of the Constitution's Territory Clause supported this result.[48] As Professor Christina Ponsa-Kraus has explained:

> The distinction between incorporated and unincorporated territories thus served as the cornerstone of a racially motivated imperialist legal doctrine: the idea of the unincorporated territory gave sanction to indefinite colonial rule over majority-nonwhite populations at the margins of the American empire ... The unincorporated territory was a judicial innovation designed for the purpose of squaring the Constitution's commitment to representative democracy with the Court's implicit conviction that nonwhite people from unfamiliar cultures were ill-suited to participate in a majority-white, Anglo-Saxon polity. With the creation of the unincorporated territory, the Court implicitly embraced the view that the theory of political legitimacy underlying the Constitution allowed for an exception, born of practical necessity and motivated by racism, permitting a representative democracy to govern people deemed inferior indefinitely without representation. The raison d'être of the *Insular Cases* was, therefore, to provide the constitutional foundation for perpetual American colonies.[49]

In sum, the *Insular Cases* rendered these territories and their overwhelmingly nonwhite residents "'doubly marginal': neither fully domestic nor fully foreign, and devoid of both voting representation in the federal government and independent status on the international stage," – relatively invisible and trapped "in a second-class status with an uncertain future."[50]

4.3 THE SSI TERRITORIAL EXCLUSION'S LEGISLATIVE CONTEXT AND THE COURT'S REJECTION OF THE EQUAL PROTECTION CHALLENGE IN *UNITED STATES V. VAELLO MADERO*

Under the circumstances governing the territories' disfavored legal and social status, and colonial-like treatment and history, created and reinforced through the *Insular Cases*, it should come as no surprise that the government extended only a second-class safety net to territorial residents as described earlier in Section 4.1. Indeed, Puerto Rico and the other principal territories were also excluded from the original 1935 Social Security Act. Although the absence of federal taxation in Puerto Rico (and presumably the other territories) was cited by the chairman of the House Ways and Means Committee, Robert Doughton, as the basis for the territorial exclusions,[51] racialized comments by members of Congress were also among the sentiments expressed in opposition to including territorial residents in the 1930s era social security legislation.[52] For example, in response to efforts to add Puerto Rico and the Virgin Islands to the contributory Social Security old age insurance program when Congress was considering the 1939 amendments that added the social security survivors program, Congressman Thomas Jenkins (R-OH) noted that "racially they are very different from the American people, generally speaking" and "their requirements and needs" were "not quite the same" as those of people in the mainland US because Puerto Ricans were "poorer" than those living in the continental United States."[53] Accordingly, "coverage of those island residents would entail "taking on a much bigger load toward them than we are toward our own people."[54]

Puerto Rico's nonvoting resident Commissioner in Congress, Santiago Iglesias, testified on the 1939 Social Security amendments and argued for Puerto Rico's inclusion in the Act and in the new amendments, pointing out that "since the Social Security Act was first considered by Congress four years ago ... Puerto Rico has been desirous that this law be extended to the island for the benefit of the people there." As such, there were "1,800,000 loyal American citizens" comprising the population of Puerto Rico, "whose exclusion from the benefits of the act was 'unfair.'"[55] Resident Commissioner Iglesias had made similar pleas in 1935 when the original social security legislation was being crafted and debated.[56] FDR's Secretary of Interior, Harold Ickes, had submitted written testimony for the hearing on the 1939 legislation, and stated that the need for social security act coverage in Puerto Rico and the other territories was "at least as great as the States."[57] Ickes also offered the opinion that "Puerto Rico has suffered particularly from legislation designed to benefit American people" but whose "benefits ... were not applicable to its citizens,"[58] and concluded that he saw "no just reason for discriminating against these possessions" by continuing to exclude them from coverage under the Social Security Act. Finally, Ickes, noting that Puerto Ricans did not have congressional representation, implored members of Congress to ensure that they "not suffer economically through their lesser political status."[59]

It would take more than another decade for Congress to add Puerto Rico and the Virgin Islands to the contributory social insurance program in amendments in 1950.[60] While there was not much legislative debate on the merits of the bill leading up to the 1950 amendment provisions, a staunch segregationist congressman from Mississippi, Willam Colmer,[61] opposed inclusion when the legislation was proposed in 1949. He stated, in comments in which he also voiced opposition to including "domestic servants" in the social security insurance program: "I do not like that provision of the bill which provides for the inclusion of Puerto Rico and the Virgin Islands into this system, a people who have possibly the lowest type of economy in the world, and yet, we would further burden our people by including them."[62] Another full additional decade passed before Congress included residents of Guam and American Samoa in the OASDI program in amendments in 1960.[63]

However, despite the long-awaited social security insurance programs' territorial inclusion amendments in 1950 and 1960, in 1972, Congress nonetheless excluded residents of the US territories (with the eventual exception of CNMI residents) from the amendments creating the SSI program – one of the most vital means-tested Social Security Act safety net programs.[64] The legislative history surrounding the territorial resident exclusion in the Social Security Act's SSI program amendment is sparse and somewhat opaque. Although the initial SSI legislation which the House passed in 1971 would have extended coverage to Puerto Rico, Guam, and the Virgin Islands with certain per capita income-ratio benefit-level restrictions, the Senate-passed version fully excluded the territories, and those exclusions remain in effect today.[65]

The chairperson of the Senate Finance Committee, Senator Russell Long of Louisiana, in describing the need to reject a proposed amendment to the Senate version to include the territories, referenced the absence of "appropriate answers to address equity and justice in those territories" as the reason to hold off on inclusion amendments until such answers could be provided.[66] Accordingly, those amendments were not taken to the conference on the final SSI legislation enacted in 1972.[67] Senator Long also offered as reasons for SSI exclusion in the territories that "[t]here is a difference in dollar level of earnings and there are tax considerations."[68] However, he supplied no further explanation of how those differences or considerations would undermine "equity and justice" if SSI were extended to territorial residents.

A House staffer on the initial SSI legislation who was a "social legislation specialist" for the Congressional Research Service, Carolyn Merck, testified years later to the House Committee on Interior and Insular Affairs, Subcommittee on Insular and International Affairs, that the primary consideration behind the SSI territorial exclusion was concern about disruption to the territorial economies; SSI receipt could create work disincentives through generous federal safety net benefit levels for low-income aged, blind, and disabled territorial residents that could approach the levels of some full-time workers' incomes.[69] In response to a statement that the concerns over SSI inclusion in the territories such as Puerto Rico were about the "disruptive" impact of "money distribution" on the "social and cultural fabric," in the territories, she stated:

> Well, it is certainly true that when you raise someone's income by tenfold there can be serious effects on the labor supply and work incentives and disincentives of the non-SSI members in the family who may not earn as much as the SSI benefit. Raising the income from $32 or whatever, tenfold a month, where the amount may be a fair wage on the part of full-time workers, or in some cases, of the primary earner in the family, has been an issue, and continues to be a primary question.[70]

In 1975, when SSI benefits were extended to CNMI in the covenant establishing its commonwealth terms, Senator Long reiterated that SSI was excluded from the other territories because "in view of the different economic and other circumstances in the territories and possessions, the Congress felt it would be inadvisable to provide the Federal SSI income guarantee level in the territories and possessions."[71] He suggested instead that it would be preferable to have "locally developed plans" for safety net assistance under the former federal-state welfare programs to low income disabled or aged persons "which can be more appropriated [*sic*] tailored to the circumstances prevailing in each area."[72] At the same time, Senator Long acknowledged that CNMI would receive SSI and full federal SSI funding and coverage for its eligible residents.[73] He made no effort to distinguish CNMI's economic circumstances, or the desirability of appropriate local tailoring under the preexisting (and far less generous) federal-state welfare programs, from those considerations pertaining to the other US territories in the sparse legislative history on the inclusion of SSI in the CNMI covenant.[74]

The government has defended the provision of SSI to CNMI residents while continuing to exclude residents of the other principal territories. It has asserted simply that "Congress had a sound reason to treat the Northern Mariana Islands differently than Puerto Rico and other Territories: the United States had committed to extend SSI to the Islands in the covenant establishing the Islands as a commonwealth, but had made no comparable negotiated commitment with respect to other Territories."[75] News accounts suggest the CNMI had greater leverage for negotiating somewhat better terms for its territorial status owing to timing and its perceived unique strategic importance to US national defense interests in the Pacific during the Cold War period.[76] Subsequent bills to extend SSI to the remaining principal US territories in 1976 and 1977 passed in the House, but were ultimately not adopted by the Senate with little debate or discussion.[77]

When the Supreme Court initially addressed the constitutionality under equal protection principles of Puerto Rico's lesser safety net in 1978, it is not surprising that it rejected the claims in extremely short summary *per curiam* decisions without oral argument or briefing – as if reasoning, analysis, or even serious consideration were wholly unnecessary. While the Court did not purport to declare the Fifth Amendment's equal protection principles inapplicable to the territories as "non-fundamental," the specter and taint of the *Insular Cases* still hovered over and infected these decisions.

First, in 1978, the Court in *Califano v. Torres* rejected a challenge to the SSI exclusion from three claimants who lost their SSI upon moving to Puerto Rico from various states.[78] In the decision's brief text, the Court rejected a right-to-travel challenge to the exclusion as predicated on an unestablished and erroneous theory that "a person who has moved from one State to another might be entitled to invoke the law of the State from which he came as a corollary of his constitutional right to travel."[79] The Court then, in two footnotes, dismissed the plaintiff's conventional equal protection claim, presenting it as almost an afterthought. In the first footnote, it expressly cited three of the principal *Insular Cases*, *Downes*, *Dorr*, and *Balzac*,[80] and at least impliedly relied on concepts emanating from them. The Court applied no perceptible scrutiny to the classification in question nor consideration of the alternative possibility of heightened equal protection scrutiny based on important factors often triggering greater judicial suspicion and closer evaluation.

Each footnote matter-of-factly supplied information with scant analysis. The Court's first relevant footnote noted:

> The complaint had also relied on the equal protection component of the Due Process Clause of the Fifth Amendment in attacking the exclusion of Puerto Rico

> from the SSI program. Acceptance of that claim would have meant that all otherwise qualified persons in Puerto Rico are entitled to SSI benefits, not just those who received such benefits before moving to Puerto Rico. But the District Court apparently acknowledged that Congress has the power to treat Puerto Rico differently, and that every federal program does not have to be extended to it. Puerto Rico has a relationship to the United States "that has no parallel in our history." *Examining Board v. Flores de Otero*, 426 U.S. 572, 596 (1976). Cf. *Balzac v. Porto Rico*, 258 U.S. 298 (1922); *Dorr v. United States*, 195 U.S. 138 (1904); *Downes v. Bidwell*, 182 U.S. 244 (1901).[81]

Then, in its next relevant footnote, the Court listed three reasons offered by the government to support the disparate exclusion of Puerto Rico from the SSI program, but supplied no analysis, reasoning, or even a conclusion of whether any of these specific reasons provided a rational basis for the distinction created. It stated:

> At least three reasons have been advanced to explain the exclusion of persons in Puerto Rico from the SSI program. First, because of the unique tax status of Puerto Rico, its residents do not contribute to the public treasury. Second, the cost of including Puerto Rico would be extremely great – an estimated $300 million per year. Third, inclusion in the SSI program might seriously disrupt the Puerto Rican economy.[82]

The Court then ended the opinion after rejecting the right-to-travel claim by restating the general principle that "[s]o long as its judgments are rational, and *not invidious*, the legislature's efforts to tackle the problems of the poor and the needy are not subject to a constitutional straitjacket."[83] Yet it also declined to consider whether any invidious considerations infected the SSI exclusion from the cited racially infused *Insular Cases* doctrines and resulting territorial history. The Court, arguably, at least impliedly relied on that history, and its consequences, to support a uniquely deferential rational basis standard not requiring any showing of a specific rational basis for the obviously disadvantaging classification's disparate impact on an overwhelmingly nonwhite population.

Two years later, the Court issued an even shorter *per curiam* opinion of only one paragraph of reasoning, in *Harris v. Rosario*,[84] rejecting an equal protection challenge to lower reimbursement levels to Puerto Rico than the states and DC under the Aid to Families with Dependent Children (AFDC) means-tested public assistance program. In *Rosario*,[85] the Court concluded in one sentence, without any citation to authority other than *Torres*, that the Territory Clause authorized Congress to treat Puerto Rico differently from the states so long as there is a rational basis for doing so.[86] It then relied solely on footnote 7 in *Torres* for the rational bases to reject the challenge, without any independent analysis or reasoning supporting the rationality of those asserted purposes.[87]

Justice Marshall issued a dissent, principally pointing out that the *Insular Cases* such as *Downes* and *Balzac*, which held that various protections of the Constitution do not apply in Puerto Rico, were of "questionable" validity.[88] He then castigated the majority for deciding for the first time, without briefing or argument, that Congress needs "only a rational basis to support less beneficial treatment for Puerto Rico" so that, presumably, "[h]eightened scrutiny" under equal protection principles "is simply unavailable" to protect "citizens who reside [in Puerto Rico] from discriminatory legislation as long as Congress acts pursuant to the Territory Clause."[89] He noted that nothing in *Torres* and its equal protection "dictum" in a footnote – the only precedent relied on by the *Rosario per curiam* majority – established these principles.[90]

Justice Marshall was particularly pointed in his rejection of the assertion in *Torres* that the extension of comparably generous safety net benefits as in the states for the most vulnerable low-income residents of Puerto Rico would disrupt the local economy. He stated:

> This rationale has troubling overtones. It suggests that programs designed to help the poor should be less fully applied in those areas where the need may be the greatest, simply because otherwise the relative poverty of recipients compared to other persons in the same geographic area will somehow be upset. Similarly, reliance on the fear of disrupting the Puerto Rican economy implies that Congress intended to preserve or even strengthen the comparative economic position of the States vis-à-vis Puerto Rico. Under this theory, those geographic units of the country which have the strongest economies presumably would get the most financial aid from the Federal Government since those units would be the least likely to be "disrupted."[91]

Accordingly, Marshall dissented from the Court's summary disposition of the case, noting "the serious issue of the relationship of Puerto Rico, and the United States citizens who reside there, to the Constitution."[92]

In 2022, the SSI exclusion for Puerto Rico reached the Supreme Court again in *United States v. Vaello Madero*.[93] As in *Torres*, the SSI claimant had lost his SSI when moving from the states (New York) back to Puerto Rico. The case arose when the SSA sought repayment from him of the benefits he continued to collect while ineligible owing to his residence in Puerto Rico.[94] He then asserted an equal protection challenge to the statutory exclusion from SSI of residents of Puerto Rico as a defense to this overpayment collection action.[95]

The case reached the Court after a unanimous First Circuit panel in an opinion authored by former Chief Judge Juan Torruella invalidated the SSI exclusion on equal protection grounds, distinguishing *Torres* as a right-to-travel case, *Rosario* as one involving a different benefits program than SSI, and each as having limited precedential value as summary *per curiam* decisions on issues other than those raised by *Vaello Madero*.[96] The First Circuit also independently analyzed each of the three proffered rationales from footnote 7 in *Torres* and found that none was rationally connected to the SSI exclusion.[97] It first flatly rejected the "economic disruption" rational basis hypothesis from the *Torres* Court's footnote 7 – the principal justification proffered in the sparse legislative history of the 1972 SSI exclusion. After pointing out that even the federal government had abandoned reliance on that justification as a rational basis for the exclusion, and quoting Justice Marshall's dissent which rejected this assertion in *Rosario*, the First Circuit stated:

> Referring back to the Court's original endorsement of this rationale in [*Torres*], one might find the Court's citation to the Report of the Undersecretary's Advisory Group on Puerto Rico, Guam and the Virgin Islands perplexing. [*Torres*], 435 U.S. at 5 n.7 (citing Dep't of Health, Educ., & Welfare, Report of the Undersecretary's Advisory Group on Puerto Rico, Guam and the Virgin Islands 6 (1976) [hereinafter 1976 report]); see Peña Martínez v. Azar, 376 F. Supp. 3d 191, 208 (D.P.R. 2019) (noting that the cited report does not support an economic theory for why Puerto Rico's inclusion in SSI would disrupt the economy and instead highlights the success of the extension of the Food Stamp Program to Puerto Rico). In fact, the 1976 report expressly rejected concerns about an influx of aid disrupting the economy as a justification for disparate treatment, concluding that "the current fiscal treatment of Puerto Rico … is unduly discriminatory and undesirably restricts the ability of these jurisdictions to meet their public assistance needs." 1976 report, supra at 6–7. Therefore, considering the dubious nature of this once-accepted rationale, we are relieved that we are not called upon to decipher it and note its abandonment only as an additional factor that weakens the relevance of [*Torres*] and [*Rosario*] for this appeal.[98]

The First Circuit also specifically found that the *Torres* Court's additional footnote 7 suggestion of a rational basis grounded in the assertion that Puerto Rico's "residents do not contribute to the public treasury" was not only "irrational and arbitrary," bearing no connection to the SSI program, but also patently false.[99] Rather, Puerto Rico "consistently contributed more than $4 billion annually in federal taxes and impositions into the national fisc" – more than six states and the CMNI.[100]

The First Circuit also rejected the third, "cost savings," rationale in *Torres*'s footnote 7, reasoning: "[C]ost alone does not support differentiating individuals. If it did, how would Congress be able to decide upon whom to bestow benefits? Presumably along the lines of its legislative priorities which, at a minimum, must be supported by some conceivable rational explanation. The circularity of this logic defeats itself."[101]

Put another way, a naked "cost savings from averting government expenditures for territorial residents" justification could support any random or arbitrary elimination or reduction in any form of government benefit, tax credit, opportunity program, or aspect of government largesse in the Territories otherwise mandated for state residents. And the government could do so without even the slightest independent rational basis for the expenditure cut. It would proceed on the assumption that any such funding cut to territory residents is rational and not arbitrary or random, simply because it involves cuts to funding for territory residents. Indeed, at oral argument before the Supreme Court, the Deputy Solicitor General [Gannon] conceded that "cost alone" would not be enough to support the SSI exclusion.[102]

However, the Supreme Court then reversed the First Circuit in another relatively short opinion. Justice Kavanaugh's majority opinion commenced by quoting the Territory Clause's text and observing that in exercising authority thereunder, "Congress sometimes legislates differently with the territories, including Puerto Rico, than it does with the States."[103] The Court then reasoned that the *Torres* and *Rosario* "precedents dictate[d] the result" and mandated that the "deferential rational basis test applies."[104] But rather than asserting a rational basis grounded in the erroneous and overbroad assertion that Puerto Rico's residents did not "contribute to the treasury" as in *Torres* and *Rosario*, the Court narrowed that contention to "the fact that residents of Puerto Rico are typically exempt from most forms of federal income, gift, estate, and excise taxes," and that "in devising tax and benefits programs, it is reasonable for Congress to take account of the general balance of benefits to and burdens on Puerto Rico."[105]

The Court's analysis, while somewhat longer than in *Torres* and *Rosario*, still falls short in addressing numerous questions raised by the application of traditional equal protection principles to the SSI territorial exclusion. In its application of this uniquely "deferential rational-basis test" based on distinctions between territories and states otherwise authorized by the Territory Clause, it required no independent justification for discrimination with respect to the specific benefit program (SSI) in question or any actual relationship, rational or otherwise, to the tax exemptions identified. Instead, by identifying the government's ability simply "to take account of the general balance of benefits to and burdens on Puerto Rico,"[106] without indicating how it had done so and the arguable relationship of that accounting to SSI exclusion, the Court relied solely on a hypothetical general tax/benefit scorecard of sorts to justify the exclusion.

While minimal-scrutiny equal protection is not a particularly "difficult standard for [government] to meet when it is attempting to act sensibly and in good faith … 'the rational-basis standard is "not a toothless one"[;] the classificatory scheme must [still] '*rationally advanc[e]* a reasonable and *identifiable* governmental objective.'"'[107] The *Dandridge v. Williams* case is often cited as an example of the most highly deferential or "low level" application of minimal-scrutiny rational basis review of social welfare legislation.[108] However, the Court in *Dandridge* still identified justifications purporting to actually relate to and establish a specific connection with the legislative classification in question (lesser per capita AFDC benefits for large families vis-à-vis small ones).[109] In contrast, the "deferential test" applied in the *Torres–Rosario–Vaello Madero* line of cases apparently needed no such specific connection or actual relationship to the tax/benefit scorecard purpose. The Territory Clause alone was seemingly enough to bridge the complete lack of a specific relationship between means and ends since it authorizes differential treatment of territories and states by definition.[110]

The result is essentially tautological: Territory-Clause-based differences between states and territories disadvantaging the latter are rational because the Territory

Clause authorizes differences in treatment between states and territories. Authorization alone, and Congressional intent to act on that authorization, denotes rationality. However, "a mere tautological recognition of the fact that [the legislature] did what it intended to do" is inadequate as a rational basis.[111] As Professor Alexander Aleinikoff has decried in critiquing the Court's same approach in *Rosario*, this reasoning "would seem to authorize virtually any discrimination against Puerto Rico residents in federal programs," and "constitutional law ought to demand more than judgment by definition."[112]

Moreover, there are several additional reasons why the relationship between the specific tax rationale and the SSI exclusion is inapposite. The claimant in this case, Jose Luis Vaello Madero, was an individual asserting his own rights as a US citizen and resident of Puerto Rico against discrimination by virtue of the SSI exclusion vis-à-vis residents of states (and DC and CNMI) who have access to SSI.[113] The question presented for the Court's disposition was whether equal protection principles require Congress to make SSI benefits "available to residents of Puerto Rico to the same extent that Congress makes those benefits available to residents of the states."[114] Viewed as a question of discrimination against putatively SSI-eligible *residents of Puerto Rico versus state residents* – as opposed solely to the broader Territory Clause-induced question of differences in Congressional treatment of *territories versus states* – the Court's federal tax exemption and tax/benefit scorecard analysis is even more attenuated from a rational basis for the challenged discrimination.[115]

Analyzed through the lens of the former question, and as Justice Sotomayor explained in her dissent, "It is antithetical to the entire premise of the [SSI] program to hold that Congress can exclude citizens who can scarcely afford to pay any taxes at all on the basis that they do not pay enough taxes."[116] Further undermining the rational connection between SSI exclusion as a means to the end of federal income tax exemption is the anomalous nonrelationship between the different classes of residents respectively benefited and burdened by these various measures. Putatively SSI-eligible low-income residents of Puerto Rico who also have no tax liability are punished with denial of access to life-support benefits because middle-income and wealthy Puerto Rico residents who would be ineligible for SSI (by being over the SSI income and/or resource limits) are exempt from federal income tax.[117] In this "reverse Robin Hood" scenario, viewing Congress's actions of giving a tax subsidy to the class of rich and relatively comfortable residents as justification for taking life-supporting benefits away from an entirely different class of disabled and elderly persons in deep poverty (i.e., "Because we subsidize Puerto Rico's rich, we can rationally starve its most vulnerable poor") is additionally irrational.

Similarly, reliance on taxes to justify the SSI exclusion is irrational from a Social Security Act and public benefits policy and law perspective. As described earlier, the Social Security system contains both contributory social insurance cash-benefit programs and noncontributory means-tested ones. SSI is a means-tested program, not a contributory social insurance program like OASDI. Indeed, SSI was designed, in part, to supply subsistence benefits to disabled and elderly persons lacking sufficient work history for contributory insurance coverage under OASDI.[118] There is no perceptible rational thread for using "a logic of contributory insurance to justify [exclusion from] a non-contributory (i.e., means-tested) program."[119]

Along those lines, Congress consolidated multiple joint federal-state public assistance programs for persons with disabilities and the elderly, previously administered by the states and with contemplated and resulting state-by-state variation and local control, into a uniform, national program when it created the SSI program in 1972. As a result, and as Justice Sotomayor also explained in her dissent, this program now "establishes a direct relationship between the recipient and the Federal Government."[120] As such, "the jurisdiction in which an SSI recipient resides has no bearing at all on the purposes or requirements of the SSI program."[121] Accordingly, "[f]or this reason alone, it is irrational to tie an individual's entitlement to SSI to that individual's place of residency."[122]

On a more basic level, the facts do not support an imbalanced tax/benefit scorecard for Puerto Rico vis-à-vis the states as a rational basis for the exclusion. The Court cited no statistical or numerical basis for its assumption that "the general balance of benefits to and burdens on the residents of Puerto Rico" suggests a negative imbalance inconsistent with the ordinary range of net tax/benefit burdens of the states.[123] A study by economists Arthur MacEwan and J. Tomas Hexner in 2016 used data from 2004 and 2010 to ascertain "net federal expenditures per capita," defined as the amount that the federal government sends to a particular state or territory less the amount that the state or territory sends to the federal government in taxes, adjusted for population. The study found that "in more than one-third of all the states … the net amount per capita received from the federal government – federal expenditures minus federal taxes – was greater than the net amount per capita received in Puerto Rico from the federal government."[124] Puerto Rico lagged behind seventeen other states (and DC) in this tax/benefit balance in the study's tables. The authors concluded: "The reality demonstrated in the tables, then, belies the conventional wisdom and indicates that, by a reasonable comparative standard, Puerto Rico is not treated 'generously' by the federal government."[125] Even looking just on the tax side of the ledger, Puerto Rico contributes more federal taxes than six states and the CNMI.[126]

The Court in *Vaello Madero* also opined that if Congress extended SSI to Puerto Rico residents it would produce a ripple effect, potentially extending all taxes to Puerto Rico too, with damaging consequences.[127] Without questioning the inevitability of wholesale extension of all tax programs by virtue of inclusion of a single additional benefit program, the assumption of net harm to Puerto Rico residents from such an occurrence is also at least questionable. While exempt from federal income tax, "residents of Puerto Rico pay every other tax known to the imagination," leading multiple commentators to point out that "Puerto Ricans on the island are the most heavily taxed of all U.S. citizens."[128] They pay FICA taxes (described in

Chapter 2, funding OASDI and Medicare); "payroll, business ... import and export taxes; commodity taxes; unemployment insurance taxes; and self-employment (SECA) taxes."[129] They are also taxed on income from sources outside Puerto Rico and on all federal employment.[130] However, since Puerto Rico residents do not pay routine federal income taxes, they cannot generally avail themselves of valuable anti-poverty programs based on tax credits, such as the Earned Income and Child Tax Credit programs.[131] Since poverty levels are unusually high and median income levels low, most residents of Puerto Rico would not shoulder much, if any, tax liability if federal income taxes were extended, but would benefit from tax credits.[132] Therefore, when evaluating the practical implications of a stateside tax/benefit package applied to Puerto Rico, many, if not most, workers in Puerto Rico "might be better off if they had to file a U.S. tax return."[133]

Finally, curiously absent from the *Vaello Madero* majority's analysis was any discussion of whether some form of heightened scrutiny might apply in an evaluation of the SSI exclusion (as suggested by Justice Marshall in *Rosario*) or the role of, or specter hovering over the case from, the *Insular Cases*. These issues are not unrelated. The Court's first *per curiam* opinion rejecting a challenge to the SSI exclusion in *Torres* cited and relied on the *Insular Cases* and, in turn, the *Vaello Madero* majority reasoned that *Torres* (and *Rosario*, which had followed and relied on *Torres*) "dictated the result." This arguably rendered the *Vaello Madero* decision "fruit of the poisonous [*Insular Cases*] tree" from a formalist, precedential perspective.[134]

More fundamentally, the issues are related because, as a result of the *Insular Cases*, residents of Puerto Rico have been historically subordinated and rendered relatively politically powerless without representation in Congress or rights to vote for the president or vice president,[135] by being placed in an amorphous "unincorporated" territory ("foreign in a domestic sense") status for over 125 years and counting, based on rationales grounded in overt racism. The inability to compete or garner meaningful attention in the national political arena and/or a history of victimization or subordination are factors significantly contributing to the Court's reasoning in applying heightened equal protection scrutiny of governmental classifications, whether characterized as strict, intermediate, or "rational basis with bite" scrutiny,[136] based on race, national origin, or gender, or burdening various groups such as immigrant "aliens,"[137] nonmarital children,[138] LGBTQ individuals,[139] and children of undocumented immigrants suffering complete deprivation of education.[140]

The case for heightened scrutiny has been succinctly summarized by former First Circuit Chief Judge Juan Torruella, noting the consequences of:

> the total national disenfranchisement and lack of national political clout of the community of 3.5 million United States citizens who reside in Puerto Rico, a condition which has lasted for the 119 years of U.S. sovereignty over the people who inhabit this territory, and even more significantly, throughout the 100 years since they were granted citizenship in 1917. This situation has, if anything deteriorated

> in recent times. This regrettable condition calls upon this court to heed the apparently forgotten advice of the Supreme Court in United States v. Carolene Products Co., 304 U.S. 144, 152 n.4, [](1938), to the effect that "prejudice against discrete and insular minorities may be a special condition, which tends seriously to curtail the operation of those political processes ordinarily to be relied upon to protect minorities, and which may call for a correspondingly more searching judicial inquiry."[141]

One could add to that reasoning the following three-step argument or syllogism for heightened scrutiny in *Vaello Madero*: (1) The SSI exclusion intentionally classifies and disadvantages persons based on "unincorporated" territorial residence; (2) the "unincorporated territory" construct is based on and a product of overt racism and historical subordination by race, which has undermined residents' ability to avert damaging national legislation and actions through disenfranchisement in national political processes; (3) therefore, heightened scrutiny should apply to such classifications since they are grounded in and only made possible through invidious racial considerations which continue to adversely injure largely politically defenseless and overwhelmingly nonwhite territorial resident populations.[142]

In short, heightened equal protection scrutiny in some form should be triggered by classifications directed at "unincorporated territory" residents. They are a class intersectionally ravaged by a confluence of historical race discrimination with ongoing present-day consequences. They also suffer from extreme and seemingly permanent political powerlessness. Altogether, their status "command[s] extraordinary protection from the majoritarian political process."[143] The tax/benefit scorecard basis offered to justify the SSI exclusion would have most definitely failed to pass muster under any of the heightened scrutiny formulations for the reasons discussed here. If the exclusion from SSI of putatively eligible territory residents lacks a specific and actual rational connection to an overall tax/benefit scorecard or ledger or other identified "legitimate" interest, then *a fortiori* it lacks a substantial or necessary/narrowly tailored relationship to any identified purpose deemed compelling, important, or substantial under recognized strict or intermediate heightened scrutiny formulations.[144]

From the perspective of equal protection heightened scrutiny doctrine, there are, however, a number of anomalies and distinctions in evaluating unincorporated territory resident classifications that could present some conceptual concern. In applying some degree of heightened equal protection scrutiny based on denial of free public education to undocumented children in *Plyler v. Doe*, the Court recognized that the class's general status as undocumented immigrants could not be declared categorically suspect or "quasi-suspect" because it is not irrelevant to many lawful classifications on that basis by definition.[145] However, the *Plyler* Court still applied heightened equal protection scrutiny, requiring a "substantial" state goal and not merely a "legitimate" one in invalidating a law denying free public education to undocumented children.[146]

Similarly, in *Vaello Madero*, pursuant to the Territory Clause, Congress has always had the constitutional power to treat territory residents differently so it could be asserted that "discrimination against residents of a territory is grounded in a distinction drawn by the Constitution itself, which, *ipso facto*, cannot be suspect."[147] However, at oral argument, the Deputy Solicitor General disclaimed insulation from usual equal protection scrutiny principles based on the Territory Clause's presence. He answered Justice Thomas's questions of whether the Territory Clause alone could supply a basis for the SSI exclusion (or the degree to which the Territory Clause might change the equal protection analysis) by asserting that the analysis would be the same; Congress could enact the same exclusion to residents of a state such as Vermont if its tax/benefits balance were similar to Puerto Rico's.[148] Of course, the principal difference in his comparison to Vermont is that Vermont is represented in Congress; it is hard to imagine Vermont senator Bernie Sanders failing to find a way to prevent such discrimination against Vermonters.[149] This political process reality buttresses the representation-reinforcement justification for heightened equal protection scrutiny for territory resident-classifications.[150]

Another anomaly is the potential transience in and out of the class.[151] Vaello Madero himself only garnered this status, and lost his SSI benefits, when he moved from New York to Puerto Rico; he could escape his loss of SSI (and lack of Congressional representation and national voting rights) simply by moving back. While somewhat problematic when compared with other classifications triggering heightened scrutiny which have greater immutability,[152] the rigid geographic territory-residence disqualification and stigma could also be viewed as further reinforcing these islands' historical subordination and lingering colonial second-class status – a factor enhancing the justification for greater scrutiny.[153]

Although neither the *Vaello Madero* majority nor its dissent addressed the *Insular Cases* in their differing conclusions on the SSI exclusion's constitutionality under the facts, Justice Gorsuch issued a concurrence, exhorting the Court to someday overrule the *Insular Cases*, and bypassing any analysis of the constitutionality of the SSI exclusion or the facts. He pointed out that the *Insular Cases* "have no foundation in the Constitution and rest instead on racial stereotypes [and] deserve no place in the law," that they originated through "support in academic work of the period, ugly racial stereotypes and the theories of social Darwinists," and no judge can properly "profess the right to draw distinctions between incorporated and unincorporated Territories, terms nowhere mentioned in the Constitution and which in the past have turned on bigotry."[154]

Justice Gorsuch implied that if any of the parties had so requested, he would have perhaps sought to overrule the *Insular Cases* right then and there. But since neither party had so requested, he was compelled to concur with the majority,[155] albeit without the slightest indication why he found the majority's equal protection analysis, and not the dissent's, the proper one. He ended his concurrence emphasizing that he "hope[s] the day comes soon when the Court squarely overrules [the *Insular*

Cases]" since "our fellow Americans in Puerto Rico deserve no less."[156] However, by joining the majority, the import of his opinion was to reinforce that what our fellow Americans from Puerto Rico and the class of vulnerable, indigent, disabled, and elderly putative SSI claimants on the island "deserve" is the continuation of a second-class safety net and deprivation of federal life-supporting benefits.[157]

At the end of the majority's opinion, the Court supplied something of a consolation prize, pointing out that "the Solicitor General has informed the Court that the President supports legislation as a matter of policy" to extend SSI to residents of Puerto Rico.[158] That legislation became part of President Biden's "Build Back Better" package of social legislation securing passage in the House; it would have extended SSI to Puerto Rico, the Virgin Islands, Guam, and American Samoa.[159] However, it stalled permanently in the Senate in May 2022, when two Democratic senators joined Republican senators in refusing to support it.[160] Although Congress passed, and the president signed into law, a considerably smaller version of this legislation later in August 2022, rethemed the Inflation Reduction Act, the package enacted did not include the SSI territory inclusion provisions.[161] Accordingly, the status quo prevails: the overwhelmingly nonwhite indigent disabled and elderly residents of these four US territories will continue to suffer extreme hardships from the deprivation of subsistence payments for a period now approaching fifty-five years since SSI's enactment, based on the consequences of doctrines grounded in racism and creating a fiction under which separate and unequal "unincorporated" territory treatment was enshrined into law and policy.

4.4 CODA

The Social Security Act's statutory exclusions and provisions examined in Chapters 1 and 4 are from different time periods more than thirty-five years apart, directed to decidedly different issues, and affecting vastly different communities of color. Yet they are bound by a common thread of the American experience emanating from our original sin: racism and white supremacy.[162] In historical context, the referenced exclusion provisions are, respectively, grounded, at least in part, in historical racism emerging from the "badges and incidents" of slavery and solicitude to protecting the postbellum plantation-sharecropping economy, or from American colonialism and imperialism around the turn of the twentieth century and indefinite separate and unequal treatment facilitated through amorphous unincorporated territory status based on theories of white Anglo-Saxon supremacy over alien races. Each exclusion was also abetted by political disenfranchisement and the relative political powerlessness of the excluded communities. Political disenfranchisement resulted from poll taxes, lynching, and myriad forms of voter intimation against African Americans at the time of New Deal legislation,[163] or the absence of Congressional representation or ability to vote for president in the territories, which continues to the present.

With respect to the SSI exclusion in the territories, the path toward reform is straightforward. The failure of "Build Back Better" in 2022 should not be viewed as the death knell of the SSI Territory Inclusion legislation. That it was approved in the House and appeared to fail (or be on the road to failure before being pulled) by only two votes in the Senate as a very small part of a far more costly overall package can be viewed as a positive political harbinger for a potentially more hospitable Congress and administration in the future.[164]

5

Race, Health Care Inequity, and Medical and Adjudicative Bias, Particularly in Evaluation of Pain and Symptomology, in the Social Security Disability Programs

5.1 INTRODUCTION TO RACIAL DISPARITIES IN THE SOCIAL SECURITY DISABILITY PROGRAMS

The remaining chapters address racial disparities (and factors contributing to such disparities and inequities) arising in the social security disability system. As described in the Introduction, the massive size of the bureaucracy created to process and adjudicate social security disability program claims, and enormous quantity of claims, further underscore the SSA disability programs' importance in the present-day American welfare state. The considerable quantitative "mass justice" challenges of SSA disability adjudication are compounded by the elasticity and imprecision of a socially constructed substantive disability legal standard. That elasticity creates further potential for disparate application in multiple respects, as is discussed later in this chapter.

Indeed, the issue of racial disparities in the SSDI and SSI programs has been the subject of much debate since 1992 when the US General Accounting Office issued a report after years of study finding unexplained racial disparities in SSDI and SSID adjudications.[1] This report, which has been touted by scholars and journalists alike as "the single most important study undertaken so far on the issue of impartiality of Social Security decisionmakers,"[2] and "the most comprehensive [study] about race and disability ever undertaken by the Government,"[3] reviewed nearly a million cases (700,000 involving white applicants and 245,000 involving Black applicants), and found unexplained statistically significant racial disparities in decision-making principally at the ALJ hearing level (where the claimants are seen in-person for the first time by disability adjudicators). That report and study found that SSA ALJs granted benefits to 66 percent of white SSDI applicants but only 55 percent of Black SSDI applicants and 60 percent of white SSI applicants as opposed to 51 percent of Black SSI applicants.[4] The only statistically significant unexplained racial disparity at the initial levels of adjudication, decided on paper at the disability determination services (DDS) offices,[5] was to young SSI applicants (those without a work history), where the agency granted benefits to 47 percent of white SSI applicants but only 34 percent of Black applicants.[6]

The GAO report recommended that the SSA Commissioner "investigate the reasons for the racial difference in allowance rates in the initial DDS decisions for young SSI applicants, as well as for all decisions at the ALJ level, and that the Commissioner act to correct and prevent any unwarranted disparities."[7] The report also recommended "that the Commissioner … look into the criteria used in adjudicating cases involving schizophrenia and 'other' mental disorders as well as neurological, sensory and respiratory disorders, all of which had a large racial difference in allowance rates."[8] Those allowance rate disparities by principal impairment were respectively: schizophrenia: 67 percent white, 55 percent Black (for SSDI applicants) and 77 percent white, 69 percent Black (for SSI applicants); "other mental disorders": 41 percent white, 31 percent Black (SSDI), and 39 percent white, 29 percent Black (SSI); respiratory disorders: 45 percent white, 32 percent Black (SSDI), and 34 percent white, 23 percent Black (SSI); and "nervous/sensory" disorders: 42 percent white, 30 percent Black (SSDI), and 42 percent white, 25 percent Black (SSI).[9]

The ranking minority member of the Senate Special Committee on Aging which oversees the SSA and who disseminated the report, Senator William Cohen (R-ME), found that "the evidence clearly supported the conclusion that race played a … major role in awarding claims" and that "there appears to be a racial bias within the administrative process of the Social Security system."[10] Around the same time as the GAO report, the Administrative Conference of the United States (ACUS) had conducted a comprehensive evaluation of the federal ALJ corps. It found that the ALJ cohort was "overwhelmingly white and male."[11] The ACUS ALJ survey found that "94% were male and 6% female" and "94% are white, 3% Hispanic and the remaining 3% divided evenly among African-Americans, Asians and Native Americans [i.e. 1 percent each]."[12] A leading Administrative Law casebook described the "overwhelming white and male ALJ cadre" as "a particular embarrassment, perhaps for SSA, whose disability program disproportionately serves women and minority groups."[13] At present, 80 percent of all federal ALJs work for the SSA and principally conduct disability hearings.[14]

Although SSA, while questioning one of the methodological aspects of the GAO report, quickly concurred with all the GAO report's recommendations,[15] it has since taken little consistent action to pursue them and, in some respects, has placed additional obstacles in the way of meeting the GAO's goals. On the positive side, for an unspecified time period after the 1992 GAO report, the agency appeared to conduct a large scale antibias training program for all of its ALJs at which approximately a quarter of all SSA ALJs participated in its first phase with a goal of eventually including all.[16] However, reports of the program's accomplishments were mixed and perhaps somewhat conflictual.

On the one hand, SSA's Deputy Commissioner, Daniel Skolar, extolled the program's success, even in reaching ALJs who had been "animated" and "critical in their opposition to the program and its premises," and who then "learn[ed] something about their own biases and preferences" and reported "an increase in knowledge."[17]

On the other hand, Professor Linda Mills – herself a former disability attorney, licensed clinical social worker and health policy scholar (and now the first woman to serve as president of New York University), who was hired to conduct antibias sessions with the ALJs – recounted a different narrative. Professor Mills suggested that ALJs were "defensive" when presented with "statistically significant evidence of their biased decision-making patterns" and then "sabotaged the consciousness-raising exercises that were offered."[18] Mills further related that:

> One senior judge read the newspaper while a diverse group of experienced trainers, myself included presented material on the judges' propensity to stereotype. When pressed, these resistant judges claimed that once ordained as judges, they were able to transcend the prejudices to which all men and women fall prey. They believed that no matter what they said or did, they could hide behind the disinterested veil of judicial impartiality.[19]

Since the GAO study, SSA has conducted a series of studies in 1995 and 1997 recruiting ALJs to serve as peer reviewers of other ALJs to evaluate their decision-making through its "quality assurance review" processes. The SSA-reviewing ALJs (RJs) concluded that the ALJs' decisions, while evincing some procedural irregularities, were largely accurate.[20] However these studies declined to seek demographic data on, discuss, or address racial disparities in decision-making in any manner.[21] Then in 2002, GAO issued a follow-up report to its 1992 report titled "SSA Decision Making: Additional Measures Would Enhance the Agency's Ability to Determine Whether Racial Bias Exists."[22] This report noted that SSA had taken some "limited steps … to address racial bias in ALJ decision making" such as by instituting a mandatory "diversity sensitivity training course for ALJs," "increased its efforts to recruit minorities for ALJ and other legal positions by attending conferences of minority bar associations," and distributed information on how to become an ALJ.[23] The 2002 GAO report also noted that SSA had established a new complaint process for ALJ misconduct, "including possible racial bias," although "the process does not include a mechanization for easily identifying complaints involving racial discrimination," does not "track the race of complainants," and "as a result, will not help SSA's … staff to identify patterns of possible racial bias among complaints filed, which might warrant further investigation or corrective action."[24]

The principal thrust of this 2002 GAO report was that SSA "has significantly scaled back its collection of race data" and that future analyses of race and racial bias in SSA decision-making "might be hindered by this."[25] The report specifically found that "the steps SSA has taken over the last decade have not appreciably improved the agency's understanding of whether or not, or to what extent, racial bias exists in its disability decision making process."[26] Among other findings, this GAO report determined that "SSA's ability to analyze racial differences in decision making will diminish due to a lack of data on race and disability"; it could not agree with SSA that its quality assurance reviews reflect "no evidence of racial bias"; and it concluded that, at present, "SSA does not have an ongoing effort to demonstrate the race neutrality of its disability programs."[27]

In 2003, the GAO issued another report of a follow-up survey of ALJ decisional disparities by race. The report found large, statistically significant disparities by race, which could not be rationalized on nonracial grounds, in decisions where claimants lacked attorney representation at hearings; specifically "the odds of being allowed benefits for African Americans were one half of the odds of being allowed for whites."[28] The GAO noted that this finding had additional salience since African Americans lacked counsel in a significantly greater percentage of the hearings than white claimants (39 percent to 29 percent).[29] However, this survey revealed no significant disparities in attorney represented cases that could not be explained by factors other than race.[30]

After reiterating the concern that SSA had scaled back its race/ethnic data collection since 1990, the 2003 report recommended, among other measures, that the SSA: "conduct ongoing analyses of ALJ decisions by race/ethnicity," and in doing so, "oversample the selection of ALJ decisions by African-American claimants, and to the extent possible other racial/ethnic groups to ensure that SSA has a sufficient number of cases to conduct analyses of ALJ decisions by race," "if needed, take actions to correct and prevent any unwarranted difference in allowance and support rates among racial/ethnic and other claimant groups," and "establish an advisory panel comprised of external experts in a range of disciplines – including statistics/econometrics, design methodology, law, medicine, vocational training, and disability – to provide leadership, oversight, and technical assistance with respect to … reviews of ALJ decisions."[31]

Since that time, SSA's Office of Retirement and Disability Policy confirmed in 2016 that SSA "discontinued the publication of data by race for the SSI program in 2002, and for the OASDI program after 2009."[32] In 2020, a group of more than forty-five nonprofit organizations as part of the Consortium for Citizens with Disabilities (CCD) wrote to SSA Commissioner Andrew Saul, requesting the SSA's recommencement of data collection and reporting on race and ethnicity in social security programs.[33] The CCD request referenced the three GAO reports and their recommendations as well as the racial/ethnic data practices of nine other federal agencies.[34]

For a short period, in following up President Biden's 2021 and 2023 Executive Orders on "Advancing Racial Equity and Support for Underserved Communities through the Federal Government,"[35] and requiring Equity Action Plans for federal agencies, the SSA's 2023 Equity Action Plan Update, building on its 2022 Equity Action Plan, acknowledged SSA's problematic declining race and ethnicity data (and some identified data decline since 2010); SSA proposed short-, medium-, and long-term steps to rectify those racial data collection and reporting deficiencies.[36] To date (in 2025), there is no indication SSA is presently pursuing implementation of those steps or furthering the GAO's recommendations from its three reports on racial differences in allowance rates in SSA disability decisions.

In 2023, pursuant to its Equity Action Plan, the SSA also initiated a study by Abt Associates of equity and bias in SSA's Quick Disability Determination (QDD) Process pursuant to its Equity Action Plan.[37] The SSA's QDD process, instituted in 2008, is a "fast track" system for a relatively small number of claims presented at the initial application (paper, nonhearing) level to identify claimants with the most severe medical disabilities and allow expedited decisions "to approve some cases in a matter of days" instead of months or years as in the full process. SSA "uses a computer-based [algorithm-AI] predictive model to screen initial applications to identify cases where a favorable disability determination is highly likely and medical evidence is readily available."[38]

The 2023 Abt study found racial and ethnic disparities in the QDD determinations, relative to white claimants, as follows: (1) Black applicants (11 percent lower for SSDI; 13 percent lower for SSI adults; 9 percent lower for concurrent SSDI/SSI; 10 percent lower for SSI children); (2) Hispanic (9 percent lower for SSDI; 6 percent lower for SSI adults; 6 percent lower for concurrent; 5 percent lower for SSI children); (3) Native American/Alaskan Native (5.6 percent lower for SSDI; 13.6 percent lower for SSI adults; 6.4 percent lower for concurrent; 6.4 percent lower for SSI children); (4) Asian American "not meaningfully different" from white applicants.[39] Abt noted that factors such as barriers to application preparation such as education, English language facility, homelessness, lack of representation, and geographic location played a role but only a "small role" in the racial/ethnic disparities in QDD determinations for "Black and Hispanic groups" of about "1–4 percentage points."[40] Although the study concluded that it lacked sufficient information to "determine conclusively whether the differences observed reflect bias within the [SSA's] QDD process, rather than sources of bias outside of the QDD process," it recommended a series of further and more targeted follow-up studies and actions by SSA.[41] However, President Trump expressly revoked President Biden's equity-based Executive Orders in his first hours in office in 2025,[42] thereby undermining further pursuit of those actions.

In short, virtually all of the major studies of racial and ethnic decisional patterns in SSA disability cases have revealed some form of disadvantaging disparity in lower approval rates for some category of Black and Brown claimants. As recently as 2022, the SSA publicly and candidly acknowledged that: "*There is evidence that although African American people are more likely to have a disability, they are less likely to be approved for disability benefits than white people.*"[43] Nevertheless, the SSA has neither pursued consistent serious efforts to isolate patterns of specific conduct fueling GAO-documented and other unexplained racial disparities in adjudications, nor taken meaningful consistent, ongoing action to address, follow up, or even better understand and assess racial disparities in its disability decisions.

The subsections of this chapter, after detailing the law and process governing SSA disability adjudications and social construction of disability and race, analyze potential and likely causes and explanations for the racial disparities in SSA disability decisions gleaned principally from medical and social science literature. These subsections also examine and analyze judicial case law in disability benefits adjudications of Black and Brown claimants raising bias issues. Finally, this chapter concludes by offering remedial suggestions to better assess the nature, extent, causes, and specific manifestations of these racial disparities, reduce adjudicative bias, and enhance more equitable program access.

5.2 THE SSA'S DISABILITY LEGAL STANDARDS AND PROCESS

The SSA essentially utilizes the same statutory definition of disability and same adjudicative process in both the OASDI and SSI disability programs. The Act's disability standard contains three principal statutory sections. First, the Act provides that the term "disability" means "the inability to engage in any substantial gainful activity by reason of any medically determinable physical or mental impairment which can be expected to result in death or which has lasted or can be expected to last for a continuous period of not less than 12 months."[44] Second, the Act further provides in relevant part that:

> [a]n individual shall be determined to be under a disability only if his physical or mental impairment or impairments are of such a severity that he is not only unable to do his previous work but cannot, considering his age, education, and work experience, engage in any other kind of substantial gainful work which exists in the national economy, regardless of whether such work exists in the immediate area in which he lives, or whether a specific job vacancy exists for him, or whether he would be hired if he applied for work. For purposes of the preceding sentence … "work which exists in the national economy" means work which exists in significant numbers either in the region where such individual lives or in several regions of the country.[45]

Third, the Act contains a specific section addressing claimant obligations to furnish evidence of their impairments and delineates the process by which pain and impairment symptomology are evaluated. It provides in relevant part that:

> An individual shall not be considered to be under a disability unless he furnishes such medical and other evidence of the existence thereof as the Commissioner of Social Security may require. An individual's statement as to pain or other symptoms shall not alone be conclusive evidence of disability as defined in this section; there must be medical signs and findings, established by medically acceptable clinical or laboratory diagnostic techniques, which show the existence of a medical impairment that results from anatomical, physiological, or psychological abnormalities which could reasonably be expected to produce the pain or other symptoms alleged and which, when considered with all evidence required to be furnished under this paragraph (including statements of the individual or his physician as to the intensity and persistence of such pain or other symptoms which may reasonably be accepted as consistent with the medical signs and findings), would lead to a conclusion that the individual is under a disability.[46]

The SSA has promulgated a five-step regulatory sequence to implement the statutory disability standards and adjudicate disability claims under the Act, and those steps operate as a flow chart. The Supreme Court has summarized this five-step substantive disability evaluation process as follows:

> *Step one* determines whether the claimant is engaged in 'substantial gainful activity.' If he is, disability benefits are denied. If he is not, the decisionmaker proceeds to *step two*, which determines whether the claimant has a medically severe impairment or combination of impairments ... If the claimant does not have a severe impairment or combination of impairments, the disability claim is denied. If the impairment is severe, the evaluation proceeds to the *third step*, which determines whether the impairment is equivalent to one of a number of listed impairments that the [Commissioner] acknowledges are so severe as to preclude substantial gainful activity. If the impairment meets or equals one of the listed impairments, the claimant is conclusively presumed to be disabled. If the impairment is not one that is conclusively presumed to be disabling, the evaluation proceeds to the *fourth step*, which determines whether the impairment prevents the claimant from performing work he has performed in the past. If the claimant is able to perform his previous work, he is not disabled. If the claimant cannot perform this work, the *fifth and final step* of the process determines whether he is able to perform other work in the national economy in view of his age, education, and work experience. The claimant is entitled to disability benefits only if he is not able to perform other work.[47]
>
> The SSA shoulders the affirmative burden of producing evidence of work that exists in significant numbers in the economy if a case reaches the *fifth step* of the process.[48]

The SSA has also issued subregulatory guidance in the form of a Social Security Ruling providing a two-step process for evaluating the supportability or credibility of pain and symptomology testimony.[49] First, it considers "whether there is an underlying medically determinable physical or mental impairment(s) that could reasonably be expected to produce an individual's symptoms, such as pain. Second, once an underlying physical or mental impairment(s) that could reasonably be expected to produce an individual's symptoms is established, [it] evaluate[s] the intensity and persistence of those symptoms to determine the extent to which the symptoms limit an individual's ability to perform work-related activities for an adult or to function independently, appropriately, and effectively in an age-appropriate manner for a child with a[n SSI disability claim]" and in doing so, assesses factors enumerated in SSA regulations, including: (i) Your daily activities; (ii) The location, duration, frequency, and intensity of your pain or other symptoms; (iii) Precipitating and aggravating factors; (iv) The type, dosage, effectiveness, and side effects of any medication you take or have taken to alleviate your pain or other symptoms; (v) Treatment, other than medication, you receive or have received for relief of your pain or other symptoms; (vi) Any measures you use or have used to relieve your pain or other symptoms (e.g., lying flat on your back, standing for 15 to 20 minutes every hour, sleeping on a board, etc.); and (vii) Other factors concerning your functional limitations and restrictions due to pain or other symptoms.[50]

The SSA system contains a four-stage adjudication process. The first two stages of the SSA administrative process include an initial application and reconsideration evaluation by the state disability determination services (DDS) agency acting under contract with SSA.[51] The latter two (third and fourth) stages include hearings before federal ALJs at local offices of the SSA Office of Hearings Operations and administrative appeals before the SSA's Appeals Council. Within SSA's Office of Analytics, Review, and Oversight, the Appeals Council considers appeals from ALJ-hearing decisions and acts as the SSA's final level of administrative review. After claimants have proceeded through all four stages, they may seek judicial review of the SSA's decision in federal district court.[52]

The high-volume, assembly line, "mass justice" challenges of SSA disability program adjudication pervade the third stage or ALJ-hearing stage of adjudication. The SSA conducts nearly 800,000 hearings annually at its local hearing offices.[53] Professor Jerry Mashaw has observed that "virtually all mass justice systems have decided that they are unable to function effectively without the active-adjudicator investigation, informal rules of evidence and procedure, and presiding officer control of issue definition and development that characterize an inquisitorial or examinational approach."[54] Courts have described the multifaceted "inquisitorial" functions of the SSA ALJ in the following manner:

> When the claimant appears before an ALJ, he or she will appear before a person not wearing a judicial robe, who is required by law to act with three hats, (1) a judge, (2) a representative of the government who cross examines the claimant, and, (3) an adviser to the claimant, required by regulation to fully develop the case to see that the claimant has a fair hearing regardless of whether the claimant is represented by counsel or otherwise ... The burden of exploring all pertinent facts and issues rests with the ALJ and in many cases, the person is not represented by counsel nor by any other person.[55]

Approximately, "50% of SSI disability claimants and 40% of all claimants [SSI and SSDI alike] lack attorney representation [at the hearing level] in a given year,"[56] and "[t]he Commissioner has no representative before the ALJ to oppose the claim for benefits."[57] The SSA's "inquisitorial" hearing system with multiple-role ALJs and without adversarial representation of competing parties "may represent a practical method of dealing with many problems encountered in agencies dispensing mass justice [;] [t]he great need is to deal efficiently and fairly with a horde of cases, rather than to preserve all the accoutrements of the courtroom."[58]

To try to ensure such a system is both efficient and fair, the courts have developed case law recognizing and enhancing statutory and regulatory obligations imposed on the inquisitorial SSA ALJs, to develop issues and evidence at hearings for the benefit of claimants, and to ensure a fair hearing, even when claimants are represented.[59] These expansive statutory, regulatory and subregulatory ALJ duties, beyond a general duty to develop the record;[60] include the obligation, in certain circumstances, to order consultative medical evaluations of claimants by doctors and obtain reports of those consultations;[61] produce vocational expert testimony;[62] identify and procure substantiation of the evidentiary bases for vocational expert testimony;[63] procure hearing testimony of a medical advisor;[64] make every reasonable effort to gather evidence from a claimant's treating medical sources and to recontact medical sources to clarify insufficient or inconsistent reports;[65] ensure unrepresented claimants are properly notified of the availability of free counsel to represent them through free legal services for indigent clients or private counsel contingent fee arrangements with fees provided only if the cases are successful with the contingent fee generally deducted from retroactive social security disability benefit payments;[66] and raise other issues *sua sponte*.[67] With respect to the evaluation of pain and impairment symptomology, ALJs have a duty to consider or inquire about reasons for inconsistent pursuance or compliance with ongoing or recommended treatment or prescribed medication, such as lack of resources or health insurance, adverse reactions to treatment, risks of medication, treatment or procedures suggested, religious objections, or mental impairment obstacles to following regimens, before drawing negative inferences that the claimant's pain/symptoms testimony is unsupportable or not credible,[68] or determining that a claimant's application should be denied and the claimant disqualified for failing to comply with prescribed treatment.[69]

In addition, the Act also provides for disqualification of an otherwise disabled clamant where substance abuse is a material cause of a claimant's disability.[70] This disqualification assessment imposes additional duties on adjudicators, particularly in a common scenario of dual diagnosed cases involving claimants with both substance abuse/drug or alcohol addiction (DAA) and a co-occurring psychiatric disorder where it may be difficult to ascertain the precise degree of psychiatric impairment in the absence of DAA. In such situations, SSA guidance provides that ALJs and agency adjudicators: should have evidence in the case record establishing whether "a claimant with a co-occurring mental disorder(s) would not be disabled in the absence of DAA"; they "*may* purchase a [consultative evaluation] to help establish whether a claimant who has no treating source records has a mental disorder(s) in addition to DAA"; and, if the record is fully developed and the adjudicators still cannot disentangle the disabling effects of DAA from the mental impairment, "they will find that DAA is not material to the determination of disability and allow the claim."[71]

5.3 THE SOCIAL CONSTRUCTION OF "DISABILITY" IN THE SSA DISABILITY SYSTEM

The Social Security disability standard is commonly misperceived as solely medical or scientific based largely on objective medical facts demonstrated through scientific and clinical methodology. For example, in *Matthews v. Eldridge*, the

Supreme Court declared, with respect to the social security disability standard and evaluation process:

> In short, a medical assessment of the worker's physical or mental condition is required. This is a more sharply focused and easily documented decision than the typical determination of welfare entitlement. In the latter, a wide variety of information may be deemed relevant, and issues of witness credibility and veracity are often critical to the decisionmaking process ... By contrast, the decision whether to discontinue disability benefits will turn, in most cases, upon routine, standard and *unbiased* medical records by physician specialists.[72]

The reality, however, is that in the social security system, adult disability embraces a specific context and frame of reference – disability from work in the labor market.[73] Under the Social Security Act, with limited exceptions, claimants are disabled if, after considering their age, education, work history, and medical limitations, they are unable to perform their past relevant work and cannot make an adjustment to other substantial and gainful "work which exists in significant numbers either in the region where [the claimant] lives or in several regions of the country."[74] Medical science alone has never been directed to the study of work environments, nor able to provide a reliable means to demonstrate the inability to adjust to and function sufficiently and consistently in a work setting.[75]

Accordingly, the disability inquiry requires either a presumptive or more individualized determination of whether a claimant's medically demonstrated impairment limitations combined with certain vocational characteristics and restrictions, and labor market conditions, preclude meaningful participation in the workforce. The statutory standard behind this inquiry considers some politically and socially approved statutory vocational factors deemed relevant to making workplace adjustments, such as age, education, and prior work experience, and whether there is a significant incidence of appropriate jobs within one's vocational-medical capacity, while excluding others such as employer preferences or structural discrimination, the prevalence of actual job openings, or distance of work from one's home. Indeed, much case law has been generated, and entire books and many articles have been written focused principally on the nonmedical, vocational, and labor market side of social security disability law and adjudication.[76] Several commentators have sharply criticized the SSA ALJs and other adjudicators' particularly wide discretion and resulting significant inconsistency and arbitrariness reflected in substantial variations in their assessment of evidence of the requisite quantum of other jobs in the labor market, and quality of supporting evidence of that job incidence data deemed sufficient to meet the statutory requirement of "work which exists in significant numbers in the economy" under the SSA's step-5 obligations under the Act and regulatory disability determination process.[77]

Far from a routine and standard medical determination, the Act and its disability criteria more realistically embody recognition that there are circumstances in which individuals should be excused from the social obligation of work.[78] Thus, the social security disability definition is a product of political compromise and reflects a degree of social consensus. As Professor Jerry Mashaw described: "SSA disability adjudications should perhaps be viewed as really concerned with difficult value judgments – individualized exemptions from the moral, social and economic constraints of the work ethic, determined by a complex of medical, vocational and environmental factors as they impinge on particular individuals."[79] Debates over whether the standard and its calculus of vocational, labor market, and medical factors continue to embody the most accepted or appropriate sociopolitical consensus and societal ethos on the meaning of disability persist, and will continue indefinitely under the legal standards adopted by Congress. Opinions on the proper social construction of disability for government benefits purposes vary widely in a diverse constitutional democracy, and "there is no epistemic answer to these value-laden questions."[80]

Moreover, even the entirely medical aspects of the disability standard are not "routine," "standard," fully "objective," unimpaired or unaffected by human "bias," or as easily verifiable as the Supreme Court suggested in *Mathews v. Eldridge* and as is sometimes mistakenly assumed by politicians. SSA disability regulations expressly incorporate the evaluation of subjective symptomology, including pain, psychiatric and other mental symptomology, and many other limiting symptoms that cannot be objectively or definitively ascertained through medical science, diagnostic testing, and technology.[81] Approximately 30 percent of SSDI claimants and over 55 percent of adult SSI claimants have mental impairments.[82] For over 50 percent of all cases, pain or other subjective symptomology is a significant issue.[83] The National Academy of Sciences has explained that "[p]ain is inherently subjective; there are no thoroughly reliable ways to measure it; and the correlation between the severity of pain and the level of dysfunction is imperfect."[84] This scientific conclusion has found resonance in judicial opinions. The Sixth Circuit has explained: "The measure of an individual's pain cannot be easily reduced to a matter of neat calculations. There are no x-rays that can be taken that would objectively show the precise level of agony that an individual is experiencing. Hence, in evaluating the intensity and persistence of pain, both physicians and layman alike, must often engage in guesswork."[85]

The Fourth Circuit has applied this reasoning to psychiatric mood disorders, reasoning that the SSA ALJs cannot rely upon the absence of objective medical evidence to discredit "a claimant's subjective complaints regarding symptoms of … *disease(s) that do … not produce such evidence*" and holding that "depression – particularly chronic depression – is one of those … diseases."[86] That is because "no laboratory test has yielded results of sufficient sensitivity and specificity to be used as a diagnostic tool for [MDD.]" and "symptoms caused by major depression can *vary from person to person*" and are "*entirely subjective*."[87]

In short, through the assessment of (1) pain and symptomology, including psychiatric symptomology, or (2) certain highly variable labor market and vocational issues, and (3) evaluation of eligibility disqualifications, such as for (a) failing to follow prescribed treatment without good cause, or (b) DAA "materiality" of otherwise disabled claimants whose drug or alcohol usage might be deemed a "material factor" in the disability; and (4) through the level of zeal or enthusiasm (or lack thereof) at which affirmative duties to develop the record and provide appropriate notice, information, and fairness to claimants is pursued, the SSA's ALJs and adjudicatory personnel have significant leeway and degrees of discretion to inject their own conscious and unconscious perspectives and personal, moral, and social constructions of disability into the decisional processes.[88] The ambiguous nature of these assessments and duties can conceal the effects of implicit and explicit racial bias.[89] In that respect, ACUS has particularly identified ALJs' assessment of pain and claimant symptomology as a potential source of bias in SSA disability adjudications, noting that "bias can manifest in credibility evaluations through inadequate record development and inappropriate consideration of factors that are irrelevant to the limitations imposed by a claimant's subjective symptoms."[90]

5.4 THE SOCIAL CONSTRUCTION OF RACE AND DAMAGING LEGACY OF BIOLOGICAL RACE

The construction of race and corresponding subordination and discriminatory treatment of African Americans and other underserved and historically subordinated communities of color also have implications for health care equity and disparities and the inequitable distribution of social security disability benefits. Race, racial categories, and the concept of "Blackness" in American society are not biologically based or scientifically determined.[91] While some people interpret "the phrase 'race is socially constructed' to mean that the biological category of race has a social meaning so that each society interprets differently what it means to belong to a biological race," that is erroneous.[92] Rather, "[t]here are no human populations with such a high degree of genetic variation that they objectively fall into races[;] [t]here is only one human race."[93] Modern science establishes that "in genetic terms, all human beings are more than 99.9 percent the same,"[94] and the up to 0.1 percent of potential genetic variation "is not grouped in discrete, genetically distinct units which scientists can identify as races."[95]

Even viewed simply as a marker of ancestral geographic origin, ancestry tests reveal that the average African American has more than 25 percent of their ancestry from Europe and elsewhere,[96] and considerably greater percentages of other (non-African) origins among the growing number of mixed-race persons socially constructed as Black, such as President Barack Obama and Vice President Kamala Harris, historical figures such as Frederick Douglass and Booker T. Washington, and prominent contemporary racial justice/health justice scholars and experts cited herein, such as Professor Dorothy Roberts (Law) and Dr. Mary T. Bassett (Medicine and Public Health-former New York State and New York City Health

Commissioner). Indeed, eminent Harvard African American Studies Scholar, Professor Henry Louis Gates, Jr., whose famous racial profiling by police and arrest for breaking into his own home provoked a national controversy and a White House "beer summit,"[97] and who created the popular *Finding Your Roots* television series, examined his own roots and discovered his ancestry was as much European as African (49 percent each).[98] Accordingly, race is better understood certainly not as a biological category but as a series of social categorizations based on certain physical markers, some degree of ancestry, identity development, and the legal and social meanings attached to those categorizations.[99]

While historical conceptions of biological races, used to elevate white supremacy and the white race as superior and to justify slavery, eugenics, sterilization, *de jure* segregation, social and legal exclusion, systematic discrimination, and other forms of exploitation,[100] have long been scientifically repudiated, persistent, present-day remnants of that biological race legacy contribute to current racial health care inequities and disability benefits disparities. In the late 1840s, a group of Louisiana physicians, led by Dr. Samuel Cartwright, Chair of the Medical Association of Louisiana and a plantation and slave owner, launched a campaign to secure independence from the medical profession dominated by northern physicians. Dr. Cartwright stressed the northern physicians' inadequate knowledge of southern medical conditions and specific "ignorance of diseases which afflicted only Negros," which he used to rationalize slavery as morally just and scientifically supportable, based on biological differences between the white and Black races.[101]

In a report issued in 1851, Dr. Cartwright made a number of findings including that Blacks possessed smaller brains and lungs and thicker skin, and suffered two diseases, *drapetomania*, a mental illness that caused enslaved Blacks to run away from confinement, and *dysaesthia aethiopica*, a disease characterized by partial insensitivity of the skin to pain, along with reduced intellectual ability and laziness.[102] More than 100 years later, doctors, medical, and other "researchers continued to experiment on black people based in part on the assumption that the black body was more resistant to pain and injury."[103] This included the secret military tests of the effect of mustard gas and other chemicals on Black soldiers during World War II and the US Public Health Service and Tuskegee Institute's also covert study of the progression of syphilis in Black men, infected with syphilis without their knowledge or consent, from 1932 to 1972.[104]

Among present day assumptions of biological racial differences with historical antecedents in slavery and the nineteenth-century racial studies by Cartwright and others, Professor Dorothy Roberts notes that "one of the most enduring and disturbing" is that Blacks "are impervious to pain."[105] In *Fatal Invention: How Science, Politics and Big Business Recreate Race in the Twenty-First Century* (2011), Roberts observed that "some modern medical experts still believe that tolerance for pain differs by race" and pointed to a 1983 Sloan-Kettering Study of pain in cancer patients which reached the conclusion that "black patients obtained relief comparable to white patients at half the morphine dose."[106] Roberts noted that many doctors share this belief and accept this finding, and cited multiple examples and studies documenting physicians' prescribing of less pain medication to Black and Latino/a patients than to white patients with various controls for other explanations of the disparities.

Since Professor Roberts' 2011 book, a 2016 University of Virginia study of the assumptions and beliefs of medical residents and medical students found that about half of those surveyed still hold false beliefs about biological differences between Black and white persons such as thicker skin and less pain among Black patients.[107] The study concluded that "individuals with at least some medical training hold and may use false beliefs about biological differences between Blacks and whites to inform medical judgments, which may contribute to racial disparities in pain assessment and treatment."[108] The study also "demonstrates that beliefs about biological differences between blacks and whites – beliefs dating back to slavery – are associated with the perception that black people feel less pain than do white people and with inadequate treatment recommendations for black patients' pain."[109]

5.5 RACE, CLASS, AND BIAS

Much discussion of racial inequities in the social security system and other systems in American society focuses on inequities grounded in obstacles and disadvantages stemming from the disproportionate poverty or socioeconomic status or class of African Americans and other historically subordinated communities of color. The deleterious financial consequences and disproportionately high levels of poverty and low levels of wealth can be traced to histories of slavery, Jim Crow, and structural and systemic discrimination as discussed in Chapter 2, along with the uniquely debilitating consequences of isolated and concentrated poverty – conditions of impecunity uniquely reinforced in Black communities through the persistence of residential segregation and more modern-day mass incarceration trends discussed in Chapter 3.[110] However, the damaging presence of ongoing, often less overt, forms of discrimination persist and continue to contribute to deleterious racial outcomes, independent of class or poverty.

For example, Black and Brown persons continue to experience discrimination and steering in the real estate and housing market, regardless of their wealth or their ratio of assets to debt as shown in housing testing in the 2000s.[111] Similarly, employment discrimination persists as demonstrated in testing, including for white collar sales management jobs by job applicants with Black-sounding names such as Lakisha and Jamal as opposed to white-sounding names such as Emily and Greg.[112] Employment testing in the lower wage labor market also reveals ongoing present-day racial discrimination.[113] Blacks and Latinos/as continue to earn significantly less in the labor market than their white counterparts even at the highest level of educational attainment.[114]

Accordingly, in examining health care inequities, disparate medical assessments, and disparate SSA disability adjudicative outcomes, not all disparities or inequities can be attributed to (or be mitigated by centering on addressing) obstacles grounded in poverty or class. Indeed, "after controlling for differences among the races in socioeconomic status, health insurance, access to health care and geographic differences, the evidence still shows that Blacks and Latinos receive fewer and inferior clinical services than whites, irrespective of whether those services are for treatment of cardiovascular disease, cancers, mental illness, prenatal care, or HIV/AIDS."[115] And the evidence of significant racial health care disparities is voluminous and growing, with numerous books, articles, reports, and studies on the topic.[116] A substantial component of that literature analyzes and documents racial and ethnic disparities in the assessment and treatment of pain and symptomology.[117]

Relying on a taxonomy of forms of discrimination developed by psychologist Joel Kovel in 1970, Professor Khiara Bridges has distinguished between two principal forms of discrimination or racism relevant to assessing present-day racial and ethnic inequities: dominative and aversive discrimination.[118] "Dominative" or "traditional" discrimination is "the species of racial discrimination most identified by the average person with the term 'racism,'" and is "characterized by a belief in the superiority of the racial in-group and the inferiority of the racial out-group," with the expectation of accompanying "feelings of hatred, malice, and/or animus towards the targeted racial groups" by actors who might be labelled "bigots," "segregationists," or "white supremacists."[119] Aversive discrimination or aversive racism is "the subtler, more modern cousin of dominative racism," by persons who "sympathize with victims of past injustice, support the principle of racial equality, and regard themselves as nonprejudiced but at the same time, possess negative feelings and beliefs about Blacks which may be unconscious" and are characterized by "implicit bias."[120]

Other scholars, such as American sociologist and Professor Eduardo Bonilla-Silva, have pointed to additional forms of ongoing racial discrimination that can neither be characterized as dominative nor aversive, is committed by persons who have neither hatred nor ill will toward people of color, nor implicit nor unconscious biases "because they *consciously* believe racial minorities to be culturally inferior (i.e. lazy, in possession of problematic values, work averse, inclined to criminality, [or substance abuse])" and other negative stereotypes about "members of a racial out-group."[121] Moreover, courts recognize that the relatively easy ways to detect overt, dominative forms of discrimination and racialized hostility are increasingly scarce. The Third Circuit observed: "[E]xtreme manifestations of discrimination are thankfully rare … [because] [i]t has become easier to coat various forms of discrimination with the appearance of propriety, or to ascribe some other less odious intention to what is in reality discriminatory behavior. In other words, while discriminatory conduct persists, violators have learned not to leave the proverbial 'smoking gun' behind."[122]

A documented factor in the disparate medical care received by Black and Brown patients across class lines is the impact of bias and stereotyping (regardless of taxonomic discriminatory classification), as well as aversive forms of discrimination, including the implicit racial biases, often of otherwise well-meaning, self-professed unbiased treatment professionals. While the degree and ultimate impact of such factors are incapable of precise quantification, a 780-page report of the National Academy of Sciences, Institute of Medicine (IOM) in 2003, reviewing over 100 studies and ten years of data, concluded that "bias, stereotyping, prejudice and uncertainty on the part of health care professionals … appear among the many patient-level, system-level and clinical encounter-level factors to contribute to racial and ethnic disparities in health care."[123] The IOM report found that "[n]egative stereotypes about minorities, held explicitly or implicitly by physicians, can contribute to healthcare disparities in a number of ways" and sometimes "healthcare providers may be *consciously aware of their negative stereotypes of minorities*, but may nonetheless view these stereotypes as accurate, functional, and appropriate for their clinical work."[124] In those situations, "the research [cited] suggests that these providers will selectively attend to and recall information that confirms their stereotypes, and will tend to allow such stereotypes to enter into clinical decisions regarding the diagnosis and appropriate course of treatment."[125]

However, the IOM report also determined that "[t]here is considerable evidence that even well-meaning whites who are not overtly biased and who do not believe that they are prejudiced typically demonstrate, on average, *unconscious implicit negative racial attitudes and stereotypes* [and] [b]oth implicit and explicit stereotypes significantly shape interpersonal interactions, influencing how information is recalled and guiding expectations and inferences in systematic ways."[126] In also pointing out the fact of and manner in which the empirical evidence suggests health care providers are influenced by patients' race and ethnicity or "primed with racial stereotypes," the IOM report also described "a survey of physicians following actual clinical encounters, demonstrating that physicians endorse stereotypes about their African-American patients (who were characterized as '*less intelligent, less educated, more likely to abuse drugs and alcohol, more likely to fail to comply with medical advice*,' and less likely '*to be … the kind of person the physician could see him/herself being friends with*'), even after controlling for patients' socioeconomic status, personality variables, and perceived social support."[127]

These types of stereotypes and assumptions "can lead to unfavorable treatment of minorities" by health care providers, even when there are no meaningful underlying differences in conditions and health care attitudes between particular minority and white patients.[128] It follows, *a fortiori*, that these types of stereotypes and biases can pervade the perspectives and decision-making of nonscientifically trained ALJs and agency adjudicators and influence disability determinations in the many interstices of discretionary judgment and affirmative adjudicative duty enthusiasm levels in the

SSA disability adjudicative process. Particularly, with respect to the assessment of pain and symptomology:

> The ambiguous nature of pain and suffering losses makes them not only difficult to measure but also an ideal place for racial bias to linger undetected. Indeed, the effects of any bias are much more difficult to observe in open-ended assessments. This is especially true when it comes to *implicit* bias. While the legal system has made notable progress in eliminating explicit or conscious bias, only limited steps have been taken to confront the more difficult challenge of eliminating the effects of implicit bias.[129]

5.6 INTERSECTIONALITY: RACE AND DISABILITY

Emerging scholarly literature and popular journalism have increasingly explored the combined and uniquely intersectional obstacles and deleterious synergies confronting persons experiencing the duality of these categories – particularly Black persons with various medical impairments.[130] This literature has included the increasing public airing of fatal or excessively injurious police encounters and mistreatment in the criminal justice system of Black and Brown persons misperceived as imminently dangerous or suspicious while manifesting common symptoms of their underlying often diagnosed (or misdiagnosed) psychiatric, cognitive, neurological, physical, and/or neuropsychological conditions.[131] For example, Professor Jamelia Morgan has observed that nonnormative or nonconforming behaviors of persons with autism spectrum disabilities may be misinterpreted as suspicious, including "certain expressions of disability – such as flapping of hands, low affect facial expressions, pacing, lack of eye contact that may be exhibited by some autistic individuals," not to mention expressions of "sensory overload" from fear and anxiety owing to police shouting commands, flashing lights, and blaring loud sirens.[132] Persons with physical impairments may stumble or lose consciousness and be viewed as drunk.[133]

Professor Morgan points out that "[u]nconscious, implicit biases may influence which behaviors are labelled unusual and even suspicious, *particularly when such behaviors are exhibited by individuals who are negatively racialized or members of historically marginalized groups*."[134] Similar writings reveal that Black and Brown children with a variety of impairments are disproportionately misevaluated and underevaluated for appropriate educational and special education placements and services and overreferred for school discipline with resulting overrepresentation in the school-to-prison pipeline and juvenile justice carceral system.[135] Black youths are also twice as likely (2:1) to be restrained upon admission to a psychiatric hospital than white youths, with Latino/a youths at a similar disparate level (1.7:1) based on assessments of dangerousness.[136]

Racialized and/or race/disability intersectional faulty assumptions and misdiagnoses by treatment professionals such as those of exaggerated dangerousness or violence, sometimes compounded by a variety of further assumptions and biases by police, correctional, or school officials in official reports, can further disparately restrict Black and Brown claimants' access to disability benefits. These misdiagnoses and assumptions form the bases of disability decisions and are undoubtedly often shared or fortified by similar biases by SSA ALJs and other adjudicative personnel in disability adjudications, with less scientific knowledge potentially to mitigate such biases. For example, a growing body of research suggests that psychiatrists and other mental health treatment professionals tend to underevaluate and underdiagnose Black patients' mood-related or affective disorders such as major depressive disorder and bipolar disorder, and then fail to record mood-related symptoms during clinical assessments.[137] At the same time, they tend to overdiagnose and misdiagnose Black patients as suffering from psychotic disorders such as schizophrenia and prescribe "anti-psychotic medication" based on assessments that Black patients are "dangerous," "aggressive," or "violent."[138] One study found that African Americans were three to four times more likely to be diagnosed with schizophrenia than whites, and significant disparities persisted even after controlling for environmental and socioeconomic stressors potentially contributing to these diagnoses.[139]

One might speculate that the impact on SSA disability assessment and decision-making might or should be the same despite this phenomenon since SSA regulations provide step-three listing (automatic medical disability) criteria for both affective disorders and psychotic disorders,[140] and it is the functional limitations stemming from the underlying conditions, regardless of the diagnosis, which are most salient in the other evaluative steps in the disability process. However, the damage from such misdiagnoses and faulty assumptions can negatively affect treatment, documentation, supportability/credibility of symptom testimony, consistency of pursuance of treatment or medication by patients feeling not properly diagnosed and experiencing adverse or undesirable side-effects from unhelpful medication and treatment regimens.

It can also affect mental health treatment professionals' assessments of patients' progress in and cooperation with treatment. These are all factors which can undermine both the patients' treatment and the psychiatric assessments and reports used in their disability determinations, even before SSA adjudicators interpose their own similar biases into the evaluative process.[141] Moreover, two of the four principal claimant impairment groups revealing the greatest racial disparities in ALJ benefit approval decisions and leading the GAO to seek further particularized follow-up, were for schizophrenia and "other mental disorders."[142]

Finally, stereotypes and assumptions about Black and Brown dangerousness and propensity to violence, assumptions about criminality and drug use and involvement, with resulting overpolicing of drug crimes in communities of color, can also lead to health care and SSA disability evaluation inequities. Black people are often stereotypically perceived as abusing drugs and engaging in drug-related conduct more often than whites and are "incarcerated 6 to 10 times more for substance related crimes."[143] In reality, several studies show that illicit drug use among persons age twelve and older is essentially the same for white and Black people and much lower for Latinos/as; Blacks and Latinos/as are less likely than whites to misuse "prescription" opiates; and the overall rate of drug-induced deaths are highest among white persons.[144]

However, researchers have identified the perception of Black and Brown drug abuse as a contributing factor to the undertreatment of Black and Brown pain with opiate medication and resulting inadequate pain management.[145] A "2012 analysis of 20 years of published research found that Blacks were 34 percent less likely than whites to be prescribed opioids for conditions such as backaches, abdominal pain and migraines, and 14 percent less likely to receive opioids for pain caused by traumatic injuries or surgery."[146] The reasons researchers have posited for these disparities include "false stereotypes, such as the assumption that blacks are more likely to abuse drugs, as well as a tendency for doctors to empathize less with patients whose race is different from their own – perhaps subconsciously – and to underestimate the severity of their pain[;] [o]nly about 4 percent of the country's practicing physicians are black."[147]

These matters have consequences in social security disability determinations. Pain treatment which is viewed as "conservative" or treated less seriously often leads to disregard or devaluing of pain symptoms by ALJs and adjudicators in disability determinations.[148] The absence of opioid treatment specifically undermines the third step, automatic medical disability eligibility for Sickle Cell Disease (SCD) for children and adults – a condition disproportionately afflicting African Americans – under revisions to listings 107.05(A) and 7.05(A) since mandatory opioid treatment was added to these listings through regulatory amendments in 2015 (as described in greater detail in Section 5.8). In addition, the perception of Black drug overuse or drug-seeking behavior or proclivities likely leads to more DAA disqualification determinations for Black disability claimants including cases with dual-diagnosed, co-occurring mental impairments, where ALJs and other adjudicators may be more likely to attribute disabling mental limitations to substance abuse rather than to a Black claimant's underlying, otherwise qualifying, psychiatric disorder.[149]

5.7 RACE, HEALTH CARE SYSTEM INEQUITY, AND MEDICAL EVIDENCE

Black and Brown patients often experience discrimination, misevaluation, and improper and inadequate treatment and diagnostic testing in the health care system. Because medical evidence plays a significant role in the SSA disability evaluation process, systematic racial disparities in medical assessment and treatment undoubtedly fuel disparities in SSA disability evaluation. Factors attributable both to disproportionate poverty-based obstacles and to bias and stereotyping-influenced misdiagnoses, undertreatment, or lesser quality clinical treatment hinder Black and Brown claimants in the health care system and in pursuit of medical assessments of their conditions. For example, Black and Brown claimants have lesser access to treating physicians or general practice physicians with familiarity of a claimant's conditions and their symptom vacillations with treatment over time; 28 percent of Blacks, and 51 percent of Latinos/as lack a regular doctor compared with 21 percent of whites, and "those differences remain statistically significant after adjusting for age, income and insurance source."[150]

Many Black and Latino/a SSDI and/or SSI claimants experience the limitations and disadvantages described here:

> Poor claimants, as well as increasingly many working-class claimants, are not likely to have the financial resources to establish an ongoing relationship with a physician of the type envisioned by the SSA regulations. Often they can only afford to go to a public clinic where physicians are not likely to have the same detailed knowledge of the patient's condition that would be expected of a private doctor. The clinic physician who sees a claimant once may not, for example, be able to describe adequately how a particular medical ailment uniquely affects the claimant's ability to function. Doctors who are unfamiliar with a patient's medical history may be less likely to perform diagnostic tests, which can be important to the claimant seeking to build a record of objective medical evidence of her impairment. *When there is no long-term relationship between a claimant and a physician, the testimony or reports of the physician can be more easily discredited by decisionmakers in the [SSA] disability determination process.*[151]

They also have lesser access to health insurance (10 percent of African Americans, 19 percent of Latinos/as, 18 percent of Native Americans/Native Alaskans as compared with 7 percent of whites);[152] proximity to high-quality care as reported by medical providers,[153] or referrals for specialized testing and treatment with medical specialists (16 percent of Blacks, 22 percent of Latinos/as, 26 percent of Asian Americans, and 8 percent of whites report difficulties or inability to access specialists).[154]

All of these obstacles produce relative deficiencies in documentation of treatment and impairment history and severity, and are health system inequities which not only impair effective medical treatment and health care with resulting adverse health consequences, but they also create disparate obstacles in the social security disability system for these claimants of color through less informative and/or persuasive medical documentation. That is, "due to barriers to patient-centered health care, marginalized people also tend to have medical records with inferior quality information."[155]

5.8 THE RACIAL IMPACT OF THE MISEVALUATION OF A UNIQUELY PAIN-PRODUCING CONDITION: SICKLE CELL DISEASE (SCD)

SCD is a hereditary disease that occurs among people from parts of the world where malaria is or was common – principally parts of Africa, but also parts of the Middle East and Mediterranean regions.[156] People living with the sickle cell trait have shown some resistance to severe forms of malaria, and this protection against malaria kept the sickle cell gene mutation in the population in malaria-prone geographic locations.[157] SCD is often erroneously viewed as a Black-race-linked biological or genetic disease, rather than what it is: a geographic-conditions-linked, evolutionary "protective adaptation."[158] Professor Dorothy Roberts explained:

> It is plain to see that malaria and sickle cell aren't restricted to Africa and much of Africa is unaffected. High frequencies of the trait occur in parts of Europe, Oceania, India, and the Middle East, all places where there is malaria. In fact, people in the town of Orchomenos in central Greece have twice the rate of [SCD] reported among African Americans … [I]f we grouped together people by the presence or absence of the sickle cell gene, we'd place Yemenites, Greeks, New Guineans, and Dinkas in one 'race,' Norwegians and several black African peoples in another. It would be more accurate to call the groups with the sickle cell gene, the anti-mosquito race.[159]

However, in the US, SCD manifests with greatest prevalence among African Americans; "over 90 percent of individuals with SCD are non-Hispanic Black or African American, and an estimated 3–9 percent are Hispanic or Latino."[160] Indeed, "SCD occurs in about 1 out of every 365 Black births," and "1 in 13 Black babies is born with sickle cell trait (SCT)."[161] While approximately 9 percent of all African Americans have SCT, only 0.2 percent of white Americans do.[162] SCD is a "chronic, lifelong condition that affects every organ system in the body"; it reduces life expectancy of those in the US to 52.6 years – twenty years shorter than the expected average.[163]

SCD manifests through "a gene mutation that causes the body to produce abnormal hemoglobin, the protein that transports oxygen in the human body," and it alters the character of the body's red blood cells.[164] Red blood cells are normally disc-shaped and flexible.[165] The sickle cell "mutation causes red blood cells to 'sickle' and clump when partially depleted of oxygen causing the clots and subsequent ischemia."[166] This condition produces "various SCD syndromes."[167] SCD symptoms and associated complications can include "anemia; acute and chronic pain; infections; pneumonia and acute chest syndrome; stroke; cognitive dysfunction; and kidney, liver and heart disease."[168]

But it is the "lifelong and unpredictable vaso-occlusive crisis pain" from SCD pain crises that "necessitates consistent management [and] also makes SCD treatment so problematic."[169] Indeed, "[r]ecurrent acute pain episodes are the hallmark of SCD and the most common cause of [emergency room/department] visits and hospitalizations for individuals living with SCD."[170] Acute SCD pain "is characterized by sudden-onset severe pain commonly located in the extremity, back, or chest," and the pain can "begin within the first year of life and continue into adult hood, leading to significant morbidity and negative effects on patients' health-related quality of life."[171]

The National Academies of Sciences, Engineering and Medicine (NASEM) pointed out in December 2025 the "growing recognition that most individuals with

SCD suffer daily or persistent pain, as well as acute pain crises."[172] The need for the evaluation and treatment of SCD pain "crises" renders the disproportionately Black SCD patient population additionally prone to the same types of bias in pain mismanagement, misdiagnosis and misevaluation described earlier. Black pain underassessments not only diminish the quality of health treatment but also the accuracy and fairness of SSA disability assessments.

In addition, relatively recent (2015) regulatory changes to SSA's step-3 listing for automatic medical disability based on SCD have further exacerbated these problems and their disparate racial impacts in SSA disability determinations by significantly raising the bar on the requirements for both children and adults with SCD. Among other restrictive changes, the newer (2015) regulations, amending (1985) regulations at listing 7.05(A) for adults and 107.05(A) for children, doubled the number of required "painful vaso-occlusive crises" from three to six in a twelve-month period and now require treatment for these pain crises with "parenteral (intravenous or intramuscular) narcotic medication."[173] An alternative basis for disability under the listing (listing 7.05(B) and 107.05(B)) requires "at least three hospitalizations within a 12-month period and occurring at least 30 days apart" and where "[e]ach hospitalization must last at least 48 hours."[174] The overwhelming majority of public comments in the notice and comment process for the Administrative Procedure Act (APA),[175] when the SSA first proposed these regulations, from medical and scientific sources including hematologists and public health officials, opposed the regulatory changes as unnecessary and unduly burdensome.[176]

Virtually all of the hematologists who addressed these requirements when first proposed explained in this language (or similarly):

> [T]he level of impairment associated with this proposed listing is significantly greater than the standard for what is considered a severe course of SCD. For painful crises, it is currently recognized that patients experiencing three or more crises in a year fall into the severe category. This has been well established at least since the publication of a seminal paper regarding the efficacy of hydroxyurea in the treatment of patients with severe sickle cell disease in the New England Journal of Medicine in 1995.[177]

The SSA's only response to this comment was simply that it did not adopt the comment because it believes the final listings "provide objective criteria that are more descriptive of our intent and more specific to listing-level determinations than the prior listings," and conditions lacking in this criteria could perhaps be addressed through other step-3 listings with separate and additional requirements.[178] It did not address the hematology community's reference to the long-recognized and established three crises standard nor the consequences from doubling that standard. The doubling of the quantum of SCD pain crises required increased the opportunity for, and possibility of, further disparate assessments of Black claimants' pain.

The hematology community in their letters also overwhelmingly objected to the proposed requirement for intravenous or intramuscular narcotic/opiate treatment for these crises in the revised listings 7.05A and 107.5A. Their letters explained:

> Moreover, these painful crises do not have to require parenteral narcotic medication in order to be considered one of the three crises. Whether a patient requires parenteral narcotics or not is not a primary indicator of severity of a painful crisis. Patients with severe SCD will often experience painful episodes that may only require oral analgesia but still cause serious disruption to their lives for days or weeks at a time.[179]

The SSA offered the same, essentially nonresponsive, reply to these comments as in its response to the hematologists' comments on doubling the SCD crises requirements.[180]

The SSA's nonresponsive reply to and blanket rejection of medical community recommendations and objections to the 2015 changes to the SCD listings stands in sharp contrast to its response to comments on its 2016 proposed changes to the cystic fibrosis (CF) listing. CF is a disease stemming from a similarly geographic, evolutionary genomic adaptation; however, unlike SCD, it disproportionately (and primarily) afflicts Caucasians with ancestry from Europe.[181] Approximately 84 percent of Americans with CF are non-Hispanic whites.[182] When the SSA proposed somewhat stricter listing criteria for CF in the regulatory notice and comment process, it accepted all five sets of major comments with recommendations or objections from members of the medical community and others to its proposed CF listing changes and modified its final listing regulations accordingly.[183]

By enhancing the requirement for opiate treatment for SCD pain and pain crises, including for very young children, the new SCD listing regulations further enhance the salience of biases against the treatment of Black patients' pain with narcotic opiates. Moreover, hematologists have more broadly expressed concern that "prolonged opioid utilization" as well as "escalating doses of opioids … can cause tolerance and opioid -induced hyperalgesia (increased sensitivity to pain)" and other "[o]pioid side effects such as respiratory depression, constipation and nausea [which] can exacerbate SCD-related complications."[184]

While disability can still be established for SCD-afflicted claimants whose conditions do not meet the criteria for automatic medical disability under the medically and scientifically nonjustified and enhanced 2015 SCD listing changes, the undermining of a more realistic "step-3" disability eligibility path has had a disparate impact on African American claimants. Not surprisingly, following the 2015 SCD regulatory changes, SSI disability approval rates for children with SCD significantly plummeted from 37 percent to 24 percent, "producing a racial disparity harming thousands of impoverished children" (overwhelmingly Black children).[185] While statistics for adults with SCD have not yet been revealed, adult disability program reductions for this population, also overwhelmingly comprising Black claimants, are estimated to have fallen by a similar margin. By way of comparison, the SSA has declined to elevate the criteria for automatic step-3 medical disability under its listings for the disproportionately white claimant population afflicted with CF in a manner contrary to the recommendations of medical treatment professionals as reflected in SSA's adoption of the major medical community recommendations and objections to the 2016 changes to the CF listings when proposed.

NASEM, at the urging of the SSA in 2024,[186] convened an ad hoc interdisciplinary committee of experts with expertise in hematology, pain management, emergency medicine, and SSA disability policy, among other areas, to conduct a study. NASEM recently issued its final report titled "Sickle Cell Disease in Social Security Disability Evaluations: Pain and Treatment Settings (Dec. 9, 2025)." The SSA's direction to NASEM sought findings and conclusions on SCD evaluation, treatment, and best practices "but not recommendations" on changes to SSA's SCD listings.[187] The NASEM report further confirmed the obstacles confronting the disproportionately African American SCD-afflicted SSD/SSID claimant population in SCD pain management, treatment, and assessment, and the lack of scientific basis for and damaging effects of the 2015 changes to the SSA's SCD listings. Among the national academies' findings were the conclusions that: (1) SSA disability determination accuracy based on SCD "can be improved" through better recognition of the variety of SCD complications and pain management approaches by different types of health care providers in a variety of settings; (2) the "full spectrum of pain experienced daily" by SCD-afflicted individuals which affect functioning "is most often managed at home or in a variety of outpatient care settings"; and (3) unlike other disorders that may require emergency room care or hospitalizations, SCD "is stigmatized in ways that may affect an individual's decision to seek care."[188]

On this conclusion, the report offered subsidiary conclusions about the shortage of health care providers who understand SCD and are well trained in its treatment and willing to care for people who have it; the racialization of SCD and broader problem of Black patients' "undertreatment for pain" in the US health care system; the reality that the severity of SCD pain can only be measured through self-report; and that while SCD pain episodes often require the use of opioids for pain management, the pursuit of such narcotics can be hindered by health care professionals' inaccurate perceptions of SCD patients' "drug seeking behavior."[189] In further explaining this final conclusion, the NASEM report stated:

> [T]he choice to prescribe or receive opioids for SCD pain management varies by institution, provider, and the person with SCD. For these reasons, the [SSA listing criteria's] types of medications or interventions used to treat an acute pain crisis in a person with SCD are too restrictive as proxies for the severity of the pain or the underlying disease process. Similarly, SCD treatment in emergency department settings and the number of times a person is hospitalized are too restrictive as measures of disease severity. Growing use of alternative models of care, including home, infusion centers, or day hospitals, has enabled similar levels of care outside of the hospital.

> However, access to different care settings varies among individuals, depending on distance from types of facilities, insurance coverage, and the availability of specialists in SCD across a broad range of disciplines. Thus, many factors other than the severity of an acute pain crisis affect an individual's decision to seek care and the provider's decision to recommend admission. In addition, whether a hospitalization lasts at least 48 hours and whether readmission occurs within 30 days are both determined by a variety of factors not specific to disease characteristics, including access to care, health care provider and individual preferences, and disease stigma.[190]

Lastly, and to further summarize and emphasize its findings, the NASEM report concluded:

> 4) the frequency of sickle cell disease treatment encounters for acute complications, such as pain crises, in the emergency department and inpatient settings, including the type or amount of pain medication, the duration of treatment, and treatment location, and disposition, is too restrictive a measure of disease severity. Growing use of alternative models of care has enabled similar levels of care in outpatient or home settings … [M]any people who do not meet [SSA's current SCD listing] criteria experience an equivalent level of disease severity and significant functional limitations that [in NASEM's opinion] also would qualify them for disability.[191]

The Medical and Research Advisory Committee of the Sickle Cell Disease Association of America has praised NASEM's report, noting that its important findings and conclusions should "enable the sickle cell disease community to initiate much needed change" in addressing the "barriers" individuals with SCD face when confronting the SSA's "overly restrictive [SCD disability listing] criteria."[192]

Another barrier confronting the overwhelmingly Black SCD patient population is the absence of proportionate attention and medical research funding vis-à-vis other disorders such as the white patient population-focused CF disease. As explained by professors and SCD treatment and research specialists Alexandra Power Hays and Patrick T. McGann in a 2020 article in the *New England Journal of Medicine* titled "When Actions Speak Louder Than Words – Racism and Sickle Cell Disease":

> Cystic fibrosis is comparable to SCD as an inherited, progressive, life-threatening disease associated with decreased quality of life and shortened life span, but it primarily affects White Americans. Cystic fibrosis affects one third fewer Americans than SCD but receives 7 to 11 times the research funding per patient, which results in disparate rates of development of medications: currently, the Food and Drug Administration has approved 4 medications for SCD and 15 for cystic fibrosis. We need to analyze the role of race and racism in the persistence of such discordant resource allocation. Federal funders, lawmakers, advocates, and health care leaders need to work together to reverse the impact of years of structural racism on SCD funding, research, and policy decisions.[193]

As separate recommendations for SCD cases in addition to this chapter's broader recommendations for addressing adjudicative bias in Section 5.9, and in light of the absence of a concrete scientific foundation for the SSA's 2015 SCD listing changes and demonstrated racially disparate impacts of those regulatory changes, the SSA should adopt new SCD listing criteria consistent with and informed by NASEM's findings and conclusions.

5.9 SSA ADJUDICATIVE BIAS AND RACIAL DISPARITIES IN DECISION-MAKING

As shown in this chapter, stereotypes, biases, and unconscious aversive assumptions can undermine medical assessment and medical treatment, which can hinder disability assessments for Black and Brown persons, and these claimants of color often face additional hurdles and obstacles in the disability adjudication process based on poverty or working-class status. Just as medical personnel often harbor the biases and stereotypical beliefs developed in the voluminous literature referenced earlier, undoubtedly so too do ALJs and adjudicative personnel. In fact, some actors in the SSA adjudicative system are physicians who may harbor the same biases as reflected in the medical literature.

There are three types of SSA or DDS-retained doctors who participate in SSA disability decisions: (1) internal agency review physicians who work at the DDS level and supply listing and functional assessments and summaries of the medical evidence (including all reports and notes supplied by a claimant's treating sources) in each case but who never see nor examine the claimants; (2) "consultant physicians" who conduct one-shot examinations of claimants when requested or ordered at one of the four levels of SSA adjudication; and (3) medical advisors (MAs), if requested by the ALJs or Appeals Council, who review the files and attend the hearing to supply an opinion and medical assessment through testimony to the ALJs usually after sitting through and listening to the claimant's testimony (or through answers to interrogatories usually supplied to the MA after the hearing).[194]

Disability claimants may then suffer the "double whammy" of the fortification of the biases and stereotypes of medical personnel when they are then shared by SSA ALJs and adjudicative decision-makers. Indeed, in light of the well-documented prevalence of medical bias and stereotyping, such as in the pain and symptom assessments of Black patients, it would be quite remarkable if ALJs and adjudicatory personnel, lacking the scientific or medical training of doctors and other treatment personnel, managed to avert the societal gravitational pull and pervasive influence of these historically based and persistent preconceptions on their conscious and unconscious perspectives. Negative stereotypes and the seeds of unconscious racial bias and stereotyping are also regularly planted and reinforced through images and presentations in popular media, advertising, local news, and various forms of entertainment (e.g., movies, television, books).[195]

Moreover, the ALJs might inject their own biases and stereotypes into the decision-making process through the many discretionary judgments and affirmative duty avenues described earlier in ways that undermine Black and Brown claimants' applications, even when the medical personnel have not done so in their medical assessments. For example, Professor Mills's own study of fully adjudicated SSA disability cases from a review of sixty-seven case transcripts found that "ALJs prejudicial emotions, creep … into the hearing process as it is currently formulated through such unconscious dynamics as hindering testimony and inflicting personal judgments."[196] The Mills study also found that in eight of the sixty-seven transcripts, the ALJs determined claimants to have failed to follow prescribed treatment – an eligibility disqualification – and seven of those eight (87.5 percent) "were racial or ethnic minorities."[197]

Mills noted that ALJs exercised their discretion, conducting the hearings in ways which precluded or discouraged some claimants from offering reasons for inconsistent treatment and in some cases, where reasons were supplied, issued adverse decisions without citing those reasons.[198] Professor Mills also found that of the nine claimants in the group of adjudicated cases studied who were unrepresented, seven were African American and one was Latino/a (approximately 89 percent Black and Latino/a; 78 percent Black).[199] Mills questioned whether the ALJs sufficiently discharged their duties of appropriate notice of free representational options or discouraged representation in their exchanges with clients from the most marginalized and "disaffected groups."[200] This is a matter the GAO had also flagged for further investigation and follow-up after finding racial disparities in allowance decisions for unrepresented claimants in its most recent study in 2003.[201]

Because courts and adjudicative agencies do not generally take action on perceived implicit bias and disclosure of overt, explicit racial biases is not commonplace in agency adjudication, there are very few reported cases or instances in which either the agency or courts have either found or intimated an ALJ's decision-making may be tainted with racial or ethnic bias. This reality underscores the difficulty of policing bias through normal appeal and agency-initiated processes. Even in cases where ALJs have explicitly "said the quiet part out loud," the path toward relief for claimants of color as a class, if any such relief is expressly provided, has still been long, arduous, and limited. For example, in *Grant v. Commissioner of Soc. Sec. Admin.*, claimants brought a class action challenge alleging bias on several grounds against an ALJ in Pennsylvania and Washington DC (ALJ Russell Rowell).[202] The case went on for twelve years, with frequent denials of bias or malfeasance by SSA after agency reviews of the record, followed by remands for further proceedings by the federal courts.[203]

Eventually, the Third Circuit, contrary to bias class action and other class action decisions in other courts,[204] issued a somewhat restrictive ruling (over a strong dissent by Judge Leon Higginbotham) determining that neither discovery nor trial was available in the federal courts in such a case in order to protect the decisional independence of ALJs and avert intrusive "probing of the mindset" or thought processes of the decision-maker.[205] Rather, for a such a class action, bias fact findings would have to take place before the agency which would then be subject to a deferential substantial evidence standard of review on appeal in federal court.[206] Judge Higginbotham, in his dissent, noted that in *Bowen v. City of New York*,[207] a district court authorized discovery and held trial in a class action in finding that SSA had engaged in a "covert" and "illegal" ("fixed clandestine") policy against claimants with mental impairments from 1977 to 1983, and ordered extensive prospective and retrospective relief; both the Second Circuit and Supreme Court affirmed the ordered relief in that case.[208]

Judge Higginbotham noted that just as the majority argued that the distinguishable reason for discovery and fact-finding in *Bowen v. City of New York* was that the SSA could not be expected to impartially adjudicate allegations of its own secret conduct and maintenance of an illegal policy, so too it cannot be expected to impartially adjudicate class action pattern and practice bias claims based on the biased conduct of an SSA ALJ in volumes of decisions which the Secretary/Commissioner adopted as the final decisions of the SSA.[209] He reasoned:

> [A]ccording to the majority, in the only instances in which the district courts engaged in fact-finding [as opposed to reserving all fact-finding to the agency per 42 U.S.C. § 405(g)], the fact in question concerned the existence of a hidden unlawful agency … practice – a question on which the Secretary could not function as an impartial fact-finder … [E]ven if one begins to imagine that the majority is correct in assuming that the Secretary develops a strange attachment to its own policies and practices, thereby rendering it incapable of being an impartial fact-finder in ruling on their legality, the fact remains that the same reasoning can be applied to an allegation of bias by an ALJ. The same Secretary that adopts a policy or practice is the same Secretary that supervises ALJs. The majority's argument seems to be that the Secretary is unable to be an impartial fact-finder with regard to the agency's unlawful policies and practices because the Secretary is not separate from the agency. If that is so, then the same can be said about the relationship between the Secretary and the ALJ. The Secretary, the ALJ and various other branches of the agency all constitute part of the same bureaucracy. To separate the Secretary, the agency, and the ALJ is to insist on pure fiction.[210]

To further concretize his argument and the implications of the majority's position in hindering resort to the federal courts to remedy pattern and practice systematic racial or invidious ALJ bias claims, Judge Higginbotham commenced his dissent with the following hypothetical:

> Suppose a class of plaintiffs alleged that the Secretary of Health and Human Services had adopted a secret policy under which claimants living in hispanic, black or poor white communities were presumed to be generally "less deserving" of social security disability benefits. Would a federal district [court] have the authority to conduct a de novo fact-finding trial in ruling on plaintiffs' claim, or would the district court only have the authority to review the Secretary's findings of facts under a limited standard of review?[211]

Nevertheless, the majority's opinion in *Grant* resulted only in a remand to the SSA for further fact-finding subject to deferential substantial evidence judicial review in federal court. On this remand from the Third Circuit, the record before the SSA, and eventually the federal district court, included an analysis of 212 of ALJ Rowell's decisions, testimony by fellow ALJs and coworkers in ALJ Rowell's office, and testimony of a Georgetown law professor who had visited and spoken with the ALJ around arranging for his clinical program at Georgetown to appear in hearings in this ALJ's office, among other witnesses. Testimony from a coworker and attorney advisor to ALJ Rowell – a position analogous to a permanent judicial law clerk – who referenced Rowell as a "close friend" revealed that the ALJ touted his ability to deny cases based on adverse credibility findings in assessing claimants' pain and symptomology. He utilized a profile of claimants he presumed to be noncredible whom he characterized as "no-goodniks," and this profile included African Americans and Hispanics (categorically, and without qualification based on class or poverty); poor whites; persons with mental impairments; those with substance addictions; and persons with obesity, among others.[212]

The ALJ's attorney advisor's testimony revealed that, when a hearing involved someone in the "no-goodnik" profile, "ALJ Rowell 'did say many times, you know this is a matter of credibility, and then he'd kind of chuckle, 'and that's bad for the claimant.' It was just – that was a normal part of the discourse."[213] With respect to the top of the "no-goodnik" list, African American claimants, the ALJ used the N-word in his office on multiple occasions and had referenced a "Senator Bilbow who allegedly introduced a Bill to Congress calling for the return of all African Americans to Africa."[214] The ALJ also claimed that Latino/a claimants feigned inability to communicate in English presumably to claim vocational disadvantage in the labor market and an easier avenue to disability benefits under SSA's medical-vocational ("grid") regulations that took lack of English language skills into account,[215] regulations in effect until 2020. He also expressed the belief that Latino/a claimants "fake mental illness [as] … a standard part of every case."[216]

The SSA panel evaluating the bias claims had initially ruled that only the ALJ's decisions would be evaluated and that none of the testimony of colleagues and witnesses regarding the ALJ's views and expressed biases should be considered.[217] Although the SSA found that 84 percent of ALJ Rowell's credibility determinations from the 212-case sample were "problematic," it consistently declined to find bias, reasoning that bias must be apparent from the face of the decision and be proven (by overcoming a virtually insurmountable proof burden) of demonstrating "that all of most of the judges' [*sic*] decisions manifest such wrongful or inappropriate dispositions."[218] The district court reversed. While applying the deferential substantial evidence standard on appeal with this record, the court eventually found on the evidence that ALJ Rowell systematically "harbored biases which rendered him unable to fulfill his duty to decide cases fairly" and it ordered new hearings for members of the class.[219] However, even on this unusually overtly racially biased record, the court declined to expressly find "racial" bias among the types of biases demonstrated; it found unlawful "biases" without specification.

In *Pastrana v. Chater*,[220] an ALJ who had openly opined about perceived laziness and lesser work ethic of Puerto Ricans was castigated by the court with a recommendation for the SSA to pursue disciplinary action for "statements that can be characterized as racist."[221] The ALJ had stated, among other musings, that in Puerto Rico, "one cannot find a person willing to do housework" or "farm work" "because Puerto Ricans consider the work undignified," "Puerto Ricans do not even want to work as mechanics because they get dirty," they "do not want to work in factories where there isn't any air conditioning," and Puerto Ricans "at age 50 … do not want to work" because "after age 50 they want to get social security."[222] The Court emphasized that a simple remand of the case was not enough because "almost 10 minutes of the claimant's one hour hearing was taken up by the ALJ's disgusting, racist rantings."

The court indicated that it would send a copy of the order and opinion along with the hearing transcript to the SSA Commissioner in the hope SSA would take appropriate disciplinary action.[223] However, unlike the *Grant* case involving ALJ Rowell who was named and identified in the published opinion, the court declined to name the ALJ whose actions it found racist and disgusting, so that future litigants and their counsel could be on notice and could take collective action to seek broader relief for other similarly affected claimants if/when confronting similar biased statements and treatment. It is unclear, and there is no public record, indicating whether SSA took any corrective or disciplinary follow-up action in response to the court's order and plea in this individual case.

A few other cases involving allegations of various forms of general (nonrace-specific) bias further illustrate the SSA's inability and sometimes resistance to policing ALJ bias and the protracted, slow, and difficult nature of judicial bias challenges and usually limited nature of relief from the courts. In *Pronti* v. *Barnhart*,[224] the court remanded a group of five consolidated cases to the SSA to determine general bias by an ALJ based on "serious" statistical and anecdotal evidence of bias in multiple cases. The allegations included assertions that ALJ Franklin T. Russell announced a "private and personal policy agenda outside of the law and contrary to Congressional intent … that too many claimants were awarded social security benefits and that he was going to protect the public treasury," that he "uses an illegal standard of proof for disability that is higher than a preponderance of the evidence," and "uses an illegal standard to determine credibility, often finding inconsistencies in claimant's testimony when none exist," among other systematic misapplications of law.[225]

In remanding the case, the court specifically referenced the inadequacies of SSA's regulations at 20 C.F.R. §§ 404.940, 416.1440 in addressing systematic bias allegations, and the counterproductive and potentially retaliation-inducing requirement that objections to an ALJ based on bias must be first asserted to the ALJ in advance of the hearing or at the "earliest possible time." It stated:

> The regulation contemplates circumstances where an ALJ has a specific bias against a particular plaintiff or has "any interest in the manner pending for decision" that would warrant his disqualification. 20 C.F.R. § 404.940. This is made clear by the requirement that a plaintiff who objects to a particular ALJ must notify the ALJ so that he can consider the specific objections and decide whether to recuse himself and withdraw from the case. If the ALJ chooses not to withdraw, the plaintiff may, after the hearing, present her objections to the ALJ to the Appeals Council "as reasons why the hearing decision should be revised or a new hearing held before another Administrative Law Judge." 20 C.F.R. § 404.940. For many reasons, this regulation is not well-suited to claims of general bias. First, it seems misguided to have to present a claim of general bias first to the very ALJ that is alleged to be biased. Assuming an ALJ was biased, it stands to reason that he would not admit as much by agreeing to withdraw from the case. Second, the Appeals Council reviews claims of bias on a case-by-case basis only, which does not take into account the nature of a claim of general bias.[226]

However, on remand, the SSA disregarded the court's remand order to determine the general bias issue and instead ordered new hearings with different ALJs for the individual claimants in the consolidated cases, thereby mooting the broader claims of general bias by the ALJ in question applicable to all, and the court, although critical of the SSA's actions and "long and tortuous process," ultimately agreed.[227]

In *Kendrick v. Sullivan*, claimants brought a class action challenge seeking to remove Manhattan (NYC) ALJ Helen Anyel based on allegations of systematic bias against claimants. The complaint alleged the ALJ systemically hindered and discouraged unrepresented claimants from seeking representation, and regularly disregarded claimant pain and symptomology testimony based on the ALJ's improper lay observations of the absence of observable pain or symptom manifestations during the short hearings.[228] The allegations also included claims that ALJ Anyel systematically disregarded controlling law such as in requiring objective proof of the extent and degree of subjective manifestations of pain – a position contrary to settled case law, agency regulations, and incapable of medical or scientific verification.[229] Ultimately, this class action, which survived SSA's motion to dismiss and opposition to class certification,[230] induced SSA to proceed in a disciplinary action against ALJ Anyel before the Merit System Protection Board (MSPB).

The Board found support for the allegations of ALJ misconduct, after identifying errors in (88.15 percent), 186 out of a survey of 211 of ALJ Anyel's decisions, and substantiation of the charge by a preponderance of the evidence that she "frequently failed to adequately extend to *pro se* claimants the right to representation during hearings held before her."[231] However, it ultimately recommended only a ninety-day suspension without pay and no further remedial action other than the ALJ's agreement to return to duty with conditions consistent with applicable law.[232] Eventually, the MSPB approved a settlement agreement between the agency and ALJ Anyel that precluded her from hearing social security disability program cases for a one-year period following her suspension and allowed her to hear and decide certain claims from the Medicare program.[233] However, Medicare claimants then also brought a class action challenge seeking to remove ALJ Anyel from presiding over Medicare adjudications owing to systemic bias in those cases.[234]

One early case, *In re Chocallo*,[235] involved somewhat greater relief in an individual MSPB proceeding against ALJ Wanda Chocallo for misconduct during three hearings and established an important principle on the limits of APA good cause and decisional independence protections in proceedings based on significant ALJ bias. SSA ALJs have often asserted arguments that inquiries into bias based on conduct during hearings or in decision-making after hearings undermine their decisional independence protected under the APA.[236] In the MSPB disciplinary decision against the SSA ALJ in this case, based on bias and misconduct allegations, the Board flatly rejected the ALJ's broad adjudicative independence assertion.

The Board reasoned that while the APA protects ALJ independence by eliminating "the conflict of interest inherent in the prosecutor and the adjudicator being vested in a single unit" and also "insulating the [ALJ] from improper outside influence which might compromise the judicial process, the Act also provided for accountability of that judge by setting forth a procedure for removal by an independent body [the MSPB]." Therefore, neither "the Act [nor] its accompanying legislative history … provide any support for the contention that conduct within the course of an adjudication may not be considered as a basis for removal or other adverse action."[237] The MSPB stated:

> [I]mportant consideration must be given to the fact that in order to carry out the decision-making process in an objective and equitable fashion an [ALJ] must be free of harassment, intimidation or improper influences from agency officials. Nonetheless, this does not give that judge carte blanche authority to conduct the government's business in a biased and destructive fashion which undermines and casts disrepute on the adjudicatory process. The fact that an [ALJ] carries out his/her duties in a hearing room rather than an office does not provide an impenetrable shield from appraisal of performance.[238]

The *In re: Chocallo* proceedings did not involve specific allegations of racial bias against the ALJ in the three cases of misconduct which formed the basis of the charges. However, in the SSA ALJ hearing proceeding in which the MSPB appeared to consider the most serious of the three, the claimant was identified as Black and the ALJ had accused the plaintiff's attorney, Jonathan Stein from Community Legal Services (CLS) of Philadelphia – who had moved to recuse the ALJ for bias before the hearing – of using the claimant in that case and Black claimants in other cases for his own causes, to the detriment of Black claimants, and effectively precluded Stein and a CLS paralegal working with him from representing the claimant in that case. The MSPB affirmed a finding that the ALJ's conduct reflected "gross bias" against the claimant's attorney in an effort to retaliate for and undermine the recusal motion. In so doing, the ALJ improperly referenced a newspaper article about the claimant's attorney outside the record, improperly rendered the claimant without representation in the hearing, and caused additional stress to the claimant through intemperate and improper questioning; and these collective actions constituted "good cause" for the ALJ's removal.[239]

Finally, the most recent known class action ALJ bias case alleged systematic general bias against claimants by five ALJs in a hearing office in Queens, New York, and resulted in somewhat broader relief in a settlement agreement of that case. In *Padro v. Astrue*,[240] the plaintiffs' record included dozens of federal court decisions reversing hearing decisions of the five ALJs and finding inappropriate "hostility" toward and "combative" questioning of claimants, numerous "arbitrary" and "illogical" decisions, "trivializing claimant impairments," mistreatment of non-English speaking claimants, and a pattern of "faulty and erroneous credibility determinations" of claimant pain and symptoms, among other patterns of violation of social security disability law and procedure.[241] While not admitting any wrongdoing on behalf of the five Queens ALJs, the SSA agreed to provide the opportunity for new hearings, with different ALJs, for an estimated 4,000+ claimants who had received unfavorable (or partially unfavorable) decisions from any of those ALJs in the period from January 11, 2008 through the date of the settlement agreement in 2013.[242]

The *Padro* settlement also provided that SSA would institute a training program in 2013 for the ALJs on the law involving evaluating treating medical source reports and opinions; assessing claimant credibility; developing the record; and conducting the hearing, and expand SSA's process options for challenging bias and unfair hearing allegations through a new Social Security Ruling (SSR).[243] That SSR (13-1p), established three options for raising bias claims.[244] First, as always, the claimant can raise such allegations stemming from the hearing, in a routine appeal to the Appeals Council within sixty days of the decision; however, the Council will not consider claims of racial bias or bias against any group or even general bias beyond bias or unfairness in the individual case and based on matters in the record.

Second, the claimant can seek review outside of individual claim adjudication by filing a complaint within 180 days of the action complained of (or of when the claimant became aware of that conduct) with SSA's Division of Quality Service (DQS) which can result in disciplinary action against the ALJ. While DQS will notify the complainants that the complaint has been processed, they will not receive any further information on the disposition of the complaint and DQS's findings are not subject to judicial review by the complainants. Third, the claimant can file a civil rights complaint within 180 days with SSA's Office of General Counsel if there are allegations of discrimination based on "race, color, national origin, (including English language ability), religion, sex, sexual orientation, age, disability, or in retaliation for having filed a civil rights complaint against the agency." The complainant will receive a copy of the decision on the complaint and can request reconsideration within thirty days.[245]

It is not apparent that the now thirteen-year-old new process and options for SSA ALJ bias complaints have been any more effective at curtailing racial bias and other biases than previous SSA procedures.[246] They still all rely on SSA investigation in policing the actions of SSA adjudicators – a process which the SSA has approached with significant reticence and a narrow view of cognizable racial or other invidious bias, as shown in the cases discussed here. In addition, the processes, along with SSA's bias regulations, to some extent function to insulate SSA from bias claims by utilizing very short time periods for filing or raising bias claims, including the regulatory "earliest opportunity" requirement for asserting bias objections to an ALJ which SSA has used to seek dismissal of ALJ bias claims in federal court actions as untimely.[247]

The processes also largely depend on bias complaint filing by aggrieved claimants whose focus is on obtaining often desperately needed benefits in their individual cases, as is the focus of most private disability benefits attorneys whose compensation is dependent on contingent fees from success on the merits. Some private attorneys have publicly advertised that while they applaud important efforts to curtail bias (mostly in actions with representation by legal services and other nonprofit organizations or pro bono counsel), they do not pursue bias claims for their clients and only focus on success in the individual cases.[248] Some have voiced fear of retaliation from ALJs in subsequent cases with other clients before such ALJs, thereby undermining the attorneys' contingent fee business model and bottom-line financial viability.[249] An ACUS report found that bias complaints are raised in fewer than 1 percent of all cases.[250] At the time of this writing, leaders of the National Organization of Social Security Claimant Representatives (NOSSCR) expressed unawareness of any pending actions or successful ALJ bias or misconduct challenges under SSR 13-1p procedures (or otherwise) since the 2013 *Padro* settlement.[251]

5.10 RECOMMENDATIONS FOR REMEDYING SSA RACIALLY DISPARATE DECISION-MAKING AND ADJUDICATIVE BIAS

5.10.1 *Resume Race/Demographic Data Collection*

First, the scope of the problem of racial bias and sources and evolution of previously identified racially disparate disability decision patterns by GAO and others cannot be meaningfully identified and evaluated without relevant demographic data. "The first step to fixing any problem is to recognize there is a problem,"[252] and the absence of data obscures identification of the sources and persistence of the problems of systemic racial disparities and potential bias uncovered by the GAO. The now revoked 2021 and 2023 Executive Orders on Advancing Racial Equity observed that lack of race and ethnicity data "has cascading effects and impedes efforts to measure and advance equity [and a] first step to promoting equity in Government action is to gather the data necessary to inform that effort."[253] Indeed, SSA itself recently acknowledged that "*[s]ince 1987, there has been a huge decline in race and ethnicity data in our records [and] [t]his makes it more difficult for us to monitor the fair treatment of people of color in our programs.*"[254] It has also proposed short-, medium-, and long-term steps to rectify those racial data collection and reporting deficiencies.[255]

Accordingly, SSA should recommence its best efforts at collection of race, ethnicity and basic demographic data on its decisions at all levels, including ALJ decisions as the GAO and several disability advocacy groups have urged for many years. For example, the 2023 Abt Associates QDD bias study noted only the present capacity to identify race/ethnicity from 60 percent of the adult SSDI and/or SSI and 17 percent of the children's SSI applications, so Abt "used an established approach – called Bayesian Improved First Name Surname Geocoding (BIFSG) – to predict claimants' race and ethnicity as proxies for missing data."[256] SSA can also supplement their efforts with disclosures from medical charts and otherwise from materials in claimants' case records.

If or when the data reflects disparate patterns, SSA should audit select decisions of highly disparate ALJ decision-makers and follow up with training and, if reflective of bias or systemically legally flawed or inadequate decisions, with discipline. Such an audit may reveal a concentrated or isolated pattern with a particular ALJ or group of ALJs. For example, a recent small study which became the subject of a law student's law review note found that three out of the twelve ALJ's whose decisions were reviewed using files and data from legal aid program case files were responsible for 77 percent of the denials of Black claimants and granted benefits to only 7.6 percent of Black claimants.[257]

5.10.2 *Resume/Expand Implicit Bias Interventions/Trainings for ALJs*

Second, as discussed, the SSA found previous efforts at racial bias awareness and reduction-focused interventions for ALJs in the early 1990s useful and successful. While the SSA's conclusions were not shared by all those conducting the interventions, and multiple recent articles critical of SSA bias procedures have recommended new implicit bias interventions,[258] significant advances in the mind science and methodology of implicit bias interventions since the early 1990s support renewed efforts as well. Moreover, as recently as 2022, SSA had recommended in its Equity Action Plan: "Conducting mandatory training on unconscious bias for all agency employees, including employees who make decisions on eligibility for DI and SSI disability benefits. The intent of this training is to disrupt and correct any negative biases that might interfere with the decision-making process."[259]

It is now fairly well accepted that implicit biases have some basic characteristics: (1) they are pervasive and affect all of us to some degree; (2) they are malleable;

and (3) they can be reduced with appropriate interventions.[260] Interdisciplinary expert teams of psychologists, neurologists, and lawyers have developed protocols for instructional interventions specifically provided to judges, prosecutors, and law enforcement officials at all levels, integrating important modern concepts of "racial anxiety"[261] and "stereotype threat"[262] into implicit bias workshops to address bias, difference, and potential discrimination issues more comprehensively and holistically. Professor Jerry Kang's summary of such methodology, in his article "*What Judges Can Do About Implicit Bias*,"[263] outlines a cogent, systematic, step-by-step approach to such interventions with judicial decision-makers. One such interdisciplinary entity, the Perception Institute,[264] has conducted several such interventions for groups of state and local ALJs in the past decade.[265] Accordingly, SSA need not recreate the wheel; a specific wheel is in place for a broader scale expansion of a modern implicit bias interventional program which should ease implementation of a national program for all SSA ALJs as originally contemplated and projected by SSA in the 1990s and as SSA itself recently recommended in its 2022 Equity Action Plan.

5.10.3 *Implement Implicit Bias Interventions for all Disability Agency (DDS) Medical and other (SSA) Medical Personnel Involved in Creating Reports and Assessments in SSA Disability Adjudications and Curtail Predominantly One-Sided and Pressured Quality Reviews of the DDSs*

Third, as mentioned earlier, there are three types of agency-employed or retained medical consultants who often create medical assessments or supply testimony in SSA disability adjudications: DDS review physicians, consultant examining physicians, and hearing level medical advisors. The agency-employed medical sources create medical reports and assessments which are often decisive evidence in these adjudications. And they are not immune from the same implicit biases described in the medical literature referred to here, which are pervasive throughout the medical profession. While SSA and the state agency DDSs which report to SSA are not in the best position to address the biases of medical personnel outside their employ, such as a claimant's treating sources, they can and should take steps to mitigate biases of those they regularly employ, hire, consult, and rely upon. Indeed, by committing in the 2022 Equity Action Plan to conduct unconscious bias training for "all agency employees" and adjudicative personnel in some form, SSA has already determined that such a program should extend to all agency-retained medical personnel involved in the disability adjudication processes.

Moreover, the recent data on the impact of implicit bias interventions with medical personnel is encouraging; a 2025 report reviewing fifty-five selected studies of implicit bias interventions determined that 96 percent of the studies "reported an overall positive association of the intervention." The "[p]ositive outcomes included increases in the knowledge, skills and attitudes around implicit biases and improved ability to identify strategies for identifying and managing one's potential biases around patients."[266]

The SSA should also take measures to avert pressuring (or from taking action which can be construed as pressuring or facilitating) DDS and other consultant medical sources to offer restrictive medical assessments, contrary to defensible professional judgment. For example, in the *Bowen v. City of New York* case, a rarely unanimous Supreme Court decision noted that the unchallenged district court findings determined that:

> SSA relied on bureaucratic instructions rather than individual assessments and overruled the medical opinions of its own consulting physicians that many of those whose claims they were instructed to deny could not, in fact, work. Physicians were pressured to reach 'conclusions' contrary to their own professional beliefs in cases where they felt, at the very least, that additional evidence needed to be gathered in the form of a realistic work assessment. The resulting supremacy of bureaucracy over professional medical judgments and the flaunting of published, objective standards is contrary to the spirit and letter of the Social Security Act.[267]

While the secret illegal policy exposed in the *City of New York* litigation has long been declared unlawful and specific illegal pressure on the DDS review physicians in mental impairment cases enjoined, the adjudicative culture may still convey messages promoting unnecessary, reflexive stringency at least when in doubt. For example, in commenting on the impact of SSA's conduct of quality review of mostly the benefits allowance decisions, as opposed to denial decisions, at the DDS (initial and reconsideration) levels of decision-making, former Social Security Advisory Board (SSAB) chairperson Sylvester J. Schieber explained:

> *[A] quality review process that targets almost exclusively allowance decisions sends an unintended message.* Only a small fraction of denied cases are selected for quality review. The chance of an insufficiently documented denial determination slipping through the system unchecked cannot be discounted … [There may be many reasons why there has been a steady decline in allowance rates in the DDS, but it certainly seems likely that inadequate investment which has led to a "start and stop" type of work environment is a major factor.] This is not about a culture of denial but about human nature. When faced with pressure to clear cases quickly, adjudicators may take shortcuts and those shortcuts can lead to unintended consequences.[268]

For the reasons discussed later in Section 5.10.5 with respect to ALJs and the hearing level adjudicative culture and similar and greater pressures on ALJs (where appearance of claimants in person makes race a more salient factor), the pressure to deny claims and to do so quickly is likely to lead to disparate denials of the applications of claimants of color at the earlier stage (DDS) levels too. These practices – especially one-sided or slanted (approval-decision-focused) quality reviews of DDS decision-making and the evaluations of DDS medical personnel – should be discontinued.

5.10.4 *Increase Efforts at Enhancing Diversity of the ALJ Corps*

Fourth, while owing to reasons of poor health care and resulting medical impairments, poverty and the consequences of historic and contemporary discrimination, Black and Brown claimants comprise a disproportionate slice of the disability claimant population, they hold only a tiny portion of the ALJ positions – last documented at 1 percent Black and 3 percent Latino/a as discussed earlier. Professor Sherrilyn Ifill has explained the importance of judicial diversity as furthering the dual purposes of promoting public confidence in the legitimacy of the courts and their decisions and in enhancing the quality of judicial decision-making.[269] On the latter, she explained:

> [T]o recognize that differing racial or ethnic groups may have different perspectives that bear on legal decisionmaking is not to assign or essentialize the experiences of different groups. To be sure, there is no one "Black perspective" or "Latino perspective." But there are shared experiences that influence how we look at the world around us – even the law. In previous articles about this I've cited polls that showed that even black and white lawyers *and judges* differ in their views about aspects of the criminal justice system. For example, in one poll 83% of white judges polled, but only 18% of black judges, believed that blacks are treated fairly in the criminal justice system.[15] This is a stark disparity. What is it that black judges see that white judges do not? What is it that white judges see that black judges do not? How do we reconcile these disparate views of our justice system held even by *judges*? Is one view illegitimate and the other legitimate? The truth is that neither of these perspectives should be disqualified from legal decisionmaking.[270]

Other scholars have pointed to how "judicial diversity can itself be a remedy to counter implicit bias; the creation of a diverse bench introduces ideas that were once viewed as foreign to becoming the norm in decision making … [and] can reflect a judicial approach that is representative of an entire nation's people."[271]

As also described earlier, the SSA for a period of time pursued efforts to try to advance diversity of its ALJ corps, and it is not clear if those efforts have been successful. As an initial matter, SSA should maintain public demographic data on its ALJ corps; such data is readily available for Article III federal judges.[272] There are a number of more fulsome actions SSA can take to try to improve diversity within the ALJ corps including developing a pipeline program, conducting targeting outreach at Minority Bar associations and minority led legal organizations, diversifying selection panels and hiring personnel, and creating more transparent application processes.[273]

5.10.5 *Curtail Predominantly One-Sided and Pressured Oversight of ALJs and Create an Independent Panel to Review a Sampling of Bias Complaints Submitted to the Three SSA Entities Receiving Bias Claims per SSR 13-1p*

For the reasons compellingly articulated by Judge Higginbotham in *Grant*, and as shown in the more than thirty-two years since the Third Circuit's *Grant* decision in the paucity of bias complaints and the arduous, exhausting, and usually minimal bias-related relief and remedies from such efforts which reach the courts, the SSA does not appear to be structurally well suited to the adjudicative policing of patterns of ALJ racial (and other) biases by its own ALJs. Historically, the SSA's focus in supervising the ALJ corps has been to pursue oversight actions – such as Appeals Council own motion review in the Bellmon Review Program – which *discouraged* ruling in favor of claimants and against the agency's initial application denial decisions in these hearings by conducting oversight and review programs that examined only claimant-favorable ALJ decisions and the decision-making only of ALJs with higher than average benefit approval rates. Several courts have noted that such one-sided review programs put pressure on and convey a message to ALJs to deny more claims.[274] The Trump administration's recent expressed belief that newer Supreme Court precedent expanding the executive branch's control over independent agencies and their ALJs permits the dismissal of ALJs at will who do not further administration priorities and policies will likely have the same chilling effect on SSA ALJ decision-making and induce more disability claim denials.[275]

The SSA has also pressured ALJs to decide cases more rapidly by meeting a goal or quota of 500 decisions annually.[276] In an effort to challenge the undesired pressure to decide cases more rapidly, the ALJ union – the Association of Administrative Law Judges – challenged the practice in court as violative of ALJ decisional independence under the APA and suggested the pressure compelled them to decide more cases against the agency and for claimants. In reality, the opposite was true as ALJ denial rates increased; the Seventh Circuit ultimately rejected this challenge as unfounded.[277]

Both the pressure to deny claims and to decide cases more rapidly can lead to racially and other invidiously biased decisions. Implicit bias research suggests that significant time pressure often leads to automaticity (automatic cognitive responses) which trigger resort to unconscious racial schemas and implicit biases.[278] When the overwhelmingly white male ALJ corps is pressured to deny more claims, and do so more promptly, a likely reflexive response would be to deny more cases including very strong but not overwhelming or "bulletproof" cases from claimants perceived as perceptively less worthy, less credible, or less socially desirable, and perhaps less understandable from the ALJ's own lived experience and perspective. That those with more social distance from the ALJs would bear a disproportionate share of the prompt denial decisions in such cases, such as Black and Brown claimants, seems likely.

And needless to say, SSA should not continue or reinstitute those types of review programs – especially review programs focusing exclusively or mostly on approval decisions or on only high-approving ALJs. But if these are some of the messages historically communicated to SSA ALJs from SSA supervision and oversight (deny more claims, decide more rapidly) – and to some extent these messages are baked into and otherwise currently reinforced in the SSA adjudicative culture and present political climate – a further message from the agency through its own usually tepid bias case oversight, now through SSR 13-1p processes, will likely produce little meaningful reform.

As such, having an independent entity review or audit samplings of those SSR 13-1p bias complaints to the three SSA components receiving them (Appeals Council, DQS, and OGC) that can also request additional information, take other investigatory steps, and recommend further remedial and corrective actions, thereby averting sole reliance on SSA to effectively police itself, would be a step in the right direction. For example, the SSAB, a bipartisan seven-member board created under the 1994 Social Security Independence and Improvement Act with members appointed by Congress and the White House to provide advice and make recommendations to SSA, Congress and the White House on Social Security and SSI matters,[279] could select and oversee a small panel of experts. The SSAB could perhaps choose such an expert panel from different nonpartisan constituencies such as the National Academy for Social Insurance, the Committee for a Responsible Federal Budget Social Security Disability Solutions Initiative, and Consortium for Citizens with Disabilities to conduct such samplings and reviews and make recommendations.

6

The Special Problem of Race-Norming and Correction in Medical Diagnostic Clinical Care Tools and Algorithms Used in Social Security Disability Assessments

6.1 A OVERVIEW OF RACE-NORMING/RACE CORRECTION

Another health system and medical diagnostic practice, with historical genesis in theories of biological race and adverse impacts on SSA disability decisional equity, is the practice of race-norming. Race-norming, also known as race correction is a practice by medical and health care professionals of inserting racialized assumptions into medical practice clinical support tools, guidelines, and diagnostic algorithms that "adjust or correct their outputs on the basis of a patient's race or ethnicity."[1] Race-normed or "corrected" outputs often understate the severity of Black patients' conditions or require greater demonstration of illness to receive treatment for a range of severe and sometimes life-threatening conditions.

The National Academies of Science, Engineering and Medicine (NASEM) in a 2023 report on the impact of race-based algorithms on patient health, observed that there are "myriad ways providers account … for race by using diagnostic algorithms with outputs adjusted according to their patient's race or ethnicity." In the words of one of the physicians in the team that brought great public attention to the problem of race-norming in a 2020 article in the *New England Journal of Medicine*, Dr. Darshali Vyas, quoted in the NASEM report: "'[W]e use these algorithms daily to risk assess our patients and guide our clinical decisions, but by embedding race into the basic data in health care decisions, these algorithms propagate race-based medicine' and one result of this practice, is that 'race-based algorithms may exacerbate existing inequities by influencing decisions in ways that direct more attention or resources to White patients than to patients from racial and ethnic minoritized populations.'"[2]

The race-normed or corrected assumptions utilized in medical tools, guidelines, and algorithms are based on nonscientific generalizations, some with roots in theories of white supremacy and others based on factors mistakenly attributed to biological race based on observed poorer health conditions and disparate health outcomes in Black and Brown communities. These assumptions are not appropriately unpacked from a nuanced, individualized assessment of the myriad social and environmental factors – often a function of a legacy of racism and racial discrimination and subordination – producing or contributing to those disparate health conditions. Professor Khiara Bridges explained:

> Although the weight of good science establishes that races are not genetically coherent entities, the myth of biological race lives on. "Race correction" algorithms, in many cases, are simply a site of the persistence of the myth of biological race. This, of course, is not to propose that black people do not have different health outcomes from their nonblack counterparts – it is undeniable that they do … If "black race" refers to a group that is genetically distinct from other racial groups, then the algorithmic model will be wrong, as the weight of good science does not support the notion that black people are genetically distinct from nonblack people. If, however, "black race" refers to a group that has lived, and continues to live, under conditions of antiblack racism, then the algorithmic model will be more precise if it uses variables that more accurately capture that disadvantage, i.e., zip code, education level, income, wealth, health insurance status, comorbidities, allostatic load, and history with anxiety and depression.[3]

The House Ways and Means Committee has issued a report reaching similar conclusions, finding that "it is not race itself" that leads to adverse health consequences for Black and Brown persons or that "explains why some research has found different levels of kidney function for different racial groups or why lung function varies between groups[;] [or] other factors, most of which are avoidable social and structural determinants of health, are the actual root causes of observed differences among racial groups. Yet this complex web is too often reduced to the fabricated, crude, and convenient construct of race."[4]

The use of race specific norms results in Black patients having diagnostic scores adjusted on the assumption that normal Black functioning in particular body system impairments is significantly diminished relative to normal white functioning in those same body systems. Impairments that are race normed include serious lung disease/pulmonary impairments,[5] kidney disease/nephrology disorders,[6] brain injury/neurological, neuropsychological and cognitive disorders,[7] heart failure/cardiac disease,[8] osteoporosis and bone fracture risk,[9] and pregnancy-related complications and obstetric disorders,[10] often commencing at a 10 percent or greater adjustment for Black patients reflecting that much less "normal" capacity than white patients. Accordingly, the scores on tests such as pulmonary function tests (PFTs) for pulmonary impairments or glomerular filtration rates (GFRs) for kidney impairments, are adjusted or "corrected" by inserting race into the guidelines or algorithms used for measuring the severity of impairments. These devices result in Black patients' impairments and conditions appearing less severe and being taken less seriously by treatment professionals. This, in turn, leads to Black patients suffering a variety of adverse health treatment and health care consequences such as less priority on transplant lists, less timely intervention and treatment, and less intensive or protective overall treatment.

These practices also result in significant and improper disadvantage for Black social security disability claimants since the testing outputs will produce functional measures reflecting significantly less severity than if race neutral norms were utilized. Indeed, multiple medical, public health, and health law scholars have specifically pointed out the negative financial consequences of the resulting underassessment of Black impairment severity from race norming and correction such as "*to seekers of disability benefits including social security*."[11] One large interdisciplinary group of eighteen medical, public health, biomedical, and other scientific and social science scholars, in a paper in the *New England Journal of Medicine*, estimated that disability payments to disabled Black veterans in the veterans disability system (which uses measures of partial disability), would increase by 17.1 percent "amounting to $1.10 Billion annually" and with increases ranging from $1,991 to $27,000 to Black veterans just from use of race neutral pulmonary testing such as through the Global Lung Function Initiative (GLI).[12]

A few examples of body impairment system guidelines and algorithms which most concretely limit eligibility in the social security disability programs will now be described.

6.2 RACE-NORMED LUNG/PULMONARY FUNCTION TESTS (PFT)/SPIROMETRY: SSA LISTING 3.03

The use of race in American clinical care and diagnostic tools for the evaluation of pulmonary functioning has perhaps the longest and best-documented history among the race-normed impairment evaluation devices. Professor Lundy Braun's 2014 book, *Breathing Race into the Machine: The Strange Career of the Spirometer from Plantation to Genetics*, chronicles that history. The book traces the belief in biologically weaker lung capacity of Black persons to Thomas Jefferson's musings in 1779 on "a different structure of the pulmonary apparatus" of enslaved Blacks from white colonists, rendering Blacks "more tolerant of heat than cold" and possessing "natural conditioning for agricultural labor."[13]

In the 1840s, a British physician and scientist named John Hutchinson refined, popularized, and named the use of a "spirometer" as a device to measure respiratory capacity.[14] Hutchinson's spirometer "consisted of a counterbalanced bell inverted in water, whereby breathing into a connected pneumatic tube resulted in measurable vertical motion of the bell measurements," reflecting degrees of fundamental respiratory volumes, including "vital capacity, which to this day still represents 'the greatest voluntary expiration, following the deepest inspiration.'"[15] Then, in 1851, Dr. Samuel Cartwright, the same Louisiana slave owner and doctor who studied biological differences of Black persons (and used his conclusions to support the institution of slavery) such as his determination that Blacks were impervious to pain, utilized the spirometer to support theories about the relative biological inferiority of "negro lungs." Professor Braun explained:

> With the spirometer, he could define the deficit quantitatively … "The deficiency in the negro," Cartwright wrote, "may be safely estimated at 20%." *Foreshadowing*

arguments for race correction in the twentieth and twenty-first centuries, Cartwright cautioned that 'to judge the negro by the spirometric observations made on the white man, would indicate in the former a morbid condition when none existed. As the deficient respiratory apparatus affected "hebetude of mind and body," lower oxygen consumption had far reaching consequences for labor. The authority of whites over Negroes was both a necessity and "a blessing." Pointing to Jefferson's observations on "pulmonary apparatus of the negro," Cartwright claimed that difference was "both anatomical and physiological."[16]

By the early twentieth century, the idea of racial biological difference in pulmonary function, with whites having greater innate lung capacity than Blacks, Asians, and Indians, became widely recognized and established as medical fact.[17] These assumptions largely continue through the present. In 1999, greater widespread public discussion of the inequity of race-norming in spirometry and pulmonary function testing emerged when in defense of a class action lawsuit against a large asbestos manufacturer (the Owens Corning Corporation), by former employees with respiratory impairments, the corporation made a motion to require demonstration of Black plaintiffs' respiratory impairments for liability and compensation purposes utilizing a racially corrected and more stringent standard of pulmonary impairment severity.[18] "The case made public a long-standing but rarely examined history of racial assumptions informing the theories and substance of lung function research."[19] The case was widely publicized and commented on in the press,[20] including when the trial judge denied the corporation's motion after apparently finding it had failed to establish a sufficient scientific or medical basis for race-normed tools in the lawsuit by a preponderance of the evidence and testimony presented.[21]

As reported in the *New England Journal of Medicine* in 2020, the still prevailing employment of standard PFTs through spirometers "uses correction factors for persons labelled as black (10–15%) or Asian (4–6%)."[22] The racially normed and (10–15 percent) adjusted PFT "implies that an African American with a given forced expiratory volume (FEV) – a measure of how much air a person can exhale during a forced breath – would be rated with a higher lung function than a White individual with the same FEV value."[23] NASEM recently explained that utilization of this pulmonary "race-based equation directly affects a clinician's assessment of whether an individual has a respiratory disease, whether additional tests are needed, whether the patient should be referred for lung transportation" or specialized medications, and, among other public and personal safety, financial and vocational consequences, "*can also impact … disability determinations.*"[24]

Figures 6.2 and 6.3 are reproductions of actual PFT results for a Black social security disability applicant used in a federal court appeal from an adverse social security disability ALJ hearing and agency decision[25] and excerpted from a federal court administrative record and transcript. Read together with the SSA's Step-3 listing for automatic medical disability based on one measure of respiratory impairment severity,

3.01 Category of Impairments, Respiratory Disorders

3.02 *Chronic respiratory disorders* due to any cause except CF (for CF, see 3.04) with A, B, C, or D:

A. FEV_1 (see 3.00E) less than or equal to the value in Table I–A or I–B for your age, gender, and height without shoes (see 3.00E3a).

TABLE I—FEV_1 CRITERIA FOR 3.02A

Height without shoes (centimeters) < means *less than*	Height without shoes (inches) < means *less than*	*Table I–A* Age 18 to attainment of age 20		*Table I–B* Age 20 or older	
		Females FEV_1 less than or equal to (L, BTPS)	Males FEV_1 less than or equal to (L, BTPS)	Females FEV_1 less than or equal to (L, BTPS)	Males FEV_1 less than or equal to (L, BTPS)
<153.0	<60.25	1.20	1.45	1.05	1.20
153.0 to <159.0	60.25 to <62.50	1.30	1.55	1.15	1.35
159.0 to <164.0	62.50 to <64.50	1.40	1.65	1.25	1.40
164.0 to <169.0	64.50 to <66.50	1.45	1.75	1.35	1.50
169.0 to <174.0	66.50 to <68.50	1.55	1.85	1.45	1.60
174.0 to <180.0	68.50 to <70.75	1.65	2.00	1.55	1.75
180.0 to <185.0	70.75 to <72.75	1.75	2.10	1.65	1.85
185.0 or more	72.75 or more	1.80	2.15	1.70	1.90

FIGURE 6.1 SSA pulmonary system listing regulation: 20 C.F.R., Pt 404, subpart P, appendix 1, listing 3.02(A), table I-B, for adults.[26]

in Figure 6.1, these figures concretely underscore the potential harm of race-normed PFT's in the SSA disability assessment.

Figures 6.2 and 6.3 are two PFTs for a Black SSA disability benefits claimant both of which denote that the claimant is "Black" or "African" as would be needed for race-norming the PFT results.[27] It is unclear how much these PFTs have been normed but the usual degree of adjustment, as described above, is 10–15 percent. The first PFT would have met the criteria for automatic medical disability at the Step-3, listing 3.02(A) for a "chronic respiratory disorder" based on the spirometry (FEV1) score of 1.71 which is 48 percent of predicted even with a race-normed and adjusted PFT. Such norming was then and still is the established PFT practice and the reason to seek and include a racial designation on the PFT results sheet as here. The second PFT is 59 percent of predicted value at 2.16 and would not satisfy the criteria for automatic medical disability at listing 3.02A.

It is entirely possibly that this claimant with the above PFT results would have been found to have a condition that either met or equaled the listing if his PFT scores had not been "race corrected" or normed, adding points to denote lesser severity. However, apart from the impact in diminishing the likelihood of a respiratory condition meeting or equaling a listing for automatic Step-3 disability, race-norming also results in a less severe medical characterization of the impairment and less medical treatment, which are factors that adjudicators consider in assessing whether a claimant's pain and impairment symptoms are credible or supportable and in assessing residual functional capacity for past work or other work in the economy. Accordingly, being normed into a less severe profile also diminishes a claimant's disability case prospects and chances for success at Step-4 and Step-5 of the five-step regulatory disability evaluation process described in Chapter 5.2.

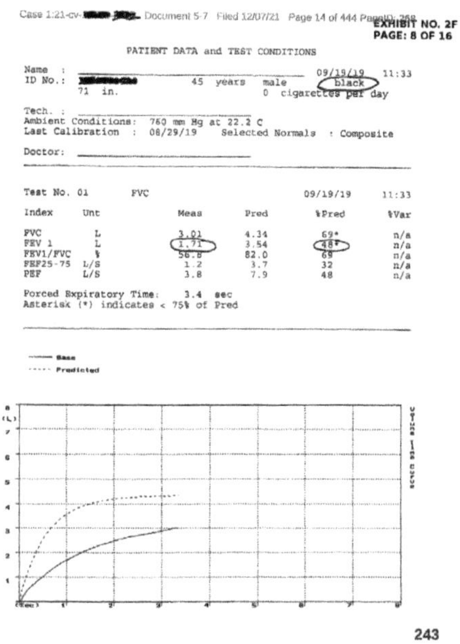
Case 1:21-cv-[redacted] Document 5-7 Filed 12/07/21 Page 14 of 444 PageID: 268
EXHIBIT NO. 2F
PAGE: 8 OF 16

PATIENT DATA and TEST CONDITIONS

Name : 09/19/19 11:33
ID No.: [redacted] 45 years male black
71 in. 0 cigarettes per day

Tech. :
Ambient Conditions: 760 mm Hg at 22.2 C
Last Calibration : 08/29/19 Selected Normals : Composite

Doctor:

Test No. 01 FVC 09/19/19 11:33

Index	Unt	Meas	Pred	%Pred	%Var
FVC	L	3.01	4.34	69*	n/a
FEV 1	L	1.71	3.54	48*	n/a
FEV1/FVC	%	56.8	82.0	69	n/a
FEF25-75	L/S	1.2	3.7	32	n/a
PEF	L/S	3.8	7.9	48	n/a

Forced Expiratory Time: 3.4 sec
Asterisk (*) indicates < 75% of Pred

FIGURE 6.2 Pulmonary function test (PFT) result for social security disability claimant in medical chart, part of federal court record in social security disability appeal.

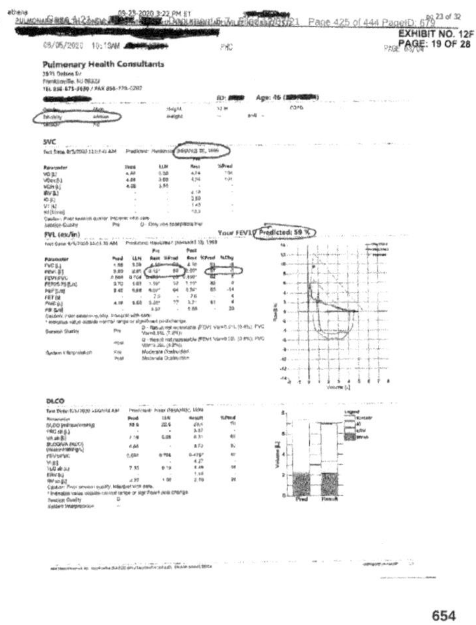
Page 425 of 444 PageID: 679
EXHIBIT NO. 12F
PAGE: 19 OF 28

[redacted]

08/05/2020 10:13AM [redacted]

Pulmonary Health Consultants

Age: 46 ([redacted])

SVC

FVL (ex/in)

Your FEV1% Predicted: 59 %

DLCO

FIGURE 6.3 Additional PFT result for social security disability claimant in medical chart, part of federal court record in social security disability appeal.

6.3 RACE-NORMED KIDNEY-FUNCTION TESTING: ESTIMATED GLOMERULAR FILTRATION RATE (eGFR): SSA LISTING 6.05 AND POMS DI 24555.005B.2

The eGFR is a laboratory formula utilized to assess kidney function taken from a simple blood test. The kidney is the body organ that functions to filter out waste and excess fluid from the body; serum creatinine is a waste product produced from the normal wear and tear of muscles and filtered from blood. The eGFR measures the speed at which one's kidneys filter out waste; if they are functioning poorly creatine builds up in the blood. Creatinine levels can be affected by other factors such as muscle mass and muscle weight.[28]

The history of race-norming of the eGFR is far more recent than the spirometer's antebellum origins. A 1999 study launched use of the "The Modification of Diet in Renal Disease (MDRD)" equation or algorithm that included race in its calculations and was introduced that year.[29] The "most widely used of the MDRD equations, estimated a race coefficient of 1.21, yielding an estimate of GFR that [was] 21% higher for Black patients than for white patients for the same serum creatinine concentration."[30] A new equation, "which included additional cohorts, was published in 2009 and estimated a modified race coefficient of 1.16, which yields an estimate of GFR that is 16% higher for Black Americans."[31]

The 1999 MDRD study had justified the inclusion of race because it had determined that "'Black ethnicity was an independent predictor of higher GFR' and 'previous studies ha[d] shown that on average, [B]lack persons have greater muscle mass than white persons."[32] The NASEM race-based algorithm report explained:

> [T]his adjustment arose from a 1999 finding that Black men and women had higher levels of serum creatinine for any measured level GFR than all other racial and ethnic groups. To account for that difference, investigators introduced an adjustment based on the debunked fallacy that Black individuals have naturally higher serum creatinine levels because they have more muscle mass, independent of physical activity. Because of this racial adjustment, Black individuals experience delays in receiving critical preventive care and increased transplant waitlist time.[33]

The potential absurdity of this assumption in application is manifest from popular culture: Does one really think that self-portrayed "scrawny" Black comedian and actor Chris Rock should be deemed to have more muscle mass than white actor and former California governor (and former bodybuilder) Arnold Schwartzenegger when assessing their respective kidney functioning?[34] As Professor Dorothy Roberts asked rhetorically in her popular TEDMED talk titled "The Problem with Race-Based Medicine": "[W]hat sense does it make for a doctor to automatically assume I have more muscle mass than [a white] female bodybuilder? Wouldn't it be far more accurate and evidence-based to determine the muscle mass of individual patients just by looking at them?"[35]

The SSA's relevant kidney function listing for automatic (step-3) medical disability for adults is at 20 C.F.R, Pt. 404, Subpt. P, Appendix 1, Listing 6.05;[36] it requires demonstration of reduced kidney functioning such as through an "eGFR of 20 ml/min/1.73m^2 or less" (6.05[A])[3]) and one of a variety of secondary complications such as fluid overload or neuropathy (6.05[B]). It is apparent that the ability to meet the eGFR principal requirement in Listing 6.05(A), would be significantly undermined by race correction equations or algorithms that scale-up the eGFR scores for Black patients by 16–21 percent beyond what the scores would be if not normed. In addition, as with the norming of PFTs, even if the non-normed eGFR would not meet or equal a step-3 listing for automatic disability, the less severe medical characterization of the impairment and less medical treatment owing to race norming the eGFR diminishes a claimant's disability case prospects and chances for success at step-4 and step-5 of the five-step regulatory disability evaluation process.

However, unlike the treatment of respiratory impairments and PFTs (and all other potentially race-normed clinical support tools, algorithms, and assessments used for any of the impairment body systems), SSA has taken some steps to move away from race-norming in the use of the eGFR based on developments and pronouncements by the leading kidney and nephrology expert bodies and societies in 2021–22. While SSA has still not altered the formal, duly promulgated regulatory listing 6.05 in any way, in August 2022, SSA issued internal subregulatory guidance to its adjudicators in the form of a Program Operations Manual System (POMS), namely POMS DI 24555.005B.2 ("Using Laboratory Testing to Evaluate Genitourinary Impairments"), announcing the following new approach for its adjudicators to race-norming in the eGFR:

> **2. Laboratory reporting of eGFR**
>
> Laboratories may report different eGFR values based on a person's race. For example, the report may contain: One eGFR value for the person's identified race, [o]ne eGFR value for African Americans and a second eGFR value for other races, or [o]ne eGFR value for other races and an instruction to multiply this value by an adjustment factor (usually recorded next to the eGFR value in the laboratory report) if the person is African American.
>
> On September 23, 2021, the National Kidney Foundation (NKF) and American Society of Nephrology (ASN), published a report recommending that laboratories should not include race in eGFR calculation and reporting. In response to this recommendation, we will use the unadjusted eGFR value for all persons, regardless of race. Some examples of how laboratories may report the unadjusted eGFR value include "eGFR," "eGFR Non-African American," "eGFR Non-Black," or "eGFR Caucasian."
>
> If the person is African American, and the laboratory reports: [1] An unadjusted eGFR value and an eGFR value for African Americans, use the unadjusted eGFR value[;] [2] An unadjusted eGFR value and an instruction to multiply this value by an adjustment factor if the person is African American, use the unadjusted eGFR value. Do not multiply the eGFR value by the adjustment factor.
>
> Contact the medical source to obtain the **unadjusted eGFR** if the person is African American and the laboratory reports: [1] One **eGFR value for African Americans**, or [2] One eGFR value and **it is unclear whether the eGFR value was adjusted for race**, **AND** All of the following conditions apply: There are no other laboratory findings in the medical evidence that satisfy the criteria in listing 6.05A, and [t]he person has at least one of the additional impairments required in listing 6.05B, and [u]sing the unadjusted eGFR value may change the determination of the claim.[37]

This internal agency guidance was issued without any publicity, fanfare, or notice. Indeed, a major Social Security blog site, *Social Security News*, maintained by veteran Social Security disability attorney, author, and commentator Charles T. Hall, suggested that the change was effectuated covertly. perhaps to reduce scrutiny and potential agency liability for past use of race-normed eGFRs. The blog noted, on June 21, 2022, that the change in the projected August 2022 POMS was initiated through an emergency message (EM-22012 SEN) to DDS adjudicators earlier in 2022 and the instructions to DDS provided: "*[POMS] DI 24555.005 includes the same instructions provided in EM-22012 SEN, Guidance on Using the Estimated Glomerular Filtration Rate (eGFR) in Cases Involving Genitourinary Disorders.*

Upon publication of the POMS, we will archive EM-22012 SEN." The blog post then stated:

> *Note* that the link to EM-22012-SEN doesn't work if you're not on Social Security's network. The SEN part may be there because this was deemed "Sensitive". In any case, it was not divulged to the public at the time these new instructions were issued to agency staff. I don't even know when the staff was told about this. This is basic stuff. It determines who wins and who loses. Why was this kept secret from claimants and their attorneys? We have an obvious need to know. *And what about African-Americans who were denied in the past under an arguably racist policy?*[38]

Nevertheless, the SSA's August 2022 POMS on use of a race-neutral eGFR is a positive and commendable first step. It reflects the SSA's first at least quasi-public recognition of the lack of scientific justification for race-norming tools and algorithms, the disparate harms to Black disability benefits claimants therefrom in SSA disability adjudication, and the agency's responsibilities to ensure a discriminatory race-norming algorithm is eliminated and nondiscriminatory eGFR tools are utilized in future adjudications. It is the SSA's first such policy statement of any kind on race-norming in disability adjudication and there are no other similar POMS applicable to lung impairments and PFTs or to race-norming in tools or algorithms in any other impairment body system. However, as discussed in Section 6.6.2, it does not go far enough to protect Black disability claimants from racially normed eGFRs and from race-norming clinical support tools and algorithms more broadly.

6.4 OTHER RACE-NORMED BODY SYSTEM IMPAIRMENT CLINICAL CARE SUPPORT TOOLS AND ALGORITHMS: COGNITIVE, CARDIAC, AND OSTEOPOROSIS IMPAIRMENTS

There are several other body system areas where clinical support tools have been and are racially normed. The race norming of Black NFL football players in neuropsychological testing for cognitive impairment and dementia that emerged from the NFL concussion and chronic traumatic encephalopathy (CTE) settlement brought significant national, high-profile, and heavily publicized attention to race-norming and its potentially deleterious impacts on Black patients.[39] To determine the severity of cognitive impairments, "neuropsychologists compare a patient's test performance to their estimated baseline cognitive abilities."[40] Race correction in cognitive testing was initially developed for seemingly benign purposes by norming the baseline "to reduce harms that can result from the overidentification of cognitive impairment among Black individuals and other marginalized racial/ ethnic groups including overpathologizing and overtreating."[41]

However, race-norming leading to underassessment or "false negatives cause even greater harm, such as when needed services are deemed unnecessary."[42] In the case of the Black NFL players suffering CTE, race-norming in cognitive testing produced harms by systematically raising the bar on the degree of impairment and distance from an upwardly normed cognitive baseline, "to make it more difficult for Black players to qualify for their rightful compensation."[43] When the NFL discontinued this practice in 2021, "many Black NFL retirees were newly qualified for compensation."[44]

Neurologist and Professor Katherine Possin has posited that the NFL case "is reminiscent of a century-long history of assuming the difference in intelligence tests (IQ) are primarily inherited and then using this false assumption to legitimize unequal distribution of resources by social class."[45] Possin advocates for "more scientifically sound alternatives to race norms" such as "regression-based normative approaches that explicitly measure social determinants of brain health" and also "address the substantial heterogeneity within race/ethnic groups." It would include "social determinants of brain health such as early life experiences, disparate educational quality, socioeconomic status, perceived discrimination, experiences of segregation, and neighborhood disadvantage."[46]

With respect to the social security disability system, as Professor Sonja Starr identified, race norming of cognitive testing leading to underdiagnosis not only risks denying access to financial support needed by those suffering cognitive decline who are civil litigants in personal injury lawsuits "like NFL players, *but more commonly, seekers of disability benefits including Social Security*."[47] It is unclear whether the IQ testing employed in the SSA's step-3 cognitive impairment listings (Listings 12.05, 112.05) have been race-normed or whether such norming is prevalent. The *Hidden in Plain Sight* authors (the Vyas team) reference the NFL concussion settlement as "extending the debate about race-norming beyond clinical medicine" and cognitive impairment tools are not among those listed in their two *New England Journal of Medicine* articles on race-norming and charts on norming in multiple body system impairment clinical support tools.[48] However, because the practice is used and has been employed in a high-profile way recently, SSA should be vigilant in ensuring race-normed cognitive testing is not employed in cases with claimants possessing cognitive impairments.

The Vyas team has also identified race-norming in a few areas that may have some utilization in SSA disability assessments. For cardiac impairments, the American Heart Association "Get with the Guidelines" heart failure score adds three points to the risk score of non Black patients admitted into a hospital, reflecting greater cardiac severity and a greater risk of death. Because "'black' is equated with lower risk, following the guidelines could direct care away from black patients."[49] The lower acknowledged impairment severity and diminished cardiac treatment from these guidelines will also reduce the strength of a Black claimant's SSA disability case.

The Vyas team has also identified race-norming in two measures of osteoporosis impairment risk assessment that are race-normed: the Osteoporosis Risk Score (Non-Blacks assigned five points); and the Fracture Risk Assessment Tool (FRAX) (Black women deemed lower fracture risk by 0.43 compared with white women;

Asian women by 0.50 compared with white women; and Hispanic women by 0.53).[50] These artificially deflated risk assessments will similarly diminish the strength of the cases of these respective claimants of color in pursuit of social security disability benefits.

6.5 RECENT DEVELOPMENTS (2020–25) IN ERADICATING RACE-NORMING

The use of race-norming or correction in clinical guidelines and algorithms became a significantly more prominent issue after an article describing inequity and problems with the practice and identifying several impairment areas where race correction was standard practice, published in the *New England Journal of Medicine* by three doctors in July 2020, "Hidden in Plain Sight – Reconsidering the Use of Race Correction in Clinical Algorithms."[51] Five years later, in the fall of 2025, in reflecting on their 2020 writing and why it resonated so significantly, the authors noted that while "concerns about the use of race in clinical care long predated 2020[,] [e]vents in the spring of 2020 escalated these concerns and created momentum for the pursuit of racial justice in medicine."[52] Those transformative events were "the twin pandemics – COVID-19, with its disproportionate impact on Black and Brown Americans and police brutality against Black Americans," further amplified after the national protest movements following the recorded and widely viewed police murder of George Floyd in May 2020.[53] Race correction guidelines and algorithms provided an "apt staging ground" for a racial reckoning with the medical profession's "complicity in structural racism," since norming and race correction assumptions were grounded in biological or genetic explanations for racial health disparities and not those attributable to racial discrimination and socioeconomic circumstances.[54]

Nevertheless, medical school instruction utilizing some biological race concepts, including race correction and race-norming guidelines and algorithms, persist as a part of mainstream medical education. A study in 2021 of "more than 880 lectures from 21 courses in one institution's 18-month preclinical medical curriculum … found five key domains in which educators misrepresent race in their discussions, interpretations of race-based data, and assessments of students' mastery of race-based science."[55] This study also found that "[r]ace-based clinical guidelines are a predictable outcome of the inaccurate use and interpretation of race" and are "taught to medical students and physicians without information about their origin and evidentiary basis." "A critical example to highlight given its relevance to preclinical curricula is the upward adjustment for persons designated as Black or African American in estimating the glomerular filtration rate (GFR), [for evaluating kidney function] which raises the threshold for concern for Black patients only."[56]

However, the increasing focus on misuse of these guidelines and algorithms in medical literature, buoyed by enhanced medical student activism,[57] has started to move medical curricula more noticeably in directions away from biological race and toward examining socioeconomic determinants of poor health, including those facilitated by the legacy and persistence of racial discrimination. For example, "an optional mini-lecture on racism in medicine was spearheaded by students at Harvard Medical School" which resulted in removal "of the race correction factor for the estimated glomerular filtration rate (eGFR)" in instruction on kidney function assessment.[58] The popularity of this lecture led to its eventual incorporation into the medical school curriculum.[59]

The authors of the 2020 "Hidden in Plain Sight" article have also pointed to steps moving in the direction of both greater "racial justice advocacy" and "evidence-based medicine" alike with respect to race-norming and correction clinical tools five years later in 2025.[60] They pointed out that since 2020, various expert bodies "have recommended removal of race from 8 out of the 13 race-adjusted clinical tools … addressed [in the 2020 article]."[61] Specifically, both the National Kidney Foundation and American Society of Nephrology joint taskforce in September 2021 "recommended moving away from race in estimates of kidney function [in the eGFR] because of the potential of delaying care to Black patients."[62] However, despite this recommendation, at the time of this writing in late 2025, "many hospitals continue to report race-adjusted eGFR."[63]

Similarly, in the spring of 2023, an American Thoracic Society (ATS) working group "recommended using race-neutral reference equations for PFT interpretation."[64] However, the ATS as of late 2025 has offered "no timeline or official guidance on how to implement these changes" and "PFT software will need to be updated in every laboratory in the country."[65] The "Hidden in Plain Sight" authors also identified "continued tensions" and "remaining barriers" to progress on removal of race from most of the other six clinical guidelines or algorithms where race neutral recommendations have been issued by various official or expert bodies.[66] Accordingly, the continued use of race-norming guidelines and algorithms remain an ongoing health care equity (and disability benefits equity) concern.

The same can be said for race-norming in cognitive testing: Despite a position paper in November 2021 by the American Academy of Clinical Neuropsychology (AACN) indicating support for "[t]he elimination of race as a variable in demographically based normative test interpretation," the AACN also "warned that this must be understood as a long-term objective because alternative norming strategies had to be developed and validated."[67] Similarly, while "the AHA released a statement acknowledging the harms of adjusting [the cardiac risk guidelines] for race," and plans to publish a new "tool for cardiovascular risk assessment that removes race as a risk factor," no such new guidelines have been published to date.[68] Finally, while the American Society for Bone and Mineral Research task force recommended in 2024 regarding osteoporosis that "fracture prediction models should not incorporate race or ethnicity adjustments," this recommendation has not yet been implemented.[69]

Congress and the Biden administration's Department of Health and Human Services (HHS) have also weighed in on race-norming since 2020. The US House Ways and Means Committee convened a hearing in the summer of 2020 and requested that more than a dozen medical societies "investigate and change clinical decision support tools that may fuel inequities in care." In summarizing the Ways and Means Committee's subsequent lengthy report on the misuse of race in clinical support tools in October 2021, its Chairmen Richard E. Neal (D-MA) stated:

> [D]ivergent understandings of the appropriate use of race and ethnicity in [clinical decision support tools] CDSTs could make it difficult to achieve consensus on the path forward. One thing is for certain: the status quo is unacceptable. Racial correction in clinical algorithms contributes to worse outcomes for patients of color receiving treatment for a broad range of conditions, from cancer, to osteoporosis, to end-stage renal disease, to child birth.[70]

Members of the Senate followed suit. Senators Elizabeth Warren (D-MA), Cory Booker (D-NJ), Ron Wyden (D-OR), and Representative Barbara Lee (D-CA) wrote a detailed letter in September 2020 to the Director of HHS's Agency for Healthcare Research and Quality urging an investigation of "race-based clinical algorithms" and practices that "adjust medical results based on a patient's race" and thereby "risk embedding racism into medical practice."[71]

In May 2024, HHS responded by adopting regulations to implement the anti-discrimination provision (Section 1557) of the Patient Protection and Affordable Care Act (ACA), 42 U.S.C. § 18116, which prohibits discrimination on the basis of race, color, national origin, sex, age, and disability in health programs and activities receiving federal funds. The regulations promulgated at 45 C.F.R.§ 92.210 (2025) provide that "covered entitles" (defined as recipients of federal assistance), must: (1) not discriminate on the basis of race, national origin, color (and the Act's other protected classes), in health programs or activities through the use of "patient care decision support tools" (PCDSTs); discharge an (2) "ongoing duty to make reasonable efforts to identify [PCDSTs] that employ input variables or factors that measure race, color, national origin [etc.]" and (3) "make reasonable efforts to mitigate the risk of discrimination resulting from [the PCDSTs] use."[72] The agency's response to comments when the regulations were first proposed explained that the final regulations used the term "PCDST" to more broadly cover not only automated computer algorithms or those powered by artificial intelligence but also any other "tools, or method, or mechanism" used to support clinical decision making including "tools that rely on assumptions, constraints, or thresholds … that have the potential to result in discrimination."[73] The agency specifically mentioned as an example:

> the race adjusted estimated glomerular filtration rate (eGFR) equation that relies not only on training data but discriminatory assumptions and thresholds such as by applying a race-adjusted co-efficient to the eGFR equation to reflect that Black people have been associated with levels of blood creatinine as compared

with non-Black people which results in a higher significance threshold for Black patients, thereby requiring more advanced kidney failure for Black patients than white patients before they can receive the same level of care.[74]

In the Social Security disability system, the state disability determination services (DDS) agencies that make initial and reconsidered disability decisions under contract with SSA are recipients of federal funds and are, therefore, "covered entities" under these regulations.[75] The DDSs employ doctors who review, interpret, and apply medical evidence generated with clinical support tools such as PFTs and eGFRs and often contract for consultant doctors to make assessments using these tools. As such, they would be subject to the prohibitions and affirmative duties in the new HHS regulations. More broadly, apart from statutory and regulatory prohibitions, the reliance on or creation of medical assessments and resulting disability decision-making with records containing or utilizing race-normed algorithms or clinical tools at any of the four levels of SSA adjudication reflects unconstitutional race discrimination under the Fifth Amendment Equal Protection guarantees when done by the SSA (at the ALJ Hearing and Appeals Council levels and in supervisory roles at other levels) or the Fourteenth Amendment's Equal Protection Clause when done by the DDSs (at the initial and reconsideration levels).

Unlike the equal protection discrimination issues analyzed in Chapters 1 and 4, requiring more developed analysis of factors triggering some degree of strict or more searching examination than the most minimal level of judicial scrutiny, the use of these race-normed tools in SSA disability adjudication reflects overt, intentionally different, and disparate treatment of Black claimants and other claimants of color based on race. As such, the Supreme Court has established that in these circumstances, "any exception to the Constitution's demand for equal protection must survive a daunting two-step examination known in [the] cases as 'strict scrutiny.' … [1] first, whether the racial classification is used to 'further compelling governmental interests.' [2] Second, if so … whether the government's use of race is 'narrowly tailored' – meaning 'necessary' – to achieve that interest."[76] No strong or compelling government purpose has been suggested for the use of race-normed clinical support tools. Indeed, expert medical bodies in increasing numbers have sharply criticized continued use of most of these tools and algorithms and recommended their abandonment and replacement with race-neutral practices.

Moreover, even if a compelling government purpose could be discovered as the actual rationale for these varieties of race-norming tools, SSA/DDS would still need to demonstrate the absence of less restrictive alternatives (such as race-neutral tools) that could be utilized to satisfy the identified compelling purpose, which appears unlikely. Professor Sonja Starr has identified race-norming as a form of disparate treatment-producing unlawful, unconstitutional race discrimination, observing that "there is no plausible justification grounded in redressing disparity" through the race-normed kidney function (eGFR) device or as to race-normed "spirometry" (PFTs), since "the practice clearly adversely affects Black patients and appears completely lacking in a medical justification"[77] Finally, the fact that HHS has identified such race-normed devices and tools as potentially unlawful race discrimination under its regulations further undermines viable defenses to an equal protection challenge.

6.6 RECOMMENDATIONS FOR ADDRESSING RACE-NORMING IN SSA DISABILITY ADJUDICATIONS

1. First, SSA should forthwith issue instructions to all adjudicators at all levels to discontinue seeking consultative evaluations created with race-normed tools or algorithms and to cease relying on assessments created in reliance on such tools. It should do so with particular attention to impairment areas in which it should be aware of prevalent race-norming discussed herein, such as respiratory impairments evaluated through race-normed PFTs. SSA can use its POMS DI 24555.005.B.2 on its approach to race-normed kidney functioning through the eGFR test as a partial model for other race-normed body system impairment clinical support tools and algorithms. However, as described in #2, this POMS needs to be fortified in a variety of ways to prevent continued discriminatory harm to Black claimants in the disability adjudication process.
2. Second, while the SSA's 2022 kidney function/eGFR POMS is a good first step, it does not go far enough to protect Black claimants in several ways.
   (a). First, while it provides that adjudicators should contact medical providers where it cannot discern if eGFRs have been race-normed and obtain unadjusted results, it does not mandate documentation that such a "contact" inquiry has taken place and the result of the inquiry. Until laboratories fully discontinue race-norming eGFRs (and present accounts reflect progress but there is still a significant way to go), such documentation is essential;
   (b). Second, the POMS only calls for the adjudicator to contact the medical source if the claimant (presumably a Black claimant whose scores may have been race-normed), meets additional requirements in Listing 6.05 for automatic medical step-3 disability based on kidney functioning. However, an erroneously and discriminatorily diminished eGFR will further diminish the perceived severity of the claimant's condition, weakening assessment of the supportability of their impairment symptoms and strength of other supportive clinical medical evidence bearing on their RFC assessment and determinations about disability based on ability to perform past work and other work at steps 4 and 5 of the SSA's evaluation process. A claimant with a record tainted with such an assessment should also be entitled to have the medical source contacted and to obtain a race-neutral, untainted eGFR assessment that does not improperly diminish

the strength of the claimant's disability case at any stage of the evaluative process; and

(c). Third, since the Supreme Court has determined that the SSA's POMS subregulatory guidelines (formerly known as the SSA Claims Manual), "is not a regulation[,] [i]t has no legal force, and it does not bind the SSA [b]ut [r]ather, it is a 13-volume handbook for internal use by thousands of SSA employees,"[78] SSA should promulgate a binding regulation pursuant to proper Administrative Procedure Act processes that has the force of law. That regulation should specify the required handling of all race-normed clinical support tools and algorithms in all SSA adjudications, such as in the manner described in POMS (DI 24555.005.B.2) for the eGFR, with the modifications of that POMS outlined earlier.

3. Third, SSA should institute an orderly process for providing notice and the opportunity for the reopening and readjudication of claims within a certain reasonably determined retroactive period for claimants whose applications were denied (or denied in part) in cases where race-normed tools or algorithms were utilized. In *City of New York v. Hecker* (described in Chapter 5), US District Court for the Eastern District of New York Chief Judge Jack Weinstein, in a remedial decree affirmed by a unanimous US Supreme Court, ordered reopening and readjudications for years of persons denied disability benefits with "tainted" improper mental impairment evidence. The Court found that the proper remedy for hearings and adjudications tainted with improper evidence that had artificially diminished measures of the claimants' impairment functional severity, necessitated notice and the opportunity for reopening and readjudication with untainted evidence.[79] By the same reasoning, this remedy is appropriate and necessary in cases with "tainted" race-normed evidence – a practice which also artificially diminished the assessed severity of claimants' impairments. SSA should commence with the cases of claimants of color where race-normed eGFRs or PFTs were employed. SSA should also conduct a wider review and investigation to determine the extent of race-norming in other impairment systems such as with respect to cognitive and cardiac impairments or for claimants with osteoporosis, and to include in this remedial provision claimants of color with adverse decisions and race-normed medical assessments in any impairment area.

Conclusion

While the Social Security Act is undoubtedly the most important and transformative anti-poverty and income security enactment in American history, it has underserved African Americans and other historically subordinated communities of color in myriad ways. The Act's promise of universal and equitable income security has been undermined by the consequences of historic statutory exclusions of Black and other minoritized communities and by benefit computation formulas that perpetuate the consequences of a legacy of slavery, Jim Crow, systemic employment discrimination, and occupational segregation and many other areas of long-term systemic inequity. Social Security retirement and disability benefits levels are lower and often fail to take Black and Brown families out of poverty and meet basic needs in view of diminished and disparate income, wealth, and retirement asset levels relative to white social security recipients.

Benefit levels and accumulated benefits are further restricted by unnecessary criminal restrictions added to the Act many decades after the OASDI programs' creation and with disparate deleterious impacts on Black and Brown claimants owing to the consequences of mass incarceration and racialized policing. Inequities and bias in health care treatment, lingering application of erroneous biological race concepts, discredited and inequitable race-norming in clinical support tools and algorithms, and misevaluation of pain and impairment symptomology, further compounded by SSA adjudicative bias, fuel further specific inequitable access to disability benefits for Black and Brown claimants.

This book proposes remedies and mitigations for many of these social security program inequities. Some can be addressed by the SSA and our lawmakers and policy makers – admittedly in the hope that we return to (or make significant progress toward) greater democratic functionality when popularly desired and needed reforms can be adopted and serve the will and needs of the people. Others will depend on longer-term movements to eradicate broader structural and systemic discriminatory trends in society at large by both government and private industry and parties, in employment, housing, education, voting, criminal justice, and health care access and treatment that cannot be meaningfully addressed solely through reforms in the social security system. To some extent, the social security system's effectiveness as an equitable bulwark against income insecurity is a function of inequity in society at large; it incorporates the racial and other invidious inequalities in several of those other major systems as shown in this book.

As in the pursuit of racial and economic justice in many other areas, the struggle for more meaningful justice and equity in the social security system is neither linear nor prompt. The challenge is in perseverance. And in recognition that even in the darkest, unlikeliest times, as prophesied by Dr. Martin Luther King Jr., "the arc of the moral universe is long, but it bends towards justice.[1]

Notes

INTRODUCTION

1. *See Never Beneficiaries, Age 60 or Older, 2020*, Soc. Sec. Admin. (discussing characteristics of the only 3.5 percent of the population who reach age 60 and never become beneficiaries); *see also* Richardson v. Perales, 402 U.S.389, 399 (1971) ("The Social Security Act has been with us since 1935 … It affects nearly all of us.").
2. Kathleen Romig, *Social Security Lifts More People Over the Poverty Line than Any Other Program*, Ctr. on Budget & Pol'y Priorities, (June 2, 2023), https://perma.cc/R9AN-K84C; *see* Elise Gould, *Social Security Kept 27 Million Americans Out of Poverty in 2013*, Econ. Pol'y Inst. (Oct. 30, 2014), https://perma.cc/Z9BN-BBB3 ("Social Security is, by far, the most effective anti-poverty program in the United States. Without Social Security, an additional 8.6 percent of Americans, or nearly 27 million, would fall below the [Supplemental Poverty Measure] poverty threshold."); *see also* The White House, Social Security Disability Insurance: A Lifeline for American Workers and Families (2015), https://perma.cc/Q28S-5UEB (The Social Security Disability program alone annually "keep[s] about 3 million Americans out of poverty, and reduces the depth of poverty for another 1.9 million Americans").
3. FDR Presidential Library, https://perma.cc/YNA4-HRHZ (archived Dec. 4, 2023) ("The crown jewel of FDR's New Deal, Social Security is his greatest legacy to the nation … 'No other New Deal measure proved more lastingly consequential or more emblematic of the very meaning of the New Deal,' notes Stanford historian David M. Kennedy. Roosevelt would have agreed. 'He always regarded the Social Security Act as the cornerstone of his administration,' Secretary of Labor Frances Perkins recalled, 'and … took greater satisfaction from it than from anything else he achieved on the domestic front.'").
4. *FDR's Statements on Social Security, Message to Congress on Social Security*, Soc. Sec. Admin. (Jan. 17, 1935), https://perma.cc/LC97-YMUN.
5. Parts of this book, namely Chapters 1 and 4, reflect reproductions of, expansions on, and updating of content from a 2024 law review article: Jon C. Dubin, *The Color of Social Security: Race and Unequal Protection in the Crown Jewel of the American Welfare State*, 35 Stan. L. & Pol'y Rev. 104 (2024). They are modified, recast, and reproduced herein with the authorization of the Stanford Law and Policy Review and the sole copyright of this article has been retained with the author for this purpose.
6. *See* 42 U.S.C. §§ 401–22 (statutory authority for OASDI).
7. *See* Social Security Administration, 2026 *Cost-of-Living Adjustment (COLA) Fact Sheet*, www.ssa.gov/news/en/cola/factsheets/2026.html#; Barry Huston, *Social Security: The Trust

Funds, 1–2 Congressional Research Service (May 23, 2024), Social Security Administration, *Contribution and Benefit Base*, www.ssa.gov/oact/cola/cbb.html. The wage base cap is adjusted each year to keep pace with average wages. *See id.*; Self-employed individuals pay 12.4 percent Self Employment Contribution Act (SECA) taxes on covered wages and net employment income up to the same cap and deduct half of these SECA taxes for income tax purposes. *Id* at 2.

8. *See* Matthew H. Hawes, *So No Damn Politician Can Ever Scrap it: The Constitutional Protection of Social Security Benefits*, 65 U. PITT L. REV. 865 (2004).
9. *See* H.R. REP. NO. 92–231, at 146–47 (1971) ("[C]ontributory social insurance should continue to be relied on as the basic means of replacing earnings that have been lost as a result of old age, disability, or blindness. But some people who because of age, disability, or blindness are not able to support themselves through work may receive relatively small social security benefits ... [which] therefore, must be complemented by an effective assistance program."); 42 U.S.C. §§ 1381–83 (providing statutory authority for SSI).
10. *See* Social Security Amendments of 1939, Pub. L. No. 76–379, 53 Stat. 1360 (1939).
11. JON C. DUBIN, SOCIAL SECURITY DISABILITY LAW AND THE AMERICAN LABOR MARKET 9 (2021).
12. *See id*. For analysis of this second concern *see id*. at *passim*.
13. *Id*.
14. *Id*. at 9–10.
15. *Id*. at 10–17.
16. *See* FRANK S. BLOCH & JON C. DUBIN, SOCIAL SECURITY LAW AND PRACTICE IN A NUTSHELL 67, 241 (2022).
17. *See* Natalie Gomez-Velez, Notice and Comment, *Socioeconomic Pedagogy and Administrative Law: Including Issues of Race/Ethnicity and Class in the Administrative Law Course*, YALE J. ON REG. (July 29, 2020), https://perma.cc/YE7K-RKXZ; *see, e.g.*, Jon C. Dubin, *Torquemada Meets Kafka: The Misapplication of the Issue Exhaustion Doctrine to Inquisitorial Administrative Proceedings*, 97 COLUM. L. REV. 1289 (1997) (analyzing the unique adjudicative model employed in SSA administrative proceedings and the resulting process implications for federal judicial review).
18. *See generally* JERRY L. MASHAW, BUREAUCRATIC JUSTICE (1983); *compare* Richard J. Pierce, Jr., *What Should We Do about Social Security Disability Appeals?*, REGULATION, Fall 2011, at 34, https://perma.cc/EWG3-PAAT (criticizing SSA ALJ adjudication as a major factor in Social Security trust fund depletion through improper ALJ benefit awards and proposing abolition of ALJ hearings), *with* Jon C. Dubin & Robert E. Rains, *Scapegoating Social Security Claimants (and the Judges Who Evaluate Them)*, 6 ADVANCE: J. AM. CONST. SOC. ISSUE GROUPS 109 (2012) (responding to and disagreeing with Professor Pierce's proposal, conclusions, and articulation of the perceived problem).
19. David Ames, Cassandra Handan-Nader, Daniel E. Ho, & David Marcus, *Due Process and Mass Adjudication: Crisis and Reform*, 72 STAN. L. REV. 1, 31–40 (2020) (describing the SSA's methods to promote adjudicative accuracy and efficiency through quality assurance reviews, including random sampling); *see also* Jonah B. Gelbach & David Marcus, *Rethinking Judicial Review of High Volume Agency Adjudication*, 96 TEX. L. REV. 1097, 1116, 1149 (2018) (analyzing the efficiency and accuracy in "problem-oriented" oversight of SSA high-volume adjudication through judicial review).
20. Schweiker v. Gray Panthers, 453 U.S. 34, 43 (1981) (quoting Friedman v. Berger, 547 F.2d 724, 727 n.7 (2d Cir. 1976), *cert. denied*, 430 U.S. 984 (1977)); White v. Shalala, 7 F.3d 296, 300 (2d Cir. 1993) (same, and also referencing the Act as "exceptionally complicated");

see also Feld v. Berger, 424 F. Supp. 1357–58 (S.D.N.Y. 1976) (Noting that the SSA's regulations were "so drawn that they have created a Serbonian bog from which the agencies seemingly are unable to extricate themselves [and] … [i]t borders on the absurd that federal, state and local officials charged with the administration of the Social Security Act cannot reach an accommodation as to the meaning of the regulations which they drafted themselves but instead force a court action for their interpretation."); *see, e.g.*, Jon C. Dubin, Social Security Disability Law and the American Labor Market 72–103 (2021) (describing the often extraordinary complexity of labor market work adjustment assessments in Social Security disability substantive law and regulations).

21. Alexandra Berzon, Nicholas Nehamas, & Tara Siegel, *The Bureaucrat and the Billionaire: Inside DOGE's Chaotic Takeover of Social Security*, N.Y. Times, (June 16, 2025).
22. *Id.*; Molly Weston Williamson, *Trump Administration Attacks on Social Security Put Kids and Families at Risk*, Center for American Progress, June 16, 2025.
23. Nancy Altman, *The Greatest Threat to Social Security in Its 90-Year History*, Times-Republican (Mar. 12, 2025), ("Donald Trump and Elon Musk are planning to utterly demolish Social Security's customer service to pay for billionaire tax cuts."). Italics added for emphasis.
24. Lisa Rein, Meryl Kornfield, & Hannah Natanson, *How Social Security Has Gotten Worse under Trump*, Washington Post (Dec. 30, 2025).
25. *Id.*
26. Berzon et al., note 21 *supra*; Alicia H. Munnell, *Scary Headlines Drive People to Claim Social Security Earlier – and that Has Real Consequences*, Marketwatch, June 2, 2025.
27. Adam Edelman & Jane C. Timm, *Fact Checking Trump's Speech to Congress*, NBC News, Mar. 5, 2025.
28. Public Law 119–21, 139 Stat. 22 (July 4, 2025).
29. *See* Committee for a Responsible Federal Budget, *OBBBA Would Accelerate Social Security and Medicare Insolvency*, June 27, 2025, www.crfb.org/blogs/obbba-would-accelerate-social-security-medicare-insolvency ("We estimate that the extension and expansion of the 2017 tax cuts, the expanded senior deduction, and other OBBBA changes would reduce total taxation of benefits by roughly $30 billion per year. This would be enough to accelerate insolvency of the Social Security Old-Age and Survivors (OASI) trust fund from early 2033 to late 2032 … Upon insolvency in 2032, we estimate that Social Security beneficiaries would face an across-the-board benefit cut of around 24 percent – even deeper than the cuts scheduled under current law.); *see also* Munnell, *supra* note 29. Without taking OBBBA into account, the 2025 Social Security Trustees report estimates that the combined OASI and Disability Insurance (DI) trust funds would become unable to pay full benefits in 2034 and face an across-the-board 19 percent cut. *See* The 2025 Annual Report of the Board of Trustees if the Federal Old-Age and Survivors' Insurance and Federal Disability Insurance Trust Funds, June 18, 2025, www.ssa.gov/oact/TR/2025/index.html; *see generally* Madeline Shepherd, *Poverty in America Remained Flat in 2024 But Will Likely Rise as the One Big Beautiful Bill Act Goes into Effect*, Center for American Progress (Sept. 9, 2025) (documenting the anticipated impact from "historic cuts" to the Medicaid and SNAP programs and loss of Affordable Care Act (ACA) tax subsidies with resulting significantly increased premium costs and loss of health insurance for millions of Americans, the failure of miniscule tax cuts available to lower income persons to offset the devastating impacts of these program reductions, and concluding that "these cuts will be more likely to harm women, people age 65 and older, Black and Hispanic families, and people without a high school diploma"). *See also* Munnell, *supra* note 26.

30. *See, e.g.*, Executive Order 14151, Ending Radical and Wasteful DEI Programs and Preferences, 90 Fed. Reg, 8339 (Jan. 28, 2025); Executive Order 14173, Ending Illegal Discrimination and Restoring Merit-Based Opportunity, 90 Fed Reg. 8633 (Jan. 31, 2025).
31. US Attorney General Memorandum, *Ending Illegal DEI and DEIA Discrimination and Preferences* (Feb. 5, 2025).
32. *See id.; see also* Anna Griffith & David D. Troutt, Rewriting Racial Equality: The State of Civil Rights Law Under Trump, Rutgers Center on Law, Inequality and Municipal Equity (Nov. 2025) (Organizing the second Trump administration's approach to turning back the clock on civil rights and the pursuit of racial equality, into "four pillars": "1. Redefining racial discrimination; 2. Dismantling the institutional framework for government support of racial equity and cancelling existing investigations; 3. Enforcing policy priorities through defunding and fining institutions; [and] 4. Encouraging racial gerrymandering of congressional districts in the guise of political gerrymandering."); *see generally* Nicole Hannah Jones, *How Trump Upended 60 Years of Civil Rights in Two Months*, N.Y. Times (June 27, 2025) ("The astounding ambit of Trump's first months has made it possible to imagine a future that looks eerily like the past. An America where the constitution still stands, but Black people and other marginalized groups receive virtually no protection from the federal government, and the actions of that government instead encourage discrimination").
33. Executive Order 14253, Restoring Truth and Sanity to American History, 90 Fed. Reg. 14563 (Mar. 27, 2025).
34. *See* Erica Green, *Trump Treats Black History Differently than Other Parts of America's Past*, N.Y. Times (June 20, 2023); Geoff Bennett, *Pentagon History Purge Highlights What Histories Are Told and Why Others Are Ignored*, PBS News, (Mar. 18, 2025).
35. *See, e.g.*, Danielle Cohen, *Florida Wants to Teach Kids that Slavery Was Good*, The Cut (July 21, 2023) (Noting that the Republican-backed Florida Board of Education approved changes to the history curriculum to teach "how slaves developed skills, which could … be applied for their personal benefit"); Tori Otten, *Oklahoma Superintendent Brazenly Claims Tulsa Race Massacre Was Not about Race*, The New Republic (July 7, 2023) ("The teaching of Black history in public schools is under serious threat … Oklahoma's far-right superintendent of public instruction thinks that schools should teach students about the Tulsa race massacre, so long as teachers don't actually acknowledge that the white supremacist attack was about race").
36. Geoff Bennett, *Pentagon History Purge Highlights What Histories Are Told and Why Others Are Ignored*, PBS News, (Mar. 18, 2025); Russell Contreras & Delano Massey, *Trump's 'Restoring Truth' Order Could Return Confederate Monuments*, Axios, March 30, 2025; *see generally* Sara Pequeno, *Opinion: No One Was Sad to See This Confederate Statue Go. Now Trump Is Bringing It Back*, USA Today (Aug. 7, 2025) ("Trump wants us to move backward, to a time when our nation's ugly, racist past was swept under the rug. Why else would he be propping up inept Confederate generals while targeting Black history?").
37. Gabe Castro-Root, *National Parks Drop Free Entrance on M.L.K. Day and Juneteenth*, N.Y.Times (Dec. 8, 2025).
38. *See* Angela Glover Blackwell, *How We Achieve a Multiracial Democracy*, Stanford Social Innovation Review (Spring 2023), https://ssir.org/articles/entry/how_we_achieve_a_multiracial_democracy ("America needs a new story – one that is honest and inspiring, and that doesn't shy away from its racial history – to guide us toward realizing a thriving multiracial democracy.").
39. *See generally* Melvin L. Oliver & Thomas M. Shapiro, Black Wealth/White Wealth: A New Perspective on Racial Inequality (2nd ed. 2006) (chronicling the practices and policies leading to dramatic racial wealth disparities and inequality and

present-day consequences); *see, e.g.*, DOROTHY BROWN, THE WHITENESS OF WEALTH: HOW THE TAX SYSTEM IMPOVERISHES BLACK AMERICANS –AND HOW WE CAN FIX IT (2022) (focusing on American tax law's impact on the racial wealth gap); RICHARD ROTHSTEIN, THE COLOR OF LAW: A FORGOTTEN HISTORY OF HOW OUR GOVERNMENT SEGREGATED AMERICA 177–93 (2017) (describing policies and practices adopted in law and leading to substantial intergenerational racial wealth disparities with focus on the effective exclusion of Black families from wealth-generating home ownership); MEHRSA BARADARAN, THE COLOR OF MONEY: BLACK BANKS AND THE RACIAL WEALTH GAP (2017) (analyzing structural racial discrimination in credit and banking and impact on racial wealth gap); DAYNA BOWEN MATTHEW, JUST MEDICINE, A CURE FOR RACIAL INEQUALITY IN AMERICAN HEALTH CARE (2015) (examining racial inequity in health care access and treatment); MICHELLE ALEXANDER, THE NEW JIM CROW: MASS INCARCERATION IN THE AGE OF COLORBLINDNESS (2010) (analyzing racial discrimination in the criminal justice system and the consequences of mass incarceration in re-creating a "racial caste system" for disproportionately Black and Brown persons incarcerated due to felony convictions who are then denied employment, housing, voting rights, educational opportunity, various public benefits, and jury service); *see also* DEBORAH N. ARCHER, DIVIDING LINES: HOW TRANSPORTATION INFRASTRUCTURE REINFORCES RACIAL INEQUALITY (2025) (examining how transportation infrastructure – including highways, roads, sidewalks and buses – has served to advance Jim Crow segregation, spatial inequality, and racial subordination); DOROTHY E. ROBERTS, SHATTERED BONDS: THE COLOR OF CHILD WELFARE (2001) (analyzing the ways in which the child protective and foster care system disproportionately damages Black families and children); DOROTHY E. ROBERTS, TORN APART—HOW THE CHILD WELFARE SYSTEM DESTROYS BLACK FAMILIES (2022) (same).

40. *See* RICHARD ROTHSTEIN, THE COLOR OF LAW: A FORGOTTEN HISTORY OF HOW OUR GOVERNMENT SEGREGATED AMERICA (2017) (explaining the exclusive focus on the Black community); *cf.* JILL QUADAGNO, THE COLOR OF WELFARE: HOW RACISM UNDERMINED THE WAR ON POVERTY (1994) (focusing on the Black community).
41. *Cf.* Jon C. Dubin, *From Junkyards to Gentrification: Explicating a Right to Protective Zoning in Low-Income Communities of Color*, 77 MINN. L. REV. 739, 743 n.15 (1993) (describing focus on the Black community with analysis of Latino/a/Hispanic/Brown community in relevant part).
42. *See* BENJAMIN W. VEGHTE, ELLIOT SCHREUR, & MIKKI WAID, NAT'L ACAD. OF SOC. INS., SOCIAL SECURITY AND THE RACIAL GAP IN RETIREMENT WEALTH (Dec. 2016); *see generally* MELVIN L. OLIVER & THOMAS M. SHAPIRO, BLACK WEALTH/WHITE WEALTH: A NEW PERSPECTIVE ON RACIAL INEQUALITY (2nd ed. 2006) (chronicling the practices and policies leading to dramatic racial wealth disparities and inequality and present-day consequences); RICHARD ROTHSTEIN, THE COLOR OF LAW: A FORGOTTEN HISTORY OF HOW OUR GOVERNMENT SEGREGATED AMERICA 177–93 (2017) (describing policies and practices adopted in law and leading to substantial intergenerational racial wealth disparities with focus on the effective exclusion of Black families from wealth-generating home ownership); *see generally* MEHRSA BARADARAN, THE COLOR OF MONEY: BLACK BANKS AND THE RACIAL WEALTH GAP (2017) (analyzing structural racial DISCRIMINATION on credit and banking and impact on racial wealth gap); DOROTHY Brown, THE WHITENESS OF WEALTH: HOW THE TAX SYSTEM IMPOVERISHES BLACK AMERICANS –AND HOW WE CAN FIX IT (2022) (focusing on American tax law's impact on the racial wealth gap).
43. *See* KILOLO KIJAKAZI, KAREN SMITH, & CHARMAINE RUNES, URB. INST., AFRICAN AMERICAN ECONOMIC SECURITY AND THE ROLE OF SOCIAL SECURITY 3–22 (July

2019); Benjamin W. Veghte, Elliot Schreur, & Mikki Waid, Nat'l acad. of Soc. Ins., Social Security and the Racial Gap in Retirement Wealth (Dec. 2016); Maya M. Rockeymoore & Meizhu Lui, Comm'n to Modernize Soc. Sec., Plan for a New Future: The Impact of Social Security Reform on People of Color, (2011); *see also* John B. Mitchell, *Suspending Prisoners' Social Security Benefits: Yet Another Blow to Financially Vulnerable African American and Hispanic Families*, 20 Seattle J. Soc. Just. 109, 150–51 (2021) (noting that Social Security "made up half or more of the incomes of 69.4% of African Americans sixty-five and older, lifting 1.3 million out of poverty" and that "the poverty rate for those Black seniors over sixty-five would have gone from 19.4% to 50.7%" without Social Security benefits, while citing similar statistics for Latino/a households and seniors).

44. *See, e.g.*, Edward D. Berkowitz, *Social Security: Origin, Accomplishments, and Threats to the 90-Year-Old Act* (Aug. 7, 2025) https://kansaspress.ku.edu/blog/2025/08/07/social-security-blog/ ("It would help things if my fellow academics recognized the program's extraordinary achievements in providing a secure base for people's retirement and keeping many out of poverty, rather than using the analytic lenses of race and gender to point out the program's perceived shortcomings. Academics are by their nature critics out to bust the conventional wisdom. In this instance, however, they undermine social progress and, despite their liberal sympathies, strengthen the conservative campaign to dismantle the program."); *see also* Nancy J. Altman, The Truth About Social Security – The Founders Words Refute Revisionist History, Zombie Lies and Common Misunderstandings 283–85 (2018) (suggesting that claims of the programs' "unfairness to African Americans" are largely manufactured by actors "hiding their ideological opposition" to social security programs with the example of President Bush who used such race-focused critique to try to bolster his failed plan to privatize social security).
45. *See* Social Security Administration (SSA), Equity Action Plan in Agreement With EO 13985 (Feb. 10, 2022); *see also* Social Security Administration, 2023 Equity Action Plan Update (Feb. 14, 2024).
46. Kilolo Kijakazi, *Join Us – SSA's Equity Action Plan Stakeholder Engagement Meeting*, Social Security Administration (May 26, 2022) (emphasis added), www.ssa.gov/news/en/advocates/2022–05-26.html (Notice of National Meeting on SSA's 2022 Equity Action Plan scheduled for June 16, 2022).
47. *See* The White House, Social Security Disability Insurance: a Lifeline for Millions of American Workers and Their Families, 10–11 (July 17, 2015).
48. Social Security Administration, Research, Statistics and Policy Analysis, *Monthly Statistical Snapshot May 2025*, www.ssa.gov/policy/docs/quickfacts/stat_snapshot/2025–05.pdf (SSA revealing that in May 2025, there were approximately 8.2 million SSDI beneficiaries, and 4.9 million SSID recipients, while the retirement program provided benefits to 55 million persons. The social security survivors' program supplies benefits to another 5.8 million persons).
49. Jonah B. Gelbach & David Marcus, *Rethinking Judicial Review of High Volume Agency Adjudication*, 96 Tex. L. Rev. 1097, 1101–02 (2018) ("Appeals from overwhelmed agency adjudicators compose a large chunk of the federal courts' docket. In 2013, for instance, claimants appealed 18,779 SSA ALJ decisions to federal district courts"); Harold J. Krent & Scott Morris, *Inconsistency and Angst in District Court Resolution of Social Security Disability Appeals*, 67 Hastings L. J. 367, 370 (2016) ("Over 10,000 Social Security Disability cases are resolved each year in the federal court system. As a consequence, almost every district court judge and magistrate decides a significant number of such appeals from claimants each year."). In the twelve-month period from September 2022–23, appeals in Social Security Disability program cases (SSDI/SSID) comprised

approximately 5 percent of all civil case filings in the U.S Courts. *See* www.uscourts.gov/sites/default/files/data_tables/jb_c2_0930.2023.pdf.

50. Paul R. Verkuil, *The Self-Legitimating Bureaucracy*, 93 YALE L.J. 780, 781 (1984) (reviewing JERRY L. MASHAW, BUREAUCRATIC JUSTICE (1983)).
51. Heckler v. Campbell, 461 U.S. 458, 461 n.2 (1983) (quoting JERRY L. MASHAW, CHARLES J. GOETZ, FRANK I. GOODMAN, WARREN F. SCHWARTZ, PAUL R. VERKUIL, & MILTON M. CARROW, SOCIAL SECURITY HEARINGS AND APPEALS: A STUDY OF THE SOCIAL SECURITY ADMINISTRATION HEARING SYSTEM xi (1978)).
52. Jon C. Dubin, *Why* Carr v. Saul *Should Signal the End of Common Law Issue Exhaustion in Inquisitorial Proceedings*, 29 GEO. MASON L. REV. 627, 637 and n. 47 (2022) (citing MASHAW ET AL., HEARINGS AND APPEALS, *supra* note 51, at xi); *see also Authorized Judgeships*, U.S. COURTS, https://perma.cc/6W39-RQX4 (reporting 860 Article III authorized judgeships in 2021); *Hearings and Appeals*, SOC. SEC. ADMIN., https://perma.cc/5DSY-M5KR (reporting the Office of the Chief Administrative Law Judge oversees more than 1,500 ALJs).
53. Dubin, *End of Issue Exhaustion*, *supra* note 52, at *id.* (citing SOC. SEC. ADMIN., ANNUAL PERFORMANCE REPORT: FISCAL YEARS 2019–21, at 44–46 (2020), https://perma.cc/4UHJ-QLVE (reporting 2.31 million completed claims, 544,000 reconsiderations, and 794,000 hearings for 2019, and targeting over 2.35 million completed claims for 2021); *see also* OFF. INSPECTOR GEN. SOC. SEC. ADMIN., AUDIT REPORT: OVERSIGHT OF ADMINISTRATIVE LAW JUDGE DECISIONAL QUALITY app. C, fig.C-1 (2017) [hereinafter OFF. INSPECTOR GEN., AUDIT REPORT], https://perma.cc/3JRS-3DN2; Mashaw et al., *Hearings and Appeals*, *supra* note 51, at xi).
54. *See, e.g., Protecting Social Security Disability Act of 2014*, S. 3003, 113th Cong. 2d Sess.; *see also* U.S. HOUSE OF REPRESENTATIVES, WAYS & MEANS COMM., SUBCOMM. ON SOCIAL SECURITY, HEARING ON EXAMINING CHANGES TO SOCIAL SECURITY'S DISABILITY APPEALS PROCESS, SERIAL NO. 115-SS11, 115 th CONG., 2D SESS.177–86 (July 15, 2018); U.S. HOUSE OF REP., WAYS & MEANS COMM., SUBCOMM. ON SOCIAL SECURITY, FOURTH IN A SERIES HEARING ON SECURING THE FUTURE OF THE SOCIAL SECURITY DISABILITY INSURANCE PROGRAM, 112 TH CONG., 2D SESS. (June 27, 2012).
55. *E.g.*, National Public Radio *Special Series, Unfit for Work: The Starting Rise of Disability in America* (Mar. 2013); Damian Paletta, *Insolvency Looms as States Drain U.S. Disability Fund*, WALL STREET JOURNAL (Mar. 22, 2011); *It Ain't Broke Yet, But Federal Disability Insurance Still Needs Some Big Fixes*, WASHINGTON POST, Editorial Bd. (July 2, 2018); Lisa Rein, *Social Security to Drop Obsolete Jobs Used to Deny Disability Benefits*, WASHINGTON POST (June 24, 2024); Lisa Rein, *Judges Rebuke Social Security for Errors as Disability Denials Stack Up*, WASHINGTON POST (May 25, 2023); Kate Davidson, *Trump Administration Weighs Tighter Requirements for Disability Payments*, WASHINGTON POST (Jan. 10, 2020).
56. *See* Kathleen Romig, *Social Security Trust Funds Would Be on Stronger Footing if Not for Trump Economic, Immigration Policies*, CENTER FOR BUDGET AND POLICY PRIORITIES (June 18, 2025); THE 2025 ANNUAL REPORT OF THE BOARD OF TRUSTEES, *supra* note 29. Based on the June 2025 Social Security Trustees Report, *supra* note 29, the OASI trust fund (prior to the passage of the OBBBA of 2025) was expected to be unable to pay full benefits as of 2033 but would be extended to 2034 if combined with the DI trust fund, which is otherwise solvent until 2098. *See id.;* Congress has transferred funds from one fund to the other in either direction multiple times before (eleven times, and such a fund transfer or consolidation would require congressional action). *See* Jon C. Dubin, *A Modest Albeit Heavily Tested Social Security Disability Reform Proposal: Streamlining the Adjudicative Process by Eliminating Reconsideration and Enhancing Initial Stage*

Development, 23 GEO J. OF POVERTY L. & POL'Y 203, 204 (2016); *see* Kathy Ruffing & Paul N. Van De Water, *Congress Needs to Boost Disability Insurance Share of Payroll Tax by 2016*, CTR. ON BUDGET AND POLICY PRIORITIES (July 31, 2014), bit.ly/4shTeWu (describing Congress's eleven reallocations between the OASI and SSDI trust funds in both directions – six from OASI to SSDI, five from SSDI to OASI – in actions in the years 1968, 1970, 1978, 1979, 1980, 1982, 1983, 1984, 1994, 1997, and 2000). The non-partisan Committee for a Responsible Federal Budget has estimated that the passage of OBBBA will now accelerate exhaustion of the combined social security OASI and DI trust fund by one year, producing "a 24 percent benefit cut in late 2032." Committee for a Responsible Federal Budget, *Retirees Face an $18,100 benefits cut in 7 years* (July 24, 2025); *see also* Rebecca Vallas, A *Letter from the CEO*, NATIONAL ACADEMY OF SOCIAL INSURANCE (July 9, 2025) (noting that passage of the OBBBA of 2025 is "estimated to move up the projected insolvency date of the Social Security Trust Fund by one full year"); the 2025 Annual Report of the Board of Trustees, *supra* note 29.

57. *See Social Security Benefit Protection and Opportunity Enhancement Act of 2015*, P.L. No. 114–74, Title VIII, Sec. 801 et seq.

58. *See Republican Proposals to Modify Social Security: Benefit Cuts, Retirement Age Increases, and Fiscal Implications*, NORTH DENVER TRIBUNE, (Mar. 25, 2025), bit .ly/4cp2wLC (discussing Republican proposals "spearheaded by the Republican Study Committee (RSC) and aligned with broader conservative initiatives like Project 2025, … to address the program's solvency concerns through … raising the full retirement age to 69 or 70, reducing benefits for future retirees, and slashing administrative funding for the Social Security Administration (SSA)"); *see also* Prem Thakker, *Republicans Are Bringing Back Their Plan to Gut Social Security and Medicare*, THE NEW REPUBLIC (June 14, 2023), https://perma.cc/86X3-RHN5; Taegan Goddard, *Desantis Went Further Than Paul Ryan on Social Security*, POL. WIRE (Feb. 13, 2023), https://perma.cc/NXY8-B7D3 (noting that as a Congressman, Ron DeSantis supported Paul Ryan's "entitlement reform" plans to partially privatize Social Security and Medicare but went further and also sought to raise the full retirement age to 70).

59. Kathleen Romig, *Trump Administration Plans Deep Cuts to Social Security Disability Insurance, Particularly for Older Workers*, CTR. ON BUDGET AND POLICY PRIORITIES (Oct. 16, 2025); *see also* JACK SMALLIGAN, UPDATING SOCIAL SECURITY DISABILITY: REGULATORY CHANGES COULD SIGNIFICANTLY REDUCE ELIGIBILITY, PARTICULARLY AMONG OLDER WORKERS, URBAN INSTITUTE 11 (Oct. 29, 2025) ("The proposed restrictions being considered would likely represent an even larger change in the number of SSDI recipients, [than cuts proposed in the 1980s by President Reagan and would reflect] the biggest change to SSDI since the program was established"). The initial plan to accomplish these massive program cuts through one large regulation or "Mega-Reg" appears to have been at least temporarily shelved, in part due to a substantial and immediate outcry against it including in republican constituencies. *See* Lisa Rein and Meryl Kornfield, *Social Security Scraps Plan to Limit Disability Benefits after Uproar*, THE WASHINGTON POST (Nov. 19, 2025); *New Survey: Vast Majority of Older Voters Oppose "Mega-Reg,"* PR NEWSWIRE (Nov. 5, 2025). However, social security, elderly, and disability rights groups remain concerned that these plans will be renewed or implemented in part through multiple, smaller actions over time. *See, e.g.*, David Camp, Senior Policy Advisor and General Counsel, National Organization for Social Security Claimant Representatives, *Dispatches from Camp*, THE NOSSCR FORUM (Nov. 20, 2025) ("Whether combined into one 'MegaReg' now or later, or gradually released through sub-regulatory updates – NOSSCR and our coalitions will work to advocate [with

SSA]"); *see also* Mark Miller. *Social Security Disability, a Protection for Some Workers, is at a Crossroads*, N.Y. TIMES (Dec. 13, 2025) ("a notice about the rulemaking process is still on the [SSA's] website … Some experts believe the work will be resumed at some point").

60. 596 U.S. 159 (2022).
61. *Id.* at 180–89 (Gorsuch, j., concurring).

1 THE SOCIAL SECURITY ACT IN RACIAL AND HISTORICAL CONTEXT: THE AGRICULTURAL AND DOMESTIC WORKER EXCLUSION IN THE OLD AGE/ RETIREMENT PROGRAM

1. Larry DeWitt, *The Decision to Exclude Agricultural and Domestic Workers from the 1935 Social Security Act*, 70 SOC. SEC. BULL. 49, 64 (2010).
2. Juan F. Perea, *The Echoes of Slavery: Recognizing the Racist Origins of the Agricultural and Domestic Worker Exclusion from the National Labor Relations Act*, 72 OHIO ST. L. J. 95, 96 (2011).
3. KILOLO KIJAKAZI, KAREN SMITH & CHARMAINE RUNES, *URB. INST.*, AFRICAN AMERICAN ECONOMIC SECURITY AND THE ROLE OF SOCIAL SECURITY 1 (July 2019).
4. *Compare* IRA KATZNELSON, WHEN AFFIRMATIVE ACTION WAS WHITE 59 (2005) ("It is not hard to see why southern members were so intensely concerned with [enactment of an expansive agricultural exclusion] and why, in order to get the Bill passed, other members were prepared to go along. The status of subaltern Black labor in agriculture – a structure that often came close to resembling nineteenth century conditions under slavery – was a consistent concern for southern members in the 1930s when [the New Deal legislation] was being debated.") *and* DAVID STOESZ, CTR. FOR SOC. DEV. RSCH., THE EXCLUDED: AN ESTIMATE OF THE CONSEQUENCES OF DENYING SOCIAL SECURITY TO AGRICULTURAL AND DOMESTIC WORKERS 10 (2016) (reaching similar conclusions and also finding nonracial administrative burden explanations for exclusion of disproportionately Black workforce from Social Security old age insurance "not … convincing" since Congress had managed to overcome any such administrative problems in the 1950s when these groups were added and other countries found ways to include agricultural and domestic workers in their old age social insurance programs), *with* DeWitt, *supra* note 1, at 64, *and* Gareth Davies & Martha Derthick, *Race and Social Welfare Policy: The Social Security Act of* 1935, 112 POL. SCI. Q. 217, 235 (1997) ("the range and probable weight of nonracial factors become so obvious when one takes the trouble to reconstruct the political debate of 1935."). *See generally* Perea, *supra* note 2, at n.1 (collecting historians' conflicting conclusions about the role of racial considerations in the enactment of agricultural and domestic exclusions in New Deal remedial legislation).
5. *See* DeWitt, *supra* note 1; Davies & Derthick, *supra* note 4.
6. *See also* NANCY J. ALTMAN, THE TRUTH ABOUT SOCIAL SECURITY: THE FOUNDERS WORDS REFUTE REVISIONIST HISTORY, ZOMBIE LIES AND COMMON MISUNDERSTANDINGS 227–28 (2018).
7. *See* KATZNELSON, *supra* 4; STOESZ, *supra* 4; *see also* REPORT OF THE COMMITTEE ON ECONOMIC SECURITY, Submitted to the President of the United States, Tbl. 16 (Jan. 1935) (listing nine countries – Austria, Belgium, Bulgaria, Czechoslovakia, France, Germany, the United Kingdom, Italy, and the Netherlands – that specifically identified the inclusion of agricultural and domestic workers in their country's social security or

contributory social insurance programs in 1933 and several others listing coverage of "all wage earners," "all employed persons," "all citizens," "workers," "wage earners," or "all workers (or persons) employed in industry or commerce."); *see generally* Wilbur Cohen, *Foreign Experience in Social Insurance Contributions for Agricultural and Domestic Workers*, 8 Soc. Sec. Bull. 5 (1945) (describing the different mechanism used by various countries to effectively account for and collect taxes and contributions for social insurance from agricultural and domestic workers and employers over the years).

8. *See* Jill Quadagno, *The Color of Welfare: How Racism Undermined the War on Poverty* 20 (1994); Robert C. Lieberman, Shifting the Color Line: Race and the American Welfare State 28 (1998). Professor Katzelson observed that "the administration was trapped … by the pervasive legacy of Jim Crow" and "any crusade to break out of its power restraints would have been doomed to fail, even if the President had been willing." Katznelson *supra* note 4, at 28. It would also "have risked the wide array of social and economic programs the New Deal advanced." Thus, while "[i]t makes no sense to write a retrospective morality tale condemning politicians and citizens who were imprisoned by Jim Crow … we also should not minimize the ugly and lasting consequences of this Faustian bargain." *Id.* at 28–29. Thus, "[b]y not including occupations in which African Americans worked, and by organizing racial patterns of administration, New Deal policies for Social Security, social welfare, and labor market programs restricted black prospects while providing positive economic reinforcement for the great majority of white citizens." *Id.* at 29.

9. In the parlance of the day, the country's failure to come to grips with issues emanating from a history of slavery, Jim Crow, and pervasive structural racial discrimination – the race problem – was sometimes characterized as "the negro problem." *See, e.g.*, Kenneth O'Reilly, *The Roosevelt Administration and Black America: Federal Surveillance Policy and Civil Rights during the New Deal and World War II Years*, 48 Phylon 12, 12 (1987) ("The nature of the federal government's response to the 'Negro problem' during the years 1933–1945 has been the subject of a lively historical debate."); *see also* Gunnar Myrdal, The American Dilemma: The Negro Problem and American Democracy (1944) (concluding that the negro problem was essentially a white man's problem). African American intellectual W. E. B. Du Bois expressed the sentiments of many in the Black community when he famously posited the rhetorical question: "How does it feel to be a problem?" W. E. B. Du Bois, The Souls of Black Folk: Essays and Sketches 2 (1903).

10. Perea, *supra* note 2, at 100.

11. Jill Quadagno, The Transformation of Old Age Security 16 (1988).

12. *Id.*

13. Harvard Sitkoff, A New Deal for Blacks 34 (thirtieth anniversary ed. 2009); *see also* Quadagno, Transformation of Old Age Security, *supra* note 11, at 16–18.

14. Walter White, A Man Called White 169–70 (1948).

15. *See* Brad Epperly, Christopher Witko, Ryan Strickler, & Paul White, *Rule by Violence, Rule by Law: Lynching, Jim Crow, and the Continuing Evolution of Voter Suppression in the U.S.*, 18 Persp. on Pol. 756, 765 (2020) ("[L]ynching and other forms of violence were tools in the widespread suppression of black political participation."); *see also* Sherrilyn A. Ifill, *Creating a Truth and Reconciliation Commission for Lynching*, 21 Minn. J. L. & Ineq. 263, 272–76 & n.98 (2003) (describing the effects of lynching and pervasive forms of voter intimidation and noting: "It took over 100 years for southern blacks to recover from the effects of this disenfranchisement[;] [a]lthough 15% of southern office holders were black in 1870, fewer than 3% were black in 1979.").

16. *See* STEVEN F. LAWSON, BLACK BALLOTS: VOTING RIGHTS IN THE SOUTH, 1944–1969 57 (1976) (noting that FDR "withdrew from his clear advocacy of [poll tax] repeal and tried to soothe the feelings of southern politicians ... [he] explained that 'at no time and in no manner did I even suggest federal legislation of any kind to deprive states of their rights directly or indirectly to impose the poll tax.'"); QUADAGNO, *supra* note 8, at 20.
17. Jon C. Dubin, *From Junkyards to Gentrification: Explicating a Right to Protective Zoning in Low-Income Communities of Color*, 77 MINN. L. REV. 739, 751–52 (1993).
18. *Id.*; RICHARD ROTHSTEIN, THE COLOR OF LAW: A FORGOTTEN HISTORY OF HOW OUR GOVERNMENT SEGREGATED AMERICA 59–75 (2017); *see also* DOUGLAS S. MASSEY & NANCY A. DENTON, AMERICAN APARTHEID: SEGREGATION AND THE MAKING OF THE UNDERCLASS 51–57 (1993) (describing redlining and other discriminatory and racially segregative practices at the time).
19. Dubin, *Junkyards to Gentrification, supra* note 17, at 752–53; *see* Joy Milligan, *Plessy Preserved: Agencies and the Effective Constitution*, 129 YALE L. J. 924, 931–32 (2020); ROTHSTEIN, *supra* note 18, at 23–24. In 1933, FDR established the Public Works Administration (PWA) which launched the first federal involvement in public housing; PWA also enforced racial segregation in all housing built and sited through a "neighborhood composition rule." *Id.*
20. Milligan, *supra* note 19, at 966–72; Dubin, *Junkyards to Gentrification, supra* note 17, at 752–53; Elizabeth K. Julian & Michael M. Daniel, *Separate and Unequal- The Root and Branch of Public Housing Segregation*, 23 CLEARINGHOUSE REV. 666, 668–69 (1989) (citing 95 CONG. REC. 4791–98, 4849–61 (1949)). In their successful advocacy against the anti-discrimination amendments, congressional supporters argued that challenging racial discrimination in public housing would provoke rejection of the entire expanded public housing program and thereby deprive Black families of much-needed housing – even though new housing would be provided on a racially discriminatory and segregated basis. *Id.*
21. Perea, *supra* note 2, at 104–07.
22. *Id.* at 105. The NIRA was invalidated in the courts and superseded by subsequent New Deal labor protection legislation. *Id.* at 104 n.50; see A.L.A. Schechter Poultry Corp. v. United States, 295 U.S. 495 (1935).
23. *Id.* at 105–06 & n.61.
24. *See id.*
25. QUADAGNO, COLOR OF WELFARE, *supra* note 8, at 22–23.
26. *Id.* at 23.
27. Perea, *supra* note 2, at 118–26.
28. Daiquiri J. Steele, *Enduring Exclusion*, 120 MICH. L. REV. 1667, 1678 (2021) (domestic workers were excluded "inasmuch as the bill defined employee as 'engaged in commerce or in the production of goods for commerce'"); Perea, *supra* note 2, at 114 & n.105 (same).
29. *Id.* at 114–16.
30. *Id.* at 115 (quoting 82 CONG. REC. 1404 (1937)).
31. KATZNELSON *supra* note 4, at 27.
32. There is ample record of additional relatively contemporaneous (to the Social Security Act) racially inequitable New Deal remedial legislation and program administration such as in the Agricultural Adjustment Act of 1933. *See* Perea, *supra* note 2, at 107–09, and the Tennessee Valley Authority (TVA) and the Civilian Conservation Corps (CCC). *See* ROTHSTEIN, *supra* note 18, at 19–20.
33. EDWIN E. WITTE, THE DEVELOPMENT OF THE SOCIAL SECURITY ACT 143–44 (1962).
34. *Id.*

35. *Id.*
36. While serving as Chairperson of the House Rules Committee when the Civil Rights Act of 1957 was before it, Congressman Smith noted that: "The Southern people have never accepted the colored race as a race of people who had equal intelligence and education and social attainments as the whole people of the South." CHARLES EUCHNER, NOBODY TURN ME AROUND: A PEOPLE'S HISTORY OF THE 1963 MARCH ON WASHINGTON 88 (2010). Others described Smith as "an apologist for slavery who cited the Greeks and Romans in its defense." *Civil Rights Act of 1964*, ENCYCLOPEDIA VA. He introduced the "Southern Manifesto" in 1956, assailing the *Brown v. Board of Education* decision: "the document attacked *Brown* as an abuse of judicial power that trespassed on states' rights and urged Southern school districts to exhaust all 'lawful means' to resist the 'chaos and confusion' that it said would result from racial desegregation." ANDREW GLASS, Smith, George Introduce "Southern Manifesto," March 12, 1956, POLITICO, (Mar. 12, 2010), *see also* David Rosenbaum, *Offending Portrait Succumbs to Black Lawmakers' Protest*, N.Y. TIMES (Jan. 25, 1995) (describing protest led by Georgia Congressman John Lewis to hanging of Howard Smith's portrait in the House Rules Committee hearing room, due to Smith's segregationist and white supremacist positions and statements).
37. *Economic Security Act: Hearings on H.R. 4120 Before the H. Comm. on Ways & Means*, 74th Cong. 974 (1935); *see also* QUADAGNO, TRANSFORMATION OF OLD AGE SECURITY, *supra* note 11, at 134 (quoting letter to Council on Economic Security member (WPA Director Harry Hopkins) from a person in Alabama, noting that if Blacks got old age assistance "the entire family would live off the money and [you] could not get them to work for us on our farms … They would be too independent if they should get a federal old age pension").
38. Economic Security Act: Hearings on H.R. 4120 Before the H. Comm. On Ways & Means, at 976.
39. Chris Pope, *Why Is Social Security Regressive?*, NATIONAL AFFAIRS, (Winter 2022); *see also* MARY POOLE, THE SEGREGATED ORIGINS OF SOCIAL SECURITY: AFRICAN AMERICANS AND THE WELFARE STATE 41 (2006) (Noting that Fred Sullens, the editor of the JACKSON DAILY NEWS, "was a personal friend of Senator Harrison").
40. WILLIAM E. LEUCHTENBERG, FRANKLIN D. ROOSEVELT AND THE NEW DEAL 1932–1940, at 131 (1963) (quoting JACKSON (MISS.) DAILY NEWS (June 20, 1935)).
41. *See* DeWitt, *supra* note 1, at 54 (describing differing perspectives of some Southern representatives such as a liberal congressman from an area in western Maryland more similar to Pennsylvania than the deep agricultural South).
42. *See also* MEHRSA BARADARAN, THE COLOR OF MONEY: BLACK BANKS AND THE RACIAL WEALTH GAP 102 (2017) (noting that with respect to New Deal legislation and Southern legislators' racialized interests in domination of Black labor, "[m]ost often Southern senators did not even have to speak against the legislation. They used their seniority position[s] on senate committees to make sure bills were drafted in such a way so as to exclude Blacks; otherwise a bill would never reach the floor for a vote").
43. *See* DeWitt, *supra* note 1, at 54.
44. *See* Pope, *supra* note 39 (noting that Senator Harrison adroitly steered the Committee "to get what he wanted" and pressed for the Title II old age insurance program (which had contained the agricultural and domestic worker exclusions) as a way to avert the "probable alternative" of a "flat, non-contributory" national, federal old age assistance benefit in Title I (or as otherwise proposed in other bills such as the Townsend plan for all elderly, or in Congressman Lundeen's occupationally inclusive, non-discriminatory unemployment insurance and social insurance plan). Although Harrison's testimony did not explicitly connect these dots, a flat national, federally administered benefit would

understandably include black farm laborers and could lead to the described impacts on the racialized southern farm economy identified by the JACKSON DAILY NEWS editorial and in Congressman Smith's testimony. *See also* Pope at *id.* ("Harrison, the son of a Confederate veteran, had been bitterly opposed to the flat benefits proposed by Townsend and others."); POOLE, *supra* note 39, at 31;

45. POOLE, *supra* note 39, at 31.
46. *Id.* (quoting Harrison's statement from, RALPH J. BUNCHE, THE POLITICAL STATUS OF THE NEGRO IN THE AGE OF FDR 207 (1973)).
47. BUNCHE, *supra* note 46, at 434–35.
48. *See* RICHARD KLUGER, SIMPLE JUSTICE: THE HISTORY OF BROWN V. BOARD OF EDUCATION AND BLACK AMERICA'S STRUGGLE FOR EQUALITY 105–280 (1975).
49. *Economic Security Act: Hearings on S. 1130 Before the S. Comm. on Finance*, 74th Cong. 641–47 (1935) (Statement of Charles Hamilton Houston, Special Counsel, NAACP); *id.* at 644 ("When you realize that out of the 5,500,000 Negro workers in this country, approximately 2,000,000 are in agriculture and another 1,500,000 in domestic service – 3,500,000 Negroes dropped through the act right away when it comes to the question of old-age annuity").
50. *See* DeWitt, *supra* note 1, at 60–61.
51. Houston Testimony, *supra* note 49, at 641–42; 643.
52. *Id.* at 641–43.
53. *Id.* at 641.
54. *Id.* at 642.
55. KATZNELSON, *supra* note 4, at 48; *see generally Text of the Lundeen Bill*, N.Y. TIMES (Mar. 9, 1935) (Providing a plan for unemployment insurance for unemployed persons "willing and able to work," and "for the immediate establishment of other forms of social insurance for the purpose of providing compensation for all workers and farmers who are unable to work because of sickness, old age, maternity, industrial injury, or any other disability" and further providing that: "The benefits of this act shall be extended to workers, whether they be industrial, agricultural, domestic, office or professional workers, and to farmers, without discrimination because of age, sex, race, color, religious or political opinion or affiliation").
56. *See* POOLE, *supra* note 39, at 21–27.
57. *Id.* at 22.
58. *See* Steele, *supra* note 28, at 1677 (quoting Editorial, *Social Security – for White Folk*, 42 CRISIS 80, 80 (1935) [emphasis in original]).
59. *Unemployment, Old Age and Social Insurance: Hearings on H.R. 2827 Before the H. Comm. on Lab.*, 74th Cong. 147 (1935) (Statement of Manning Rudolph Johnson, League of Struggle for Negro Rights); *see also Economic Security Act: Hearings on S. 1130 Before the S. Comm. on Fin.*, 74th Cong. 479–91 (1935) (Statement of George Edmund Haynes, Executive Secretary for race relations, Federal Council of Churches; pointing out that three-fifths of all African Americans will be excluded from coverage due to the exclusions and also urging adoption of an anti-discrimination provision in the bill).
60. *See generally* QUADAGNO, COLOR OF WELFARE, *supra* note 8, at 20.
61. KATZNELSON, *supra* note 4, at 192 n.57.
62. Haynes, George Edmund (1880–1960), SOC. WELFARE HIST. PROJECT, https://socialwelfare.library.vcu.edu/social-work/haynes-george-edmund/.
63. *Economic Security Act: Hearings on H.R. 4120 Before the H. Comm. on Ways & Means*, 74th Cong. 602 (1935) (statement of George Edmund Haynes, Executive Secretary for race relations, Federal Council of Churches); *see generally* KATZNELSON, *supra* note 4, at 37, 38–39 (noting that FERA Administrator Harry Hopkins – also a principal member of the Committee on Economic Security that produced the Social Security legislation

and FDR's closest advisor – in administering the FERA program "soon discovered that 'he had to tailor relief ... to accommodate the demands of southern plantation owners for cheap farm labor by curtailing [the level] of relief payments to agricultural laborers and sharecroppers,'" and describing widespread and pervasive racial discrimination in the distribution of federal relief funds by the local unit of government in numerous southern states administering the FERA funds).

64. Steele, *supra* note 28, at 1677.

65. Frances Fox Piven, *Why Welfare is Racist*, in RACE AND THE POLITICS OF WELFARE REFORM 327 (Sanford F. Schram, Joe Soss, & Richard C. Fording Eds., 2003) (citations omitted). *See also* QUADAGNO, TRANSFORMATION OF OLD AGE SECURITY, *supra* note 11, at 132–37 (providing myriad examples of southern discrimination against African Americans in the administration of the 1935 Social Security Act's old age assistance and other welfare programs to preserve prevailing wages and "intrude as little as possible on the planter–tenant relationship," including cutting benefits to Black recipients in half "when Black labor was in heavy demand ... while payments to white recipients were made on the usual basis"); Henry A. Freedman, *The Welfare Advocate's Challenge: Fighting Historic Racism in the New Welfare System*, 36 J. POVERTY L. & POL'Y 31, 31 & n.2 (2002) (describing lawsuit successfully challenging Georgia's policy of cutting off Aid to Families with Dependent Children (AFDC) benefits to able-bodied Black women "at cotton-picking time" in Anderson v. Burson, 300 F. Supp. 410 (N.D. Ga. 1968)). For examples of judicial evaluation of subsequent discriminatory Southern-state administration in the Act's locally administered, means-tested (Title I (Old Age), Title IV (Aid to Dependent Children) and Title X (Aid to the Blind)) programs (along with the Aid to the Permanently and Totally Disabled program adopted in the 1950 Social Security Act Amendments), *compare* Whitfield v. Oliver, 399 F. Supp. 348, 355–57 (M.D. Ala. 1975) (three-judge court finding unconstitutional systemic racial discrimination in the provision and allocation of welfare benefits among these programs in Alabama) *with* Jefferson v. Hackney, 406 U.S. 535 (1972) (rejecting claims of systemic race discrimination in the administration and allocation of welfare benefits in Texas's programs after a trial court finding that local welfare officials were fully unaware of the disparate racial impact of their actions).

66. In 1950, Congress "extended coverage to farm and domestic workers regularly employed by a single employer, but not to farmers themselves or farm labor or domestic servants who worked for multiple employers. These latter groups were brought under coverage in 1954." DeWitt, *supra* note 1, at n.16; *see also*, *Notes and Brief Reports: Employment Covered Under the Social Security Program* 1935–84, 48 SOC. SEC. BULL. 33, 34–35 (Apr. 1985) (describing the series of amendments in the 1950s reversing these exclusions).

67. *See* STOESZ, *supra* note 4, at 10 (arguing that "problems enrolling farm workers and domestics ... is not a convincing explanation for their exclusion from a government pension [since] [a]fter all, these groups were folded into Social Security during the early 1950s when the South had not changed appreciably with regard to the nature of low-wage work" and "several European nations – Great Britain, France, Germany, Sweden, and Austria – had encountered similar problems in enrolling farm workers yet had contrived creative ways to enhance the economic security of their farm workers"). On the other hand, DeWitt stresses the administrative difficulties in including these two excluded occupational groups, the significant costs and burdens encountered by the SSA when finally reversing these exclusions in the 1950s, and the recurrence in relatively modern times of tax evaders such as President Clinton's first Attorney General-nominated candidate, Zoe Baird, whose nomination was undermined by her failure to pay social security payroll (FICA) taxes for two domestic and personal employees and workers. *See* De Witt,

supra note 1, at 56, 62–63. DeWitt's reference to Zoe Baird's situation is perhaps not the best example of administrative difficulties with payroll tax reporting for domestic workers. Indeed, Baird's decision to evade tax law was not attributable to administrative difficulty but to her desire to honor her employees' wishes to knowingly avoid such tax reporting obligations and system involvement. *See id.* at 56. Baird's employees' wishes are fully understandable since they were each undocumented Peruvian immigrants who would be ineligible for social security and whose formal identification to the government could potentially have led to adverse immigration consequences. *See* Clifford Krauss, *The New Presidency: Justice Department; Nominee Pays Fine for Hiring of Illegal Aliens*, N. Y. Times (Jan. 17, 1993). In short, tax evasion is an ongoing pervasive issue, with considerably more far-reaching consequences beyond payroll tax nonreporting in the social security system owing to allegations of administrative inconvenience. *See generally*, Mathew Desmond, Poverty By America 125 (2023) (discussing yearly accounts of the amount of general tax nonreporting and tax evasion and pointing out that "[t]he IRS now estimates that the United States loses more than $1 trillion a year in unpaid taxes, most of it owing to tax avoidance by multinational corporations and wealthy families"). More fundamentally, the prospect or even inevitability of some significant degree of illegal tax evasion is a reality that lawmakers seek to curb; not a valid justification for limiting the broader Social Security payroll tax system (or other tax systems) or exempting specific occupations from coverage and taxation.

68. Lieberman, Shifting the Color Line, *supra* note 8, at 115–16.
69. *Id.* at 116.
70. *Id.* at 117.
71. *See id.* at 116–17.
72. *See also id.* at 109 (noting that as to the earlier 1950 inclusion amendment, the debate on it "produced the strongest demand yet from black organizations for inclusion as well as evidence of continuing Southern resistance. Clarence Mitchell of the NAACP reminded the Finance Committee of the predominance of blacks in these occupations, and he pointed out the pattern of agricultural exclusion from federal labor protection such as minimum wage and the National Labor Relations Act. Mitchell received unusually dismissive treatment from [House Ways and Means Chairman Robert] Doughton [from North Carolina] who repeatedly challenged his testimony and told him flat out that his statement was 'exactly contrary to the experience of most people'").
73. Lieberman, Shifting the Color Line, *supra* note 8, at 113–16. Some scholars have questioned why if the 1935 Act's exclusions, among the many considerations behind them, also included racial considerations such as the protection of the Southern post-bellum agricultural economy and racially subordinative political, economic and social order, why wouldn't those same considerations and forces be at play and as influential in the equally racially turbulent 1950s? *See, e.g.*, Nancy J. Altman, The Truth About Social Security – The Founders Words Refute Revisionist History, Zombie Lies and Common Misunderstandings 227–28 (2018) ("If the exclusion of domestic and farm workers was racially motivated in 1935, it is hard to explain why those forces would not be equally at play in 1950. It's hard to argue that 1950 was substantially less racist than 1935"). For one, those considerations and forces persisted and were at play; but as shown above, the southern legislative contingent asserting them in 1954 (including Congressman Howard Smith, Senators John Stennis, Harry Byrd, and others) was not as dominant or united on Social Security program structure issues as in 1935, and ultimately failed to carry the day. *See* Lieberman, *supra* note 8, at 117. Further, while the country's racial climate was still quite hostile and resistant to principles of racial equality, it had evolved somewhat by the time of the 1954 principal inclusion amendment. A unanimous

Supreme Court handed down the landmark *Brown v. Bd. of Education* decision in 1954, more than three months before passage of the 1954 Social Security inclusion amendment. The *Brown* decision had ended legal and constitutional sanction for Jim Crow and the pervasive system of racial apartheid and racial subordination established thereunder and was a result that would have been unthinkable in 1935. It was the culmination of a series of cases, and social circumstances, gradually chipping away at the constitutional and social foundation of Jim Crow throughout that nineteen-year period from 1935 to 1954. *See*, KRUGER, SIMPLE JUSTICE *supra* note 48.

74. DeWitt, *supra* note 1.
75. *See id.*
76. Professors Gareth Davies and Martha Derthick have catalogued these reasons:

> To summarize the nonracial factors that contributed [to excluding agricultural and domestic workers from the Social Security Old Age Insurance program (Title II)]: legislators had been told that these groups had always been [initially] excluded from new social insurance programs [in other countries], and that the Treasury was not capable of administering the [initial legislation which had included agricultural and domestic workers]; the most active private advocate for social insurance had told them that the inclusion of these groups might endanger the long-term prospects of the entire social security program; Roosevelt was suspected of favoring the Morgenthau amendments [FDR Treasury Secretary's Amendments containing these exclusions, contrary to the intent and wishes of FDR's Labor Secretary Frances Perkins and Works Progress Administration head, Harry Hopkins, in the initial inclusive Bill]; and administration officials, at pains to appear deferential, emphasized that their bill could only benefit from careful congressional scrutiny. If race contributed to the enthusiasm of southern legislators for revision, then it was joined with these other factors.

Davies & Derthick, *supra* note 4, at 226.

77. DeWitt conceded that important administrative observers of the Act's passage identified racial bias behind the Title I Old Age program's enactment. *See* DeWitt, *supra* note 1, at 64. ("It is not as if observers of these events were oblivious to the issue of race as it influenced particular provisions of law … [They] recounted how race was a factor in the development of Title I of the 1935 act … [and] pointed an accusing finger at Southern Democrats in Congress when it came to the Title I program." But they "did not report any such influence on the Title II program coverage issue").
78. Harmony Goldberg, *The Long Journey Home: The Contested Exclusion and Inclusion of Domestic Workers from Federal Wage and Hour Protections in the United States*, INT'L LAB. ORG. 11–12 (2015).
79. *See* Davies & Derthick, *supra*, note 4, at 224 (emphasis added).
80. The Fifth Amendment's Due Process clause incorporates equal protection doctrine to the federal government and federal legislation. *See* Bolling v. Sharpe, 347 U.S. 497, 499–500 (1954); *see also* Adarand Constructors, Inc. v. Pena, 515 U.S. 200, 224 (1995) ("Equal protection analysis in the Fifth Amendment area is the same as that under the Fourteenth Amendment").
81. *See generally* Washington v. Davis, 426 U.S. 229 (1976).
82. 429 U.S. 252 (1977).
83. *Id.* at 265.
84. *Id.* at 265–66.
85. *Id.* at 270 n.21.

86. *See, e.g.*, Williams v. City of Dothan, 745 F.2d 1406, 1414 (11th Cir. 1984); Dowdell v. City of Apopka, 698 F.2d 1181, 1185 (11th Cir. 1983); Baker v. City of Kissimmee, 645 F. Supp. 571, 586 (M.D. Fla. 1986); Ammons v. Dade City, 594 F. Supp. 1274, 1300 (M.D. Fla. 1984), *aff'd per curiam*, 783 F.2d 982 (11th Cir. 1986) (en banc); Johnson v. City of Arcadia, 450 F. Supp. 1363, 1378–79 (M.D. Fla. 1978).
87. *Arlington Heights*, 429 U.S. at 264–68; *see* Lodge v. Buxton, 639 F.2d 1358, 1363 n.8 (5th Cir. 1981) (observing that one cannot expect to find a "smoking gun" in discrimination cases), *aff'd*, 458 U.S. 613 (1982).
88. *See, e.g.*, Katie Rader, No, The New Deal Wasn't Racist, JACOBIN (Sept. 24, 2024); Samuel Hammond, No, The New Deal Wasn't Racist, AMERICAN COMPASS (Oct. 12, 2020).
89. *See, e.g.*, Adolph Reed, Jr., The New Deal Wasn't Intrinsically Racist, THE NEW REPUBLIC (Nov. 26, 2019).
90. *See* Ch. 5.5 *infra* and accompanying text (discussing "dominative" or "traditional" discrimination as "the species of racial discrimination most identified by the average person with the term 'racism,'" and as "characterized by a belief in the superiority of the racial in-group and the inferiority of the racial out-group," with the expectation of accompanying "feelings of hatred, malice, and/or animus towards the targeted racial groups" by actors who might be labelled "bigots," "segregationists," or "white supremacists" (citing Khiara Bridges, *Excavating Race-Based Disadvantage among Class-Privileged People of Color*, 53 HARV. CIV. RTS-CIV. LIB. L. REV. 65, 86 (2018) and Joel Kovel, WHITE RACISM: A PSYCHOHISTORY (1970)).
91. Of course, the previously discussed rhetoric of influential Southern legislators about Black workers' differential character and resulting appropriate lower wage scales, and importance and desirability of tethering Black workers to farm work, unsupported by social security pensions, in discussions of new deal labor laws and Title I of the Social Security Act, respectively, would satisfy most popular and colloquial understandings of expressions of "racism." The same could be said for rhetoric in opposing the proposed occupational inclusion amendment to Title II of the Act in 1954, referencing the "irresponsible and reckless" character of the domestic and farm workers finally proposed for full inclusion in the Social Security program in these disproportionately Black-worker occupational categories. Moreover, the economic, social, and political circumstances rendering Black workers vulnerable to significant exploitation in these occupational categories, precluding meaningful access to political processes through lynching and other disenfranchisement devices, and thereby rendering Black interests in the design and coverage of the Social Security Act and other New Deal legislation fully expendable, was also undoubtedly a product of American racism.
92. *Arlington Heights*, 429 U.S. at 266–68. Admittedly, equal protection race discrimination doctrine was far more restrictive in the 1930s than in the 1970s and thereafter as *Plessy v. Ferguson*'s "separate but equal" doctrine was still the law. *See* KLUGER, *supra* note 48. It is also conceded that the present Supreme Court has and likely will render equal protection and anti-discrimination doctrine less protective of the rights and interests of African Americans and other historically subordinated persons of color for the foreseeable future. *See generally* Russell K. Robinson, *Unequal Protection*, 68 STAN. L. REV. 151 (2016) (asserting that the Court has become less vigorous in protecting the rights of racial minorities under the Equal Protection Clause); *see, e.g.*, Students for Fair Admissions, Inc. v. President & Fellows of Harvard Coll., 600 U.S. 181, 407 (2023) (Jackson, J., joined by Sotomayor and Kagan, JJ., dissenting) (noting that the Court's current majority, in "deeming race irrelevant in law does not make it so in life"); *see also* Dep't of Homeland

Sec. v. Regents of the Univ. of Cal., 591 U.S. 1, 34–35 (2020) (applying *Arlington Heights* factors and paradigm and rejecting discriminatory intent claims based on rescission of the Deferred Action for Childhood Arrivals (DACA) program, notwithstanding numerous derogatory statements about Mexican immigrants by President Trump before and after taking office and an abrupt change in policy contrary to the usual sequence of events in rescissions); *cf.* Trump v. Hawaii, 585 U.S. 667, 696–710 (2018) (rejecting a challenge asserting religious discrimination against Muslims through a third version of the Executive Order, relabeled a presidential proclamation, restricting travel from seven predominantly Muslim countries as rationally related to legitimate national security and immigration purposes); *id.* at 739–40 (Sotomayor, J., joined by Ginsburg, J., dissenting) ("Ultimately, what began as a policy explicitly 'calling for a total and complete shutdown of Muslims entering the United States' has since morphed into a 'Proclamation' putatively based on national security concerns. But this new window dressing cannot conceal an unassailable fact: the words of the President and his advisers create the strong perception that the Proclamation is contaminated by impermissible discriminatory animus against Islam and its followers"); *see generally* William D. Araiza, *Cleansing Animus: The Path through Arlington Heights*, 74 Ala. L. Rev. 541, 553 (2023) (analyzing equal protection discriminatory intent or animus doctrine through 2023, finding that "the *Arlington Heights* factors have become generally accepted as the ostensible guide to determining discriminatory intent," and proposing that the *Arlington Heights* methodology also be used in *Trump v. Hawaii*-type fact patterns involving evaluation of whether reenacted policies or laws, initially adopted with discriminatory statements or stronger background indicia of invidious intent, have been sufficiently "cleansed" of the taint of the discriminatory intent evidence from the earlier similar enactment). Equal protection doctrine, as developed in modern times and not yet overruled, is applied and discussed in this chapter principally as a lens within which to evaluate the salience of racial considerations in the 1935 Act's exclusions.

93. Columbus Bd. of Educ. v. Penick, 443 U.S. 449, 464–65 (1979).
94. *See, e.g.*, Rogers v. Lodge, 458 U.S. 613, 624–26 (1982); *see also* Ammons v. Dade City, 783 F.2d 982, 988 (11th Cir. 1984) (*per curiam*) (affirming trial court's reliance on evidence of discrimination "covering practically every aspect of municipal conduct in Dade City throughout its history" to support a finding of intentional discrimination in municipal services).
95. In discussing the initial Social Security legislative proposal, Edwin Witte, the Executive Director of FDR's Committee on Economic Security that drafted the bill, explained:

> It is a fact that, as the bill stands, it attempts to cover the entire employed population. It is a fact that we cannot overlook that no matter whether a person works in a small establishment or a large establishment, whether he works on a farm or whether he works as a domestic servant, or whether he works in a factory, there is one common characteristic, which is that everybody grows old … [W]e are presenting a program which would cover the entire employed population.

Economic Security Act: Hearings on H.R. 4120 Before the H. Comm. on Ways & Means, 74th Cong. 108 (1935) (Statement of Dr. Edwin. E. Witte, Executive Director, Committee on Economic Security); *see also* Committee on Economic Security Report to the President, *supra* note 7 (stating "we are opposed to any exclusions of any specific industries within the Federal act" and recommending the inclusion of all workers earning under $250 per month, and explaining that "agricultural workers, domestic workers, home workers and the many self-employed people constitute large groups in the population who have received little attention [and] [i]n these groups there are many who are at the very bottom of the economic scale.").

96. *See* Jessica A. Clarke, *Explicit Bias*, 113 Nw. U. L. Rev. 505, 557–58, 584 (2018) (In *Arlington Heights*, "the Supreme Court adopted a burden-shifting framework to address concerns about the mixed motives of legislators[,] … rejected an inquiry that would have required a showing of sole purpose or primary purpose … and call[ed] for a holistic review of evidence of discriminatory intent, considering history, context, effects on minority groups, and statements by decisionmakers"); *see also* W. Kerrel Murray, *Discriminatory Taint*, 135 Harv. L. Rev. 1190, 1244 (2022) (noting that "[i]n the normal case where a plaintiff shows the action was motivated in part by proscribed intent," or "where taint supports a prima facie case, the government … need only show that legitimate reasons support the policy, that it has accounted for the problematic history, and that any persisting disparate impact is unavoidable and outweighed by the benefits of the legitimate justifications").
97. *See, e.g.*, Fisher v. Sec'y of Health, Educ. & Welfare, 522 F.2d 493, 499–503 (7th Cir. 1975); Doe v. Hodgson, 344 F. Supp. 964 (N.D. Cal. 1970), *aff'd*, 478 F.2d 537 (2d Cir. 1973), *cert. denied*, 414 U.S. 1096 (1973); Romero v. Hodgson, 319 F. Supp. 1201 (N.D. Cal. 1970), *summarily aff'd*, 403 U.S. 901 (1971). Admittedly, these cases were decided a few years before *Arlington Heights*.
98. 406 U.S. 535 (1972).
99. *Id.* at 547–48 ("The depositions of Welfare officials conclusively establish that the defendants did not know the racial make-up of the various welfare assistance categories prior to or at the time when the orders here under attack were issued … Appellants are thus left with their naked statistical argument: that there is a larger percentage of Negroes and Mexican-Americans in AFDC than in the other programs"); *see Fisher*, 522 F.2d at 501 (in *Jefferson*, "welfare officials did not know the racial make-up of the categories of recipients and the reduction was not the result of racial or ethnic prejudice"); *id.* at 500 (In *Romero*, "no allegation of racial, sexual or economic discrimination was made in the lower court"); *see also Doe*, 344 F. Supp. at 968 (relying on *Romero* and *Jefferson*).
100. Whitfield v. Oliver, 399 F. Supp. 348, 353 (M.D. Ala. 1975). The three-judge court in *Whitfield v. Oliver* reached its conclusion even without the benefit of the later decided guidance of *Arington Heights*, on mixed motive challenges and the delineation and use of identified categories of circumstantial evidence to discern a decisive unconstitutional racial taint behind a law or governmental action. A body of additional lower court decisions reveals how comparable circumstantial evidence demonstrates equal protection violations in various governmental entities' provision of services or benefits under *Arlington Heights* and its progeny. *See, e.g.*, Williams v. City of Dothan, 745 F.2d 1406, 1414 (11th Cir. 1984); Dowdell v. City of Apopka, 698 F.2d 1181, 1185 (11th Cir. 1983); Baker v. City of Kissimmee, 645 F. Supp. 571, 586 (M.D. Fla. 1986); Ammons v. Dade City, 594 F. Supp. 1274, 1300 (M.D. Fla. 1984), *aff'd per curiam*, 783 F.2d 982 (11th Cir. 1986) (en banc); Johnson v. City of Arcadia, 450 F. Supp. 1363, 1378–79 (M.D. Fla. 1978).
101. *See* Whitfield v. Oliver, 399 F. Supp. 348, 355–57 (M.D. Ala. 1975).
102. DeWitt, *supra* note 1, at 51 (citing Davies & Derthick, *supra* note 4, at 217–35); *id.* at 64 (acknowledging substantial support and feedback from Derthick in drafting the article on the SSA website).
103. Davies & Derthick, *supra* note 4, at 235 (emphasis added).
104. Robert C. Lieberman, *Race and the Organization of Welfare Policy*, in Classifying Race 156, 161 (Paul E. Peterson ed., 1995).
105. Kijakazi et al., *supra* note 3, at 2.
106. *See* Stoesz, *supra* note 4, at 5 (referencing similar impacts from these exclusions on Latino/a agricultural and domestic workers in the southwest).
107. *Id.* at 14.
108. *Id.*

2 CONTEMPORARY RACIAL INEQUITY FOR BENEFICIARIES OF THE SOCIAL SECURITY OLD AGE/RETIREMENT PROGRAM: CAUSES, REMEDIES, AND IMPENDING CHALLENGES

1. Frank Bloch and I have described the formula for applying the AIME to determine the PIA (and ultimately the monthly benefit amount) as set out in SSA's regulations as follows:

> AIMEs are calculated by indexing earnings to adjust for the upward trend in wages over the years. *See generally* 20 C.F.R. § 404.210; *see also* 20 C.F.R. § 404.211. Wage earners' earnings for years creditable for Social Security purposes are indexed by comparing those earnings in each year with the average earnings in that year, and then adjusting the earnings to reflect average increases in earnings in the relevant time period. *See* 20 C.F.R. § 404.211(d). Each year in which the wage earner had sufficient earnings to qualify for "insured status" is used, except that up to five of those years with lower earnings can be deducted to arrive at the required number of "benefit computation years." 20 C.F.R. § 404.211(e). The AIME is then calculated by adding together the indexed earnings in the benefit computation years; dividing that sum by the number of months in those years; and rounding down to the next dollar. 20 C.F.R. § 404.211(f). For an example of indexing a worker's earnings see 20 C.F.R. § 404.211(d). SSA then uses a formula to convert wage earners' AIME to their PIA, which becomes the base amount of a wage earner's monthly benefit.
>
> This formula revolves around the use of certain "bend points," which operate by paying x percent of a first prescribed amount of the AIME, y percent of a next prescribed amount of the AIME, and so on. The practical reality of these bend points is to favor wage earners with lower AIME amounts, as can be seen by looking at the percentage of the AIME at each bend point that is included in the wage earner's PIA. The bend point amounts are adjusted each year. For example, in the year 2021, the formula adds together 90% of the AIME equal to or less than $996, 32% above $856 and up to $6002, and only 15% over $6002. As a result, the higher a wage earner's AIME, the less the percentage of that amount is included in the wage earner's PIA and thus in the amount of monthly benefits the wage earner actually receives. *See generally* 20 C.F.R. § 404.212.

   FRANK S. BLOCH & JON C. DUBIN, SOCIAL SECURITY LAW AND PRACTICE IN A NUTSHELL 223–24 (2022); *see* Social Security Administration, Primary Insurance Amounts, www.ssa.gov/oact/cola/piaformula.html

2. *What Is the Maximum Social Security Retirement Benefit Payable* (Jan. 2, 2025), www.ssa.gov/faqs/en/questions/KA-01897.htmlc ("if you retire at full retirement age in 2025, your maximum benefit would be $4,018. However, if you retire at age 62 in 2025, your maximum benefit would be $2,831. If you retire at age 70 in 2025, your maximum benefit would be $5,108."); *see also* Katie Brockman, *Here's the Max Social Security Benefit for 2026 – and Exactly What You Need to Do to Get It*, THE MOTLEY FOOL (Nov. 2, 2025) (providing updated maximum social security monthly figures for 2026: For early retirement at age sixty-two, the maximum is $2,910 per month; at full retirement age of sixty-seven, the maximum is $4,156 per month; at age seventy, the maximum is $5,251 per month); *see generally* Kathleen Romig & Dave Shoffner, *Understanding the Social Security Family Maximum*, (Aug. 2015), www.ssa.gov/policy/docs/ssb/v75n3/v75n3p1.html ("The family maximum formula for Old-Age and Survivors Insurance (OASI) benefits is based on a beneficiary's primary insurance amount (PIA) [as applied to a somewhat complex formula] … Ultimately, this formula yields a maximum for each family that is between 150 percent and 188 percent of the worker's basic Social Security benefit, or PIA.").

3. Black workers in the US earn 84 cents, and Latino/a's 76 cents for every $1 earned by white workers. *See* Xactly, *How the Racial Wage Gap Has Fallen – and Risen – Over the Past Two Decades* (Apr. 30, 2024), www.xactlycorp.com/blog/benchmarking/how-racial-wage-gap-has-fallen-and-risen-over-past-two-decades. Even more recently, the US Bureau of Labor Statistics reports that median earnings of Hispanics who worked full time ($947) were lower than those of Blacks ($991), and whites ($1,225), and by gender, "median weekly earnings for Black men were $1,053, or 77.6 percent of the median, for White men ($1,357). Median earnings for Hispanic men were $1,005, or 74.1 percent of the median for White men. The differences were smaller among women, as Black women's median earnings were $942, or 85.6 percent of those for White women ($1,100), and earnings for Hispanic women were $880, or 80.0 percent of those for White women." BUREAU OF LABOR STATISTICS, USUAL WEEKLY EARNINGS OF WAGE AND SALARY WORKERS, FIRST QUARTER2025 (Apr. 16, 2025).
4. *See* MAYA M. ROCKEYMOORE & MEIZHU LUI, COMM'N TO MODERNIZE SOC. SEC., PLAN FOR A NEW FUTURE: THE IMPACT OF SOCIAL SECURITY REFORM ON PEOPLE OF COLOR 12 (2011) ("Discrimination and segregation in hiring, pay and employment were common and largely legal practices until the 1960's when civil rights legislation outlawed employment discrimination. And structural racism in the labor market persists today."); *see also* Mark Miller, *America's Retirement Race Gap, and Ideas for Closing It,* N.Y. TIMES (Nov. 23, 2023); RICHARD W. JOHNSON & KAREN E. SMITH, LIMITATIONS ON SOCIAL SECURITY BENEFITS FOR BLACK RETIREES: EXPLORING STRUCTURAL RACISM'S IMPACT v–vii,1–5, URBAN INSTITUTE (Apr. 2023); KILOLO KIJAKAZI, KAREN SMITH & CHARMAINE RUNES, URBAN INSTITUTE, AFRICAN AMERICAN ECONOMIC SECURITY AND THE ROLE OF SOCIAL SECURITY 13–15 (July 2019).
5. After documenting the transformation of low wage employment in a largely industrial manufacturing economy to a heavily service-based economy at present, one field study utilizing "testers" seeking lower wage service positions, concluded:

   > We find that minority job applicants are routinely overlooked in favor of equally qualified white applicants. In jobs requiring interaction with customers, employers seem particularly averse to hiring minorities, and blacks in particular. In these positions, we see rising barriers to entry or frequent channeling into positions requiring less customer contact and more manual work than positions offered to their white counterparts. These results underscore the consequences of industrial shifts over the past three decades, with new job growth dominated by the service sector. Given employers' reluctance to hire racial minorities for positions involving customer contact, these broader patterns do not bode well for the employment prospects of young minority men.

   Devah Pager, Bruce Western, & David Pedulla, *Employment Discrimination and the Changing Landscape of Low-Wage Labor Markets*, 1 U. CHI. LEGAL F. 317, 340 (2009); *see also* Marianne Bertrand and Sendhil Mullainathan, *Are Emily and Greg More Employable than Lakisha and Jamal? A Field Experiment on Labor Market Discrimination*, 94 AM. ECON. REV. 991 (2004) (Study with testing based on white- and Black-identified names for positions in both lower wage and higher skill and wage positions categories such as "sales management," persons with Black-identified names received 50 percent fewer callbacks and even continued to experience disparate treatment when improving credentials and observable skills beyond those of candidates with white-identified names).
6. *See* Mark Miller, *America's Retirement Race Gap, and Ideas for Closing It,* N.Y. TIMES (Nov. 23, 2023).
7. *Id.*; *see generally* Joeseph Robinson Jr., *Note, Live Black … Retire Poor … Die Early: How Social Security as an Institution Continues to Perpetuate the Social Racism of the 1930's*, 24

ELDER L. J. 487, 504 (2017). The Social Security system by "[u]sing a benefits structure that makes distributions based on earnings[,] effectively incorporates a policy of social discrimination into the Act itself. This systematic discrimination has been best characterized as, 'Congress incorporat[ing] the effects of … discrimination against African-Americans into the very program designed to ameliorate the economic devastation caused by old age, disability, or early death of the wage earner.'" (quoting Phoebe Weaver Williams, *Social Security Reform: Transformative Opportunities for African Americans*, 3 ELDER'S ADVISOR 23, 27 (2001)).

8. KIJAKAZI ET AL., *supra* note 4, at 15; MAYA M. ROCKEYMOORE & MEIZHU LUI, COMM'N TO MODERNIZE SOCIAL SECURITY, PLAN FOR A NEW FUTURE: THE IMPACT OF SOCIAL SECURITY REFORM ON PEOPLE OF COLOR 27–28; 40–42 (Oct. 2011); *see also* WENDY L. MACIAS-KONSTANTOPOLOUS, et al., *Race, Healthcare, and Health Disparities: A Critical Review and Recommendations for Advancing Health Equity*, 24 WESTERN J. OF EM. MED. 906 (Sept. 2023) (documenting racial inequity in health care provision and providing remedial recommendations).

9. *See* William Baldwin, *Is Social Security Racist,?* FORBES (Aug. 26, 2021) ("Two elements of Social Security contribute to racial inequality. One is that the system rewards Marriage. The other is that it rewards longevity. Black people get shortchanged on both scores."). Lower marriage rates reduce benefits through the absence of spouses with higher earnings records on which to base benefits. *See* Richard W. Johnson & Karen E. Smith, *How Can Changes to Social Security Improve Benefits for Black and Hispanic Beneficiaries*, CENTER FOR RETIREMENT RESEARCH 1, 22–23 (Dec. 2023); Richard W. Johnson, *Policy Options to Reduce the Black-White Gap in Retirement Security*, 1 J. OF ELDER POL'Y 85 (Spring 2021); ROCKEYMOORE & LUI, *supra* note 4, at 27 ("Given the way that Social Security works, a widowed spouse who has never worked could receive benefits greater than those of a single person who has worked for low wages his or her entire adult life if that widowed spouse was married to a high earning spouse."); *see also* Dorothy A. Brown, *Social Security and Marriage in Black and White*, 65 OHIO ST. L.J. 111, 116–21; 137–43 (2004) (noting that white wives are more likely than Black wives to be eligible for the greatest spousal and survivors benefits and Black wives are more likely than white wives to receive no spousal benefits and the lowest survivor benefits since they are more likely than white wives to earn close to or exceeding 50 percent of the family income, precluding spousal benefits, and since, in any event, spousal benefits are generally lower for equal wage earning couples and Black couples are more likely to earn equal amounts); *see generally* Social Security Admin., *Benefits for Spouses*, www.ssa.gov/oact/quickcalc/spouse.html (describing spousal social security benefits based on a worker-spouse's earnings as follows):

> When a worker files for retirement benefits, the worker's spouse may be eligible for a benefit based on the worker's earnings. Another requirement is that the spouse must be at least age 62 or have a qualifying child in her/his care. By a qualifying child, we mean a child who is under age 16 or who receives Social Security disability benefits. The spousal benefit can be as much as half of the worker's "primary insurance amount," depending on the spouse's age at retirement. If the spouse begins receiving benefits before "normal (or full) retirement age," the spouse will receive a reduced benefit. However, if a spouse is caring for a qualifying child, the spousal benefit is *not* reduced. If a spouse is eligible for a retirement benefit based on his or her own earnings, and if that benefit is higher than the spousal benefit, then we pay the retirement benefit. Otherwise we pay the spousal benefit.

For a discussion of eligibility for survivor's benefits for a spouse or, in certain circumstances, former spouse or dependent child upon death of a wage earner, with benefits up to 100 percent of the wage earner's PIA at the spouse's full retirement age or earlier if caring for a dependent child under sixteen or disabled, and with lesser benefits at age sixty unless at least fifty and disabled, *see* Social Security Admin., *Survivors' Benefits*, www.ssa.gov/pubs/EN-05–10084.pdf

10. Richard W. Johnson, *Policy Options to Reduce the Black-White Gap in Retirement Security*, 1 J. of Elder Pol'y 83, 85 (Spring 2021) ("Black people are especially likely to serve as primary caregivers of their grandchildren, which can interfere with paid work, raise spending needs, and reduce retirement savings."); *see generally* Meredith Minkler & Esme Fuller-Thompson, *African American Grandparents Raising Grandchildren: A National Study Using the Census 2000 American Community Survey*, 60 Journals of Gerontology: Series B S82 (2005).
11. *See* discussion of these issues in Chapter 3.
12. *See* Benjamin W. Veghte, Elliot Schreur, & Mikki Waid, Social Security and the Racial Gap in Retirement Wealth (National Academy of Social Insurance, Dec. 2016), 2–5; *see also* Dorothy Brown, The Whiteness of Wealth: How the Tax System Impoverishes Black Americans -And How We Can Fix It 3–4 (2022); Richard Rothstein, The Color of Law: A forgotten History of How Our Government Segregated America (2017); Jon C. Dubin, *From Junkyards to Gentrification: Explicating a Right to Protective Zoning in Low-Income Communities of Color*, 77 Minn. L. Rev. 739 (1993).
13. *See* Benjamin W. Veghte, Elliot Schreur, & Mikki Waid, Social Security and the Racial Gap in Retirement Wealth (National Academy of Social Insurance, Dec. 2016), 2–5; *see also* Edward N. Wolff, *The Decline of African-American and Hispanic Wealth since the Great Recession* 1, 33 (Nat'l Bureau of Econ. Res., Working Paper No. 25198, 2018), https://perma.cc/AF3Z-DNXF (documenting an increase in the wealth gap between Black/Latino/a and white Americans after the recession of 2007–10, with the Black/white ratio falling to 0.14 in 2016 and Latino/a/white ratio falling to 0.19 in 2016. The study concluded by "highlighting the importance of Social Security in the minority community[;] [i]n 2016, Social Security made up a much greater share of total (augmented) wealth of minorities than of whites." Specifically, "[i]n 2016, Social Security wealth comprised 46% of the augmented wealth of [B]lacks and 44% among Hispanics, compared to 20% among whites."); Nathalie Martin, *Bad Apples or a Rotten Tree: Ameliorating the Double Pandemic of COVID-19 and Racial Economic Inequality*, 82 Mont. L. Rev. 105 (2021) (describing how the COVID-19 Pandemic (commencing in March 2020) has exacerbated the racial wealth gap with particularly deleterious and disproportionately fatal consequences for Black and Brown communities); *see generally* Melvin L. Oliver & Thomas M. Shapiro, Melvin L. Oliver & Thomas M. Shapiro, Black Wealth/ White Wealth: A New Perspective on Racial Inequality (2nd ed. 2006); Brown, Whiteness of Wealth, *supra note* 12.
14. Kijakazi et al., *supra* note 4, at 5–9; Veghte et al., *supra* note 13, at 2–5; Rockeymoore & Lui,. Et Al; *supra* note 13, at 14–21; *see also* Ariel Education Initiative and Aon/Hewitt, 401(k) Plans in Living Color: A Study of 401(k) Savings Disparities Across Racial and Ethnic Groups (2012); *see* Richard W. Johnson, *Policy Options to Reduce the Black-White Gap in Retirement Security*, 1 J. of Elder Pol'y 83, 87 (Spring 2021) (noting that two-thirds of white elderly (over 65) adults "received asset income in 2015, compared with less than 1/3 of Black people and Latinos."); Brian Vines, *Retiring While Black*, Consumer Reports (Apr. 13, 2021) ("Blacks are less likely to have retirement savings accounts like 401(k)'s or pensions, partly because they are less likely to work for an employer that offers them … [and] [r]etirement accounts held by Blacks have little more than a third of the balance of accounts owned by whites, according to a 2016 analysis of Federal Reserve data.").

15. *See* Johnson, *supra* note 9, at 87. The 2023 comparative poverty rates by race/ethnicity reported by the Census Bureau are: Native American: 21.2 percent; Black 17.9 percent;, Latino/a 16.6 percent, and white 7.7 percent. *See* Emily A. Shrider, *Poverty in the U.S. 2023*, Tbl. A-3, UNITED STATES CENSUS BUREAU (Sept. 10, 2024); The July 2025 comparative unemployment rates reported by the Bureau of Labor Statistics were: Black 7.2 percent, Latino/a 5.0 percent, white 3.7 percent. US Department of Labor, Bureau of Labor Statistics, *News Release – The Employment Situation – July 2025* (Aug. 1, 2025). Whereas 10.8 percent of all households have zero or negative wealth owing to debt ("net debt"), "[d]isproportionate numbers of Black (18.9%) and Hispanic/Latino (11.3%) households were in net debt." TASHFIA HASAN, KATHERINE LUCAS MCKAY, & JOANNA SMITH-RAMANI, DISPARITIES IN DEBT: WHY DEBT IS A DRIVER OF THE RACIAL WEALTH GAP, ASPEN INSTITUTE 2 (FEB. 2022). This Aspen Institute racial debt report summarized comparative debt issues of persons of color as follows:

> Three aspects of the debt held by people of color demonstrate the significant contribution of racial disparities in debts to racial wealth gaps. Compared to white people, the debt held by people of color is: (1) more likely to be harmful [i.e., not asset building debt such as prime home mortgages]; (2) more likely to involve the court system; and (3) more likely to have spillover nonfinancial consequences. These characteristics undermine households' wealth by disrupting cash flow, chronically constraining accumulation of savings. and stripping away existing wealth.

Id. at 6.

16. BENJAMIN W. VEGHTE, ELLIOT SCHREUR, & MIKKI WALD, SOCIAL SECURITY AND THE RACIAL GAP IN RETIREMENT WEALTH, at 2–5; KIJAKAZI ET AL., *supra* note 4, at 14; *see also* Mark Miller, *America's Retirement Race Gap*, *supra* note 6, at *id.* ("[W]orkers of color earn less, have lower life expectancy and tend to work in physically demanding occupations that become more difficult to continue at older ages. For example, 50 percent of Black workers ages 55 to 62 reported in 2014 that they have jobs requiring 'lots of physical effort' compared with just 32 percent of whites."); *see generally* Wendy L. Macias-Konstantopolous, et al., *Race, Healthcare, and Health Disparities: A Critical Review and Recommendations for Advancing Health Equity*, 24 WESTERN J. OF EM. MED. 906 (Sept. 2023) (documenting racial inequity in health care provision and providing remedial recommendations).
17. *See* NATIONAL ACADEMY OF SOCIAL INSURANCE, A REPORT OF THE OLDER WORKERS' RETIREMENT SECURITY TASK FORCE, OLDER WORKERS IN PHYSICALLY CHALLENGING JOBS NEED STRONGER SOCIAL INSURANCE SUPPORTS 1–9, 11 (SEPT. 2023); *see also* Elvis Guzman and Nakia Gladden, *Why Raising the Retirement Age Would Hurt African Americans*, CENTER FOR GLOBAL POLICY SOLUTIONS 3–4 (July 2015) (noting that African Americans retire earlier owing to higher unemployment and poorer health); KIJAKAZI ET AL., *supra* note 4, at 13.
18. *See generally* Social Security Administration, *Retirement Benefits*, 2–5 (2025), www.ssa.gov/pubs/EN-05–10035.pdf (describing differences in benefit level calculation percentages based on early or delayed retirement).
19. Structural changes in the "new economy" leading into the twenty-first century do not appear to mitigate racial inequity in employment and earnings in the American labor market. *See* Lesley Williams Reid & Beth A. Rubin, *Integrating Economic Dualism and Labor Market Segmentation: The Effects of Race, Gender, and Structural Location on Earnings, 1974–2000* 44 THE SOCIOLOGICAL QUARTERLY 405, 420 (Summer 2003) ("Overall, these trends suggest that although the new economy has benefitted women and minorities, this benefit has not lessened employment and earnings inequality.");

see also Devah Pager, Bruce Western, & David Pedulla, *Employment Discrimination and the Changing Landscape of Low-Wage Labor Markets,* 1 U. Chi. Legal F. 317, 340 (2009) (revealing significant race discrimination in the new, service-dominated low wage employment sector of the economy based on field study with Black and white testers).

20. Johnson & Smith, Center For Retirement Research, *supra* note 9, at 1.
21. Johnson & Smith, Exploring Structural Racism's Impact, *supra* note 4, at xi.
22. *Id.*
23. Social Security Administration (SSA), Equity Action Plan in Agreement With EO 13985 11 (Feb. 10, 2022).
24. H.R. Comm. on Ways & Means, 64th Cong., Rep. of the 1979 Advisory Council on Social Security 136 (Comm. Print 1979).
25. *See* Social Security Administration, Research, Statistics and Policy Analysis, *Monthly Statistical Snapshot May 2025*, www.ssa.gov/policy/docs/quickfacts/stat_snapshot/2025-05.pdf (SSA revealing that in May 2025, there were approximately 8.2 million SSDI beneficiaries, and 4.9 million SSID recipients, while the retirement program provided benefits to 55 million persons. The social security survivors' program supplies benefits to another 5.8 million persons).
26. *See* Johnson & Smith, Exploring Structural Racism's Impact, *supra* note 4, at xi; *see also* C. Eugene Steuerle, Karen E. Smith, & Caleb Quakenbush, *Has Social Security Redistributed to Whites from People of Color?* Urban Institute (Nov. 2013) ("Social Security redistributes from Hispanics, blacks, and other people of color to whites. This effect is least ambiguous when examining only old age and survivors (OASI) benefits. The addition of disability benefits (DI) restores some progressivity for blacks, but combined OASDI transfers continue to favor whites for several decades.").
27. Chris Pope, *Why Is Social Security Regressive?*, National Affairs [American Enterprise Institute] (Winter 2022), www.nationalaffairs.com/publications/detail/why-is-social-security-regressive
28. Johnson & Smith, Exploring Structural Racism's Impact, *supra* note 4, at 3.
29. SSA, Equity Action Plan, *supra* note 23, at 3.
30. *See* Phoebe Weaver Williams, *Social Security Reform: Transformative Opportunities for African Americans*, 3 Elder's Advisor 23, 26–28 & 35 nn.68 & 70 (2001).
31. *See id.* (citing Law of Aug. 1, 1956, ch. 836, tit. 1, § 102(a), 70 Stat. 809).
32. Califano v. Webster, 430 U.S. 313, 314–16 (1977) (citations omitted).
33. *Id.* at 318 (citations omitted).
34. *Id.* (citations omitted).
35. *Id.* (citations omitted).
36. *Id.* at 316–20.
37. *See, e.g.*, Students for Fair Admissions, Inc. v. President & Fellows of Harvard Coll., 600 U.S. 181 (2023).
38. *See* Williams, *supra* note 7, at 27–28 (citing H.R. Comm. on Ways & Means, 64th Cong., Rep. of the 1979 Advisory Council on Social Security 132 (Comm. Print 1979)).
39. H.R. Comm. on Ways & Means, 64th Cong., Rep. of the 1979 Advisory Council on Social Security 126 (Comm. Print 1979).
40. *See supra* Introduction note 39 (collecting books highlighting those injuries to the Black community through numerous federal, state, and local government policies and their intergenerational consequences).
41. *See* Alfred L. Brophy, *Reconsidering Reparations*, 81 Ind. L. J. 811, 835 (2006).
42. *See* Introduction *supra*.

43. *See* Prem Thakker, *Republicans Are Bringing Back Their Plan to Gut Social Security and Medicare*, The New Republic (June 14, 2023), https://perma.cc/86X3-RHN5; *see also* Taegan Goddard, *Desantis Went Further than Paul Ryan on Social Security*, Pol. Wire, https://perma.cc/NXY8-B7D3 (noting that as a Congressman, Ron DeSantis supported Paul Ryan's "entitlement reform" plans to partially privatize Social Security and Medicare but went further and also sought to raise the full retirement age to 70); *cf.* Kijakazi et al., *supra* note 4, at 22–30 (evaluating proposals to address trust fund solvency and Social Security reform, and outlining options without disparate racial impacts); Rockeymoore & Lui, *supra* note 4, at 35–44 (same).
44. *See generally* Latoya Hill & Samantha Artiga, *What Is Driving Widening Racial Disparities in Life Expectancy?*, Kaiser Fam. Found. (May 23, 2023); https://perma.cc/TY4W-WMMX (noting that in 2021, white life expectancy was 76.4 years whereas Black life expectancy was only 70.8 years).
45. H.R. Comm. on Ways & Means, 64th Cong., Rep. of the 1979 Advisory Council on Social Security 137 (Comm. Print 1979).
46. *Id.*
47. *See* note 1 *supra* (describing the use of "bend points" to calculate the AIME and determine the PIA and social security benefits formula).
48. Johnson & Smith, Center For Retirement Research, *supra* note 9, at 3–4.
49. *Id.*
50. *Id.* at 15–16.
51. *Id.* The benefit formula modification suggested herein is admittedly modest, acknowledging the possibility that a significantly more progressive formula alteration might jeopardize public support for the program as reflecting a departure from its universal, essentially contributory, nonmeans-tested historic character and design.
52. Social Security Amendments of 1972, Pub. L. No. 92–603, § 101, 86 Stat. 1329, 1333–35; *see* Zhe Li, Cong. Research Service, R43615, *Social Security: Minimum Benefits*, Summary, 1–2 (2021) (describing the minimum benefit provision); Kelly A. Olsen & Don Hoffmeyer, *Social Security's Special Minimum Benefit*, 64 Soc. Sec. Bull. 1, 2 (No. 2, 2001) (same).
53. Li, *supra* note 52, at 2–3.
54. *Id.*
55. Social Security Administration, Annual Statistical Supplement, 2024, 5.21 tbl.5.A8 (Dec. 2024).
56. Kathryn L. Moore, *Gender Disparity in Social Security*, 32 Elder L.J. 1, 21–22 (2025).
57. Johnson, *supra* 9, at 92.
58. *See, e.g.*, Areeba Haider & Justin Schweitzer, *The Poverty Line Matters, But It Isn't Capturing Everyone It Should*, Center for American Progress (Mar. 5, 2020) (The poverty line and official government poverty statistics, "do … not reflect the economic reality of America today. The calculation doesn't take into account housing, transportation, child care, or medical costs. It doesn't consider geographical differences, even though costs of living vary significantly across the country. And it doesn't align with the lived experiences of millions of U.S. residents, especially given that 43 percent of people can't afford to pay for basic necessities, 40 percent would struggle to find $400 in an emergency, and almost one-third of respondents to a recent Center for American Progress poll said that they or a family member did not have enough money to buy food at some point in the past year."); *see also* Shawn Fremstead, *The Defining Down of Economic Deprivation: Why We Need to Reset the Poverty Line*, The Century Foundation (Sept. 30, 2020) (describing the ways in which the 1860s-era official poverty measure and the more recent supplemental poverty measure both "set the 'poverty line' much lower than what the public perceives as what

it means to be poor and lower than the poverty line of other similar economically developed countries.").

59. Johnson & Smith, Center for Retirement Research, *supra* note 9, at 4–5; *see also* The Social Security 2100 Act, H.R. 4583, 118th Cong. § 103 (2023); S. 2280, 118th Cong. § 103 (2023) (same);
60. Johnson & Smith, Center for Retirement Research, *supra* note 9, at 5.
61. *Id.* at 14–15.
62. *Id.* at 16.
63. *See* Jack A. Smalligan, *Increasing SSI Benefits Is a More Effective Approach to Reducing Poverty than an Enhanced Social Security Minimum Benefit*, BROOKINGS INSTITUTION (May 14, 2024), www.brookings.edu/articles/increasing-ssi-benefits-is-a-more-effective-approach-to-reducing-poverty-than-an-enhanced-social-security-minimum-benefit/
64. *Id.*
65. *Id.*
66. *Id.*
67. *See* Supplemental Security Income Restoration Act of 2021, H.R. 3763, S.2065 117th Cong. (2021).
68. *See* SSI Savings Penalty Elimination Act of 2025, H,R. 2450, S. 1234, 119th Cong. (2025).
69. These last two proposed modifications to the SSI program are from the Brookings paper although they have been advocated in some form in the SSI Restoration Act as well. *See* Jack A. Smalligan, *Increasing SSI Benefits Is a More Effective Approach to Reducing Poverty than an Enhanced Social Security Minimum Benefit*, BROOKINGS INSTITUTION (May 14, 2024).
70. Kathleen Romig, *Policymakers Can Expand SSI to Cut Poverty for Seniors and People with Disabilities*, CENTER FOR BUDGET AND POLICY PRIORITIES (Sept. 10, 2021); *see also* Chantel Boyens, Danielle Kwon, Elaine Maag, & Jack Smalligan, *How Four Proposals to Reform Supplemental Security Income Would Reduce Poverty*, URBAN INSTITUTE (Sept. 2021).
71. *See* Johnson, *supra* note 9, at 94; *see also* Kathleen Romig and Sam Washington, *Policymakers Should Expand and Simplify Supplemental Security Income*, CENTER FOR BUDGET AND POLICY PRIORITIES 4, Fig. 2 (May 4, 2022) (listing demographics of SSI population over age sixty-five as follows: 31 percent Latino; 19 percent African American; 18 percent other; 32 percent white).
72. *See generally* Madeline Shepherd, *Poverty in America Remained Flat in 2024 But Will Likely Rise as the One Big Beautiful Bill Act Goes into Effect*, CENTER FOR AMERICAN PROGRESS (Sept. 9, 2025) (documenting the anticipated impact from "historic cuts" to the Medicaid and SNAP programs and loss of Affordable Care Act (ACA) tax subsidies with resulting significantly increased premium costs and loss of health insurance for millions of Americans, the failure of minuscule tax cuts available to lower income persons to offset the devastating impacts of these program reductions, and concluding that "these cuts will be more likely to harm women, people age 65 and older, Black and Hispanic families, and people without a high school diploma.").
73. *See* Rebecca Vallas, *Testimony: After Decades, It's Past Time to Bring SSI into the Twenty-First Century*, THE CENTER FOR AMERICAN PROGRESS (Sept. 21, 2021) (citing *Voters Overwhelmingly Support Strengthening SSI*, DATA FOR PROGRESS AND THE CENTURY FOUNDATION, May 2021) (available at bit.ly/SSI polling).
74. *Id.*
75. *See* Moore, *supra*, note 56, at 29 and n. 218 (citing, among other sources: Patricia A. Seith, *Congressional Power to Effect Sex Equality*, 36 HARV. J. L & GENDER 1, 54–59 (2013) "(explaining how Economic Equity Act, which included Social Security caregiver

credit bills, sought to revise and reconstruct federal laws 'grounded in gendered notions of women's role in society.)'; Nancy C. Staudt, *Taxing Housework*, 84 GEO. L.J. 1571, 1573 (1996) (seeking to obliterate the 'false and gendered distinction between paid work outside the home and unpaid work inside of it' and proposing that homemakers pay tax on their imputed income and receive independent Social Security benefits upon retirement); *cf.* Naomi Cahn, [Clare Huntington & Elizabeth S. Scott], *Family Law for the One-Hundred-Year Life*, 132 YALE L.J. 1691, 1759 (2023) (endorsing proposed Social Security Caregiver Act of 2021 that would treat familial caregiving as work for purposes of Social Security)."

76. *See* Moore *supra* note 56, at *id.* (citing Seith, *supra* note 75, at 54–56); *see generally* note 9 *supra* (describing eligibility for SSA spousal and survivors benefits and racially disparate impact from lesser marriage rates, and more equal earnings among spouses in Black families).
77. Johnson & Smith, CENTER FOR RETIREMENT RESEARCH, *supra* note 9, at 7,
78. VEGHTE et al., *supra* 13, at 11.
79. *Id; see also* Tracey Gronniger, *The Intersections of Inequity in Aging*, GENERATIONS (Jan. 15, 2021), https://generations.asaging.org/intersections-inequity-aging/ (Noting that for women of color, the types of financial and economic inequities facing women generally "are amplified, with systemic racism leading to lower incomes, more precarious housing and poorer health outcomes … than white men and women" and advocating for "legislative proposals that would provide Social Security caregiver credits to people who take time out of the workforce to care for children or other relatives.").
80. VEGHTE et al., *supra* 13, at 11.
81. *Id.*
82. *See* John Jankowski, *Caregiver Credits in France, Germany, and Sweden: Lessons for the United States*, 71 SOC. SEC. BULL. 61, 65 (No. 4 2011) (caregiver credits have become a near-universal component of public pension systems in higher-income OECD [Organization for Economic Cooperation and Development] countries."); *see also* ELAINE FULTZ, PENSION CREDITING FOR CAREGIVERS: POLICIES IN FINLAND, FRANCE, GERMANY, SWEDEN, THE UNITED KINGDOM, CANADA, AND JAPAN, INSTITUTE. FOR WOMEN'S POLICY RESEARCH 1 (2011) (noting that in 2009, only four OECD countries out of thirty – the US, Turkey, Mexico, and Australia – did not provide caregiver (Pension Crediting for Caregiver, PCC) credit systems).
83. Moore, *supra* note 56, at 27.
84. *Id.* at 27–28.
85. *Id.* at 30–32.
86. Johnson & Smith, CENTER FOR RETIREMENT RESEARCH, *supra* note 9, at 6.
87. *Id.*; *see also* Mark Zandi, *Evaluating Senator Warren's Social Security Plan*, MOODY'S ANALYTICS 3 (Sept. 2019), www.economy.com/mark-zandi/documents/2019–09-19-Warren-Social-Security-Reform.pdf
88. *Id.*
89. S.1211, 118th Cong.; H.R. 3729, 118th Cong. (2023) (requiring a minimum of 80 caregiving hours to children under 12, or to relatives needing assistance for activities of daily living; offering caregiving credits for up to 60 months which is available at the maximum level (1/2 of AWI) to caregivers who earn zero wages; caregivers who work and earn less than the average national wage are also eligible but the credit is adjusted based on an income based sliding scale, decreasing as the caregiver's wages reach the average national wage.).
90. Johnson & Smith, CENTER FOR RETIREMENT RESEARCH, *supra* note 9, at 16.
91. *Id.*
92. *Id.*

93. Veghte et al., *supra* note 13, at 11.
94. *See* Adam Hofri-Winogradow & Richard L. Kaplan, *Property Transfers to Caregivers: A Comparative Analysis*, 103 Iowa L. Rev. 1997, 2018 (2018) (citing, Associated Press-NORC Center for Public Affairs Research, *Long-Term Care in America: Expectations and Preferences for Care and Caregiving* 11 (2016), www.longtermcarepoll.org/PDFs/LTC%202016/AP-NORC%20Long%C20Term%20Care_2016.pdf).
95. National Academy of Social Insurance, A Report of the Older Workers' Retirement Security Task Force, Older Workers in Physically Challenging Jobs Need Stronger Social Insurance Supports 1–9 (Sept. 2023); *see also* NASI Press Release, *Older Workers in Physically Challenging Jobs Need Stronger Social Insurance Supports* (Sept. 6, 2023).
96. *See* National Academy of Social Insurance, A Report of the Older Workers' Retirement Security Task Force, Older Workers in Physically Challenging Jobs Need Stronger Social Insurance Supports 1–9, 16–18 (Sept. 2023).
97. *Id.* at 1–2.
98. *Id.* at 11; *see also* Elvis Guzman & Nakia Gladden, *Why Raising the Retirement Age Would Hurt African Americans*, Center for Global Policy Solutions 3–4 (July 2015) (noting that African Americans retire earlier owing to higher unemployment and poorer health); Kijakazi et al., *supra* note 4, at 13.
99. NASI Task Force, *supra* note 95, at 11.
100. *Id.*
101. *Id.*
102. *Id.*
103. *Id.* at 18–19.
104. *Id.*
105. *Id.* at 2,
106. Id. at 36 (citing Christian Weller, Rebecca Vallas, & Steph Lessing, *Bridge Benefit for Older Workers*, National Academy of Social Insurance and AARP Social Security Policy Innovation Challenge (Dec. 2019)).
107. *See* NASI Task Force, *supra* note 95, at 36.
108. Weller, Vallas, & Lessing, *supra* note 106, at 2.
109. NASI Task Force, *supra* note 95, at 37.
110. *Id.*
111. *See* Weller, Vallas, & Lessing, *supra* note 106, at 3 ("We propose to finance our new [Bridge] benefit with general revenue transfers. Specifically, we suggest changing the way the tax code incentivizes private retirement savings to both free up revenue that can pay for the new benefit and offer lower-income savers more effective savings matches."); *id.* at 7 ("We propose to fully pay for the new benefit with general revenue transfers.").
112. National Academy of Social Insurance, Social Security at 90: A Bipartisan Roadmap for the Program's Future 31 (Jan. 2025).
113. Johnson, *supra* note 9, at 67; Johnson & Smith, Exploring Structural Racism's Impact, *supra* note 4, at 31.
114. *See* Stacy Brown, *New Social Security Rules Could Leave Black Retirees Further behind*, The Washington Informer (Oct. 23, 2025).
115. *See generally* Dorothy A. Brown, Karen C. Burke, & Grayson M. P. McCouch, *Social Security Reform: Risks, Returns, and Race*, 9 Cornell J.L. & Pub. Pol'y 633 (2000) (concluding that despite specific elements of the social security system that disadvantage Black and Brown families such as by linking benefits to wages and centralizing marriage, the system's generally progressive structure and thrust is preferable to proposals to create

unknown significant risks in retirement security to such families through privatization and personal social security account proposals and lawmakers should work on improving distributional equity within the existing social security system and structure); *see also* Colleen E. Medill, *Challenging the Four "Truths" of Personal Social Security Accounts: Evidence from the World of 401(k) Plans*, 81 N.C. L. Rev. 901, 975 (2003) (concluding that under President Bush's Commission to Strengthen Social Security's proposal to introduce market privatization and personal social security accounts, there would be "winners and losers" but "the cumulative effect of the Commission's proposal is likely to be lesser total benefits for low-income and minority workers than under today's traditional Social Security system. They will be the group most likely to 'lose' under a reformed personal Social Security account system."); Kathryn L. Moore, *Partial Privatization of Social Security: Assessing Its Effects on Women, Minorities, and Lower-Income Workers*, 65 Mo. L. Rev. 341 (2000) (reaching similar conclusions). As Economics Professor and former Assistant Secretary of Labor for Policy, William Spriggs, explained:

> Privatizing the retirement program, and separating the integrated elements of Social Security, would split America. The divisions would be many: between those more likely to be disabled and those who are not; between those more likely to die before retirement and those more likely to retire; between children who get survivors' benefits and the elderly who get retirement benefits; between those who retire with high-yield investments and those who fare poorly in retirement. The "horizontal equity" of the program (treating similar people in a similar way) would be lost, as volatile stock fluctuations and the timing of retirement could greatly affect individuals' rates of return. The "vertical equity" of the program (its progressive nature, insuring a floor for benefits) would be placed in greater jeopardy with the shift from social to private benefits. Social Security works because it is "social." It is America's only universal federal program. The proposed changes would place Social Security in the same political space as the rest of America's federal programs – and African Americans have seen time and again how those politics work.

William E. Spriggs, *African Americans and Social Security – Why the Privatization Advocates are Wrong*, Dollars & Sense (Nov. 1, 2004).

116. *See* Kijakazi et al., *supra* note 4, at 26; Elizabeth Warren, *Expanding Social Security*,Medium (Sept. 12, 2019).
117. *See* Kijakazi et al., *supra* note 4, at 26.
118. Warren, *supra* note 116.
119. Josh Bivens & Elise Gould. *A Record Share of Earnings Was Not Subject to Social Security Taxes in 2021: Inequality's Undermining of Social Security Has Accelerated*, Economic Policy Institute, (Jan. 2023).
120. *See id*; *see also* S. Hrg. 118–422, Social Security Forever: Delivering Benefits and Protecting Retirement Security, Hearing Before the Committee on the Budget, United States Senate, 118th Cong, 2d Sess., pg. 68, Prepared Written Testimony of Rebecca D. Vallas, CEO of National Academy of Social Insurance (Sept. 11, 2024).
121. *See id. see also* S. HRG. 118–84, Protecting Social Security For All: Making the Wealthy Pay Their Fair Share, Hearing Before the Committee on the Budget, United States Senate, 118th Cong, 1st Sess., pg. 65, Prepared Written Testimony of Kathleen Romig, Director of Social Security and Disability Policy, Center for Budget and Policy Priorities (July 12, 2023).
122. *See* Testimony of Vallas, *supra* note 120, at id.

123. Gayle L. Reznik, Dave Shoffner, & David A. Weaver, *Coping with the Demographic Challenge: Fewer Children and Living Longer* 66 Soc Sec. Bull. 37, 37 (2005/2006); *see also* Testimony of Romig, *supra* 121 at 64.
124. Anne Marie D. Lee, *America is Hitting "Peak 65" in 2024 as Record Number of Boomers Reach Retirement Age. Here's What to Know*. CBS News (Jan. 29, 2024).
125. *See* Kathleen Romig, *Increasing Payroll Taxes Would Strengthen Social Security* 7, Center for Budget and Policy Priorities, (Sept. 27, 2016) ("Two prominent deficit-reduction committees have proposed raising the tax cap so that it covers 90 percent of all earnings and then pegging it to that level in the future. Others have proposed eliminating the tax cap altogether.").
126. *See* Vallas, *Testimony*, *supra* note 120, at 68–69.
127. Warren, *supra* note 116.
128. *Id.*
129. *See* Medicare and Social Security Fair Share Act of 2025, S. 1690, 118th Cong. (May 7, 2025).
130. *See id.*; Letter from Stephen Goss, SSA Chief Actuary to Social Security Administration, to Senator Sheldon Whitehouse and Congressman Brendan Boyle, (July 11, 2023), www.ssa.gov/oact/solvency/WhitehouseBoyle_20230711.pdf; *see also* Vallas Testimony, *supra* note 120, at 69.
131. Letter from Goss to Whitehouse and Boyle, *supra* note 130.
132. *See* Suzanne Blake, *Social Security Update: Lawmakers' New Plan Would Expand Benefits by* $2,400,Newsweek (Feb. 28, 2025);
133. *See* Letter from Steven C. Goss, SSA Chief Actuary, to Senator Bernie Sanders (on The Social Security Enhancement Act) (Feb. 13, 2023).
134. *See id.*
135. *See* National Academy of Social Insurance, Social Security at 90: A Bipartisan Roadmap for the Program's Future 24 (Jan. 2025) ("A strong majority – 68 percent of respondents – favor eliminating the cap altogether. A similar share – 65 percent of respondents – favor applying payroll taxes to all wages over $400,000. Again, strong bipartisan support emerged for both options, with 65 percent of Republicans, 73 percent of Democrats, and 63 percent of Independents supporting eliminating the tax cap altogether and 60 percent of Republicans, 73 percent of Democrats, and 57 percent of Independents supporting applying payroll taxes to earnings above $400,000.").
136. A number of proposals, such as Representative Larson's 2019 version of the Social Security 2100 Act bill (with Senators Richard Blumenthal and Chris Von Hollen), and NASI's recent bipartisan polling, propose or reflect bipartisan polling support for increasing the payroll tax rate from 6.2 percent to approximately 7.2 or 7.4 percent (total rate employee/employer from 12.4 percent to 14.4 or 14.8 percent). *See* Letter from Stephen S. Goss, SSA Chief Actuary to Representative John Larson, Senator Richard Blumenthal and Senator Chris Von Hollen, Sept. 19, 2019 analyzing the 2019 Social Security 2100 Act bill; NASI, *Social Security at 90*, *supra* note 27, at 23 (providing bipartisan positive polling on this issue). Because an across-the-board tax increase would be regressive and increase racial and economic social security inequity, it is not recommended herein. *See generally*, Pope, *Why Is Social Security Regressive?*, *supra* note 27 (describing FICA tax rate increases as ultimately regressive). Of course, if no consensus can be reached and solvency assured without the proposed tax rate increase or a similar increase, (and considering its bipartisan popularity), it may require inclusion in a package of reform proposals to avert the adoption of even more regressive actions and cuts to the program, with even deeper racially and economically inequitable impacts.
137. *See* Johnson & Smith, Center for Retirement Research, *supra* note 8, at 21–23.

3 MASS INCARCERATION AND THE RACIAL IMPACT OF CRIMINAL JUSTICE SYSTEM-INVOLVED STATUTORY RESTRICTIONS IN SOCIAL SECURITY PROGRAMS

1. Emily Widra, *States of Incarceration: The Global Context 2024*, PRISON POLICY INITIATIVE (June 2024).
2. *See* The Sentencing Project, *Report, Mass Incarceration Trends* (May 21, 2024).
3. *Id.; see also* Jessica M. Eaglin, *The Drug Court Paradigm*, 53 AM. CRIM. L. REV. 595, 600–01 (2016) (describing impact of the "War on Drugs" on the exponential increase in incarcerations between 1972 and 2010).
4. Lisa Ly, *Federal Policies and Mass Incarceration in America*, 30 POLICY PERSPECTIVES 1, 4–6 (2023); *see also* Shon Hopwood, *Clarity in Criminal Law*, 54 AM. CRIM. L. REV. 695, 706 (detailing expansion of federal criminal statutes from about 3,000 in the 1980s to 4,500 in 2008).
5. Terry-Ann Craigie, Ames Grawert, & Cameron Kimble, *Conviction, Imprisonment and Lost Earnings: How Involvement With the Criminal Justice System Deepens Inequality*, BRENNAN CENTER FOR JUSTICE 6 (Sept. 15, 2020); *see also* Don Stamen, *The Prison Paradox: More Incarceration Will Not Make Us Safer* 1–2 VERA (July 2017) (noting that incarceration rates have risen even when crime rates have declined and that "[r]esearch consistently shows that higher incarceration rates are not associated with lower violent crime rates.").
6. *See* MICHELLE ALEXANDER, THE NEW JIM CROW: MASS INCARCERATION IN THE AGE OF COLORBLINDNESS xxvi–xxvii (2D ED. 2020).
7. *See* CRAIGIE et al *supra* note 5, at 7.
8. *See* Nazgol Ghandnoosh, *One in Five: Ending Racial Inequity in Incarceration*, THE SENTENCING PROJECT (Oct. 11, 2023).
9. *See id.; see also* Nazgol Ghandnoosh, Celeste Barry, & Luke Trinka, *One in Five: Racial Disparity in Imprisonment Causes and Remedies*, THE SENTENCING PROJECT (Dec. 7, 2023).
10. Ghandnoosh, *Ending Racial Inequity in Incarceration, supra*, note 8, at 3.
11. Kyleigh Clark-Moorman & Tracy Velázquez, *Racial Disparities Persist in Many U.S. Jails: Despite Narrowed Gap in Incarceration Rates, Black People Remain Overrepresented in Jail*, PEW (May 2023).
12. Ghandnoosh, *Ending Racial Inequity in Incarceration, supra* note 8, at 3.
13. The Sentencing Project, *Mass Incarceration Trends, supra* note 2.
14. *See* Clark-Moorman & Velazquez, *supra* note 11 (citing statistics from the Jail Data Initiative).
15. *See* Becky Pettit and Carmen Gutierrez, *Mass Incarceration and Racial Inequality*, 77 AM J. ECON. SOCIO. 1153, 1158 (May 2018); *see, e.g.*, Sam McCann, *What Is Stop and Frisk? And Is It Constitutional*, VERA, (Feb. 21, 2025) ("A 2003–2023 analysis of New York City's stop-and-frisk practices found that 90 percent of people stopped by police were people of color, with Black people making up more than half of stops despite constituting less than a quarter of the population. Historically, New York Police Department (NYPD) officers have also been more likely to use force against people of color, themselves reporting use of force in at least 23 percent of stops of Black and Latinx people under the city's robust stop-and-frisk program from 2004 to 2012.").
16. Petit & Gutierrez, supra note 15, at *id.; see generally* Gregory M. Lipper, *Racial Profiling*, 38 HARV. J. ON LEGIS. 551, 562 (2001) (Citing a study indicating that police stopped African American motorists in New Jersey to a disproportionate degree and "corroborating

the claim that the state's law enforcement officials engage in racial profiling" and leading to several studies in other states and large cities, such as Maryland, New York City, Los Angeles, and Dallas, all confirming disproportionate stopping of Black motorists in those jurisdictions as well); *see also* David A. Harris, *The Stories, the Statistics, and the Law: Why "Driving While Black" Matters*, 84 MINN. L. REV. 265, 268–69 (1999) (noting that the New Jersey study which "observed almost 6,000 cars over approximately 42 randomly distributed hours, concluded that blacks and whites drove no differently; the percentages of blacks and whites violating the traffic code were virtually indistinguishable" yet "although 17.5% of the population violating the traffic code on the road [was] black, more than 72% of those stopped and searched were black. In more than 80% of the cases, the person stopped and searched was a member of some racial minority. The disparity between 17.5% black and 72% stopped includes 34.6 standard deviations." The study concluded that "[s]uch statistical significance … is literally off the charts" and "strongly support[s] the assertion that the state police targeted the community of black motorists for stop, detention, and investigation.").

17. *See* Katheryn K. Russell, *"Driving While Black": Corollary Phenomena and Collateral Consequences*, 40 B.C. L. REV. 717, 721–25 (1999) (Supplying examples of each form of "___ while Black" racial profiling); *see also* Taja-Nia Y. Henderson & Jamila Jefferson-Jones, *#LivingWhileBlack: Blackness as Nuisance*, 69 AM. U. L. REV. 863 (2020) (describing the phenomenon of "Living while Black" and of white people calling authorities to initiate police interaction with Black persons based on unfounded allegations of wrongdoing or suspicion); Chan Tov McNamarah, *White Caller Crime: Racialized Police Communication and Existing While Black*, 24 MICH. J. RACE & L. 335 (2019) (describing the same problem as one of "existing while Black" and also framing the practice as "a systematic phenomenon" of "racialized police communication.").
18. *See* Russell, *supra* note 17, at *id.* (noting that these forms of racial profiling "increase … the probability that Blacks will be targeted for arrest. This in turn increases the probability that Blacks will be convicted and incarcerated for crimes."). For discussion and documentation of racial profiling in Latino/a communities *see* Anthony Mucchetti, *Driving While Brown: A Proposal for Ending Racial Profiling in Emerging Latino Communities*, 8 HARV. LATINO L. REV. 1 (2005) (noting particularly disproportionate rates of police stops of Latinos/as in communities with emerging large Latino/a populations); Kevin R. Johnson, *The Case for African American and Latina/o Cooperation in Challenging Racial Profiling, in Law Enforcement*, 55 FLA. L. REV. 341 (2003) (describing similarities and commonalities in racial profiling of African Americans and Latinos/as).
19. *See* Ghandnoosh, Barry, & Tripka *supra* note 9, at 5–24; *see also* Wendy Sawyer, *Visualizing the Racial Disparities in Mass Incarceration*, PRISON POLICY INITIATIVE (July 27, 2020) (finding that "racial inequality is evident in every stage of the criminal justice system" and supplying statistical charts to highlight a series of system disparities fueling racialized mass incarceration).
20. Carrie Johnson, *The Vast Majority of Criminal Cases End in Plea Bargains, a New Report Finds*, NPR, (Feb. 22, 2023) ("In any given year, 98% of criminal cases in the federal courts end with a plea bargain – a practice that prizes efficiency over fairness and innocence, according to a new report from the American Bar Association … The deals also exacerbate racial inequality, with Black defendants more often subject to prosecutors' stacking of multiple charges in drug and gun cases. Altogether, defendants face stiffer punishments for going to trial – known as a trial penalty – that can add seven to nine years or more to their sentence. But most stark in the report is research that cites innocent defendants who agree to falsely plead guilty, sometimes on the advice of their own lawyers.") (referencing AMERICAN BAR ASSOCIATION, REPORT OF THE ABA PLEA BARGAIN TASK FORCE (2023)).

21. Lindsey DEVERS, PLEAS AND CHARGE BARGAINING RESEARCH SUMMARY, United States Department of Justice, Bureau of Justice Assistance, 3 (2011).
22. *See* Ghandnoosh, Barry, & Tripka, *supra* note 9, at *id.*; Sawyer, *supra* note 19, at *id.*
23. *See, e.g.*, SELECTIVE ENFORCEMENT: RACIALLY DISPARATE POLICING OF LOW-LEVEL OFFENSES IN NEW JERSEY, A REPORT OF THE AMERICAN CIVIL LIBERTIES UNION OF NEW JERSEY (DEC. 2015).
24. Stephanie Hunter McMahon, *Inmates May Work, But Don't Tell Social Security*, 72 S. CAR. L. REV. 757, 757 (2021).
25. Craigie, et al., *supra* note 5, at 19; *see also* Lucius Couloute & Daniel Kopf, *OUT OF PRISON & OUT OF WORK: UNEMPLOYMENT AMONG FORMERLY INCARCERATED PEOPLE*, Prison Policy (July 2018), www.prisonpolicy.org/reports/outofwork.html (noting that in 2018, the unemployment rate for formerly incarcerated persons was nearly five times higher than the general US unemployment rate at a rate of 27.3 percent in comparison with 5.2 percent for the general population; that employers discriminate against people with criminal records and "having a record reduces employer callback rates by 50%"; and formerly incarcerated Black men (35.2 percent) and Black women (43.6 percent) face substantially higher unemployment rates in comparison to formerly incarcerated white women (23.2 percent) and white men (18.4 percent) and even when they are able to find work, the jobs are often unsecure and low-paying positions).
26. *Id.* at 773.
27. *Id.* at 760.
28. In the means-tested SSI program, Congress has precluded payment of benefits to persons confined to penal and other public institutions since the program's enactment in 1972. *See* 42 U.S.C.§ 1382(e)(1)(A). The fully means-tested SSI subsistence benefits program raises different policy considerations and rationale for exclusion based on the provision of subsistence in the public institution, as opposed to the contributory, earnings-based nature of the social security insurance programs. Those differences are discussed later.
29. *See* Social Security Act Amendments, Pub. L. No. 96-473, 94 Stat. 2263, 2265 (1980); Social Security Amendments of 1983, Pub. L. No. 98-21, § 339(a) 97 Stat. 65, 133–34, (1983). In contrast to the hearings and approximately 100-page report of hearing proceedings and materials on the 1980 law analyzed later, there were no hearings on the 1983 law extending the benefits suspensions to incarcerations of old age/retirement and survivor program recipients. *See* John B. Mitchell, *Suspending Prisoners' Social Security Benefits: Yet Another Blow to Financially Vulnerable African American and Hispanic Families*, 20 SEATTLE J. SOC. JUST. 109, 116 and n.31 (2021).
30. *See id.*
31. *See* "The Ticket to Work and Work Incentives Improvement Act," effective April 1, 2000. Pub. L. No. 106-170, § 402, 113 Stat. 1860, 1907-09 (1999) (codified as amended at 42 U.S.C. § 402(x)). There is also scant legislative history behind the 1999 amendment beyond a House Report, describing a desire to provide monetary incentives to state and local correctional institutions to improve reporting and information sharing between the SSA and correctional institutions on as many inmates as possible who are potentially subject to the benefits exclusion provision as soon as possible, and to maximize savings from extending the OASDI exclusion to inmates convicted of a wider range of crimes. *See* H.R. Rept. No. 106-220, 106 th Cong. 1st Sess. 23-24 (July 1, 1999). In 2009, Congress passed the "No Social Security Benefits for Prisoners Act of 2009," Pub. L. No. 111-115, §§ 1-2 (2009) (codified at 42 U.S.C. § 404(a)(1)(B); 42 U.S.C. §1383(b)), filling the asserted "glitch" or "loophole" in §402(x) to explicitly prohibit retroactive payments that might have accumulated before or during the period of incarceration (or owing to fleeing felon restrictions

in another provision discussed later), in the OASDI and SSI programs. The legislative history of this 2009 provision reflects a focus primarily on court decisions narrowing the scope of subsequent laws excluding SSI and then OASDI benefits from fleeing felons and persons in violation of parole or probation conditions, and only referencing the extension of this law to the exclusion of retroactive benefits under the incarceration exclusion provision as simply another cost savings measure. *See* 155 Cong. Rec. H13596-97, 111th Cong. 1st Sess. (Dec, 8, 2009).

32. *See* 42 U.S.C. § 402(x). The incarceration benefits exclusion provision contains a narrow regulatory exception solely for incarcerated social security disability beneficiaries who are satisfactorily participating in a vocational rehabilitation program provided two additional stringent conditions are met: (1) A court of law has specifically approved the program; and (2) the SSA Commissioner has determined that the program is expected to result in the individual being able to do substantial gainful activity upon release and within a reasonable time. *See* 20 C.F.R. § 404.468(d). This provision and these conditions have proven extremely difficult to meet. *See, e.g.*, Social Security Ruling 87-2a (The "vocational rehabilitation exception" requires persuasive "evidence to show that the claimant had actively and satisfactorily participated in a rehabilitation program which had been approved for him by a court of law and which could be expected to result in the claimant being able to engage in substantial gainful activity upon his release from prison and within a reasonable time.").
33. *See* Social Security Act Amendments, Pub. L. No. 96-473, 94 Stat. 2263, 2265 (1980).
34. 42 U.S.C. § 423 (d)(6)(B) provides a temporary preclusion in the disability evaluation process of considering impairments arising in connection with an individual's confinement in a jail, prison, or other penal institution or correctional facility pursuant to such individual's conviction of an offense (committed after Oct. 19, 1980) constituting a felony under applicable law, or which is aggravated in connection with such a confinement (but only to the extent so aggravated) but limited only to "benefits payable for any month during which such individual is so confined." Since SSDI benefits are already more broadly suspended for periods of incarceration pursuant to § 402(x), it is unclear what additional purposes are currently served through suspension under § 423 (d)(6)(B). Other significant system-involved benefit provisions include: 42 U.S.C. §§ 1382(e)(4)(A), and 402(x)(1)(A)(iv)-(v) (rendering ineligible for SSI (after 1996) or OASDI benefits (after 2004) anyone who is: (1) "fleeing to avoid prosecution" for a felony; (2) "fleeing to avoid … custody or confinement after conviction" for a felony; or (3) "violating a condition of probation or parole" for any offense. Much class action litigation has limited the scope of these provisions. In 2009, in the settlement of the *Martinez v. Astrue* class action, SSA agreed to limit the felony warrants triggering a benefits suspension to only three felonies involving active fleeing: "escape from custody," "flight to avoid prosecution or confinement," and "flight-escape." *See* Social Security Admin., *Notice of Final Settlement in the Martinez Court Case*, (Eff. Apr. 1, 2009), www.ssa.gov/martinezsettlement/. SSA has also posted a notice following a final relief order – after the Second Circuit held that "the Social Security Administration's practice of treating a warrant alleging that a recipient is violating a condition of probation or parole (PPV) as sufficient and irrebuttable evidence that the recipient is in fact violating a condition of probation or parole (PPV) is inconsistent with the plain meaning of the Social Security Act," – enjoining SSA from suspending benefits solely based on the warrant allegation of a PPV. Social Security Admin., *Notice of Final Relief Order in Clark Court Case, Clark Relief Order*, www.ssa.gov/clark_relief_order/ (citing Clark v. Astrue, 602 F.3d 140 (2d Cir. 2010)).
35. 20 C.F.R. § 404.1506 (c)(2); *see also* Social Security Ruling 83–21, *Title II: Person Convicted of a Felony*, at *2 (same).

36. 363 U.S. 603 (1960).
37. *Id.* at 610; *see also id.* at 628 (Black, J., dissenting) ("A basic constitutional infirmity of this Act, in my judgment, is that it is a part of a pattern of laws all of which violate the First Amendment out of fear that this country is in grave danger if it lets a handful of Communist fanatics or some other extremist group make their arguments and discuss their ideas."); *see generally*, Karen Tani, *Flemming v. Nestor: Anticommunism, the Welfare State, and the Making of "New Property,"* 26 L. & HIST. REV. 379 (2008) (describing the influence of the "red scare," Cold War, McCarthyite period on this decision and the decision's impact on social welfare law more broadly). Indeed, the first discussion of adding potential provisions to the Social Security Act, stripping incarcerated persons of their benefits, occurred in the 1950s when authorities disclosed that an official of the Communist Party convicted under the Smith Act for being an official of an organization alleged to be devoted to pursuing subversive activities was receiving Social Security old age/retirement benefits while incarcerated. CONG. STAFF REPORT. 96-63, SOCIAL SECURITY BENEFITS FOR PRISONERS, BEFORE THE HOUSE COMMITTEE ON WAYS AND MEANS, SUBCOMMITTEE ON SOCIAL SECURITY, 96th CONG, 2D SESS., 2 (June 18, 1980). Legislation was then "enacted in 1956 which allowed a judge as part of the sentence, upon conviction of certain federal crimes dealing with subversion of the Government, to deny social security benefits to the individual convicted." *Id.; see* 42 U.S.C. § 402(u).
38. *Flemming v. Nestor*, 363 U.S. at 610–11 (citing and quoting 42 U.S.C. § 1304, reserving "the rights to alter, amend or repeal any provision of the Act.").
39. *Id.* at 611.
40. *Id.* at 612.
41. *Id.*
42. *Id.* at 612–13.
43. *Id.* at 613–20.
44. *See id.*
45. *See* notes 2–5 *supra* (and accompanying text).
46. *See* H.REP. 96–103, RECEIPT OF SOCIAL SECURITY BENEFITS BY PERSONS IN PENAL INSTITUTIONS, HEARING BEFORE THE HOUSE COMMITTEE ON WAYS AND MEANS, SUBCOMMITTEE ON SOCIAL SECURITY, 96th CONG, 2D SESS., 36, Testimony of SSA Associate Commissioner for Policy, Lawrence H. Thompson (June 20, 1980); *see also* David Koitz, *Social Security Benefits for Prisoners*, THE LIBRARY OF CONGRESS, CONGRESSIONAL RESEARCH SERVICE (CRS), ISSUE BRIEF NO. IB81163 1 (updated version, Aug. 4, 1983) (reiterating the absence of any limitation on benefits based solely on incarceration prior to 1980). Both SSA Associate Commissioner Thomson's testimony and the CRS report cited earlier, noted the presence of a few other criminal or subversive activities related restrictions on benefits prior to 1980 such as: 20 CFR § 404.344 (1979) (preventing persons convicted of the felonious and intentional homicide of an insured individual from receiving monthly benefits (or the lump-sum death payment) based on the earnings record of the deceased (killed) person); 42 U.S.C. § 402(u) (1956 amendment allowing a judge, as part of a sentence, to deny payment of a portion of social security benefits of any type to an individual convicted of subversive crimes against the US government (espionage, sabotage, treason, sedition, etc.) and the provision in *Flemming v. Nestor* (42 U.S.C. § 402(n)) providing for the termination of social security benefits upon the deportation of the insured worker following violation of certain provisions of the Immigration and Nationality Act). In addition, the Act has precluded benefits to undocumented immigrants since at least 1996. *See* 42 U.S.C. § 402 (y) ("unlawful aliens").

47. *See* Jonathan Wolfe, *New York Today: Son of Sam, 40 Years Later*, N.Y. TIMES (July 28, 2017).
48. *See id.*
49. *See, e.g.*, Richard Haitch, *Follow-Up on the News; Convict Benefits*, N.Y.TIMES (July 26, 1981) ("After newspaper articles had disclosed that many imprisoned criminals were receiving monthly Social Security benefits – including David Berkowitz, the so-called Son of Sam killer in New York – President Jimmy Carter last October signed into law legislation restricting the benefits. The law applied only to prisoners convicted of felonies, and it banned payment to them of one type of Social Security: disability insurance.").
50. *See, e.g.*, 125 CONG. REC. 24119-22 (SEPT. 11, 1979) ("*Cons Drawing Social Security Checks*," Statement of Representative Frank Thompson (D-NJ), enclosing in the congressional record, four 1979 articles in THE TRENTONIAN by staff writer Ed Leefeldt, titled: "*Getting Rich in Jail: Cons Drawing Social Security Checks*," "*Social Security Checks: Taxpayers 'Reward' Cons*," "*Sex Offender's Paid: Satan's Tale Nets a Check*," and "*Crafty Cons Know This: Craziness Can Pay Off*"; *see also More Prisoners Get U.S. Benefits*, N.Y. TIMES (Sept. 2, 1979); *see also* U.S. GOV'T ACCOUNTABILITY OFF., GAO/HRD-82-43, PRISONERS RECEIVING SOCIAL SECURITY AND OTHER FEDERAL RETIREMENT, DISABILITY, AND EDUCATION BENEFITS 1-2 (1982) (since the SSDI benefits were not providing for inmates' basic subsistence, which was already provided by the public through the prisons, the inmates could "buy things that many other prisoners cannot afford [and] ... accumulate savings while incarcerated. This situation drew public attention during 1979 and 1980, when prison guards and officials complained about prisoners' use of these benefits and the news media publicized examples of certain prisoner benefits. In the Social Security disability examples, usually the disability began during or after the time of the crime, and the severity of impairment appeared questionable.").
51. *See, e.g.*, H.REP. 96-103, RECEIPT OF SOCIAL SECURITY BENEFITS BY PERSONS IN PENAL INSTITUTIONS, HEARING BEFORE THE HOUSE COMMITTEE ON WAYS AND MEANS, SUBCOMMITTEE ON SOCIAL SECURITY, 96h CONG, 2D SESS., 3,8, 10–12, 14–20, 25, 48, 61, 81, 86, 93 (June 20, 1980) (Testimony of multiple witnesses).
52. *See id.* at 3 (Statement of Representative Barber B. Conable, D-NY).
53. *Id.* at 67–70 (Testimony of Sargeant Earnest P. Davis).
54. *Id.*
55. RECEIPT OF SOCIAL SECURITY BENEFITS BY PERSONS IN PENAL INSTITUTIONS, HEARING, *supra* note 51, at 8 (Testimony of Representative William G. Whitehurst, R-VA) ("it is ridiculous for someone like David R. Berkowitz, New York City's 'Son of Sam' mass murderer, to be allowed to collect several hundred dollars each month in social security benefits because of some asinine qualification procedure. For what possible reason can there be in paying an animal like this from our country's already strained social security fund? What must the families of this creature's victims think? Have our laws become so inflexible that our social security administrators must bend over backwards to make sure that another parasite is added to suck the life out of the social security host? I hope to God they are not. And I cannot help but wonder how many other mass murderers are on the rolls of social security who are shielded from public scrutiny by privacy laws.").
56. *Id.*at 10.
57. *Id.* at 61 (Testimony of James Trout).
58. The only additional reasoning supplied in support of the 1983 amendment's provision, extending the incarceration extension to the Social Security old age/retirement and survivor's programs in addition to the disability program, was a passing reference to program financing concerns. *See* Koitz, *supra* note 46, at 5. ("As part of the major legislation

designed to solve social security's financing problems, the Senate Finance Committee on March 10, 1983, recommended a provision to eliminate all benefits (including retirement and survivor benefits) to convicted felons during incarceration."). Courts evaluating challenges to the latter 1983 amendment rely on legislative history and reasons proffered for the former 1980 SSDI legislation to assess the constitutional rationality of this 1983 OASI benefit suspension extension. *See, e.g.*, Zipkin v. Heckler, 790 F.2d 16, 18–19 (2d Cir. 1986) ("In enacting section 202e (x) [applicable to all OASDI programs], Congress apparently based that legislation on the policy rationales underlying a former statute … suspending *disability* payments to incarcerated recipients … The mere fact that Congress did not expressly restate these rationales in enacting section 202(x) [in the 1983 extension of this provision to the social security retirement program] is of no moment … We thus hold that section 202(x) rationally reflects the policy that prisoners' Social Security retirement benefit payments be suspended since their substantial economic needs are already met. Any contemporaneous payment of Social Security funds in our view would be wasteful.").

59. Receipt of Social Security Benefits by Persons in Penal Institutions, Hearing, *supra* note 51, at 83 (Statement of Representative Robert W. Daniel, Jr, R-VA); *see also id.* at 84 (Statement of Representative Dave W. Evans, D-IN) ("We have spent much time since I have been in Congress discussing ways to ensure the viability of the Social Security system. We have sought methods to end the drain on SS funds and restore the confidence of those who have earned their benefits through years of honest labor. It is certainly a well-placed step to wipe out this intolerable drain on an already flagging system.").
60. *See* Mitchell, *supra* note 29, at 152–53.
61. *See id.*
62. The only suggestion of racially disparate and deleterious consequences from the bill to arise in the hearing was a passing reference in a letter in the hearing record by Charles Sullivan, the Executive Director of a nonprofit prison reform organization in Texas, Citizens United for Rehabilitation of Errants. Mr. Sullivan pointed out that "minorities (Black and Mexican American) were overrepresented in Vietnam and are now overrepresented in prison (Over 60% out of a general population of less than 30%)." Receipt of Social Security Benefits by Persons in Penal Institutions, Hearing, *supra* note 51, at 88. (Letter from Charles Sullivan, Executive Director, Citizens United for Rehabilitation of Errants).
63. Receipt of Social Security Benefits by Persons in Penal Institutions, Hearing, *supra* note 51, at 36–44 (Testimony of SSA Associate Commissioner for Policy Steven Thompson).
64. *Id.* at 43.
65. *Id.* at 36–37.
66. 424 U.S. 319, 340–43 (1976). It has often been pointed out, then and now, that the nation's wealthiest residents (such as current mega-billionaires, Elon Musk or Jeff Bezos for example), would have an unquestioned right and expectation to receive OASDI benefits. *See, e.g.*, Matt Frankel, *Do Billionaires Still Collect Social Security? The Answer Might Surprise You*, USA Today, (June 27, 2025) ("Do billionaires qualify for Social Security benefits? The short answer is yes. Under the current law, an individual's wealth or current income level has no impact on their eligibility to receive a Social Security retirement benefit. In other words, even if you have $10 billion in assets, you could qualify for Social Security as long as you meet the requirements.").
67. *See* Cong. staff Report. 96–63, Social Security Benefits For Prisoners, Before the House Committee on Ways and Means, Subcommittee on Social Security, 96h Cong, 2d Sess., 7 (June 18, 1980).

68. *See* 42 U.S.C.§ 1382(e)(1)(A) (with limited exceptions, "no person shall be an eligible individual or eligible spouse for purposes of this subchapter with respect to any month if throughout such month he is an inmate of a public institution."); *see* Levings v. Califano, 604 F.2d 591, 592–94 and n.3 (8th Cir. 1979) (construing the SSI public institution exclusion not to extend to a resident of a nursing home responsible for payment of services there and not receiving support from the home and noting that "the only example of the 'inmate' exclusion appearing in the legislative history of the SSI program states that '(n)o assistance benefits will be paid to an individual in a penal institution.' H.R. Rep. No. 92–231, 92d Cong., 1st Sess., reprinted in (1972) U.S. Code Cong. & Ad. News 4989, 5136").
69. When a wage earner is entitled to disability or retirement benefits, a dependent of the wage earner – a spouse or child – can receive up to 50 percent of the wage earner's PIA as separate dependent/auxiliary benefits from the wage earner, subject to a family maximum cumulative amount of 150–75 percent of the wage earner's PIA. *See* Frank S. Bloch & Jon C. Dubin, Social Security Law and Practice in a Nutshell 225–30 (2022).
70. *See* Receipt of Social Security Benefits by Persons in Penal Institutions, Hearing, *supra* note 51, at 38 (Testimony of SSA Associate Commissioner for Policy Steven Thompson). Although there are several state-to-state criminalization variation issues triggering varying application of the original (1980s era) incarceration benefits suspension rule in 42 U.S.C. § 420(x) in different jurisdictions, the issue of felony definition variation has been largely mooted as applied to that rule since Congress expanded the law to all crimes resulting in incarceration in 1999. *See* note *supra* and accompanying text (describing the 1999 amendment to this statute, extending OASDI benefit suspension to beneficiaries incarcerated for any crime, not just felonies/crimes with sentences greater than one year). However, the felony definition variation issue is still quite salient as applied to the rule in 42 U.S.C. § 423(d)(6)(A), precluding consideration in the SSDI evaluation process, of an impairment arising "in connection with" a felony. This statute, and its racial impact, is further analyzed later in this chapter.
71. *See* Receipt of Social Security Benefits by Persons in Penal Institutions, Hearing, *supra* note 51, at 36–44 (Testimony of SSA Associate Commissioner for Policy Steven Thompson).
72. *See* Jon C. Dubin, Social Security Disability Law and the American Labor Market 133–50 (2021). Nor had any study documented a greater prevalence of benefit fraud or attempted social security fraud in the incarcerated population. Indeed, one of the most high-profile examples of fraud and corruption in the SSDI program was committed not by incarcerated persons but by police officers who were convicted after bribing doctors to supply fraudulent medical evidence to support fake SSDI claims, and then secretly moonlighting as security guards at a strip club. *See id.* at 149–50. Nevertheless, despite the data, the accounts of medical and psychiatric treatment professionals, and unanimous position statement of the bipartisan group of SSA Commissioners, a fraud and "disability con" narrative was amplified in the first Trump administration, with an initiative instituted to review the social media accounts of disabled beneficiaries for evidence of fraud or disability faking. *See* Doron Dorfman, *Fear of the Disability Con: Perceptions of Fraud and Special Rights Discourse*, 53 Law & Soc'y Rev. 151, 1085–86 (2019) (describing the tightening of SSA disability approval process in 2017 to make it "harder to qualify for benefits or appeal rejections" that was "spurred by fear of the disability con perpetuated by massive media attention," and leading to the 2019 Trump administration SSA disability social media review initiative).

73. Cong. staff Report, 96–63, Social Security Benefits For Prisoners, Before the House Committee on Ways and Means, Subcommittee on Social Security, 96h Cong, 2d Sess., 1 (June 18, 1980).
74. *Id.*
75. Receipt of Social Security Benefits by Persons in Penal Institutions, Hearing, *supra* note 51, at 45–56 (Testimony and Statement of Stephen Ney, Director, ACLU National Prison Project).
76. *Id.* at 51–56.
77. *See* Cong. staff Report. 96-63, Social Security Benefits For Prisoners, Before the House Committee on Ways and Means, Subcommittee on Social Security, 96h Cong, 2d Sess., 9-11 (June 18, 1980); *id.* at 2-22 App. C (enclosing article: Marc Levinson, "'Pay As You Stay' or Stay Longer," *Corrections Magazine* (Dec. 1979) (describing Florida's program to make prisoners pay for portions of their prison stays enacted in 1979). Since that time, many additional states have adopted similar programs. *See* Britany L. Deitch, *Pay-to Stay Laws and Private Prisons*, 28 U. Pa. J. L. & Soc. Change 1 (2024) ("As of June 2023, forty-six states, regardless of their current or historical political party leanings, have some form of pay-to-stay law"). However, the Supreme Court has held that the Social Security Act's anti-garnishment provision in 42 U.S.C. § 407(a), essentially supersedes state laws to the contrary under the supremacy clause and preempts attempts to garnish social security benefits to pay for or reimburse prison maintenance and care expenses under these state programs. *See* Bennett v. Arkansas, 485 U.S. 395, 397 (1988) ("Section 407(a) unambiguously rules out any attempt to attach Social Security benefits … We reject the State's attempt to avoid this conclusion by arguing that the federal statute contains an 'implied exception' that would allow attachment of otherwise exempted federal payments simply because the State has provided the recipient with 'care and maintenance.'") Nevertheless, the extractive and impoverishing nature of pay-to-stay laws has a racially disparate impact on Black and Brown inmates in light of mass incarceration trends, which undermines reentry objectives and "promotes recidivism and reincarceration." Deitch, *supra* note 77, at 11–17.
78. Aaron Littman, *Free-World Law Behind Bars*, 131 Yale L.J. 1385, 1411–12 (2025) (footnotes and citations omitted); *see generally* Belinda Lee, *Note, Bolstering Benefits Behind Bars: Reevaluating Earned Income Tax Credit and Social Security Benefits Denials to Inmates*, 98 NYU L. Rev. 331, 360 (2023) ("In demarcating whether a provision should be imputed income [in tax law], we ask whether the provision is a net-benefit or a net-detriment. Employees may accept salary reductions for a net-benefit, like a penthouse apartment. Employees may demand salary increases for net-detriments, like being forced to live inside a bank building. Generally, prison living conditions and meals are subpar, and would be considered a net-detriment. The net-detriment nature invalidates justifying Social Security benefit denials to prisoners on the grounds that they already receive care.").
79. Receipt of Social Security Benefits by Persons in Penal Institutions, Hearing, *supra*, note 51, at 51. Ney's reentry concerns were amplified in a letter from the Executive Director of the American Correctional Association, Anthony P. Travisono. *See id.* at 92 ("[w]e feel very strongly that denying incarcerated offenders social security benefits would have a further deteriorating effect on our efforts to effectively utilize available resources to prepare the successful reentry of offenders back into the mainstream of society."). The importance of a financial cushion or nest egg to fall back upon to facilitate successful reentry upon release from incarceration and to avert recidivism has been echoed with greater resonance in present times as decarceration movements

have emerged and focused on compassionate release advocacy, particularly for elderly and infirm inmates likely eligible for some form of OASDI. *See, e.g.*, Lee, *supra* note 78, at 366 ("Financial instability is highly correlated with recidivism. As the number of released older inmates increases and states consider implementing compassionate release policies, it is important to consider the resources available to older inmates.").

80. *See also* Wendy Sawyer & Peter Wagner, *Mass Incarceration: The Whole Pie 2025*, PRISON POLICY INITIATIVE (Mar. 11, 2025) (documenting in 2025 that only a small percentage of the almost 2 million incarcerated individuals have been convicted of murder).
81. RECEIPT OF SOCIAL SECURITY BENEFITS BY PERSONS IN PENAL INSTITUTIONS, HEARING, *supra* note 51, at 51 (Testimony and Statement of Stephen Ney, Director, ACLU National Prison Project).
82. *Id.* at 53; 66.
83. *Id.* at 66; *cf.* Lee, *supra* note 78, at 349 (noting that "carceral status does not preclude retired government employees from receiving public pensions, which are similarly drawn out of a limited and shrinking fund pool.").
84. Hearings, *supra* note 51, at 52 (ACLU/Ney); *id.* at 92–95 (Statement of the Lawyers' Committee for Civil Rights Under Law).
85. *Id.* at 94 and n.2 (quoting a blackletter law annotation on bill of attainder as "any legislative act which takes away the life, liberty or property, of a particular person named or an easily ascertainable person or group of persons because the legislature thinks them guilty of conduct which deserves punishment.").
86. *See* Mitchell, *supra* note 29, at 115–17 and nn. 22–30.
87. *See, e.g.*, Jensen v. Heckler, 766 F.2d 383, 385 (8th Cir. 1985) (citing and quoting *Flemming v. Nestor* to reject due process and bill of attainder challenges to the application of the incarceration benefits suspension statute); Pace v. United States, 585 F. Supp. 399, 401 (S.D. Tex. 1984) (reaching similar conclusions in express reliance on *Flemming v. Nestor*).
88. *See, e.g.*, Belinda Lee, *Note, Bolstering Benefits Behind Bars: Reevaluating Earned Income Tax Credit and Social Security Benefits Denials to Inmates*, 98 NYU L. REV. 331 (2023); John B. Mitchell, *Suspending Prisoners' Social Security Benefits: Yet Another Blow to Financially Vulnerable African American and Hispanic Families*, 20 SEATTLE J. SOC. JUST. 109 (2021); Jennifer D. Oliva, *Son of Sam, Service-Connected Entitlements, and Disabled Veteran Prisoners*, 25 GEO. MASON L. REV. 302 (2018).
89. *See* Mitchell, *supra* note 88.
90. *See* Oliva, *supra* note 88 (Veterans Disability program); Lee, *supra* note 88 (Earned Income Tax Credit program).
91. Professor Mitchell stated:

> [I]t is now nearly forty years later (after enactment of this law), and dozens and dozens of courts have sustained the constitutionality of 42 U.S.C. § 402(x) without even a hint of a dissenting thought. No court in this land now would do otherwise than summarily deny any attempt at appealing the 1980 or 1983 amendments. So, why take the time to go through this legal analysis, even if one of the offered two grounds have never yet been raised? The answer is that this analysis is integral to the argument for repeal. § 402(x) is petty, unfair, and harmful to members of communities of color, and legislative repeal is more likely if its legal failings are initially highlighted.

Mitchell, *supra* note 29, at 117–18. I am persuaded that an additional full blown due process rational basis and/or bill of attainder analysis here would not be fruitful. While

Chapter 4 develops equal protection rational basis and heightened scrutiny arguments in analyzing the weakness of rationales supporting the statutory exclusion of the US territories from the SSI program and corresponding deficiencies in the Court's reasoning in its relative recent decision in rejecting challenges to the law in U.S. v. Vaello Madero, 596 U.S. 159 (2022), at least there, a unanimous panel of the First Circuit had held in 2020 that those proffered public policy justifications for the statutory SSI US territory exclusions were both irrational and unconstitutional. *See* United States v. Vaello-Madero, 956 F.3d 12 (1st Cir. 2020). In contrast, the many challenges to the OASDI incarceration benefits suspension provision have yet to even garner a dissent or a stray distinct court decision calling the provision's constitutionality into question. In Chapter 4, equal protection arguments are developed to further elucidate the injustice of the SSI benefits exclusion in the territories (Puerto Rico, Virgin Islands, Guam, American Samoa) and to support repeal of that statutory exclusion after also examining historical racism and white supremacy and their lingering role, through the *Insular Cases*, in the territories' separate and unequal social welfare safety nets.

92. *See* Mitchell, *supra* note 29, at 118–36.
93. *See id.* at 118–23.
94. *See Id.* at 118–36. Professor Mitchell noted that when the Supreme Court first rejected constitutional challenges to the Social Security Act of 1935, the majority's explanation of the Act's purpose through Justice Cardozo, reflected a greater focus on averting the debilitating circumstances of extreme elderly poverty during the great depression and under 1930s-era historical and social circumstances. The opinion stated:

> [There is no difference if] men are thrown out of work because there is no longer work to do, or because the disabilities of age make them incapable of doing it … The hope behind this statute is to save men and women from the rigors of the poor house, as well as from the haunting fear that such a lot awaits them when journey's end is near.

Id. at 120 (quoting Helvering v. Davis, 301 U.S. 619, 641 (1937)).

95. *See generally*, VOYA, *In 2020, about 1 in 6 People in the U.S. were Age 65 and Over; 20% Still Are Working* (Feb. 1, 2024), www.voya.com/article/2020-about-1-6-people-us-were-age-65-and-over-20-still-are-working ("According to newly released Census and Bureau of Labor Statistics data, about 20% of Americans over age 65 – a total of 10.6 million people – are either working or looking for work, representing a 57-year high."); Social Security Admin., *Receiving Benefits While Working*, www.ssa.gov/benefits/retirement/planner/whileworking.html (describing receipt of full social security retirement benefits while working if beyond one's full social security retirement age).
96. *See* Mitchell, *supra* note 29, at 123–34.
97. *See id.*
98. *See* Lee, *supra* note 88, at 352 and n.126 (citing Creasie Finney Hairston, *Prisoners and Families: Parenting Issues during Incarceration* 4–5 (Urb. Inst. "From Prison to Home" Conference Working Paper, 2002)).
99. *See* Mariam A. Hinds, *The Shadow Defendants*, 113 Geo. L.J. 823 (2025).
100. *Id.* at 827.
101. *Id.* at 859–60; *see, e.g.*, New Jersey Wealth Disparity Task Force, New Jersey – Building a State of Opportunity: A Report of the Wealth Disparity Task Force to Close Opportunity Gaps and Repair Structural Disparities 25 (Feb. 2025) ("Far too many Black and Hispanic families living in New Jersey have a relative or close friend who is incarcerated, a burden which is partially borne by family members and their communities. During the listening sessions, many individuals shared

stories about the mounting fines and fees and the onerous costs associated with communicating with an incarcerated loved one."); *id.* at 59 (detailing specific financial burdens borne by the "disproportionately Black and Hispanic women" who assume the emotional and financial support of the household of the incarcerated individuals).

102. Mitchell, *supra* note 29, at 141.
103. *See id.* at 131–32.
104. *See id.* at 141–58; *see also* Lee, *supra* note 88, at 163–72 (describing societal harm from the disparate racial impact of the OASDI and EITC incarceration exclusions).
105. Mitchell, *supra* note 29, at 157–58 (citations and footnotes omitted).
106. *See* JESSICA T. SIMES, PUNISHING PLACES: THE GEOGRAPHY OF MASS IMPRISONMENT 144 (2021) (Owing to mass incarceration, "community losses yield significant economic … costs, as large numbers of prime age men and women cannot contribute to the neighborhood or community's economic viability (let alone their own family).").
107. Alexis Karteron, *Family Separation Conditions*, 142 COLUM. L. REV. 649, 663 (2022); *see also* TODD R. CLEAR, IMPRISONING COMMUNITIES: HOW MASS INCARCERATION MAKES DISADVANTAGED NEIGHBORHOODS WORSE 64 (2007) ("Because housing in the United States is economically and racially segregated, incarceration that concentrates by socioeconomic status and race also concentrates by location. Some neighborhoods have dominant numbers of residents either on their way to prison, in prison, or recently released.").
108. *See* Karteron, *supra* note 107, at 663; Laura Bliss, *Mapping Chicago's "Million Dollar Blocks,"* BLOOMBERG (July 24, 2015) (Quantifying the costs of incarceration at over $22,000 per inmate annually and noting that "[t]he costs of incarceration are concentrated in low-income, predominantly black communities in the city").
109. *See* American Disability Action Group, *Explained Social Security Disability Payment Chart* (Nov. 21, 2025), www.americandisabilityactiongroup.com/social-security-disability-payment-chart/
110. Again, when Congress is next in a position to rationally examine the impacts of laws before adoption and can legislate for the public good consistent with principles of democracy perhaps it can address this issue. Because the SSI program is a means-tested subsistence-based program, the SSI incarceration benefits suspension law discussed in note 28 *supra* (42 U.S.C.§ 1382(e)(1)(A)) is not inconsistent with the Act's SSI-program's thrust and the same powerful arguments for repeal of the OASDI's provision in 42 U.S.C. § 402(x) do not similarly apply to the SSI provision. *See* note 67 *supra* and accompanying text (citing Congressional Staff Report). However, there are many obstacles to SSI benefit restoration upon release and substantially delayed or permanently terminated SSI benefits for disabled and elderly previous SSI recipients can produce significant and counterproductive obstacles to successful reentry. SSA can and should take steps to ensure previous SSI recipients can have benefits promptly restored upon release from incarceration, such as through automatic reentitlement (or presumptive reentitlement for a six-month or specific period of time). *See generally* COMMUNITY LEGAL SERVICES OF PHILADELPHIA, ACCESS IS EQUITY: ADDRESSING THE CRISIS IN ACCESS TO SOCIAL SECURITY DISABILITY BENEFITS 6–7 (NOV. 2022) (describing obstacles to SSI benefit reinstatement and "perpetuation of cycles of trauma, poverty and incarceration" from the inability to restore SSI benefits after release from incarceration, and suggested measures to improve prompt SSI access upon release); *see also* Jeffrey Abramovitz & T. J. von Oehsen, *The Feds Make It Too Hard for Former Inmates to Access Social Security Benefits*, PENNSYLVANIA CAPITAL-STAR (Nov. 18, 2022) ("The [SSI] application and renewal process is unnecessary difficult for people coming out

of jail and prison" and without SSI, "they may end up homeless, reincarcerated, or in worse health.").

111. Receipt of Social Security Benefits by Persons in Penal Institutions, Hearing, *supra* note 51, at 96 (Letter from Peter W. Hughes, Legislative Counsel, National Retired Teachers' Association and American Association for Retired Persons, to Hon. J.J. Pickle, Chairman, Subcommittee on Social Security. Committee on Ways and Means, June 27, 1980).
112. *Id.*
113. *Cf.* Schmidt v. Northern Life Ass'n, 112 Iowa 41, 44–45, 83 N.W. 800, 801 (1900) ("Certainly one who sets fire to his own building cannot recover the insurance thereon, and we know of no reason why the maxim, '*Nullus commodum capere potest de injuria sua propria*,' should not apply. Indeed, the unbroken voice of authority is to the effect that a beneficiary in an insurance policy who murders the insured forfeits his rights thereunder.").
114. *See* Cong. staff Report. 96–63, Social Security Benefits For Prisoners, Before the House Committee on Ways and Means, Subcommittee on Social Security, 96th Cong, 2d Sess., 9 (June 18, 1980).
115. *Id.* at 9, 18–19 and App. B.
116. *See* Adam F. v. Comm'r of Soc. Sec., 2019 WL 13201890, *4–5 (E.D. Wash. 2019); *see also* Hixson v. Colvin, 2016 U.S. Dist. LEXIS 132506, *9 (W.D. Wash. 2016) (in concurrent SSI/SSDI case, noting that the ALJ had approved the claimant's SSI but denied the SSDI application after considering his severe knee impairment for SSI purposes but excluding consideration of this impairment for SSDI purposes under the SSDI felony-related impairment rule).
117. *See* 21 U.S.C. § 861a (imposing lifetime bans on SNAP and TANF after drug felony convictions as described); *see generally* Margaret Love and Nick Sibilia, Access to SNAP and TANF Benefits After a Drug Conviction: A Survey of State Laws (Dec. 2023) (surveying states' responses to this PRWORA provision and the state option to mitigate or abrogate the lifetime SNAP/TANF drug felony bans through subsequent affirmative state legislation).
118. *See* Receipt of Social Security Benefits by Persons in Penal Institutions, Hearing, *supra* note 51, at 38 (Testimony of SSA Associate Commissioner for Policy Steven Thompson).
119. Oliva, *supra* note 88, at 320 (emphasis in original, referencing Harvey Silvergate, Three Felonies a Day: How the Feds Target the Innocent (2009) and citing L. Gordon Crovitz, *Information Age: You Commit Three Felonies a Day*, Wall St. J. A21 (Sep. 28, 2009)); *see also* Douglas Husak, *Is the Criminal Law Important?*, 1 Ohio St. J. Crim. L. 261, 268 (2003) (noting that "[it] is hard to believe that many of us have not committed countless state and federal offenses").
120. Oliva, *supra* note 88, at *id.*
121. Tennessee v. Garner, 471 U.S. 1, 14 (1985) (citations omitted); *see* Oliva, *supra* note 88, at *id.*
122. *See* Receipt of Social Security Benefits by Persons in Penal Institutions, Hearing, *supra* note 51, at 50–51 (Stephen Ney, Director, ACLU National Prison Project).
123. *See generally* Tianna Herring. *How Inflation Makes Your State's Criminal Justice System Harsher Today than It Was Yesterday*, Prison Policy Initiative (June 10, 2020) (describing the problem of increasing felonization of property crimes owing to inflation); Bill Rice, A *Reform Long Overdue: Raising Virginia's Felony Grand Larceny Threshold*, 21 Rich. Pub. Int. L. Rev. 1 (2018) (raising similar concerns).
124. *See* Herring, *supra* note 123, at *id.*; *see also* N.J.S. § 2C:20-2b (New Jersey Statutes, Title: 2C, The New Jersey Code of Criminal Justice, Chapter 20: Theft, Section

2C:20-2: Consolidation of theft and computer criminal activity offenses); Jason A. Volet, *Are Theft Crimes in New Jersey a Misdemeanor or Felony?* (July 15, 2025) www.criminallawyer-nj.com/blog/are-theft-crimes-in-new-jersey-a-misdemeanor-or-felony/

125. *See* US Inflation Calculator, www.usinflationcalculator.com/ (last accessed Dec. 31, 2025) ($200 in 1978=$994.24 today).
126. *See* Herring, *supra* note 123, at *id.*; *Felony Theft Amount by State 2025*, World Population Review, worldpopulationreview.com/state-rankings/felony-theft-amount-by-state, (last accessed Oct. 3, 2025); *see also* Ashe Huang, *Permanent Punishment: A Policy Critique of the Felony Related Impairment Rule* 12–13 (Nov. 11, 2023) (unpublished law student paper on file with author – making a version of this argument as to this rule in paper submitted in the author's Fall 2023 Social Security Disability Law seminar at NYU law School).
127. *See supra* notes 19–21 and accompanying text.
128. Access to and quality of counsel is also a factor with racially disparate consequences, and it is likely that many defense counsel are unaware of the SSDI felony-related impairment exclusion rule prior to counseling clients during plea bargaining. It is unclear whether defense attorneys have an ethical obligation to counsel defendants on the rule's application as another potentially damaging collateral consequence of a felony plea, after the Supreme Court's decision in Padilla v. Kentucky, 559 U.S. 356 (2010), holding that owing to the serious and integral nature of deportation, the Sixth Amendment right to effective assistance of counsel mandated counseling on potential deportation consequences before an immigrant defendant entered a guilty plea.
129. *See* Satterwhite v. Astrue, 886 F. Supp. 2d 809, 815–16 and n.2 (S.D. Ohio 2012).
130. *See* Ramirez v. Comm'r of Soc. Sec., 2011 U.S. Dist. LEXIS 11980, *31–34, 42–45 (D. Or. 2010), *aff'd* 463 Fed App'x 640, 642 (9th Cir. 2016). Another potential issue with defendants with psychiatric or cognitive impairments deemed "severe" by SSA (such as Ms. Ramirez in the above case, *id.* at *30), is whether their very impairments might induce greater stress and/or receptivity to an excessive or false guilty plea. *See generally*, Brian D. Johnson, Ryan D. King, & Cassia Spohn, *Sociolegal Approaches to the Study of Guilty Pleas and Prosecution*, 12 Ann. Rev. L. & Soc. Sci. 479, 481 (2016) ("for those with mental illness, the rate of false guilty pleas can exceed 40%"); Allison D. Redlich, Alicia Summers, & Steven Hoover, *Self-Reported False Confessions and False Guilty Pleas among Offenders with Mental Illness* 34 Law & Human Behavior 79, 81–82 (Feb. 2010) ("Compared to prevalence rates in the general population, persons with serious mental illness are over-represented both in the criminal justice system and in the pool of identified false confessors. A combination of psychologically manipulative police interrogation tactics, a complex legal system, and inherent vulnerabilities that typify mental disorders (e.g., proneness to confusion, lack of assertiveness) make this population at risk for miscarriages of justice, including wrongful convictions … For these same reasons, persons with serious mental illness are also likely to be at risk for FGPs [False Guilty Pleas].") (citations omitted).
131. Social Security Ruling 83-21. By regulation, Social Security Rulings (SSRs) "are binding on all components of the [SSA]. These rulings represent precedent final opinions and orders and statements of policy and interpretations that we have adopted." 20 C.F.R. §402.35(b)(1); *see* Heckler v. Edwards, 465 U.S. 870, 873 n.3 (1984).
132. *Id.*
133. Yes, lifting expensive amounts of baby formula from Walmart is apparently a thing. *See, e.g.*, Aaron Chatman, *Police: Thieves Caught Stealing 20k Worth of Baby Formula from Local Walmart*, 14 News (Mar. 23, 2024), www.14news.com/2024/03/23/police-thieves-caught-stealing-20k-worth-baby-formula-local-walmart/

134. *See generally*, Michael S. Moore, *The Metaphysics of Causal Intervention*, 88 CALIF. L. REV. 827 (2000) (analyzing the criminal and civil law of proximate cause and theories of and distinction between intervening consequential events which do or do not break the causal chain of liability in assessing liability for such events); H.L.A. HART & TONY HONORÉ, CAUSATION IN THE LAW (2D ED. 1985) (same).
135. *See* Eric A. Johnson, *Two Kinds of Coincidence: Why Courts Distinguish Dependent from Independent Intervening Causes*, 25 GEO. MASON L. REV. 77, 78 (2017) (explaining the role of the traditional distinction between dependent and independent intervening causes in the law of proximate cause, summarized as recognition that: "[a]n independent intervening cause … 'will break the chain of legal cause unless it was foreseeable[;]' [a] dependent intervening cause will not break the causal chain unless it was downright 'abnormal' or freakish.") (citations omitted); *see also* WAYNE R. LAFAVE, CRIMINAL LAW 364–653(5th ED. 2010) ("a coincidence will break the chain of legal cause unless it was foreseeable, while a response will do so only if it is abnormal (and, if abnormal, also unforeseeable.").
136. Moore, *supra* note 134, at 834 (explaining intervening causation liability example from H.L.A. HART & TONY HONORÉ, CAUSATION IN THE LAW, *supra* note 134, at 77–79).
137. *See* Kimberly A. Kaiser & Sierra Molina, *Analyzing State-Level Variation in the Felony Murder Rule Using a Systematic Statutory Content Analysis Approach*, AM. J. CRIM. JUST. (July 3, 2025), https://doi.org/10.1007/s12103-025-09817-8
138. *See id; see also* Guyora Binder, *Making the Best of Felony Murder*, 91 B.U. L. REV. 403, 404 (2011) (noting that "most jurisdictions" condition the offense at least on "negligence through a combination of culpability requirements, dangerous felony limits, foreseeable causation requirements, and complicity standards … and require felonious motive through a combination of enumerated felonies, causation standards, and merger limitations.").
139. *See id; see also* Kaiser & Molina, *supra* note 137.
140. 2019 U.S. Dist. LEXIS 124978 (S.D. Fla. 2019).
141. *Id.* at *7–8. The court noted that it was unclear if the conviction was for drug possession or possession with intent to distribute and observed that "[n]o court records of the conviction itself were cited and the Court is unaware of any such record evidence." *Id.* at *6–7.
142. *Id.* at *6–8.
143. *See id.* at *8, 10.
144. 731 F. Supp.1009, 1011 (D. Kans. 1989).
145. *Id.*
146. *See id.*
147. *Id.* at 1011.
148. *See id; see also* Huang, *supra* note 126, at 15–19 (citing the *Leach* and *Moore* case examples and arguing for a causation requirement for the felony-related impairment rule).
149. *See, e.g.*, Aboud v. Comm'r of Soc. Sec., 2021 WL 1962006, *2–3 (E.D.N.Y. 2021) (after noting the rule's inclusion of "nontraumatic impairments" and nonnecessity of a "causative relationship between the commission of the felony and the impairment," the court remanded for consideration of application of the felony-related impairment rule to a claimant's mental impairment and psychiatric symptomology arising after her felony embezzlement charge and subsequent conviction (and her job termination after the felony charge), and their connection with the impairment which "might have a dispositive impact" on the SSDI application); Iglesias v. Colvin, 2016 U.S. Dist. LEXIS 39939, *6–7 (D. Or. 2016) (affirming ALJ's application of the felony-related impairment rule and

noting "there is ample evidence in the record to support the ALJ's conclusion that even if Iglesias' mental impairments existed prior to her arrest, they were substantially aggravated by her arrest and subsequent conviction."). In the *Ramirez* case, *supra* note 130, and accompanying text, the district court asserted that the ALJ had found the claimant's aggravated mental impairment to be "in connection with the commission of the felony" and not in connection with the prosecution or "conviction of the felony." *Ramirez*, 2010 U.S. Dist LEXIS, at *44. However, the ALJ had expressly found that "the claimant's psychological condition was … exacerbated in 2002–2004 [a two-year period after commission of the felony] due to the circumstances surrounding her felony commission/conviction." *Id.* at *44–45. In affirming the district court, the Ninth Circuit found that the claimant's psychiatrically aggravated symptoms arose "days after being arrested" and then she entered a guilty plea and had "depression over the last nine months secondary to the arrest and resulting threat of job loss." *Ramirez*, 463 Fed. App'x at 642.

150. *See, e.g.*, Smith v. Kijakazi, 14 F. 4th 1108, 1114 (9th Cir. 2021) (for purpose of SSDI mental impairment evaluation, it is important to recognize that "in many mental conditions, [c]ycles of improvement and debilitating symptoms are a common occurrence."); Estrella v. Berryhill, 925 F.3d 90, 98 (2d Cir. 2019) ("a one-time snapshot of a claimant's status may not be indicative of her longitudinal mental health."). For these reasons, SSA regulations call for acquisition and the evaluation of longitudinal evidence of mental impairments and their fluctuating symptomology and severity, stating:

> 5. Need for longitudinal evidence.
>   a. *General*. Longitudinal medical evidence can help us learn how you function over time, and help us evaluate any variations in the level of your functioning. We will request longitudinal evidence of your mental disorder when your medical providers have records concerning you and your mental disorder over a period of months or perhaps years.

Section 12.00 C.5.a, 20 C.F.R., Pt 404, Appendix I (2025).

151. *See* note 149 *supra* (citing and discussing the *Aboud*, *Iglesias*, and *Ramirez* SSDI felony-related impairment rule mental impairment cases).
152. *Id.*
153. *Id.*
154. *Mapping Police Violence*, Campaign Zero (2025), https://mappingpoliceviolence.org/ (last updated July 2025); *U.S. Police Violence in 2024, Year-end Report*, Campaign Zero (2024), https://campaignzero.org/wp-content/uploads/campaign-zero-mpv-2024-fact-sheet.pdf (Feb. 2025). Despite the disproportionate rate in which African Americans are killed by the police, they are also least likely to be armed at the scene during a fatal police encounter. *See* Reed T. DeAngelis, *Systemic Racism in Police Killings: New Evidence from the Mapping Police Violence Database, 2013–2021*, 14 RACE AND JUSTICE 419, fig.2 (2024), https://journals.sagepub.com/doi/epub/10.1177/21533687211047943
155. Cato T. Laurencin & Joanne M Walker, *Racial Profiling Is a Public Health and Health Disparities Issue*, 3 (2021), https://pmc.ncbi.nlm.nih.gov/articles/PMC7231642/pdf/nihms-1582568.pdf
156. Vilissa Thompson, *Understanding the Policing of Black, Disabled Bodies*, Center for American Progress (Feb. 10, 2021), www.americanprogress.org/article/understanding-policing-black-disabled-bodies/
157. *Id.*
158. *See generally* John H. Blume & Rebecca K. Helm, *The Unexonerated: Factually Innocent Defendants Who Plead Guilty*, 100 CORNELL L. REV. 157, 185–86 (2014) ("the

current law in most jurisdictions, barring a defendant from bringing a civil action if he pleads guilty, could be modified [;] [a]llowing civil suits even if a defendant pleads guilty [and] would *discourage the practice of forcing innocent defendants to plead guilty*, or in some cases, would allow the individual to recoup some damages for the loss of liberty. If the defendant prevailed in such a suit, it would also serve to restore a person's civil rights.") (emphasis added); *see also* note 20 *supra* and accompanying text (discussing the racially disparate incidence of false guilty pleas by putatively innocent defendants).

159. Hixson v. Colvin, 2016 U.S. Dist LEXIS 132668, *5–14 (W.D. Wash. 2016).
160. Finkbeiner v. Comm'r of Soc., Sec 2015 WL 668058, *10 and n.4 (E.D. Mich. 2015).
161. *See generally* Sunita Patel, *Jumping Hurdles to Sue the Police*, 104 MINN. L. REV. 2257 (2020) (describing many of those obstacles or hurdles).
162. *See supra* notes 137–39 and accompanying text.
163. *See* Guyora Binder, *Making the Best of Felony Murder*, 91 B.U. L. REV. 403, 404 (2011).
164. *See, e.g.*, Ian P. Farrell, *Abolishing Felony Murder: An Empirical Perspective*, 62 AM. CRIM. L. REV. 25, 30–32 (2025).
165. *Id.* at 28–29 and nn.3, 4.
166. *See* Farrell, *supra* note 164, at 30.
167. *See* Guyora Binder, *Racially Disparate and Disproportionate Punishment of Felony Murder: Evidence from New York*, 110 IOWA L. REV. 1055, 1112 (2025) (noting, in study of New York convictions, that "Black people were 12.3 times as likely to be convicted of non-felony-murder second-degree murder as white people … the Black/white conviction likelihood ratio for the confirmed and identified felony murder conviction dataset was 19.7:1 … [and therefore] the Black/white disparity for felony murder convictions was 60% greater than the Black/white disparity for other forms of second-degree murder.").

4 THE EXCLUSION OF THE SUPPLEMENTAL SECURITY INCOME BENEFITS PROGRAM FROM THE PRINCIPAL US TERRITORIES AND THE RACIAL ORIGINS AND IMPLICATIONS OF AMERICAN COLONIALISM IN THE WELFARE STATE

1. *See* 42 U.S.C. § 410(h); *see* notes 60–63 *infra*.
2. The maximum SSI monthly benefit for an individual in 2026 is $994 and a beneficiary with no other income would receive the full amount, but the receipt of other countable income would usually reduce the base amount dollar for dollar. *See* Social Security Administration, *SSI federal payment amounts for 2026*; *see generally* FRANK S. BLOCH & JON C. DUBIN, SOCIAL SECURITY LAW AND PRACTICE IN A NUTSHELL, 227 (2022). There is a resource limit of only $2,000 in countable assets or savings and a claimant with excess resources is ineligible for benefits. *Id.* at 31.
3. *See* JON C. DUBIN, SOCIAL SECURITY DISABILITY LAW AND THE AMERICAN LABOR MARKET 9–10 (2021) (discussing consolidation of the Social Security Act's historic 1935 New Deal, locally administered, federal-state public assistance programs, and 1950 federal-state ATPD public assistance program into the entirely federal, uniform, and nationally administered SSI program in 1972).
4. Rebecca Vallas, *Testimony: After Decades, It's Past Time to Bring SSI into the Twenty-First Century*, THE CENTURY FOUNDATION (Sept. 21, 2021).
5. *Id.* (citing S. Rept. No. 92–1230, Social Security Amendments of 1972, Committee on Finance, U.S. Senate (Sept. 25, 1972), p. 384.
6. United States v. Vaello Madero, 596 U.S. 159, 163 (2022) (citing 42 U.S.C. §§ 1382c(a)(1)(B)(i), 1382c(e)).

7. *See id.* (citing 48 U.S.C. § 1801 (note); 90 Stat. 268).
8. The poverty rates of these territories for "all individuals" or "all people" are: American Samoa – 54.6 percent; Puerto Rico – 43.5 percent; Guam – 20.2 percent; and Virgin Islands – 18.6 percent. *See 2020: DECIA American Samoa Demographic Profile*, U.S. Census Bureau (archived Jan. 7, 2024); *2020: DECIA Guam Demographic Profile*, U.S. Census Bureau (Jan. 7, 2024); *2020 Island Areas Censuses Data on Demographic, Social, Economic and Housing Characteristics Now Available for the U.S. Virgin Islands*, U.S. Census Bureau (Oct. 20, 2022). In contrast, the national poverty rate in 2021 is 11.6 percent (not including Puerto Rico and the other territories) and the closest state to the territories in poverty rate is Mississippi at 19.6 percent. *See ACS 1-Year Estimates Data Profiles* [Puerto Rico, 2010–2022], U.S. Census Bureau, Poverty in the United States, U.S. Census Bureau (Sept. 13, 2022).
9. *See generally* Diane Haase, *Hurricane Recovery Forest and Conservation Nurseries*, U.S. Dep't of Agric. (Jan. 13, 2020) ("Hurricanes, typhoons and cyclones have caused devastating damage to nearly all of the American-Affiliated islands during the past few years. In 2017, Hurricanes Irma and Maria struck the U.S. Virgin Islands and Puerto Rico. Just a year later, Typhoons Yutu and Mangkhut hit Guam and the Northern Mariana Islands, and then in 2019, Cyclone Gita impacted American Samoa.").
10. *Policy Basics: Aid to the Aged Blind and Disabled*, Ctr. on Budget & Pol'y Priorities (Jan. 15, 2021) (Puerto Rico's "AABD benefits comprise a 'basic benefit' of up to $64 a month and a 'secondary benefit' equaling 50 percent of actual shelter costs up to $100 per month.").
11. Javier Balmaceda, *Build Back Better Permanently Extends Economic Security to Puerto Rico and Other Territories*, Ctr. on Budget & Pol'y Priorities 3 (Dec. 14, 2021).
12. Puerto Rico and American Samoa have a program called NAP (Nutrition Assistance Program), funded at lower levels, offering maximum food assistance benefits that "are roughly 60% of the monthly maximum benefits under SNAP." Andrew Hammond, *Territorial Exceptionalism and the American Welfare State*, 119 Mich. L. Rev. 1639, 1669–72 (2021).
13. Staff, A *Reckoning for "Rational" Discrimination: Rethinking Federal Welfare Benefits in the United States Occupied Islands*, 43 U. Haw. L. Rev. 265, 274–75 (2020).
14. *See* Dubin, SSDL and the American Labor Market, *supra* note 3, at 118, 129.
15. *See Policy Basics – Aid to the Aged Blind and Disabled*, *supra* note 10, at 2–3.
16. *See* Social Security Advisory Board, Supplemental Security Income and United States Territories 11–13 (June 2025).
17. *See The Population of Puerto Rico Exceeds the Population of 20 States*, P.R. Rep. (June 25, 2020). Puerto Rico's size reflects the greatest number of fully unrepresented Americans of any territory or nonstate/district. The smallest population of any state is that of Wyoming, at approximately 600,000 residents. *Id.* The smallest Congressional district in 2020 is Montana's 1st District, at 542,704 residents, and Congressional districts average 761,169 residents. *See* Cong. Rsch. Serv., Apportionment and Redistricting Process for the U.S. House of Representatives 2, 9 (2021). The remaining territories of Guam (153,836); Virgin Islands (82,146); American Samoa (49,710), and CNMI (47,329) total approximately 339,000 residents. *See* Stephen Wilson, William Koerber & Evan Brassell, *2020 Population of U.S. Island Areas Just Under 339,000*, U.S. Census Bureau (Oct. 28, 2021), The population of the unrepresented residents of the District of Columbia is 712,836. *See id.*
18. *Decennial Census: Race*, U.S. Census Bureau (2020). The 2020 census reflects a significant change in the self-identification of race by residents of Puerto Rico and a substantial decrease in those identifying as "white alone" from the 2010 and 2000

censuses. *See generally* Syra Ortiz-Blanes, *In 2000 Most Puerto Ricans Identified as White*, MIA. HERALD (Oct. 19, 2021) (attributing changed Puerto Rican residents' self-identification away from "white" designation to greater use of mixed-race or multiple race and "other" categories on the revised census, to "historical events that rocked Puerto Rico and local efforts to educate people about race and racism."). The 2020 census reflects greater consistency with mainland constructions of race, where whiteness is historically exclusive of other races. *See id.*; *see generally* NELL IRVIN PAINTER, THE HISTORY OF WHITE PEOPLE (2010) (analyzing and documenting the history of white identity in the West and US); HENRY LOUIS GATES, JR. & ANDREW S. CURRAN, WHO'S BLACK AND WHY-A HIDDEN CHAPTER FROM THE EIGHTEENTH-CENTURY INVENTION OF RACE (2022) (analyzing social construction of race and Black identity including historical "one-drop" rule in the US in which Black identity follows one drop of Black blood or any known African ancestry);F. JAMES DAVIS, WHO IS BLACK?: ONE NATION'S DEFINITION (1991)) (same). It is also consistent with some American historical constructions of race in Puerto Rico and racism which follows that construction. For example, the former Speaker of the House, Representative Joseph G. Cannon of Illinois, in opposing the 1917 legislation granting citizenship to Puerto Ricans noted as relevant to his position that the island "is populated by a mixed race. About 30 percent are pure African … [and fully] 75 to 80 percent of the population … was pure African or had an African strain in their blood." José A. Cabranes, *Citizenship and the American Empire*, 127 U. PA. L. REV. 391, 481 (1978) (quoting Remarks of Rep. Joseph G. Cannon, 53 CONG. REC. 1036 (1916)). However, there are potential equality-hindering consequences from the new census categories and 2020 census results in Puerto Rico. *See generally* TANYA KATERÍ HERNÁNDEZ, RACIAL INNOCENCE: UNMASKING LATINO ANTI-BLACK BIAS AND THE STRUGGLE FOR EQUALITY 129 (2022) (analyzing the manner in which the new census categories and dramatic drop in 2020 in the "white alone" census population in Puerto Rico, and in categorizing Latinos elsewhere, has hindered efforts to address pervasive anti-Black discrimination against Afro-Latinos by obscuring colorism and other distinctions between the treatment of predominantly European-phenotype and predominantly African-phenotype Latinos).

19. *2020: DECIA U.S. Virgin Islands Demographic Profile*, U.S. CENSUS BUREAU (2020).
20. *2020: DECIA Guam Demographic Profile*.
21. *2020: DECIA American Samoa Demographic Profile*.
22. The term "insular" as applicable to "Insular Area" (and as the descriptor for the "Insular Cases") is "the U.S. government's organizational term for jurisdictions that are not part of the fifty U.S. states or the District of Columbia. Insular areas include all of the U.S. territories and the freely associated states." Staff, *supra* note 13, at 267 n.10 (citing Off. of Insular Affs., *Definitions of Insular Area Political Organizations*, U.S. DEP'T OF THE INTERIOR).
23. Staff, *supra* note 13, at 267. The US acquired American Samoa in the Tripartite Convention of 1899 with Germany and Great Britain, and the Virgin Islands were purchased from Denmark in 1916. *See id.*; *see also* Hammond, *supra* note 12, at 1656–58. The Jones Act of 1916 promised eventual independence to the Philippines and that pledge was finally vindicated after World War II in 1946. *See* The Jones Act of 1916, ch. 416, 39 Stat. 545 (1916) (preamble); 22 U.S.C. § 1394 (recognition of Philippine independence). The Spanish-American War commenced with American fighting in Cuba and Spain also relinquished sovereignty over Cuba in the 1898 Treaty of Paris. *See* ADA FERRAR,

CUBA: AN AMERICAN HISTORY 165 (2021). Because fighting in Cuba against Spain had commenced as a revolutionary war by Cubans seeking independence from Spain, the Spanish-American War has been alternatively referenced as "the American intervention in the Cuban War for Independence." *Id.* at 157–66. It led to extended American intervention and involvement in Cuba's governance albeit without formal territorial acquisition as with the other former Spanish colonies relinquished by Spain in 1898. *See id.* at 167–81.

24. RUBIN FRANCIS WESTON, RACISM IN U.S. IMPERIALISM: THE INFLUENCE OF RACIAL ASSUMPTIONS ON AMERICAN FOREIGN POLICY, 1893–1946 15 (1972).
25. University of Puerto Rico Law School Dean Emeritus Efren Rivera Ramos has sorted the *Insular Cases* into two groupings: the nine initial such cases in 1901 and subsequent ones decided up to 1922, culminating in Balzac v. Porto Rico, 258 U.S. 298 (1922). *See* EFRÉN RIVERA RAMOS, THE LEGAL CONSTRUCTION OF IDENTITY: THE JUDICIAL AND SOCIAL LEGACY OF AMERICAN COLONIALISM IN PUERTO RICO 74–76 (2001).
26. Alejandro Agustin Ortiz & Adriel I. Cepeda Derieux, *The Most Racist Supreme Court Cases You've Probably Never Heard of*, ACLU NEWS & COMMENT (Feb. 10, 2022); *see also* Sanford Levinson, *Why the Canon Should be Expanded to Include the Insular Cases and the Saga of American Expansionism*, 17 CONST. COMMENT 241, 242–44 (2000) (confessing that even as a preeminent constitutional scholar, leading constitutional law casebook coauthor/editor, and professor of constitutional law at the University of Texas for over two decades, Levinson had not yet read the *Insular Cases*, nor had colleagues at other schools, and arguing now that they should be added to three major law school/legal community "canons").
27. Anthony M. Ciolli, *Territorial Constitutional Law*, 58 IDAHO L. REV. 206, 212 (2022).
28. *See, e.g.*, Juan Torruella, *The Insular Cases: The Establishment of a Regime of Political Apartheid*, 77 REV. JUR. U.P.R. 1, 15–24 (2008) (describing overlapping lineup of Justices and their backgrounds in *Plessy* and the 1901–04 *Insular Cases*); *see also* Hammond, *supra* note 12, at 1659–60 ("It is not a coincidence that eight of the Supreme Court justices who decided *Downes v. Bidwell*, one of the more infamous *Insular Cases*, also decided *Plessy v. Ferguson*. Indeed, the Court's racist language in *Downes* rhymes with its Jim Crow decisions when it characterizes the people of Puerto Rico as an 'alien race'").
29. Downes v. Bidwell, 182 U.S. 244, 287 (1901) ("If those possessions are inhabited by alien races, differing from us in religion, customs, laws, methods of taxation, and modes of thought, the administration of government and justice, according to Anglo-Saxon principles, may for a time be impossible.").
30. *Id.* at 306 (White, J., concurring).
31. *Id.*
32. *Id.* at 287 (holding that "the island of Porto Rico is a territory appurtenant and belonging to the United States, but not a part of the United States within the revenue clauses of the Constitution"; as such the Uniformity Clause in Article I, Section 8, Clause 1, did not apply to it and Congress could tax its goods at different rates from products in the states). Second Circuit Judge José A. Cabranes has noted that "[b]etween 1900 and 1932, Puerto Rico was officially misspelled as 'Porto Rico' – a result of the incorrect spelling of the island's name in the English version of the Treaty of Paris … It took the Puerto Ricans 32 years to persuade Congress that the island should have its rightful name restored. Congress changed the island's name to 'Puerto Rico' by joint resolution on May 17, 1932."

José A. Cabranes, *Citizenship and the American Empire*, 127 U. PA. L. REV. 391, 391 n.1 (1978) (citing Act of May 17, 1932, ch. 190, 47 Stat. 158 (1932)).

33. *See* Dorr v. U.S., 195 U.S. 138, 148 (1904) (rejecting extension of the Sixth Amendment and Article III, Section 2 rights to trial by jury in a "territory peopled by savages" since it is impracticable and the right is not "fundamental"). In Balzac v. Porto Rico, 258 U.S. 298, 310 (1922), usually identified as the last *Insular Case*, the Court held that the Jones Act of 1917, granting citizenship to Puerto Ricans, had not incorporated Puerto Rico into the US; therefore, the Sixth Amendment right to trial by jury still did not apply in unincorporated territories such as Puerto Rico based on the Court's earlier reasoning in *Dorr* and reaffirmance of assumptions that Puerto Ricans still lacked capacity or training to navigate or understand a jury system derived from an "institution of Anglo-Saxon origin").
34. De Lima v. Bidwell, 182 U.S. 1, 219 (1901) (McKenna, J., joined by Shiras and White, JJ., dissenting).
35. *Id.* ("There may be no ready test of the civilized and uncivilized, between those who are capable of self-government and those who are not, available to the judiciary or which could be applied or enforced by the judiciary. Upon what degree of civilization could civil and political rights under the Constitution be awarded by courts? The question suggests the difficulties, and how essentially the whole matter is legislative, not judicial.").
36. Cabranes, *supra* note 32, at 431–32 & nn.157–59 (quoting remarks of Sen. William B. Bate, 33 CONG. REC. 3613, 3616 (1900)).
37. Cabranes, *supra* note 32, at 432 & n.160 (quoting remarks of Sen. Chauncey M. Depew, 33 CONG. REC. 3622 (1900)).
38. Cabranes, *supra* note 32, at 462.
39. *Id.* at 481 (quoting remarks of Rep. Joseph G. Cannon, 53 CONG. REC. 1036 (1916)).
40. Cabranes, *supra* note 32, at 481 (noting recorded applause of other members of Congress in attendance).
41. Downes v. Bidwell, 182 U.S. 244, 341–42 (1901) (White, J., concurring) ("The result of what has been said is that whilst in an international sense Porto Rico was not a foreign country, since *it was … owned by the United States*, it was *foreign to the United States in a domestic sense*, because the island has not been incorporated into the United States, *but was merely appurtenant thereto as a possession*.") (emphasis added).
42. 8 U.S.C. § 1408.
43. *See, e.g.*, Dorr v. U.S., 195 U.S. 138 (1904).
44. *See* Fitisemanu v. United States, 1 F.4th 862, 865–68 (10th Cir. 2021) (rejecting applicability of the 14th Amendment Citizenship Clause to persons born in American Samoa in reliance on the *Insular Cases* and noting: "Congress has conferred American citizenship on the peoples of all other inhabited unincorporated territories – Puerto Rico, Guam, the U.S. Virgin Islands, and others – but not the people of American Samoa. American Samoans are instead designated by statute 'nationals, but not citizens, of the United States.' … [E]very extension of citizenship to inhabitants of an overseas territory has come by an act of Congress … Without such an act, no inhabitant of an overseas territory has ever been deemed an American citizen by dint of birth in that territory"), *cert. denied*, 143 S. Ct. 362 (2022); *see also* Tuaua v. United States, 788 F.3d 300, 308 n.7 (D.C. Cir. 2015), *cert. denied*, 579 U.S. 902 (2016) (same). A spirited academic and political debate has emerged around the potential for repurposing the *Insular Cases* to respect Indigenous culture, as has been asserted by American Samoan leadership and relied on by the courts in *Fitisemanu* and *Tuaua*. *Compare* Christina D. Ponsa-Kraus, *The* Insular Cases *Run Amok: Against Constitutional Exceptionalism in the Territories*, 131 YALE L. J. 2449, 2455 (2022) ("[T]he *Insular Cases* gave rise to nothing less than a crisis of political legitimacy

in the unincorporated territories, and … no amount of repurposing, no matter how well-intentioned – or even successful – can change that fact."), *with* Stanley K. Laughlin, Jr., *Cultural Preservation in Pacific Islands: Still a Good Idea – and Constitutional*, 27 U. HAW. L. REV. 331, 374 (2005) ("The genius of the [*Insular Cases' doctrine*] is that it allows the insular areas to be full-fledged parts of the United States but, at the same time, recognizes that their cultures are substantially different from those of the mainland United States and allows some latitude in constitutional interpretation for the purpose of accommodating those cultures."), *and* Rose Cuison-Villazor, *Problematizing the Protection of Culture and the Insular Cases*, 131 HARV. L. REV. F. 127 (2018) (developing a nuanced, middle-ground position). Further exploration of this issue is beyond this book's scope. However, whatever can be said in support of refashioning historically odious doctrines for the laudable purpose of respecting Indigenous culture, the same is not true for the purpose of denying equal access to important government benefits, against the wishes of the same Indigenous populations. *See House Passes BBB with Over $1 Billion in Local Hospital, Medicaid, SSI and Other Funds*, CONGRESSWOMAN AUMUA AMATA COLEMAN RADEWAGEN (Nov. 19, 2021) (American Samoa's Congressional-delegate Aumua Amata, lauding as a "historic first," proposed legislation extending SSI to the principal US territories including American Samoa "to help make ends meet" for thousands of disabled and elderly Island residents and an "important step … to equality with the states in key areas that provide help to our people.").

45. Ponsa-Kraus, *The Insular Cases Run Amok, supra* note 44, at 2455; *see also* Igartúa de la Rosa v. U.S., 417 F.3d 145, 163 (1st Cir. 2005) (Torruella, J., dissenting) (characterizing the *Insular Cases* as "anchored on theories of dubious legal or historical validity, contrived by academics interested in promoting an expansionist agenda").
46. Ponsa-Kraus, *The Insular Cases Run Amok supra* note 44, at 2452; *see also* Cabranes, *supra* note 32, at 411 ("For the first time in American history, 'in a treaty acquiring territory for the United States, there was no promise of citizenship … [nor any] promise, actual or implied, of statehood. The United States thereby acquired not "territories" but possessions or "dependencies" and became, in that sense, an "imperial" power.'" (alteration in original)) (quoting LUELLA GETTYS, THE LAW OF CITIZENSHIP IN THE UNITED STATES 144–45 (1934)).
47. Ponsa-Kraus, *The Insular Cases Run Amok, supra* note 44, at 2453.
48. Territory Clause, Article IV, Section 3, Clause 2, provides: "The Congress shall have Power to dispose of and make all needful Rules and Regulations respecting the Territory or other Property belonging to the United States; and nothing in this Constitution shall be so construed as to Prejudice any Claims of the United States, or of any particular State." The *Insular Cases* reflected a "departure from the original meaning of the Territory Clause, according to which territorial status was understood as temporary." Ponsa-Kraus, *The Insular Cases Run Amok, supra* note 44, at 2454 n.11; *see also* Cesar A. Lopez-Morales, *Making the Constitutional Case for Decolonization: Reclaiming the Original Meaning of the Territory Clause*, 53 COLUM. HUM. RTS. L. REV. 772 (2022) (documenting the clause's original intent and the impact of the *Insular Cases*' Territory Clause interpretations on unequal treatment of territory residents).
49. Ponsa-Kraus, *The Insular Cases Run Amok, supra* note 44, at 2454–55; *see also* Ciolli, *supra* note 27, at 212 (explaining that the *Insular Cases* clearly did permit Congress to draw distinctions between "incorporated" and "unincorporated" territories based on a belief that the "savage," "half-civilized," "ignorant and lawless" "alien races" inhabiting the so-called unincorporated territories warranted different treatment than white Americans in the states and the so-called incorporated territories).

50. Christina Duffy Ponsa, *When Statehood Was Autonomy*, *in* RECONSIDERING THE INSULAR CASES: THE PAST AND FUTURE OF THE AMERICAN EMPIRE 1, 2 (Gerald L. Neuman & Tomiko Brown-Nagin eds., 2015).
51. *See* WILLIAM R. MORTON, CONG. RSCH. SERV., CASH ASSISTANCE FOR THE AGED, BLIND, AND DISABLED IN PUERTO RICO 12–13 (2016).
52. *See* Emma Amador, *Women Ask Relief for Puerto Ricans: Territorial Citizenship, the Social Security Act, and Puerto Rican Communities, 1933–1939*, 13 LABOR: STUDIES IN WORKING-CLASS HISTORY OF THE AMERICAS, 105, 122 (Dec. 2016) (noting that "[t]here were numerous such reflections on Puerto Ricans as an inferior people, one that was distinct from the mainland population" and "[i]mperialism and the racialized understandings of Puerto Rican people that it engendered were crucial components of deciding how, and in what way, Puerto Rico should be treated under social policy.").
53. *Id.*
54. *Id.*
55. *Id.* at 121.
56. 79 CONG. REC. 5528, 5563 (Apr. 12, 1935) (Iglesias stated: "I request … the incorporation of Puerto Rico in the definition of the United States into this humanitarian measure through a proper amendment. Certainly, Puerto Rico, an organized Territory, whose people are citizens of the United States, is an integral part of the United States, and in all fairness and justice the people of Puerto Rico should be permitted to participate in the obligations, duties, and benefits, as well as in the obligations and responsibilities, of so far-reaching a social program."); *see also* 79 CONG. REC. 6037, 6068 (Apr. 19, 1935) (Iglesias offering an amendment to the social security bill to add Puerto Rico).
57. Amador, *supra* note 52, at 121.
58. *Id.* at 121 (quoting and citing Social Security Act Amendments of 1939, 76th Cong., 1st Sess., H.R. Rep. No. 728, Comm. on Ways and Means, June 2, 1939, Rep. to Accompany H.R. 6635, 1595–1596).
59. *Id.*
60. Pub. L. 81–734, 81st Cong., 2d Sess., 64 Stat. 477 (Aug. 28, 1950).
61. *See* Eric Katz, *Civilian Federal Buildings Are Named after Confederates, KKK Members and Segregationists, Too*, GOVERNMENT EXECUTIVE (June 22, 2020) (identifying the William Collmer Federal Building and US Courthouse in Hattiesburg, Mississippi, on a list of federal buildings named after persons with racist pasts, and noting that Congressman Colmer, in his long career in Congress, helped spearhead what became the "Southern Manifesto" imploring Southerners to resist school integration; fighting "tooth and nail" to block the passage of the Civil Rights Acts and the Voting Rights Act in the 1960s, and lamenting that the Supreme Court desegregation rulings would produce "an even increasing intermingling of negroes and whites in public places.").
62. 95 CONG. REC. 13807, 13813 (Oct. 4, 1949); *see generally* EXTENSION OF SOCIAL SECURITY TO PUERTO RICO AND THE VIRGIN ISLANDS: HEARINGS BEFORE A SUBCOMMITTEE OF THE COMMITTEE ON WAYS AND MEANS, HOUSE OF REPRESENTATIVES, 81 CONG., 1ST SESS. (Nov. 15, 16, 17 and 22nd, 1949) (containing discussion on the inclusion amendments with representative from Puerto Rico and Virgin Islands).
63. Pub. L. 86–778, § 103, 86th Cong., 2d Sess., 74 Stat. 994 (Sept. 13, 1960); *see also* William L. Mitchell, *Social Security Legislation in the Eighty-Sixth Congress*, 23 SOC. SEC. BULL. 3 (Nov. 1960) (describing 1960 amendment adding Guam and American Samoa to the OASDI program).
64. *See* Hammond, *supra* note 12, at 1675–76 (tables of safety net programs in territories); Staff, *supra* note 13, at 273 (same).

65. *See* William R. Morton, Cong. Rsch. Serv., Cash Assistance for the Aged, Blind, and Disabled in Puerto Rico 15 (2016).
66. *Id.* (citing and quoting 118 Cong. Rec. S33991 (daily ed. Oct. 5, 1972) (statement of Sen. Quentin N. Burdick and Sen. Russell B. Long)).
67. *See id.*
68. Morton, *supra* note 65, at 16 (citing and quoting 118 Cong. Rec. S33991 (daily ed. Oct. 5, 1972) (statement of Sen. Jacob K. Javits and Sen. Russell B. Long)).
69. *See Briefing on Puerto Rico Political Status by the General Accounting Office and the Congressional Research Service: Hearing before the Subcomm. On Insular & Int'l Affs. of the H. Comm. on Interior & Insular Affs.*, 101st Cong. 34 (1990) (statement of Carolyn Merck, Specialist in Social Legislation).
70. *Id.*
71. Morton, *supra* note 65, at 16–17 and n.72 (quoting 122 Cong. Rec. 6244–45 (1976) (statement of Sen. Russell B. Long)).
72. *Id.*
73. *Id.*
74. *See id.*
75. Petition for Writ of Certiorari at 19, United States v. Vaello Madero, 596 U.S. 159 (2022) (No. 20-303), 2020 WL 5441159, at *19.
76. *See, e.g.*, Aurora Kohn & Mar-Vic Cagurangan, *How the CNMI Managed to Negotiate SSI into the Covenant*, Pac. Island Times (May 5, 2022) ("Unlike Guam or Puerto Rico, the Northern Marianas directly negotiated their political status with the U.S. – during the Cold War era" and had more leverage for inclusion of some beneficial federal legislation for its residents because "[i]t was all about U.S. national defense … [and] the … islands are vital to the defense of their nation."); *see also* Zaldy Dandran, *Variations, Tinian and the Covenant*, Marianas Variety (Mar. 2, 2023) (noting that the only reason CNMI was able to have political status negotiations in the 1970s with the US was the political circumstances of the Cold War; the US, focusing on defense of the Pacific in that era, wanted another major US defense installation in the key strategic location of the CNMI island of Tinian in the Pacific. The US authorities "wanted Tinian so bad [they] could taste it."); *see generally* Howard P. Willens & Deanne C. Siemer, An Honorable Accord: The Covenant Between the Northern Mariana Islands and the United States (2002) (analyzing and detailing the CNMI covenant negotiations); *cf.* note 23 supra and accompanying text (describing the markedly different manner and time periods in which the US acquired Puerto Rico, Guam, Virgin Islands, and American Samoa as spoils of war or through purchase from former colonial European governments).
77. *See* Morton, *supra* note 65, at 17–19.
78. 435 U.S. 1 (1978).
79. *Id.* at 5.
80. *See supra* notes 28–35 and accompanying text.
81. *Torres*, 435 U.S. at 3 n.4 (further citations omitted)
82. *Id.* at 4 n.7.
83. *Id.* at 4 (quoting Jefferson v. Hackney, 406 U.S. at 546 (1972)) (emphasis added).
84. 446 U.S. 651 (1980).
85. I refer to these cases as "*Torres*" and "*Rosario,*" as opposed to their more common designations as "*Califano*" and "*Harris,*" for a few reasons: the low-income challengers are often erased in the history of these efforts, and they are the more unique and distinct parties in these cases. Additionally, using the challengers' names averts confusion with the multitude of other reported cases designated by the surnames of these cabinet secretaries, who were sued several times each day.

86. *Rosario*, 446 U.S. at 651–52.
87. *See id*. at 652.
88. *Id*. at 653.
89. *Id*. at 654.
90. *Id*. at 655.
91. *Id*. at 655–56.
92. *Id*. at 656.
93. 596 U.S. 159 (2022).
94. United States v. Vaello Madero, 956 F.3d 12, 15–16 (1st Cir. 2020).
95. *Id*. at 16.
96. *Id*. at 19–21.
97. *See id*. at 21–32.
98. *Id*. at 21–23. In its brief before the Supreme Court, the government argued that it had not really abandoned this argument; instead, it had "briefly argued" in the certiorari petition that "extending SSI benefits to Puerto Rico might discourage people from working." Brief for Petitioner at 24 n.2, United States v. Vaello Madero, 596 U.S. 159 (2022) (No. 20–303). It noted that "that proposition, however, has been disputed as an empirical matter. *See* DEP'T OF HEALTH, EDUC., & WELFARE, REPORT OF THE UNDERSECRETARY'S ADVISORY GROUP ON PUERTO RICO, GUAM AND THE VIRGIN ISLANDS 22 (1976)." *Id*. Accordingly, it recast that argument, "following the change in Administration," as the assertion that "economic conditions in Puerto Rico are more appropriately considered as a further justification for Congress's decision to respect Puerto Rico's fiscal autonomy and to leave it to the Commonwealth's legislature to determine the appropriate level of benefits for its aged, blind, and disabled residents." *Id*. However, the government failed to identify how the withdrawal of billions of dollars per year in federal support provided directly to desperately impoverished disabled children and adults, and the elderly would promote greater territorial autonomy – particularly since none of the territories sought, and most all expressly oppose, such an "autonomy without meaningful funding" approach to subsistence support for their most vulnerable residents. The SSA's Office of the Chief Actuary has estimated expenditures of $1.8 to $2.5 billion per year in the ten-year period from 2021–30, a total of $23 billion, for extending SSI to Puerto Rico, American Samoa, Guam, and the Virgin Islands. *See generally* Memorandum from Michael Stephens, Supervisory Actuary, Off. of the Chief Actuary, Soc. Sec. Admin., to Steve Goss, Chief Actuary, Off. of the Chief Actuary, Soc. Sec. Admin. (June 11, 2020). Indeed, at oral argument before the Supreme Court, Justice Sotomayor questioned how the denial of this substantial SSI funding "can be a plus with respect to the self-governance of Puerto Rico" since "it's not as if it could take this federal money, Puerto Rico, and distribute it in some other way or put this money to use in some other way because the money's going directly to the people, not to the government." *See* Transcript of Oral Argument, United States v. Vaello Madero, 596 U.S. 159 (2022) (No. 20–303), 2021 WL 6051137, at *12. The Deputy Solicitor General [Gannon] conceded in response: "That – that's true, Justice Sotomayor, with respect to the money that's coming back from the federal government to the recipients – of the program." *Id*. at *12–13.
99. *Vaello Madero*, 956 F.3d at 23–29.
100. *Id*. at 24.
101. *Id*. at 29.
102. *See* Transcript of Oral Argument, United States v. Vaello Madero, 596 U.S. 159 (2022) (No. 20–303), 2021 WL 6051137, at *11–12.

103. United States v. Vaello Madero, 596 U.S. 159, 162 (2022).
104. *Id.* at 164–65
105. *Id.* at 165.
106. *Id.*
107. Logan v. Zimmerman Brush Co., 455 U.S. 422, 439 (1982) (emphasis added) (quoting Schweiker v. Wilson, 450 U.S. 221, 234 (1981)); *see also Vaello Madero*, 596 U.S. at 194 (Sotomayor, J., dissenting) (offering similar formulation of the rational basis standard); *see* Raphael Holoszyc-Pimentel, Note, *Reconciling Rational-Basis Review: When Does Rational Basis Bite?*, 90 N.Y.U. L. Rev. 2070, 2076 n.34 (2015) (collecting eighteen cases where the Supreme Court invalidated legislative action under the rational basis standard); *see generally* Katie R. Eyer, *Protected Class Rational Basis Review*, 95 N.C. L. Rev. 975, 1053 (2017) (explaining how and why "there are reasons to believe that protected class rational basis review may once again hold real potential" in equal protection litigation on policies disparately disadvantaging racial minorities and women but not meeting an intent standard for strict or intermediate scrutiny purposes, and eluding "the ultra-deferential [rational basis] formulation that became common in the 1990s and early 2000.").
108. 397 U.S. 471 (1970). *See, e.g.*, Donald L. Beschle, *Kant's Categorical Imperative: An Unspoken Factor in Constitutional Rights Balancing*, 31 Pepp. L. Rev. 949, 949 n.4 (2004) (citing *Dandridge* as "the essence of what today is commonly referred to as the low-level rational basis test"); Comment, *O'Neil v. Baine*: *Application of Middle-Level Scrutiny to Old-Age Classifications*, 127 U. Pa. L. Rev. 798, 801 n.17 (1979) (explaining that *Dandridge* represents "low level" rational basis test).
109. Those justifications included avoiding the undermining of work incentives which would occur when large family welfare budgets without family maximum-size caps would approach minimum wage salaries and promoting equity between low-income workers and welfare recipients. *Dandridge*, 397 U.S. at 486 and n.19. Further underscoring the need for an actual, specific, at least rational connection between means and ends, even in minimal-scrutiny rational basis equal protection challenges to Congressional classifications in public benefits/social welfare programs, the Court found that a "fraud prevention" justification for a Congressional amendment removing food stamps eligibility from indigent households with unrelated household members was insufficiently rationally related to the specific restriction enacted. *See* Moreno v. U.S. Dep't of Agric., 413 U.S. 528, 535–38 (1973).
110. Natalie Gomez-Velez, *De Jure Separate and Unequal Treatment of the People of Puerto Rico and the U.S. Territories*, 91 Fordham L. Rev. 1727, 1747 (2023) ("[I]n *Vaello Madero*, the Court not only ignored the *Insular Cases*' influence on its interpretation of the Territorial Clause, but also interpreted the clause to permit a form of rational basis review so weak as to render the Equal Protection Clause meaningless as applied to the U.S. territories. Under this approach, the Court accepts whatever justification the U.S. government offers for its differential treatment of the territories as rational simply because it applies to the territories.").
111. *Logan*, 455 U.S. at 441 (citations omitted).
112. T. Alexander Aleinikoff, *Puerto Rico and the Constitution: Conundrums and Prospects*, 11 Const. Comment. 15, 22–24 (1994).
113. *See Leading Case: Fifth Amendment – Due Process Clause – Equal Protection – U.S. Territories – United States v. Vaello Madero*, 136 Harv. L. Rev. 360, 365–67 (2022) [hereinafter *Leading Case*].
114. *Vaello Madero*, 596 U.S. at 162.

115. *See Leading Case*, *supra* note 113, at 366 (noting that the *Vaello Madero* "majority considered only the territory-state distinction" and not the "islander–mainlander distinction" but "the government needed a rational basis for both distinctions to prevail").
116. *Vaello Madero*, 596 U.S. at 196 (Sotomayor, J., dissenting) (citation omitted); *see also* Carolyn Fergus-Callahan, *United States v. Vaello-Madero: A "Shameful" Failure to Protect Needy American Citizens Living in the U.S. Territories*, 100 DENV. L. REV. F. 1, 33–34 & nn.260–63 (2023) (noting that 57 percent of SSI recipients report no income and pay no federal taxes and that for SSI recipients that do report income, the average amounts are so low that "the vast majority of SSI recipients would not meet even the standard deduction" and have "little, if any, tax liability.").
117. *See Leading Case*, *supra* note 113, at 368.
118. *See* Hammond, *supra* note 12, at 1683; *supra* note 5 (citing SSI legislative history explaining need to supply assistance to persons lacking OASDI contributory insurance); *cf.* Zobel v. Williams, 457 U.S. 55, 63 (1982) ("Appellants' reasoning would … permit the State to apportion all benefits and services according to the past tax [or intangible] contributions of its citizens. *The Equal Protection Clause prohibits such an apportionment of state services*." (emphasis added by the Court in *Zobel* quoting *Shapiro v. Thompson*, 394 U.S. 618, 632–33 (1969)); *see also* United States v. Vaello Madero, 956 F.3d 12, 26 n.20 (1st Cir. 2020) (applying rational basis test and explaining that "the Court in Zobel invalidated a government scheme distributing monetary benefits which were based on the length of residency in the state, rejecting as impermissible the state's argument that the scheme was justified by 'past contributions' to the state" (quoting *Zobel*, 457 U.S. at 60–61, 63)); *see also id.* ("[T]he relationship between residence and contribution to the State [is] so vague and insupportable, that it amounts to little more than a restatement of the criterion for the discrimination it purports to justify. (Brennan, J., concurring) (citing *Zobel*, 457 U.S. at 71)).
119. Hammond, *supra* note 12, at 1683.
120. *Vaello Madero*, 596 U.S. at 195 (Sotomayor, J., dissenting).
121. *Id.* at 196.
122. *Id.*
123. *Id.* at 165.
124. Arthur MacEwan and J. Tomas Hexner, *Puerto Rico: Quantifying Federal Expenditures* 3–4 (Ctr. for Glob. Dev. & Sustainability, Working Paper No. 2016–10, 2016).
125. *Id.* at 2.
126. *Vaello Madero*, 596 U.S. 196–97 and n.5 (Sotomayor, J., dissenting).
127. *Id.* at 165–66.
128. LUIS FUENTES-ROHWER & GUY-URIEL CHARLES, AM. CONST. SOC'Y, ISSUE BRIEF, THE US CONSTITUTION MEETS DEMOCRATIC THEORY: THE PUZZLING CASES OF PUERTO RICO AND D.C. 14 (2020) (quoting Nelson A. Denis, *Taxing Puerto Rico to Death*, ORLANDO SENTINEL (Jan. 10, 2018)); *but cf. id.* (noting that "D.C. residents pay more federal taxes per capita than any other state and it's not even close" and reaffirming the "colonial-era phrase, no taxation without representation" in commenting on the lack of political representation for Puerto Rico and the District of Colombia).
129. *Id.* at 14.
130. United States v. Vaello Madero, 956 F.3d 12, 25 (1st Cir. 2020).
131. FUENTES-ROHWER & CHARLES *supra* note 128, at 14.
132. *Id.* at 15.
133. *Id.* at 15.
134. The "fruit of the poisonous tree" doctrine "anchors the Fourth Amendment's exclusionary rule, which generally requires that evidence (the fruit) acquired from a

Fourth Amendment violation (the poisonous tree) is inadmissible at trial. *See* Wong Sun v. United States, 371 U.S. 471, 503 (1963)." Devon W. Carbado and Russell K. Robinson, SFFA: Bakke's *Chickens Coming Home to Roost*, 113 CALIF. L. REV.1031, 1049 and n.83 (2025) (suggesting by analogy to that doctrine that Justice Powell erred in the *Bakke* decision by not recognizing that racism operates as "a 'poisonous tree' from which the 'fruit' of Black inequality grows."); *see, e.g.*, Joseph E. Sung, *Redressing The Legal Stigmatization of American Samoans*, 89 S. CAL. L. REV. 1309, 1328-29 (2016) (arguing that "just because the Court embraced and developed an incorrectly decided precedent in the past [through the Insular Cases and the mistreatment of territorial residents] does not make the 'fruits of the poisonous tree' [of that discredited precedent] any less poisonous.").

135. *See* Igartúa-de la Rosa v. United States, 417 F.3d 145 (1st Cir. 2005) (en banc).
136. *See generally* Mario L. Barnes & Erwin Chemerinsky, *The Once and Future Equal Protection Doctrine?*, 43 CONN. L. REV. 1059, 1077–80 (2011) (analyzing strict, intermediate, and rational basis levels of equal protection scrutiny as "essentially balancing tests – each test determin[ing] how the weights on the scale are to be arranged"); Kenji Yoshino, *The New Equal Protection*, 124 HARV. L. REV. 747, 755–63 (2011) (examining categories generating heightened equal protection scrutiny and various tiers of review and suggesting that "with respect to federal equal protection jurisprudence, this canon has closed"); Holoszyc-Pimentel, supra note 107, at *passim* (exploring application of heightened level of scrutiny falling outside defined tiers, identified as "rational basis with bite").
137. *See* Graham v. Richardson, 403 U.S. 365, 372 (1971).
138. *See* Clark v. Jeter, 486 U.S. 456, 461 (1988).
139. *See* United States v. Windsor, 577 U.S. 744, 754 (2013); *see generally* Russell K. Robinson, *Unequal Protection*, 68 STAN. L. REV. 151 (2016) (analyzing how the Court has applied heightened equal protection scrutiny to address discrimination directed against LGBTQ individuals and couples).
140. *See* Plyler v. Doe, 457 U.S. 202, 217& n.17 (1982).
141. Igartúa v. Trump, 868 F.3d 24, 25–26 (1st Cir. 2017) (Torruella, J, dissenting from denial of rehearing en banc); *see also* Fergus-Callahan, *supra* note 116, at 21–29 (arguing for strict equal protection scrutiny of territorial residency classifications based on history of unequal treatment and political powerlessness); Adriel I. Cepeda Derieux, Note, *A Most Insular Minority: Reconsidering Judicial Deference to Unequal Treatment in Light of Puerto Rico's Political Process Failure*, 110 COLUM. L. REV. 797, 827–39 (2010) (developing argument for heightened equal protection scrutiny of Congressional actions toward Puerto Rico based on political process theory stemming from *Carolene Products*' footnote 4 and JOHN HART ELY, DEMOCRACY AND DISTRUST: A THEORY OF JUDICIAL REVIEW (1980)).
142. *See* Ponsa-Kraus, *The Insular Cases Run Amok, supra* note 44, at 2533–36 (characterizing Vaello Madero's brief as raising these points in similar terms and as justifying strict equal protection scrutiny).
143. San Antonio Indep. Sch. Dist. v. Rodriguez, 411 U.S. 1, 28 (1973) (describing criteria for "strict" equal protection scrutiny based on classifications directed to suspect classes and noting "the traditional indicia of suspectness: the class is … subjected to such a history of purposeful unequal treatment, or relegated to such a position of political powerlessness as to command extraordinary protection from the majoritarian political process").
144. *See generally* Barnes & Chemerinsky, *supra* note 136, at 1077–80 (describing scrutiny standards and their origins); *see also* United States v. Virginia, 518 U.S. 515, 533 (1996) (noting that on heightened, intermediate equal protection scrutiny of legislation,

"[t]he justification must be genuine, not hypothesized or invented *post hoc* in response to litigation … [a]nd it must not rely on overbroad generalizations").

145. *See Plyler*, 457 U.S. at 220–24 ("[U]ndocumented status is not irrelevant to any proper legislative goal. Nor is undocumented status an absolutely immutable characteristic since it is the product of conscious, indeed unlawful, action.").
146. *Id.* at 224–25.
147. Ponsa-Kraus, *The Insular Cases Run Amok*, *supra* note 44, at 2536.
148. *See* Transcript of Oral Argument at 5–8, United States v. Vaello Madero, 596 U.S. 159 (2021) (No. 20–303), 2021 WL 6051137 (The DSG [Gannon] noted that "the balance of federal benefits and burdens … apply in the territory differently than they do in the states. And so, if Vermont had a different relationship with the federal government on the one side, then it might be easier for the federal government to alter it on the other side. And in this instance, it doesn't"). As a factual matter, the tax/benefit scorecard actually appears even more generous for Vermont than Puerto Rico. In 2015, Puerto Rico sent $3,524,557 in combined federal taxes to the federal government and received $1,314 per person in federal funds in return in 2016; Vermont sent $4,495,280 in taxes but received a substantially greater $8,965 per person in Federal funds in 2016. *See Puerto Rico Lags in Federal Funding*, P.R. Rep. (Aug. 16, 2017); *see also* MacEwan & Hexner, *supra* note 124, at 4 (noting that Puerto Rico was nineteenth and Vermont was twelfth among the fifty states and DC (and Puerto Rico), and therefore Vermont received a more favorable federal expenditure/tax balance in "net federal transfers per capita" in 2010 than Puerto Rico).
149. The *Vaello Madero* majority expressly reserved the question of whether Congress possesses the same power to selectively exclude states from various otherwise national federal benefit programs based on this tax/benefit scorecard rationale, noting that "Congress has not done so, and that question is not presented in this case." *See Vaello Madero*, 596 U.S. at 166 n.1. In so doing, the Court rendered ambiguous and unresolved the question of whether a different and lesser (second-class) form of watered-down equal protection rational basis doctrine applied to the territories and not the states by virtue of the Territory Clause's presence.
150. *See* Gomez-Velez, *supra* note 110, at 1739; Derieux, *supra* note 141, at 827–39.
151. *See* Ponsa-Kraus, *The Insular Cases Run Amok*, *supra* note 44, at 2536.
152. *See* Susan R. Schmeiser, *Changing the Immutable*, 41 Conn. L. Rev. 1495, 1507–12 (2009) (describing immutability as a factor contributing to criteria triggering heightened equal protection scrutiny).
153. *See* Derieux, *supra* note 141, at 838–39.
154. *Vaello Madero*, 596 US. at 180–87 (Gorsuch, J., concurring).
155. *Id.* at 189.
156. *Id.*
157. *See* Cari Alonso-Yoder, Response, *United States v. Vaello Madero and the Insulation of the Insular Cases*, Geo. Wash. L. Rev. on the Docket (May 24, 2022).
158. *Vaello Madero*, 596 U.S. at 166.
159. Balmaceda, *supra* note 11, at 1.
160. *See* Connor O'Brien, *Manchin and Sinema 'Sabotaged' Biden's Plans, Sanders Says*, Politico (May 15, 2022).
161. *See Congress Leaves Disability Community Priorities Out of Inflation Reduction Act*, Autistic Self Advocacy Network (Aug. 12, 2022) ("It also does not provide fixes to SSI and Medicaid for people with disabilities living in US territories like Puerto Rico. Once again, the policies that our community needs most urgently were left on

the cutting room floor."). It is unclear why SSI territorial inclusion was deleted in the transition from the Build Back Better Act (BBB) legislation to the Inflation Reduction Act beyond the general insistence of Senators Manchin and Sinema to substantially reduce BBB's total price tag. The original BBB had a $3.5 trillion projected cost and Senator Manchin eventually indicated that he would not support a bill with a total cost greater than $1.5 trillion. *See* Lindsey McPherson, *How Build Back Better Started and How It's Going: A Timeline*, ROLLCALL (Jul. 21, 2022). He also expressed concerns about the BBB's energy provisions, suggesting that "the bill will also risk the reliability of our electric grid," "increase our dependence on foreign supply chains," and try to facilitate a transition to clean energy and emission reduction "at a rate that is faster than technology or the markets allow [which] will have catastrophic consequences for the American people like … in both Texas and California in the last two years." Press release, Joe Manchin, US Senate, Statement on Build Back Better (Dec. 18, 2021). Senator Sinema strongly opposed BBB's reliance on increasing taxes on the wealthy to pay for its spending provisions. *See* Alex Shephard, *Kyrsten Sinema's Joe Manchin Moment*, THE NEW REPUBLIC (July 28, 2022). Neither Senator voiced public opposition to the BBB's SSI territorial inclusion provision; nor is there any other accessible public opposition or public reasoning for this provision's omission from the IRA.

162. *See generally* Jim Wallis, AMERICA'S ORIGINAL SIN: RACISM, WHITE PRIVILEGE, AND THE BRIDGE TO A NEW AMERICA (2017) (describing origins and nature of America's original sin of racism).
163. *See supra* Ch.1.1 notes 14–16 and accompanying text (discussing lynching and poll taxes); *see also supra* Ch. 1.3 notes 103–104 and accompanying text (discussing implications of Black political disenfranchisement during the new deal).
164. Admittedly, this measure as a stand-alone bill would likely not pass the now-Republican-majority House as presently constituted.

5 RACE, HEALTH CARE INEQUITY, AND MEDICAL AND ADJUDICATIVE BIAS, PARTICULARLY IN EVALUATION OF PAIN AND SYMPTOMOLOGY, IN THE SOCIAL SECURITY DISABILITY PROGRAMS

1. U.S. GEN. ACCOUNTING OFFICE, GAO/HRD-92-56, SOCIAL SECURITY: RACIAL DIFFERENCE IN DISABILITY DECISIONS WARRANTS FURTHER INVESTIGATION (1992).
2. LINDA MILLS, A PENCHANT FOR PREJUDICE: UNRAVELING BIAS IN JUDICIAL DECISIONMAKING 53 (1999).
3. Stephen Labaton, *Benefits Are Refused More Often to Disabled Blacks, Study Finds*, N.Y. TIMES (MAY 11, 1992).
4. GAO, SOCIAL SECURITY: RACIAL DIFFERENCE IN DISABILITY DECISIONS, *supra* note 1, at 5.
5. As discussed *supra* note 5 in chapter two and *infra* in this chapter, studies using Black and white identified names (i.e., Lakisha and Jamal vs. Emily and Greg) have produced racially disparate outcomes in employment tests even without in-person contact by employers with the applicants. In addition, medical records reviewed at the initial levels as part of the "paper" files sometimes include racial identifiers, particularly if the medical source utilizes or received racially normed or race corrected medical assessments and measures, as described below in chapter six.

6. GAO, Social Security: Racial Difference in Disability Decisions, *supra* note 1, at 5.
7. *Id.*
8. *Id.*
9. *See* United States General Accounting Office, Social Security: Racial Difference in Disability Decisions, Statement of Lawrence H. Thompson, SSA Assistant Comptroller General, Human Resources Division, Before the Subcommittee on the Oversight of Government Management, Committee on Government Affairs, U.S. Senate, pp. 7–9, tbls 2, 3 (Sept. 22, 1992).
10. Labaton, *supra* note 3.
11. Paul R. Verkuil, Daniel J. Gifford, Charles H. Koch, Richard J. Pierce and Jeffrey S. Lubbers, ACUS Report for Recommendation 92–7, Vol. II, The Federal Administrative Judiciary 863, 882 (1992).
12. *Id.* at 882; *see also* Elaine Golin, Note, *Solving the Problem of Gender and Racial Bias in Administrative Adjudication*, 95 Colum. L. Rev. 1532, 1533 (1995) ("The administrative judiciary is particularly susceptible to being perceived as biased as it is overwhelmingly male (94.59% in 1990) and white (94.32%)."). Current statistics on the racial composition of the federal ALJ corps generally and the SSA ALJ corps more specifically, are not publicly available. In my own anecdotal observations over a thirty-five-year period from 1990 through the present (2025), in which I have supervised law school clinical education programs providing free social security disability representation in Newark, New Jersey (twenty-six years) and San Antonio, Texas (nine years) and represented several hundred mostly Black and Latino/a claimants in SSA hearing offices in those majority minority cities at administrative hearings in that period, we have only conducted one such hearing before an African American ALJ.
13. Peter L. Strauss, Tood D. Rakoffand Cynthia R. Farina, Gellhorn and Byse's Administrative Law: Cases and Comments 375, n.1 (10th Ed. 2002).
14. *See* Kathleen Romig, *Trump Administration Action against Social Security Judges Threatens Fair Access to Benefits*, Center on Budget and Policy Priorities (Mar. 14, 2025).
15. GAO, Social Security: Racial Difference in Disability Decisions, *supra* note 1, at 5.
16. Daniel L. Skoler, *Fighting Racial Bias: How One Federal Agency Confronted the Problem*, 21 Hum. Rts. 18, 19–21 (Winter 1994).
17. *Id.* at 21.
18. Mills, Penchant for Prejudice, *supra* note 2, at 3.
19. *Id.*
20. *Id.* at 55–16, 153.
21. *See id.*
22. *See* United States General Accounting Office, SSA Decision Making: Additional Measures Would Enhance the Agency's Ability to Determine Whether Racial Bias Exists 3 (Sept. 2002).
23. *Id.* at 3–4.
24. *Id.*
25. *Id.* at 3.
26. *Id.* at 18.
27. *Id.* at 18.
28. United States General Accounting Office, SSA Disability Decision Making, Additional Steps Needed to Ensure Accuracy and Fairness of Decisions at the Hearings Level, 13–14 (Nov. 2003). This GAO report also found

that the "differences by race persisted after controlling for nonattorney representatives" such as paralegals, lay representatives, counselors, friends or family. *Id.* at 15–16 and n.32.

29. *Id.* at 14–15. Professor Mills's own study of fully adjudicated SSA disability cases from review of sixty-seven case transcripts, found that in nine cases where claimants were unrepresented in her sample, seven of them were African American (77.77%) and one was Latino. MILLS, A PENCHANT FOR PREJUDICE, *supra* note 3, at 75–76.
30. *Id.* at 14.
31. *Id.* at 23–24.
32. Patricia P. Martin, *Why Researchers Now Rely on Surveys for Race Data on OASDI and SSI Programs: A Comparison of Four Major Surveys*, SOCIAL SECURITY ADMINISTRATION, OFFICE OF RETIREMENT AND DISABILITY POLICY, OFFICE OF RESEARCH, EVALUATION AND STATISTICS, RESEARCH AND STATISTICS, Note No. 2016–01, 1 (Jan. 2016).
33. *See* Consortium for Citizens with Disabilities, Letter to Andrew Saul, Commissioner of Social Security Administration (Oct. 1, 2020).
34. *See id.*
35. *See* Executive Order 13985, 86 Fed. Reg. 7009 (Jan. 20, 2021); Executive Order 14091, Further Advancing Racial Equity and Support for Underserved Communities, 88 Fed. Reg. 10825 (Feb. 16, 2023).
36. SOCIAL SECURITY ADMINISTRATION, 2023 EQUITY ACTION PLAN UPDATE 20–21(Feb. 14, 2024); *see also* SOCIAL SECURITY ADMINISTRATION (SSA), EQUITY ACTION PLAN IN AGREEMENT WITH EO 13985 2 (Feb. 10, 2022) (Identifying race/ethnic SSA data deficiencies for several decades, the manner in which they impede monitoring to ensure equitable treatment of claimants of color, and commitment to increase race/ethnic data collection).
37. *See* ABT ASSOCIATES, AN INVESTIGATION ON BIAS IN THE QUICK DISABILITY DETERMINATIONS MODEL, FINAL REPORT 5 (AUG. 8, 2023); *see* SSA EQUITY ACTION PLAN, *supra* note 36, at 15 and n.31 (2022) (recommending a research study to assess potential bias by DDS adjudicators under contract with SSA in the QDD process).
38. Social Security Administration, Quick Disability Determinations (QDD), www.ssa.gov/disabilityresearch/qdd.htm. SSA identified 7.1% of all initial disability applications for QDD consideration in 2020. *See* Sika Koudou and Jethro Dely, *Research and Statistics Note No. 2022–02, Quick Disability Determination Cases: Descriptive Statistics for Fiscal Years 2015–2020*, SOCIAL SECURITY ADMINISTRATION 4 (Sept. 2022).
39. ABT ASSOCIATES, *supra* note 37, at 8–9.
40. *Id.* at 12.
41. *Id.* at 11; *see also id.* at 14–15 ("Options for SSA Follow-Up").
42. *See* Executive Order 14151, Ending Radical and Wasteful DEI Programs and Preferences, 90 Fed. Reg. 8339 (Jan. 28, 2025) ("Pursuant to Executive Order 13985 and follow-on orders, nearly every Federal agency and entity submitted "Equity Action Plans" to detail the ways that they have furthered DEIs infiltration of the Federal Government. The public release of these plans demonstrated immense public waste and shameful discrimination. That ends today.").
43. SSA, EQUITY ACTION PLAN (2022), *supra* note 36, at 3 (emphasis added).
44. 42 U.S.C. § § 423 (d)(1)(A) (SSDI); 1383c(a)(3)(A) (SSID).
45. 42 U.S.C. § § 423 (d)(2)(A) (SSDI); 1383c(a)(3)(B) (SSID).
46. 42 U.S.C. § 423(d)(5)(A) (SSDI); *see* 42 U.S.C.§ 1382c(a)(3)(D) (SSID) ("a physical or mental impairment is an impairment that results from anatomical, physiological, or psychological abnormalities which are demonstrable by medically acceptable clinical and laboratory diagnostic techniques.").
47. Bowen v. Yuckert, 482 U.S. 137, 140–42 (1987) (citations omitted).

48. *Id.* at 146, n.5. The SSA utilizes a similar but distinct sequential process for children's SSI disability claims which does not assess the fourth and fifth adult steps on functional ability to adjust to past relevant work or significant other work in the labor market, but whether the child has an impairment which meets or is medically or functionally equivalent to a step-3 listing, utilizing child-specific criteria for assessing functional equivalence. *See* Frank S. Bloch & Jon C. Dubin, Social Security Law and Practice in a Nutshell, 90–96 (2022).
49. A 1996 SSR that used the term "credibility" in reference to pain and symptom evaluation has been replaced with a 2016 SSR deleting reference to "credibility" and utilizing the term "supportability" of pain and symptoms. *Compare* Social Security Ruling 96–7p, with Social Security Ruling 16–3p, 81 Fed. Reg. 14166 (Mar. 28, 2016). The ostensible purpose of this change in language was to signal that the pain and symptom assessment was not one grounded in extraneous assessments of "character" but focused on the factors relevant to symptom supportability. *See* SSR 16-3p. The change in terminology has not appeared to have meaningfully changed the manner of ALJ assessment of pain and symptoms beyond a substitution of the word "credibility" with some version of "supportability" in the SSA decisional boilerplate templates utilized in ALJ decisions. *See* Carolyn A. Kubitschek and Jon C. Dubin, Social Security Disability Law and Procedure in Federal Court § 6:28 (2025 ed.) (analyzing cases utilizing SSA's decisional templates for evaluating credibility or supportability of pain and symptomology both before and after adoption of SSR 16-3p).
50. Social Security Ruling 16-3p; *see* 20 C.F.R. §§404,1529(c)(3) (SSDI); 416.929(c)(3) (SSID).
51. Jon C. Dubin, *Why* Carr v. *Saul Should Signal the End of Common Law Issue Exhaustion in Inquisitorial Proceedings*, 29 Geo. Mason L. Rev. 627, 638 (2022).
52. *Id.*
53. *Id.*
54. Jerry L. Mashaw, *Unemployment Compensation: Continuity, Change, and the Prospects for Reform*, 29 U. Mich. J.L. Reform 1, 16 (1996).
55. Salling v. Bowen, 641 F. Supp. 1046, 1053 (W.D. Va. 1986); *see also* Carr v. Saul, 593 U.S. 83, 90–91 (2021) ("[I]t is the ALJ's duty to investigate the facts and develop the arguments both for and against granting benefits." (quoting Sims v. Apfel, 530 U.S. 103, 111 (2000) (plurality opinion))); Rausch v. Gardner, 267 F. Supp. 4, 6 (E.D. Wis. 1967) (describing the SSA hearing judge, 3-hat, multiple-role, model).
56. Dubin, *End of Issue Exhaustion, supra* note 51, at 643, n.86; *id.* at 643–44 ("A total of 295,916 claimants lacked attorney representation at their ALJ hearings in fiscal year 2018"); *id.* at 671, n.207 (noting that in the same fiscal year, "82,496 claimants were represented by non-attorneys.").
57. *Sims*, 530 U.S. at 111.
58. Bernard Schwartz, Administrative Law § 5.29, at 285 (3d ed. 1991).
59. *See* Heckler v. Campbell, 461 U.S. 458, 471 (1983) (Brennan, J., concurring) ("[T]here is a 'basic obligation' on the ALJ in these nonadversarial proceedings to develop a full and fair record." (quoting Broz v. Schweiker, 677 F.2d 1351, 1364 (11th Cir. 1982))); *see also Campbell*, 461 U.S. at 471 n.1 ("The 'duty of inquiry' derives from claimants' basic statutory and constitutional right to due process in the adjudication of their claims").
60. *See generally* Carolyn A. Kubitschek and Jon C. Dubin, Social Security Disability Law and Procedure in Federal Court §§ 6:8-6:9 (2025 ed.) (collecting cases and analyzing the ALJ's duty to develop the record).
61. *See* 20 C.F.R. §§ 404.1519, 416.919 (2025); Kubitschek & Dubin, *supra* note 60, at § 6.12 (identifying circumstances when ALJs should or must procure consultative evaluations of claimants).

62. *See* KUBITSCHEK & DUBIN, *supra* note 60, at §§ 3:90, 3:92, 3:94 (identifying circumstances when ALJs must produce vocational expert hearing testimony).
63. *See* Social Security Ruling 24-3p, 89 Fed. Reg. 97158 (Dec. 6, 2024; eff. date Jan. 6, 2025).
64. Social Security Ruling 18-01p, 83 Fed. Reg. 49,613 (Oct. 2, 2018).
65. *See* 42 U.S.C. §§ 423(d)(5)(B), 1382c(a)(3)(H)(i); 20 C.F.R. §§ 404.1512(b), 416.912(b) (2025); *How We Collect and Consider Evidence of Disability*, 77 Fed. Reg. 10,651, 10,651-57 (Feb. 23, 2012).
66. *See* KUBITSCHEK & DUBIN, *supra* note 60, at § 6.7 (collecting and analyzing cases on ALJs' affirmative duties regarding proper, nondiscouraging, notice of availability of free representation); *see also* HALLEX I-2-1-80(B) (SSA's subregulatory guidance on notice duties regarding representation).
67. *See Carr v. Saul*, 593 U.S. at 96 (Thomas, J., concurring in part and concurring in the judgment) ("ALJs can raise new issues *sua sponte*" (citing 20 C.F.R. §§ 404.944, 404.946)).
68. *See* Social Security Ruling 16-3p, 82 Fed. Reg. 49462 (Oct. 25, 2017); KUBITSCHEK & DUBIN, *supra* note 60, at § 6:32 (collecting and analyzing cases on this issue).
69. *See* Social Security Ruling 18-3p, 83 Fed. Reg. 49616 (Oct. 29, 2018) (supplying guidance on the disqualification from eligibility for failing to comply with prescribed treatment without good cause); KUBITSCHEK & DUBIN, *supra* note 60, at § 2:5 (collecting and analyzing cases on this issue).
70. *See* 42 U.S.C. §§ 423(d)(2)(C); 1382c(a)(3)(J).
71. Social Security Ruling 13-2p, 78 Fed. Reg. 11939 (Feb. 20, 2013); *see generally* Max Selver, *Note, Disability Benefits and Addiction: Resolving an Uncertain Burden*, 91 N.Y.U. L. REV. 954 (2016) (discussing proof burdens in disability benefit cases involving decoupling substance abuse disorders from other potentially disabling impairments in dual-diagnosed, co-morbidity cases under the Social Security Act's amendments and regulations).
72. Matthews v. Eldridge, 424 U.S. 319, 343-44 (1976).
73. *See* JON C. DUBIN, SOCIAL SECURITY DISABILITY LAW AND THE AMERICAN LABOR MARKET, 2 (2021). For discussion of the somewhat different disability standards for children, lacking consideration of ability to work in the labor market, *see* note 48 *supra*.
74. Social Security Act Amendments of 1967, Pub. L. No. 90-248, 81 Stat. 821 (1967) (codified at 42 U.S.C. § 423(d)(2)(A) (2006)).
75. DUBIN, SSDL AND THE AMERICAN LABOR MARKET, *supra*, note 73, at 3.
76. *See, e.g.*, DUBIN, SSDL AND THE AMERICAN LABOR MARKET, *supra* note 60, at *passim*; KUBITSCHEK & DUBIN, *supra* note 60, at Ch. 3 (collecting and analyzing cases on vocational factors and labor market assessments in social security disability program federal court decisions); Kevin Liebkemann, *Job Incidence Numbers in Social Security Disability Claims: A Case Study and Analysis*, 44 J. NAT'L ASS'N ADMIN. L. JUDICIARY 15 (2024). The disability program labor market job incidence questions alone have caused much uncertainty and expressions of inconsistency and indeterminacy, even among Supreme Court Justices with widely divergent judicial perspectives. *See* Biestek v. Berryhill, 587 U.S. 97, 111 (2019) (Opinion of Gorsuch, joined by Ginsburg, JJ., dissenting) ("As part of your application for disability benefits, you've proven that you suffer from serious health problems and can't return to your old construction job. Like many cases, yours turns on whether a significant number of other jobs remain that someone of your age, education, and experience, and with your physical limitations, could perform. When it comes to that question, the Social Security Administration bears the burden of proof. To meet its burden in your case, the agency chooses to rest on the testimony of a vocational expert the agency hired as an independent contractor. The expert asserts there are 120,000 "sorter" and 240,000 "bench assembler" jobs nationwide that you could perform even with your disabilities. Where did these numbers come from?").

77. *See, e.g.*, Liebkemann, *supra* note 76, at 26–32; Brief *Amici Curiae* of the National Organization of Social Security Claimant Representatives, AARP and the AARP Foundation in support of the Petitioner in Biestek v. Berryhill, 17-1184, at 4–12 (Sept. 4, 2018); Andrew T. Palestini, *Jobs Which Exist in Significant Numbers – How Many, How Far from Home?*, 4 O.H.A.L.J. 7 (1994).
78. DUBIN, SSDL AND THE AMERICAN LABOR MARKET, *supra* note 73, at 4 and 170, n.15 (using "the term 'social obligation to work,' mindful that there are elements in society in a wealth or leisure class who elude comparable scrutiny as socially non-functional, undignified or non-productive when not employed). *See*, e.g., Ezra Klein, *Mitt Romney Flashback: Stay-at-Home Moms Need to Learn the Dignity of Work*, WASHINGTON POST (Apr. 15, 2012) (Discussing contradiction in then-Presidential candidate Mitt Romney's assertion that low-income mothers need to leave the home and child care duties and assume mandatory employment obligations in the labor market to have 'the dignity of work,' while defending his wife Ann from charges she had 'not worked [a] day in her life' because serving as a stay-at-home mom and caring for the Romney children was real 'work' and should be viewed as such.)."
79. *See* Jerry Mashaw, *The Supreme Court's Due Process Calculus for Administrative Adjudication in Mathews v. Eldridge: Three Factors in Search of a Value*, 44 U. CHI. L. REV. 28, 45 (1976) Thus, the notion that a person might be quite disabled, but still capable of doing some things for which others will pay, is not inconsistent with the Act's conception or recognition of a normative justification for an exemption from the social obligation of work. *See* Lance Liebman, *The Definition of Disability in Social Security and Supplemental Security Income: Drawing the Bounds of Social Welfare Estates*, 89 HARV. L. REV. 833, 852 (1976) ("[V]irtually every disabled person can do something for which another person will pay. He is 'totally' disabled because the market value of his labor, given such alternatives as machines and healthy persons, is so low."); EDWARD D. BERKOWITZ, DISABLED POLICY: AMERICA'S PROGRAMS FOR THE HANDICAPPED: A TWENTIETH CENTURY FUND REPORT 100 (1989) (noting that, while a person who suffered "loss of his arms and legs, his eye and his hearing, [...] might have his trunk conveyed to a busy street corner and make a little money by selling such small objects as post cards, candy or cigars," Congress would not require as much under the SSA's disability standard); Smith v. Califano, 637 F.2d 968, 971 (3d Cir. 1981) ("[S]tatutory disability does not mean that a claimant must be a quadriplegic or an amputee. Similarly, shopping for the necessities of life is not a negation of disability and even two sporadic occurrences such as hunting might indicate merely that the claimant was partially functional on two days. Disability does not mean that a claimant must vegetate in a dark room excluded from all forms of human and social activity."); Butler v. Flemming, 288 F.2d 591, 594 (5th Cir. 1961) ("I do not interpret the Act to apply only to the totally helpless and bedridden nor to those at death's door.").
80. DUBIN, SSDL AND THE AMERICAN LABOR MARKET, *supra* note 73, at 165.
81. The courts have recognized that at a certain, albeit difficult to quantify point, it is reasonable for society to excuse workers from enduring further pain, suffering or substantial discomfort in the job market. In a series of early cases shortly after the Act's passage, courts rejected Judge Learned Hand's "now famous aphorism" in a case under the War Risk Insurance Act, that "[a] man may have to endure discomfort or pain and not be totally disabled; much of the best work of life goes on under such disabilities.'" Page v. Celebrezze, 311 F.2d 757, 762 (5th Cir. 1963) (quoting Theberge v. United States, 87 F.2d 697, 698 (2d Cir. 1937)). In *Page*, the Fifth Circuit observed that the notion that pain must be endured, that pain, no matter how severe or overpowering, is not disabling unless it will "substantially aggravate" a condition, is "contrary to the standard announced in" cases from this

and other Circuits since "the purpose of much social security legislation" including this Act, "is to ameliorate some of these rigors that life imposes." *Id.*; *see generally* Jon C. Dubin, *Poverty, Pain and Precedent: The Fifth Circuit's Social Security Jurisprudence*, 25 St. Mary's L.J. 81, 112–16 (1993) (analyzing judicial and regulatory history and treatment of pain in SSA disability programs).

82. Based on 2014 data, 31% of DI beneficiaries had mental impairments (4.1% cognitive; 26.9% psychiatric and other mental impairment) and 57.4% of adult SSI beneficiaries (18.8% cognitive; 38.6% psychiatric and other mental impairments), see *Social Security Advisory Board, Disability Chartbook* Ch.6, Chart 2 (Jan. 24, 2017), www.ssab.gov/research/disability-chartbook/
83. *See generally* Commission on the Evaluation of Pain, U.S. Dep't Of Health & Human Servs., Report 79 (1986) (The proper evaluation of pain is an issue in as many as half of the social security disability cases pending before the federal courts).
84. National Academy of Sciences, Institute of Medicine, Pain and Disability: Clinical, Behavioral and Public Policy Perspectives 11 (Marian Osterweis et al. eds., 1987). *See generally* David B. Morris, The Culture of Pain 21 (1991) (lamenting that "despite our high-tech laboratories and surgical innovations, pain remains one of the most perplexing mysteries of our time"); Elaine Scarry, The Body in Pain 6–7 (1985) ("If the only external sign of the felt experience of pain (for which there is no alteration of the blood count, no shadow on the X-ray, no pattern on the CAT scan) is the patient's verbal report (however itself inadequate), then to bypass the voice is to bypass the bodily event, to bypass the patient, to bypass the person in pain."); Deborah Stone, The Disabled State 134 (1984) ("Pain, fatigue, shortness of breath – and one might add, anxiety – are real and very powerful subjective phenomena, but they defy measurement.").
85. Jones v. Secretary, Health and Human Servs., 945 F.2d 1365, 1369 (6th Cir.1991); *see* Bunnell v. Sullivan, 947 F.2d 341, 347 (9th Cir.1991) (*en banc*) ("We cannot conclude Congress intended to require medical evidence to fully corroborate the severity of pain while aware of the inability of medical science to provide such evidence.").
86. Shelley C. v. Com'r of Soc.Sec., 61 F.4th 341, 361 (4th Cir. 2023) (emphasis in original).
87. *Id.* (emphasis in original and citations omitted).
88. *See* Mills, Penchant for Prejudice, *supra* note 2, at 53 ("because the clinical evidence on which the system relies is highly flexible and standards for applying that evidence are imprecisely defined, the system may, in this way, implicitly encourage decision makers to inject their personal views (and hence their biases) into the disability decision-making process."). Indeed, at least one ALJ has openly extolled the desirability for even greater "flexibility and quasi-judicial discretion for ALJs to determine if disability is really warranted in a particular case" by eliminating the regulations that dictate decisional outcomes in certain situations such as the medical-vocational "grid" regulations. *See* John M. Meisburg, Jr., *Ten Ways to Improve the Social Security Law and Save Billions of Dollars*, 47 Fed. Lawyer 38, 40 (2000).
89. *Accord.* Maytal Gilboa, *The Color of Pain: Racial Bias in Pain and Suffering Damages*, 56 Ga. L. Rev. 651, 685 (2022) ("the ambiguous nature of pain and suffering damages … can easily conceal the effects of implicit racial bias."); *id.* at 655 (racial discrepancies in pain and suffering damages in civil tort judgments, "are the result of implicit racial bias hiding in the shadows of the ambiguous assessment of pain and suffering losses."); *see also* Shawn Trabanino, *Health Law, and Ethnicity: The Disability Administrative Law Judge and Health Disparities for Disadvantaged Populations*, 108 Cal. L. Rev. 2079, 2092 (2020) ("ALJs are tasked to use their ample discretion to assess the credibility and deceitfulness of a claimant, which inherently involves some human bias.").

90. *See* Administrative Conference of the United States, Evaluating Subjective Symptoms in Disability Cases 48 (Mar. 12, 2015); *see also id.* at 30 (noting that 17 of the 81 sample bias referrals provided to ACUS from SSA involved allegations of bias "related to subjective symptom evaluation."). For an example of some of the many ways ALJs can use their somewhat invisible duties and discretionary determinations to produce biased decisions, including through the assessment of credibility or supportability of pain and symptomology, *see* Small v. Sullivan, 820 F. Supp. 1098, 1108 (S.D.Ill.1992) (certified class action challenging alleged biased decisions by ALJ "through the use of various procedural devices designed to insure denials in a large percentage of cases ...[including] adverse credibility determinations against claimants, their doctors, and their witnesses; failing to consider, or misstating the medical evidence; engaging in *ex parte* communications with doctors; questioning claimants in a leading manner; drawing impermissible medical conclusions based upon application of the discredited "sit and spin" test; and failing to fulfill his obligation to assist unrepresented claimants in developing the facts.").
91. *See* Henry Louis Gates, Jr. & Andrew S. Curran, Who's Black and Why-A Hidden Chapter from the Eighteenth-Century Invention of Race (2022) (analyzing the social construction of race and Black identity including historical "one-drop" rule in the US in which Black identity follows one drop of Black blood or any known African ancestry);F. James Davis, Who is Black?: One Nation's Definition (1991)) (same); *see also* Nell Irvin Painter, The History of White People (2010) (history of white identity in the West and U.S).
92. Dorothy Roberts, Fatal Invention, How Science, Politics and Big Business Re-Create Race in the Twenty-First Century, 4 (2011).
93. *Id.*
94. Roberts, Fatal Invention, *supra* note 92, at 50–51 (quoting US president Bill Clinton's statement after release of the Human Genome Project's map and report).
95. *Id.* at 51.
96. *See* Carl Ximmer, *White? Black? A Murky Distinction Grows Murkier*, N.Y. Times (Dec. 24, 2014) (noting study from scientists at "23 & Me" found Black Americans on average with 73.6% African ancestry and of the remaining 26.4%: approximately 24% European and 1% Native American).
97. *See* David Marchese, *Henry Louis Gates, Jr. on What Really Happened at Obama's "Beer Summit,"* N.Y. Times (Feb 7, 2020).
98. *See* Vivian Manning-Schafel, *Henry Louis Gates, Jr., Talks Finding His Roots*, Shondaland (Jan. 2, 2024) (49% European; 49% Sub-Saharan African; 2% Native American).
99. *See* Miriam R. Hill & Volker Thomas, *Strategies for Racial Identity Development: Narratives of Black and White Women in Interracial Partner Relationships*, 49 Fam. Rel. 193 (2000) ("[R]ace is not a typology of concrete, mutually exclusive categories. We can best understand it within a social constructionist framework as the negotiated interaction between a societal phenomenon of categorization based on physical markers ... and a personal phenomenon of identity development."); Audrey Smedley, *"Race" and the Construction of Human Identity*, 100 Am. Anth. 690, 690 (1998) ("Scholars in a variety of disciplines are increasingly holding that 'race' is a cultural invention, that it bears no intrinsic relationship to actual human physical variations, but reflects social meanings imposed upon these variations.")
100. *See* Devon W. Carbado, *Critical What What?* 43 Conn L. Rev. 1563, 1610 (2011); *see also* Dorothy Roberts, Fatal Invention, How Science, Politics and Big Business Re-Create Race in the Twenty-First Century 5 (2011) (Race is "a political grouping," with "roots in slavery and colonialism," it has "served a political

function for the four hundred years since its inception, and its boundary lines – how many races there are and who belongs to each one – have shifted over time and across nations to suit those political purposes.... Who qualifies as white, black, and Indian has been the subject of countless rules changes and judicial decisions [and] [t]hese racial reclassifications did not occur in response to scientific advances in human biology, but in response to sociopolitical imperatives."); *see also* Jessica P. Cerdeña, Marie V. Plaisime, & Jennifer Tsai, *From Race-Based to Race-Conscious Medicine*, 396 THE LANCET 1125, 1125 (2021) (the hypotheses "that Black and Brown people are genetically distinct from White people ... descends from European colonization, at which time race was developed as a tool to divide and control populations worldwide. Race is thus a social and power construct, with meanings that have shifted over time to suit political goals, including to assert biological inferiority of dark-skinned populations."); Khiara Bridges, *The Dangerous Law of Biological Race*, 82 FORDHAM L. REV. 21, 24 (2013) ("Biological race is a dangerous invention because it has dangerous consequences. The extermination of racialized groups of people thought to be biologically inferior is one such consequence. Biological race is also dangerous because it argues that racial minorities – namely, black people – remain subordinated because of genetic inferiority, and not because of structural and institutional processes.").

101. *See* James Denny Guillory, *The Pro Slavery Arguments of Dr. Samuel A. Cartwright*, 9 LOUISIANA HISTORY: THE JOURNAL OF THE LOUISIANA HISTORICAL ASSOCIATION 209, 210–16 (1968); see also LUNDY BRAUN, BREATHING RACE INTO THE MACHINE: THE SURPRISING CAREER OF THE SPIROMETER FROM PLANTATION TO GENETICS 28 (2014).
102. *See id* (describing Samuel A. Cartwright, *Diseases and Peculiarities of the Negro Race*, DEBOW'S REVIEW XI (1851), 66); Zinzi D. Bailey, Justin M. Feldman and Mary T. Bassett, *How Structural Racism Works – Racist Policies as the Root Cause of U.S. Health Inequities*, 384(8) THE NEW ENGLAND JOURNAL OF MEDICINE 768, 770 (Feb 25, 2021); ROBERTS, FATAL INVENTION, *supra* note 100, at 89–90.
103. Kelly M. Hoffman, Sophie Trawalter, Jordan R. Axt, and N. Norman Oliver, *Racial Bias in Pain Assessment and Treatment Recommendations, and False Beliefs about Biological Differences between Blacks and Whites*, 113 PROC. NAT'L ACAD. SCI. 4296, 4297 (2016).
104. *Id.*; Rene Bowser, *Racial Profiling in Health Care: An Institutional Analysis of Medical Treatment Disparities*, 7 MICH. J. OF RACE & L. 79, 108 (2001) ("Contemporary racialized research continues the historical construction of Black patients as degenerate in relation to the White norm. Such research falsely treats as a default rule an inherent biologic difference between Blacks and Whites, and errs by attributing a complex physiological or clinical phenomenon to arbitrary aspects of physical appearance. These perceived differences are often outcome-determinative in medical treatment."); *see generally*, Linda Villarosa, *Myths about Physical Racial Differences Were Used to Justify Slavery – and Are Still Believed by Doctors Today*, N.Y. TIMES (Aug. 14, 2019) ("Over the centuries, the two most persistent physiological myths – that black people were impervious to pain and had weak lungs that could be strengthened through hard work – wormed their way into scientific consensus, and they remain rooted in modern-day medical education and practice.").
105. ROBERTS, FATAL INVENTION, *supra* note 100, at 92.
106. Hoffman, et al., *supra* note 103, at 4296–4301.
107. Hoffman, et al., *supra* note 103, at 4296–4301; Bailey et al., *supra* note 102, at 770 (describing the University of Virginia study and its significance); ANUSHAY HOSSAIN, THE PAIN GAP: HOW SEXISM AND RACISM IN HEALTH CARE KILL WOMEN 47 (2021) (same).

108. *Id.* at 4296; *see also* Jessica P. Cerdeña, Marie V. Plaisime, and Jennifer Tsai, *From Race-Based to Race-Conscious Medicine*, 396 The Lancet 1125, 1125 (2021) (describing pervasive racial pseudoscience in medical training, such as the "racialized belief in diminished pain sensitivity of Black patients," which "translates to consistently inadequate pain management.").
109. Hoffman, et al., *supra* note 103, at 4300; *see also* Uche Blackstock, Legacy: A Black Doctor Reckons with Racism in Medicine 90 (2024) ("The meta analysis of 20 years of studies that looked at different sources of pain in numerous settings found that Black patients were 22 percent less likely than white patients to receive pain medication when they needed it.").
110. *See* Ta-Nehisi Coates, *The Enduring Solidarity of Whiteness: Black Poverty Is Fundamentally Distinct from White Poverty and So Cannot be Addressed without Grappling with Racism*, The Atlantic (Feb. 8, 2016).
111. *See* Office of Pol'y Dev. and Research, U.S. Dep't Housing & Urban Dev., Housing Discrimination Against Racial and Ethnic Minorities 31, 55–56 (2013); George C. Galster and Erin Brooke Godfrey, *By Words and Deeds: Racial Steering by Real Estate Agents in the U.S. in 2000*, 71 J. Am. Plan. Ass'n 251, 260 (2005); Margery Austin Turner and Stephen L. Ross, Housing Discrimination in Metropolitan America: Findings from the Latest National Paired Testing Study (Feb. 2003) ("In both rental and sales markets of metropolitan areas nationwide, black and Hispanic homeseekers experience significant levels of adverse treatment, relative to comparable white homeseekers."); *see also* Bart Landry and Kris Marsh, *The Evolution of the New Black Middle Class*, 37 Ann. Rev. Soc. 373, 388 (2011) (observing that African American middle class families live in less affluent neighborhoods than white middle class families).
112. *See* Marianne Bertrand and Sendhil Mullainathan, *Are Emily and Greg More Employable Than Lakisha and Jamal? A Field Experiment on Labor Market Discrimination*, 94 Am. Econ. Rev. 991, 997–98 (2004).
113. Devah Pager, Bruce Western, and David Pedulla, *Employment Discrimination and the Changing Landscape of Low-Wage Labor Markets*, 1 U. Chi. Legal F. 317, 343 (2009) (Concluding that "discrimination remains a significant barrier to employment facing minority low-wage workers.").
114. *See* Eduardo Bonilla-Silva, Racism Without Racists: Color-Blind Racism and The Persistence of Racial Inequality in America 55 (4 th ed. 2013) (citing studies demonstrating that "blacks earn less than whites at every educational level" and that "even as blacks move up the occupational hierarchy, their income falls further behind their white peers"). More specifically, other studies found that Black income only amounted to only "85 percent" of white incomes "among upper-middle-class black and white males and females in 1988," "79% among black and white dentists and lawyers in 1990; and 76.3% among black and white professionals in 1990" and "[B]lack males with post-baccalaureate degrees received only 74% of their white peers' income in 2000." Landry & Marsh, *supra* note 111, at 385.
115. Dayna Bowen Matthew, *A New Strategy to Combat Racial Inequality in American Health Care Delivery*, 9 DePaul J. Health Care L. 793,794 (2005) (citing studies as to each cited condition).
116. *See, e.g.*, Uche Blackstock, Legacy: A Black Doctor Reckons with Racism in Medicine (2024); Dayna Bowen Matthew, Just Medicine, A Cure for Racial Inequality in American Health Care (2015); Holly Mead, Lara Cartwright-Smith, Karen Jones, Christal Ramos, Kristy Woods,

and Bruce Siegel, Racial and Ethnic Disparities in Health Care: A Chartbook, The Commonwealth Fund (2008); Institute of Medicine of the National Academies, Unequal Treatment – Confronting Racial and Ethnic Disparities in Health Care (Brian Smedley, Adrienne Y. Stith, and Alan R. Nelson, eds 2003); Khiara M. Bridges, *Race in The Machine: Racial Disparities in Health and Medical AI*, 110 Va. L. Rev. 243 (2024); Nambi Ndugga, Latoya Hill and Samantha Hill, *Key Data on Health Care by Race and Ethnicity*, KFF (June 11, 2024); Bettina M. Beech, *Poverty, Racism, and the Public Health Crisis in America*, 9 Frontiers in Pub. Health 1 (Sept. 2021); Zinzi D. Bailey, Justin M. Feldman and Mary T. Bassett, *How Structural Racism Works – Racist Policies as the Root Cause of U.S. Health Inequities*, 384(8) The New England Journal of Medicine 768 (Feb 25, 2021); Jessica Cerdeña et al., *From Race-Based to Race-Conscious Medicine*, 396 The Lancet 1125 (2021) Sofia Carratala and Connor Maxwell, *Health Disparities by Race and Ethnicity*, Center for American Progress (May 7, 2020); Khiara M. Bridges, *Implicit Bias and Racial Disparities in Health Care*, 43 Hum. Rts. 19 (2018); William Hall et al., *Implicit Racial/Ethnic Bias among Health Care Professionals and Its Influence on Health Care Outcomes*, 105 Am. J. Pub. Health 60 (2015); Dayna Bowen Matthew, *A New Strategy to Combat Racial Inequality in American Health Care Delivery*, 9 Depaul J. Health Care L. 793 (2005); Elizabeth Chapman et al., *Physicians and Implicit Bias: How Doctors May Unwittingly Perpetuate Health Care Disparities*, 28 J. Gen. Internal Med. 1504 (2013); David R. Williams and Michelle Sternthal, *Understanding Racial-Ethnic Disparities in Health: Sociological Contributions*, 51(Suppl) J. Health & Soc. Behav. S15 (2010); Elizabeth Brondolo et al., *Race, Racism and Health: Disparities, Mechanisms, and Interventions*, 32 J. Behav. Med. 1 (2009); Alexander R. Green et al., *Implicit Bias among Physicians and Its Prediction of Thrombolysis Decisions for Black and White Patients*, 22 J. Gen. Internal Med. 1231 (2007); William W. Dressier et al., *Race and Ethnicity in Public Health Research: Models to Explain Health Disparities*, 34 Ann. Rev. Anthropology 231 (2005);.Rene Bowser, *Racial Profiling in Health Care: An Institutional Analysis of Medical Treatment Disparities*, 7 Mich. J. or Race & L. 79 (2001); David R. Williams and Toni D. Rucker, *Understanding and Addressing Racial Disparities in Health Care*, 21 Health Care Finan. Rev. 75 (Summer 2000).

117. *See, e.g.*, Anushay Hossain, The Pain Gap: How Sexism and Racism in Healthcare Kill Women (2021); Anastasia Jones, et al., *Racial and Ethnic Differences in Acute Post- Operative Pain Management: Systemic Review and Meta-Analysis*, 104 Journal of Clinical. Anesthesia 1 (Apr. 2025); Maytal Gilboa and Tamar Kricheli Katz, *Biased Evaluation of Pain and Suffering Damages*, 0(0) Journal of Law and Empirical Analysis 1 (2025); Muhammad Hamza Habib, *Under-Treatment of Pain in Black Patients: A Historical Overview, Case-Based Analysis, and Legalities as Explored through the Tenets of Critical Race Theory*, 20 Ind. Health L. Rev. 63 (2023); Jonathan W. Huntsman, et al., *Race Based Biases in Psychological Distress and Treatment Judgments*, 18 PLoS One, Vol. 10 (Oct. 19, 2023); Dan Ly, *Association of Patient Race and Ethnicity with Differences in Opioid Prescribing by Primary Care Physicians for Older Adults with New Low Back Pain*, 2 JAMA 2333, 7–8 (2021); Natalie H. Strand, et al., *Racism in Pain Medicine: We Can and Should Do More*, 96 Mayo Clin Proc. 1394 (June 2021); Mary E. Morales and R. Jason Yong, *Racial and Ethnic Disparities in the Treatment of Chronic Pain*, 22 Pain Medicine 75 (Dec. 23, 2020); Oluwafunmilayo Akinlade, *Taking Black Pain Seriously*, 383 The New England Journal of Medicine 10 (Sept. 3, 2020); Vidya Rao, *'You Are Not Listening to Me': Black Women on Pain and Implicit*

Bias in Medicine, TODAY (July 27, 2020); Nevert Badreldin et al., *Racial Disparities in Postpartum Pain Management*, 134 OBSTETRICS & GYNECOLOGY 1147 (2019); Kelly M. Hoffman et al., *Racial Bias in Pain Assessment and Treatment Recommendations, and False Beliefs about Biological Differences between Blacks and Whites*, 113 PROC. NAT'L ACAD. SCI. 4296 (2016); Dan Vergano, *How Many Doctors Hold Racist Beliefs about How Black People Feel Pain*, WASHINGTON POST (APR. 27, 2016); Monika Goyal et al., *Racial Disparities in Pain Management of Children with Appendicitis in Emergency Departments*, 169 JAMA Pediatrics 996 (2015); Sophie Trawalter and Kelly Hoffman, *Got Pain? Racial Bias in Perceptions of Pain*, 9 SOC. & PERSONALITY PSYCHOLOGY COMPASS 146 (2015); Adam Waytz, et al. *A Superhumanization Bias in Whites' Perceptions of Blacks*, 6 SOCIAL PSYCHOLOGY & PERSONALITY SCIENCE 352 (2015); Sophie Trawalter, et al., *Racial Bias in Perceptions of Others' Pain*, 7 PLOS ONE 1 (Nov. 2012); Laurent Glance et al., *Racial Differences in the Use of Epidural Analgesia for Labor*, 106 ANESTHESIOLOGY 19 (2007); Lisa J. Staton et al., *When Race Matters: Disagreement in Pain Perception between Patients and Their Physicians in Primary Care*, 99 J. OF THE NAT'L MED. ASS'N. 532 (May 2007); Miriam O. Ezenwa, et al., *Racial and Ethnic Disparities in Pain Management in the United States*, 38 JOURNAL OF NURSING SCHOLARSHIP 225 (2006); Marisa Nguyen, et al., *Access to Care for Chronic Pain: Racial and Ethnic Differences*, 6 THE JOURNAL OF PAIN 301 (2005); Camren R. Green et al., *The Unequal Burden of Pain: Confronting Racial and Ethnic Disparities in Pain*, 4 PAIN MED. 277 (2004); Timothy S. Carey and Joanne Mills Garrett, *The Relation of Race to Outcomes and the Use of Health Care Services for Acute Low Back Pain*, 28 SPINE 390 (2003); Charles S. Cleeland et al., *Pain and Treatment of Pain in Minority Patients with Cancer: The Eastern Cooperative Oncology Group Minority Outpatient Pain Study*, 127 ANNALS INTERNAL MED. 813 (1997).

118. Khiara Bridges, *Excavating Race-Based Disadvantage among Class-Privileged People of Color*, 53 HARV. CIV.RTS-CIV. LIB. L. REV. 65, 86 (2018) (citing an influential taxonomy of individual racial discrimination developed in a book by a psychologist: JOEL KOVEL, WHITE RACISM: A PSYCHOHISTORY (1970)).
119. *Id.*
120. Bridges, *Excavating Race*, *supra* note 118, at 87 (citing John F. Dovodio & Samuel L. Gaertner, *Aversive Racism*, 36 ADVANCES EXPERIMENTAL SOC. PSYCHOL. 1,3 2004).
121. *See* Bridges, *Excavating Race*, *supra* note 118, at 88–89 (emphasis in original) (citing BONILLA-SILVA, *supra* note 114, at 1–4).
122. Aman v. Cort Furniture Rental Corp., 84 F.3d 1074, 1081–82 (3d Cir. 1996).
123. INSTITUTE OF MEDICINE OF THE NATIONAL ACADEMIES, UNEQUAL TREATMENT – CONFRONTING RACIAL AND ETHNIC DISPARITIES IN HEALTH CARE 178 (BRIAN SMEDLEY, ADRIENNE Y. STITH, AND ALAN R. NELSON, EDS 2003); ROBERTS, FATAL INVENTION, *supra* note 100, at 96–97 (noting the IOM report, defined "disparities" in health care as "racial or ethnic differences in health care that are not due to access-related factors or clinical needs, preferences or appropriateness of intervention" and "concluded after factoring these access-related differences, [that] remaining disparities can be attributed to discrimination by the medical professions – physician prejudices, biases, or stereotyping of their minority patients.").
124. IOM, UNEQUAL TREATMENT, *supra* note 123, at 172 (emphasis added).
125. *Id.*
126. *Id.* at 177 (emphasis added and citations omitted); *see* William Hall et al., *Implicit Racial/Ethnic Bias among Health Care Professionals and Its Influence on Health Care Outcomes*, 105 AM. J. PUB. HEALTH 60 (2015) (after analysis of fifteen studies report

concludes that "[m]ost health care providers appear to have implicit bias in terms of positive attitudes toward Whites and negative attitudes toward people of color."); Elizabeth Chapman, Anna Kaatz and Molly Carnes, *Physicians and Implicit Bias: How Doctors May Unwittingly Perpetuate Health Care Disparities*, 28 J. GEN. INTERNAL MED. 1504 (2013) ("disparities in health care persist. The [IOM] notes that these differences result from multiple factors, but "bias, stereotyping, [and] prejudice … on the part of the health care providers" play a role."); *see also* Alexander R. Green et al., *Implicit Bias among Physicians and Its Prediction of Thrombolysis Decisions for Black and White Patients*, 22 J. GEN. INTERNAL MED. 1231 (2007) ("Results [of study with implicit bias testing] suggest that physicians' unconscious biases may contribute to racial/ethnic disparities in use of medical procedures such as thrombolysis for myocardial infarction.").

127. IOM, UNEQUAL TREATMENT, *supra* note 123, at 177–78 (citations omitted).
128. *See id.* at 174; *see also* DAYNA BOWEN MATTHEW, JUST MEDICINE, A CURE FOR RACIAL INEQUALITY IN AMERICAN HEALTH CARE 48–49 (2015) ("With some justification drawn from his past limited experiences, the doctor may assume this [elderly black woman] patient has limited means, less education than himself, and has had few opportunities to take care to eat well, exercise or rest over the course of her lifetime. Most likely, the physician will not even be aware that his judgments about the patient have been reached subconsciously, and certainly without any actual information about the individual woman who sits before him. … Even in those instances when the physicians react with sympathetic compassion in response to the negative stereotypes in their subconscious, the evidence is that the treatment choices they make as a result, such as withholding complex information or deferring expensive treatments, are more likely to harm rather than improve a minority patient's health.").
129. Gilboa, *The Color of Pain*, *supra* note 89, at 662.
130. *See, e.g.*, BLACKNESS AND DISABILITY: CRITICAL EXAMINATIONS AND CULTURAL INTERVENTIONS (CHRISTOPHER BELL ED. 2011); Jamelia Morgan, *On the Relationship between Race and Disability*, 58 HARV. C.R.-C.L. L. REV. 663 (2023); Jasmine E. Harris, *Reckoning with Race and Disability*, 130 YALE L.J. FORUM 916 (2021); Camille A. Nelson, *Racializing Disability, Disabling Race: Policing Race and Mental Status*, 15 BERKELEY J. CRIM. L. 1 (2010); *cf.* Kimani Paul-Emile, *Blackness as Disability?*, 106 GEO. L. J. 293 (2018).
131. *See* Camille Nelson, *Frontlines: Policing at the Nexus of Race and Mental Health*, 43 FORDHAM URB. L. J. 615 (2016); Camille Nelson, *Racializing Disability, Disabling Race: Policing Race and Mental Status*, 15 BERKELEY J. CRIM. L. 1 (2010); Lily Robin & Evelyn F. McCoy, *Policing Is Killing Black Disabled People. Centering Intersectionality Is Critical to Reducing Harm*, THE URBAN INSTITUTE (Nov. 15, 2021); Vilissa Thompson, *Understanding the Policing of Disabled Black Bodies*, CENTER FOR AMERICAN PROGRESS (Feb. 10, 2021).
132. Jamelia Morgan, *Essay, Disability's Fourth Amendment*, 122 COLUM. L. REV. 489, 527–28 (2022).
133. *Id.* at 526–27.
134. *Id.* at 528 (emphasis added).
135. *See, e.g.*, Jenna Wechsler, *The Intersection of Race, Gender, Special Education Status, and School Discipline: A Multifaceted Approach for Closing the School-to-Prison Pipeline for the Most Vulnerable Youth*, 58 N. ENG. L. REV. 79 (2023); U.S. COMM. ON CIVIL RIGHTS, BEYOND SUSPENSIONS: EXAMINING SCHOOL DISCIPLINE POLICIES AND CONNECTIONS TO THE SCHOOL-TO-PRISON PIPELINE FOR STUDENTS OF COLOR WITH DISABILITIES (2019); Leah Hill, *Disrupting the Trajectory: Representing Disabled*

African American Boys in a System Designed to Send Them to Prison, 45 Fordham Urb. L.J. 201 (2017); Torin Togut, *The Gestalt of the School-to-Prison Pipeline: The Duality of Overrepresentation of Minorities in Special Education and Racial Disparity in School Discipline on Minorities*, 20 Am. U. J. Gender Soc. Pol'y & L. 163 (2011); Daniel Losen et al., *Disturbing Inequities: Exploring the Relationship between Racial Disparities in Special Education Identification and Discipline*, 5 J. Applied Rsch. on Child 1, No. 2, Art. 15 (2014).

136. *See* Holly Mead, Lara Cartwright-Smith, Karen Jones, Christal Ramos, Kristy Woods, and Bruce Siegel, Racial and Ethnic Disparities in Health Care: A Chartbook, The Commonwealth Fund 71 (Chapter 6.6) (2008).

137. *See* Bridget Kennedy *Pathologizing Bias: Racial Disparities in the Diagnosis of Schizophrenia*, Brandeis University 12 (May 3, 2022); Judith Warner, *Psychiatry Confronts Its Racist Past and Tries to Make Amends*, N.Y. Times (May 21, 2021) ("by the 1970's. the diagnosis of psychosis was handed out so often that the profession was essentially 'turning schizophrenia into a Black man's disorder of aggression and agitation.'"); Roberts, Fatal Invention, *supra* note 100, at 90–91 (noting that by the 1960s, psychiatrists had started describing schizophrenia as a "protest psychosis" whereby Black men developed "hostile and aggressive feelings" and "delusional anti-whiteness" and "schizophrenia became a metaphor for any black dissatisfaction with racial inequality."); *see generally* Jonathan M. Metzl, The Protest Psychosis: How Schizophrenia Became a Black Disease (2009) (same).

138. Kennedy, *supra* note 137, at 11; Warner *supra* note 137.

139. Kennedy, *supra* note 137, at 7–8; Warner *supra* note 137. ("numerous studies have shown that an almost all-white [psychiatry] profession's lack of attunement to Black expressions of anger–has led to an under-diagnosis of major depression, particularly in Black Men, and overreliance on the use of antipsychotic medications. Black patients are less likely than white patients to receive appropriate medication for their depression.").

140. *See* 20 C.F.R., Pt. 404, Subpart P. Appendix 1, Listing 12.03 (Step-3 listing for psychotic disorders including schizophrenia); Listing 12.04 (Step-3 listing for affective (mood) disorders including depression and bipolar disorder).

141. The suggested negative impacts on SSA disability assessment from misdiagnosed Black and Brown patients with psychiatric impairments, is not gleaned from SSA data or medical literature but from anecdotal observations over a 35-year period in which the author also supervised law school clinical programs providing free social security disability representation in Newark, New Jersey and San Antonio, Texas and which represented many such claimants in that period.

142. *See* notes 8–9 *supra* and accompanying text.

143. Muhammad Hamza Habib, *Under-Treatment of Pain in Black Patients: A Historical Overview, Case-Based Analysis, and Legalities as Explored through the Tenets of Critical Race Theory*, 20 Ind. Health L. Rev. 63, 79 (2023).

144. *See* Salimah H. Meghani, et al., *Advancing a National Agenda to Eliminate Disparities in Pain Care: Directions for Health Policy, Education, Practice and Research*, 13 Pain Medicine 5,12 (2012); Habib, *supra* note 143, at 79; Dan Ly, *Association of Patient Race and Ethnicity with Differences in Opioid Prescribing by Primary Care Physicians for Older Adults with New Low Back Pain*, 2 JAMA 2333, 7–8 (2021).

145. *See, e.g.*, Habib, *supra* note 143, at 79; Meghani, et al., *supra* note 144, at 12.

146. Abby Goodnough, *Finding Good Pain Treatment Is Hard. If You're Not White, It's Even Harder*, N.Y. Times (Aug. 9, 2016).

147. *Id.*
148. *See, e.g.*, Smith v. Colvin, 756 F.3d 621, 626 (8th Cir. 2014) (ALJ found the claimant pain's and symptom testimony "not credible" and the benefits denial was affirmed by the Eighth Circuit, noting, among other factors that, the pain treatment had been "'essentially routine and/or conservative in nature,' and that [the claimant] did not take narcotic medications for pain relief."); Parra v. Astrue, 481 F.3d 742, 751 (9th Cir. 2007) (the ALJ noted "that [the claimant's] physical ailments were treated with an over-the-counter pain medication. We have previously indicated that evidence of 'conservative treatment' is sufficient to discount a claimant's testimony regarding severity of an impairment.").
149. Again, the prevalence of this scenario, as in note 141 *supra* and accompanying text, is not gleaned from the SSA statistical data or other literature but from anecdotal observations over a 35-year period in which the author also supervised law school clinical programs providing free social security disability representation in Newark, New Jersey and San Antonio, Texas and which represented many such claimants in that period.
150. *See* Mead, et al., *supra* note 136, at 47 (Chapter 4.1); *see also* IOM, Unequal Treatment, *supra* note 123, at 109 (noting that "minorities" report greater difficulty in locating a "usual source" of medical care or obtaining medical care at a consistent location and "African American and Latinos were more likely than their white counterparts to receive care in hospital outpatient departments (particularly teaching and public hospitals), community based clinics and emergency rooms as usual sources of care."); Ananya Mandal, *Disparities in Access to Health Care*, News Medical Life Sciences (last updated Jan. 30, 2024), www.news-medical.net/health/Disparities-in-Access-to-Health-Care.aspx ("Compared to white individuals, ethnic or racial minorities are less likely to be able to visit the same doctor on a regular basis and tend to rely more on clinics and emergency rooms. Without a regular healthcare source, people have more difficulty obtaining their prescriptions and attending necessary appointments.").
151. Peter Lee, Sherri Porath and Joan E. Shaffner, *Engendering Social Security Determinations: The Path of a Woman Claimant*, 68 Tul. L. Rev. 1477, 1521 (1994) (emphasis added).
152. *See* Nambi Ndugga, Latoya Hill and Samantha Hill, *Key Data on Health Care by Race and Ethnicity*, KFF (fig. 6) (June 11, 2024).
153. *See* Mead, et al., *supra* note 136, at 66 (Chapter 6–1); IOM, Unequal Treatment, *supra* note 123, at 77 ("Racial and ethnic minority patients are found to receive a lower quality and intensity of healthcare and diagnostic services across a wide range of procedures and disease areas … In studies where patients' sociodemographic characteristics (e.g., education level, income), insurance status (e.g., public or privately funded insurance) and clinical factors (e.g., co-morbid illness, severity of disease) are controlled, these racial and ethnic differences are generally attenuated, but rarely disappear completely … [T]hese disparities in care have been linked to poorer clinical outcomes and higher mortality among minorities.").
154. *See* IOM, Unequal Treatment, *supra* note 123, at 112.
155. *See* Elizabeth Levy, *Record of Injustice: Medical Records, Marginalization and the Consultant Gap*, 37 Berkeley J. Gender L. & Just. 169, 171–72 (2022).
156. Roberts, Fatal Invention, *supra* note 100, at 113.
157. Julie Scott, *Sickle Cell and Malaria: What's the Link?*, Verywellhealth (Aug. 23, 2024).
158. *See* Sonora Windermere, et al., *The Medical and Legal Plight of Sickle Cell Patients-A Case Study of Racial Disparities in Health Care and Potential Legal Remedies*, 21 Ind. Health L. Rev. 83, 94 (2024).

159. Roberts, Fatal Invention, *supra* note 100, at 113.
160. National Academies of Sciences, Engineering, and Medicine (NASEM), Sickle Cell Disease in Social Security Disability Evaluations: Pain and Treatment Settings 11 (Dec. 9, 2025).
161. *Sickle Cell Disease (SCD)*, Centers for Disease Control & Prevention, https://perma.cc/7Y4L-USB4
162. *See* John S. Gibson and David C. Ree, *How Benign Is Sickle Cell Trait?* 11 Bio-Medicine 21, 21 (2016).
163. NASEM, SCD in SSD Evaluations, *supra* note 160, at 11.
164. *Id.*
165. *Id.*
166. Windermere, *supra* note 158, at 84.
167. *Id.*
168. NASEM, SCD in SSD Evaluations, *supra* note 160, at 11–12.
169. Windermere, *supra* note 158, at 84.
170. Melissa Azul and Amanda M. Brandow, *Beyond IV Push: Alternative Methods for Management of Acute Pain in SCD*, 1 Hematology Am Soc Hematol Educ Program 611, 611(2024).
171. *Id.*
172. NASEM, SCD in SSD Evaluations, *supra* note 160, at 6.
173. *See* 20 C.F.R., Pt. 404, Subpt P, Appendix 1, Listings 7.05(A); 107.05 (A) (2025). The original 1985 SCD listings are contained and discussed at 50 Fed. Reg. 50068, 50097 (Dec. 6, 1985). The 2015 changes to the SCD listings are contained and discussed at 80 Fed. Reg. 21159 (Apr. 17, 2015).
174. *See* 20 C.F.R., Pt. 404, Subpt P, Appendix 1, Listings 7.05(B); 107.05(B) (2025).
175. *See generally* Administrative Conference of the United States, *Information Interhange Bulletin No. 014, Notice-and-Comment Rulemaking* (May, 2021) (describing Administrative Procedure Act (APA) public notice, comment and agency consideration requirements in basic APA regulatory rulemaking); Dubin, *End of Issue Exhaustion, supra* note 51, at 672 n.213 (describing applicability of APA rulemaking provisions and processes to SSA benefits programs).
176. *See*, e.g., Letter from A. Kim Ritchey, MD President, American Society of Pediatric Hematology/Oncology (ASPHO) to Cheryl A. Williams, Director SSA Office of Medical Listings Improvement (Jan. 21, 2014); Martin H. Steinberg, MD, Director, Center of Excellence for Sickle Cell Disease, Boston University School of Medicine (Jan. 17, 2014); Daniel E. Bauer, MD, Ph.D., Hematology, Dana-Farber Boston Children's Cancer and Bood Disorders Center, Harvard Medical School Teaching Hospital, (Jan.16, 2014); *see also* Community Legal Services of Philadelphia, Racial Disparities in Access to Supplemental Security Income Benefits for Children, 11–12 & nn.59–67 (Dec. 2020) (critiquing as insufficiently scientifically supported, 2015 changes in SSA's sickle cell disease listing regulations).
177. *Id.* (all three above letters among other similar letters submitted to SSA as comments).
178. *See* note 176, *supra* (Letters at *id.*).
179. *See* note *supra*.
180. *See* note 176, *supra* (Letters at *id.*).
181. *See* Philip Farrell, *Tracking Down the Origins of Cystic Fibrosis in Ancient Europe*, Smithsonian (Sept. 20, 2018) ("CF is the most common genetic disease among Caucasians, and how it became so widespread is something of a mystery."); *see also* Sam Moxon, *Cystic Fibrosis Chronicle: Why has the often-deadly CF gene not passed*

out of the human genome? And what new treatments are being developed?, GENETIC LITERACY PROJECT (Jan. 31, 2023) (suggesting based on studies of mice with CF "that carrying one copy of the gene for CF actually conferred an evolutionary benefit to prevent people from dying of tuberculosis and cholera" due to diarrhea and dehydration, and they "had a higher resistance to cholera and, in a weird symbiosis, may have found symptomatic relief from CF if infected.").

182. *See* Erin T. Welsh, *Underrepresented groups with cystic fibrosis less likely to be eligible for CFTR modulators*, HEALIO (Feb. 15, 2021) (based on "the 2018 CF Foundation Patient Registry, which includes 81% to 84% of U.S. patients with cystic fibrosis … 25,918 (84.2%) were non-Hispanic white, 1,351 (4.4%) were Black/African American, 2,763 (9%) were Hispanic and 743 (2.4%) were other races.").
183. *See* 81 Fed. Reg. 37141 (June 9, 2016) (SSA stated and explained that: "we adopted these recommendations" with respect to all of the five major sets of recommendations and objections from the medical community and from others to the proposed changes to the CF listings at listings 3.04 (adults) and 103.04 (children), promulgated at 20 C.F.R., Pt. 404, Subpt B Appendix 1).
184. Azul and Brandow, *supra* note 170, at 612.
185. Letter from David Camp, Chief Executive Officer, National Association of Social Security Claimant Representatives, to Martin O'Malley, Commissioner of Social Security (Dec. 24, 2023); *see also* Letter from Darcy Milburn, Sandy Chung, Jonathan Stein, Richard Weishaupt, Linda Landry and Steve Weiss to SSA Commissioner Martin O'Malley, January 4, 2024 (on file with the author) (noting that the 2015 change in the SCD listing "led to nearly 1,500 additional children, largely Black children, who would have been eligible for SSI, to be denied between 2015 and 2020 according to an Analysis by Dr. David Weaver, former SSA Associate Commissioner for the Office of Research.").
186. NASEM, SCD IN SSD EVALUATIONS, *supra* note 160, at 6.
187. *Id.* at 4.
188. *Id.* at 110–12; *see* Carlton Haywood, Jr., et al., *Perceived Discrimination in Health Care is Associated with a Greater Burden of Pain in Sickle Cell Disease*, 48(5) Journal of Pain Management 934, 935–43 (Nov. 2014) (Identifying both SCD "disease based and race-based discrimination" as "independent" obstacles to persuading health care providers about the severity of SCD pain but finding greater patient comfort in attributing SCD stigma and disease- based reasons, as opposed to race, for such obstacles); *see also* Lakeya S. McGill, et al., *Impact of Disease- and Race-Based Discrimination in Health Care on Pain Outcomes among Adults Living with Sickle Cell Disease in the United States: The Mediating Roles of Internalized Stigma and Depressive Symptoms*, 30 STIGMA AND HEALTH 1037 (2024); Ariel O. Blakey et al., *Effects of Experienced Discrimination in Pediatric Sickle Cell Disease: Caregiver and Provider Perspectives*, 10(6) JOURNAL OF RACIAL AND ETHNIC HEALTH DISPARITIES 3095 (2023); Megan M. Miller et al., *Pain-Related Injustice Appraisals, Sickle Cell Stigma, and Racialized Discrimination in Youth with Sickle Cell Disease: A Preliminary Investigation*, 22 PAIN MEDICINE 2027 (2021).
189. *Id.* at 112.
190. *Id.* at 113.
191. *Id.* at 113–14.
192. Sickle Cell Disease Association of America, *SCDAA Response to the National Academies Release of Final Report on Sickle Cell Disease and Social Security Disability Evaluations* (Dec. 15, 2025).

193. Alexandra Power-Hays and Patrick T. McGann, *When Actions Speak Louder than Words – Racism and Sickle Cell Disease*, 383 N. Eng. J. Med. 1902, 1902 (Nov. 13, 2020).
194. *See* Kubitschek & Dubin, *supra* note 60, at §§ 2:27, 2:28, 2:29 (analyzing and collecting cases on the respective roles of consultant physicians, review physicians and medical advisors in SSA disability adjudications).
195. *See generally*, Jerry Kang, *Trojan Horses of Race*, 181 Harv. L. Rev. 1489, 1539 (2005) ("racial meanings can arise from what I call 'vicarious experiences,' which are stories of or simulated engagements with racial others provided through various forms of the media or narrated by parents and our peers."); *id.* at 1509 ("implicit mental processes may draw on racial meanings that, upon conscious consideration, we would expressly disavow. It is as if some "Trojan Horse" virus had hijacked a portion of our brain."); Rupert Brown, Prejudice: Its Social Psychology 83 (1995) (noting that stereotypes are embedded in culture, and reinforced through socialization and "repeated exposure to images in books, television and newspapers").
196. *See* Mills, A Penchant for Prejudice, *supra* note 2, at 100; *see also id.* at 88–100 (describing myriad ways in which ALJs can exercise discretion influenced by biases in performing their duties and applying standards for the evaluation of credibility in the assessment of pain and claimant symptomology).
197. *Id.* at 86–87.
198. *Id.* at 87–88.
199. *Id.* at 74–76.
200. *See id.* at 76.
201. *See supra* notes 28–29 and accompanying text.
202. 111 F. Supp. 2d 556 (M.D. Pa. 2000).
203. Grant v. Sullivan, 720 F. Supp. 462 (M.D.Pa.1989); Grant v. Sullivan, 131 F.R.D. 436 (M.D.Pa.1990); Grant v. Sullivan, 134 F.R.D. 107 (M.D. Pa. 1990), *rev'd sub nom.*, Grant v. Shalala, 989 F.2d 1332 (3d Cir.1993), *on remand sub nom.*, Grant v. Comm'r of Soc. Sec. Admin., 111 F. Supp. 2d 556 (M.D.Pa. 2000).
204. *See, e.g.*, Small v. Sullivan, 820 F.Supp. 1098 (S.D. Ill. 1992); Kendrick v. Sullivan, 784 F. Supp. 94 (S.D.N.Y. 1992); *see also Bowen v. City of New York* (discussed *infra* note 207 and accompanying text).
205. *See* Grant v. Shalala, 989 F.2d 1332. 1344–60 (3d Cir.1993).
206. *Id.*
207. Bowen v. City of New York, 476 U.S. 467 (1986), *aff'g sub nom.*, City of New York v. Heckler, 742 F.2d 729 (2d Cir.), *aff'g*, City of New York v. Heckler, 578 F. Supp. 1109 (E.D.N.Y. 1984).
208. *Id.* at 1355–57 (Higginbotham, J., dissenting); *Bowen v. City of New York*, 476 U.S. at 474–75.
209. In 1994, Congress established the SSA as an independent agency with a single Commissioner and removed SSA from the Department of Health and Human Services headed by the HHS Secretary. *See* Social Security Independence and Program Improvement Act of 1994, P.L. 103–296 (eff. Mar. 31, 1995).
210. *Id.* at 1353 (Higginbotham, J., dissenting).
211. *Id.* at 1346.
212. Grant v. Comm'r of Soc. Sec. Admin., 111 F. Supp. 2d 556, 559–60 (M.D. Pa. 2000).
213. *Id.* at 560.
214. *Id.*
215. *Id.* at 559.

216. *Grant*, 111 F. Supp. 2d at 559. ALJ Rowell's invidious stereotype about Latino/a's faking mental illness was shared by at least one other ALJ (a former ALJ in the Newark, SSA hearing office, now deceased). A medical advisor, retained by the SSA and called to testify by that Newark ALJ in one of his cases involving a Puerto Rican claimant manifesting psychiatrically limiting symptomology, became a whistle-blower of sorts on this issue – an extremely rare occurrence. The Medical Advisor, Dr. Myron Brazin, prepared a sworn affidavit and supplied it to the claimant's counsel in that case in which Dr. Brazin swore that the ALJ sought to speak with the doctor/advisor before the hearing, and without counsel present, (*ex parte*) and in a manner the doctor interpreted as "pressuring me to give testimony adverse to [the claimant]." When the doctor "pointed out that [the claimant] had been experiencing hallucinations," reflected in treatment records at a mental health clinic, the ALJ remarked: "you can't believe that; Puerto Ricans always say they are hallucinating." Affidavit of Dr. Myron Brazin, dated May 20, 1997 (on file with the author).
217. *Grant*, 989 F.2d at 1336.
218. *Grant*, 111 F. Supp. 2d at 564.
219. *Id.* at 570.
220. 917 F.Supp. 103 (D.P.R. 1996).
221. *Id.* at 110–11 and n.4.
222. *Id.*
223. *Id.* at 111. That the ALJ in question was Puerto Rican as was the federal district court judge (Juan Perez-Gimenez), were of no moment in the court's decision. For discussion of the presence and potential causes of in-group prejudice, bias and discrimination *see* Castaneda v. Partida, 430 U.S. 482, 503 (1977) (Marshall, J., concurring) ("Social scientists agree that members of minority groups frequently respond to discrimination and prejudice by attempting to disassociate themselves from the group, even to the point of adopting the majority's negative attitudes towards the minority. Such behavior occurs with particular frequency among members of minority groups who have achieved some measure of economic or political success and thereby have gained some acceptability among the dominant group."); *see also* TANYA KATERÍ HERNÁNDEZ, RACIAL INNOCENCE: UNMASKING LATINO ANTI-BLACK BIAS AND THE STRUGGLE FOR EQUALITY (2022) (describing anti-Black biases against more phenotypically Black Latino/as by other Latino/as).
224. 339 F. Supp. 2d 480, 491–501 (W.D.N.Y. 2004).
225. *Id.* at 492–94.
226. *Id.* at 495–96 (citing Small v. Sullivan, 820 F. Supp. 1098, 1106 (S.D.Ill.1992); Kendrick v. Sullivan, 784 F. Supp. 94, 100 (S.D.N.Y. 1992)).
227. *See* Pronti v. Barnhart, 441 F. Supp. 2d 466, 472–77 and n.9 (W.D.N.Y. 2006).
228. *See* Kendrick v. Sullivan, 784 F. Supp. 94, 97 (S.D.N.Y. 1992); *see also id.* at 102–04 (citing Spears v. Heckler, 625 F. Supp. 208, 209 (S.D.N.Y. 1985) and noting that "ALJ Anyel insisted that a mentally impaired claimant whose Legal Aid attorney was temporarily unavailable due to a strike go forward with her hearing unrepresented or face the prospect of having her claim dismissed."); Lora v. Bowen, 1987 WL 16151 (S.D.N.Y. 1987) (an opinion finding that ALJ Anyel's patently unsupported determination that the claimant wished to proceed without counsel, failure to evaluate the unrepresented claimant's many allegations of subjective pain, mandated remand for a new hearing before a different ALJ).
229. *See Kendrick*, *supra* note 228, at *id.*; *see also* Smith v. Heckler, 1985 WL 3845 (S.D.N.Y. 1985) (noting that the "case was remanded to ALJ Anyel because her initial denial of the

claim was based on the erroneous view that an allegation of disabling pain must be supported by objective clinical findings" and she essentially committed the same error at the remanded second hearing); *see generally, supra* notes 83–87 and accompanying text (discussing inability of medical science to ascertain degrees of pain and certain symptoms).
230. Kendrick v. Sullivan, 784 F. Supp. 94 (S.D.N.Y. 1992).
231. *See* Social Security Administration Office of Hearings and Appeals v. Helen Anyel, 58 M.S.P.R. 261 (1993).
232. *See id.*; *see also* Social Security Administration Office of Hearings and Appeals v. Anyel, 66 M.S.P.R. 328 (1995) (approving final settlement of the proceeding, imposing 90-day suspension, and return to duty with conditions "consistent with applicable law.").
233. *See* Crisci v. Shalala, 169 F.R.D. 563, 566 (S.D.N.Y. 1966).
234. *See id.* at 565–73.
235. In re Chocallo, 2 MS.P.B. 23 (1978), *aff'd*, 1 M.S.P.R. 605 (1980), aff'd, No. 80–1053 (D.D.C. 1980), *aff'd in part, vacated in part on other grounds and case remanded*, Chocallo v. Prokop, 673 F.2d 551 (D.C. Cir.) (Table), *cert. denied*, 459 U.S. 857 (1982).
236. *See* 5 U.S.C. § 7251 (extending good cause, tenure-like protection to ALJs, permitting removal of ALJs only for "good cause" shown); *see also* 5 U.S.C. § 554(d)(2) (ALJs may not have or be subject to both prosecutorial and judicial functions).
237. In re Chocallo, 1 M.S.P.R. 605, 610–11 (1980).
238. *Id.*
239. *See id.* (affirming In re Chocallo, 2 M.S.P.B. 23, 43–53 (1978)).
240. 2013 WL 5719076 (E.D.N.Y. 2013).
241. *See* Complaint in Padro v. Astrue, 11-cv-1178 (E.D.N.Y., Apr. 11, 2011) at American Association of Disability Policy Reform. *Padro v. Astrue*, http://aadpr.org/padro.html
242. *See id.*; Padro v Astrue, 2013 WL 5719076, *1–2 (E.D.N.Y. 2013).
243. *Id.* at *2; *see* Settlement Agreement in Padro v. Astrue, 11-cv-1178 (E.D.N.Y., Oct. 18, 2013) at American Association of Disability Policy Reform. *Padro v. Astrue*, http://aadpr .org/padro.html
244. Social Security Ruling 13–1p, 78 Fed. Reg.6168 (Jan. 29, 2013).
245. *See id.*
246. *See* Frank S. Bloch and Jon C. Dubin, Social Security Law, Policy and Practice: Cases and Materials 804–05 (2016) (questioning whether SSA's new procedures in SSR 13–1p reflect "meaningful improvement over those described in the twelve-year *Grant* litigation"). Three law student law review notes between 1995–2020 have critiqued the efficacy of bias procedures in the 1990's, the early 2000's, and in 2020. *See, e.g.*, Golin, *supra* note 12, at 1551–57 (1995); Jason D. Vendel, *General Bias and Administrative Law Judges: Is There a Remedy for Social Security Disability Claimants?*, 90 Cornell L. Rev. 769, 786–96 (2005); Trabanino, *supra* note 89, at 2091–96 (2020).
247. *See, e.g.*, *Kendrick*, 784 F. Supp. at 99–101 (court rejects SSA argument of bias issue waiver due to untimeliness); *see also Pronti*, 339 F. Supp. 2d at 495–96 (suggesting the "earliest opportunity" to raise bias clauses in the regulations (20 C.F.R.§§ 404.940; 416.1440) are "not well-suited to claims of general bias" [or systemic racial bias or other systemic biases] because "it seems misguided to have to present a claim of general [or systemic] bias first to the very ALJ that is alleged to be biased. Assuming an ALJ was biased, it stands to reason that he would not admit as much by agreeing to withdraw from the case. Second, the Appeals Council reviews claims of bias on a case-by-case basis only, which does not take into account the nature of a claim of general [or systemic] bias.").
248. *See, e.g.*, Laporte Law Firm, Social Security Disability Attorneys, *New Ruling Addresses ALJ Bias*, (Feb. 21, 2013), www.laportelawfirm.com/blog/new-ssa-ruling-addresses-alj-bias/

("It is our office policy to not file complaints of ALJ bias, as we feel that we most effectively advocate for our clients in our appellate work by clearly pointing out the specific legal errors and mistakes by ALJs in evaluating medical and vocational evidence, without resort to claims of bias. However, we provide this article on ALJ bias for informational purposes for the reader, in light of the important victory obtained in the Queens, NY ODAR [*Padro v. Astrue*] case.").

249. *See generally* Lowry v. Barnhart, 329 F.3d 1019, 1022 (9th Cir. 2003) (rejecting attorney's lawsuit and mandamus action to compel SSA to recuse an ALJ in all future cases who had retaliated against him in response to bias complaints and concluding that, "the bias procedures are not judicially enforceable" although also noting that "[t]he Administration's unexplained decade-long delinquency in promulgating final procedures and its lackadaisical handling of Lowry's [the attorney's] complaint raise serious concerns about its commitment to the values the procedures purport to embrace. Unfortunately for Lowry, not every agency shortcoming is subject to correction in the courts."). The attorney representing the claimant in the case in footnote 216 *supra*, – where the SSA medical advisor provided a whistle blowing account of racial bias in an *ex parte* meeting with the ALJ before the hearing – also informed the author of a pattern of retaliation from that ALJ in subsequent cases and the SSA also denied a request to recuse that ALJ from hearing subsequent cases handled by that attorney. *See also supra* 235–39 and accompanying text describing the *In re Chocallo* case and retaliation even against a nonprofit, legal services attorney who had sought to recuse the ALJ for bias.
250. *See* ACUS, Evaluating Subjective Symptoms, *supra* note 90, at 30.
251. Email from David Camp, immediate past President and CEO of NOSSCR dated October 22, 2025; E-mail from Thomas Krause, immediate past Director of Litigation of NOSSCR, dated October 23, 2025.
252. Habib, *supra* note 143, at 85.
253. E.O. 13985, *supra* note 135.
254. SSA, Equity Action Plan (2022), *supra* note 36, at 2 (emphasis added).
255. SSA, 2023 Equity Action Plan Update, *supra* note 36, at 20–21.
256. Abt Associates, *supra* note 37, at 6, n.2.
257. *See* Trabanino, *supra* note 89, at 2082–83; 2098.
258. *See, e.g.*, Frank Griffin, *Implicit Disability Bias Disinterred by Zombie Factors in Social Security Disability Determinations*, 21 Nev. L.J. 161, 190–204 (2020) (recommending program of implicit bias training and discipline to address pervasive faulty ALJ assessments of credibility of claimant pain and symptomology based on "zombie factors" – discrediting claimants for activities of daily living that are basic to survival and without which one would be a zombie such as eating, bathing, living, handling personal hygiene and living alone); Trabanino, *supra* note 89, at 2101–02.
259. SSA, Equity Action Plan (2022), *supra* note 36, at 15.
260. *See* Matthew, Just Medicine *supra* note 115, at 155–58.
261. Professors Rachel Godsil and Song Richardson have explained:

> In social psychological literature, "racial anxiety" refers to the concerns that often arise both before and during interracial interactions … For people of color, racial anxiety is experienced as the concern that they will be negatively stereotyped and subjected to hostile, distant and discriminatory treatment on the basis of their race or ethnicity. Examples of people of color experiencing discrimination in intergroup interactions are found in every life domain. The most documented can be found in health care, education, and criminal justice. In light of the ever-growing evidence that discriminatory treatment continues to be prevalent even among

> people who purport to hold egalitarian values, this anxiety is realistic and unsurprising. For Whites, racial anxiety is experienced as the concern that they will behave in ways that will be evaluated as racist by a person of color. It may be surprising that the fear of being perceived as racist triggers anxiety. However, for Whites, accusations of racism are experienced as immoral. While standards may have shifted to some degree in the 2016 election cycle, being labeled a racist often has significant negative consequences, including the loss of one's livelihood.

Rachel D. Godsil and L. Song Richardson, *Racial Anxiety*, 102 IOWA L. REV. 2235, 2240, 2241 (2017). Because the very process of an implicit bias intervention can invoke racial anxiety and or stereotype threat among participants, addressing these phenomena should be planned and incorporated into such programs. *See id.* at 2256–62 (discussing planning for positive intergroup contact and specific, concrete strategies for minimizing racial anxiety).

262. Center for Policing Equity Senior Research Scholar Kim Shayo Buchanon and Professor Phillip Atiba Goff have explained the concept of "stereotype threat" as:

> When a person fears being judged in accordance with a negative stereotype about some important aspect of their group identity, they can experience concern that their features or behavior will be taken to confirm the stereotype in the eyes of others, or even in their own. Stereotype threats, including racist stereotype threat (RST), operate as evaluative threats. Just as excessive anxiety about being evaluated can diminish performance on a difficult test or public speaking assignment, stereotype threats can also interfere with performance of difficult tasks, often in ways that tend to confirm the stereotype. For example, when black students fear being judged according to racist stereotypes about race and intelligence, they are likely to perform less well on tests of academic ability and to experience diminished self-esteem; a black person who is anxious about being stereotyped by police as criminal may engage in behaviors that are viewed by police as suspicious, such as "looking nervous," "trying to avoid looking nervous," "avoiding eye contact," or "freezing up." A woman or girl who fears being judged according to sexist stereotypes is likely to perform less well on a test of quantitative ability and is less likely to aspire to a STEM career. In the same way, a white person who fears being judged in accordance with a stereotype that white people are racist is likely to experience emotional discomfort that interferes with optimal performance in a difficult interracial interaction. In particular, a person who anticipates being judged racist is more likely to behave in racially disparate ways.

Kim Shayo Buchanon and Phillip Atiba Goff, *Racist Stereotype Threat in Civil Rights Law*, 67 U.C.L.A. L. REV. 316, 325–26 (2020).

263. *See* Jerry Kang, *What Judges Can Do about Implicit Bias*, 57 COURT REVIEW 78 (2021).

264. The Perception Institute's website explains that it was founded:

> to understand why holding egalitarian values doesn't always translate into behavior that aligns with those values. We turned to social psychology and neuroscience and identified three intersecting unconscious phenomena that explain this paradox: implicit bias, identity anxiety, and stereotype threat. But individuals can't solve societal challenges alone, and our unconscious minds are shaped by the world around us. This work requires understanding the interplay of structural, institutional, and interpersonal dynamics, and how they affect us as individuals. Genuine "mind science" research includes insights from social psychology and neuroscience, as well as law, sociology, political science, anthropology, and

> history. As mind science research analysts and data interpreters, we use this knowledge to analyze how implicit bias, identity anxiety, and stereotype threat interrupt interpersonal dynamics in varied environments. The information we gather helps us improve everyday interactions and better understand how narratives influence structures and institutions, as well as social identities. These insights help us develop interventions.

https://perception.org/solutions/. It describes its work "with a wide range of organizations to help them promote fairness, dignity, and belonging and to address implicit bias, identity/inter-group anxiety, and stereotype threat." It has worked with "Courts, Prosecutors, Public Defenders, and other criminal justice organizations to promote fairness in the justice system and help reduce implicit bias and discrimination in their practices" as well as "Healthcare Providers, hospitals, and other healthcare organizations striving to improve the quality of care for all patients, regardless of their race, ethnicity, or other identity differences." *See* https://perception.org/our-work/

265. Conversation with Professor Rachel Godsil, Perception Institute Co-Founder and Senior Research Advisor, November 13, 2025.
266. Tiana Walker, Melis Lydon, Brian Smedly and Taylor Nelson, *Research Suggests Implicit Bias Training Has Positive Impacts on Health Care Workers' Knowledge, Skills and Attitudes*, Urban Institute 14 (May 2025).
267. 476 U.S. at 474, n.5,
268. Clearing the Disability Backlog – Giving the Social Security Administration the Resources It Needs to Provide the Benefits Workers Have Earned: Hearing Before the H. Comm. on Ways and Means 229-30 (Apr. 23, 2008) (statement of Sylvester J. Scheiber, Chair, SSAB), www.ssab.gov/portals/0/documents/SchieberWaysandMeans042308.pdf (emphasis added).
269. *See* Sherrilyn Ifill, *Judicial Diversity*, 13 Green Bag 2d 45, 48 (2009).
270. *Id.* at 54; *see also* Sherrilyn Ifill, *Racial Diversity on the Bench: Beyond Role Models and Public Confidence*, 57 Wash. & Lee L. Rev. 405 (2000).
271. Melissa Breger, *Making the Invisible Visible: Exploring Implicit Bias, Judicial Diversity, and the Bench Trial*, 53 Rich. L. Rev. 1039, 1079 (2019) (citing Pat K. Chew and Robert E. Kelley, *The Realism of Race in Judicial Decision Making: An Empirical Analysis of Plaintiffs' Race and Judges' Race*, 28 Harv. J. on Racial and Ethnic Just. 91, 115 (2012)).
272. *See* American Bar Association, Profile of the Legal Profession, Ch. 5 (2023).
273. *See* Kate Berry, Building a Diverse Bench: Selecting Federal Magistrate and Bankruptcy Judges, Brennan Center for Justice (2017); Ciara Torres-Spelliscy, Monique Chase, and Emma Greenman, Improving Judicial Diversity, Brennan Center for Justice (2d Ed. 2010). Among all of the recommendations herein, this one likely would perhaps face the greatest immediate obstacles at present in light of President Trump's anti-diversity, equity and inclusion Executive Order and the DOJ's new anti-discrimination focus described in the Introduction above.
274. *See* Barry v. Bowen, 825 F.2d 1324,1327,1330 (9th Cir. 1987) ("When Bellmon Review was initiated, the SSA targeted for review those ALJs having an allowance rate of 66 $^2/_3$% or higher … Thus a program or policy that creates systemic, structural bias plainly falls outside the range of appropriate own motion review. Bellmon Review was such a program. Indeed, every court that has addressed the issue has concluded that the program did have this pernicious effect.") (collecting cases); Stieberger v. Heckler, 615 F.Supp. 1315, 1390-91 (S.D.N.Y. 1985) (the fact that claimants only appeal unfavorable decisions to the Appeals

Council dees not justify the one-sided Appeals Council own motion Bellmon review process of reviewing only approval decisions and of high approving ALJs' decisions as the latter conveys a far different message and *chilling effect* than routine, everyday claimant appeals).

275. *See* Kathleen Romig, *Trump Administration Action against Social Security Judges, supra* note 14.
276. Ass'n of Administrative Law Judges v. Colvin, 777 F. 2d 402, 403 (7th Cir. 2015).
277. *Id.* at 405–06.
278. *See* Kang, *Trojan Horses, supra* note 195, at 1498–1514.
279. *See* www.ssab.gov/about/

6 THE SPECIAL PROBLEM OF RACE-NORMING AND CORRECTION IN MEDICAL DIAGNOSTIC CLINICAL CARE TOOLS AND ALGORITHMS USED IN SOCIAL SECURITY DISABILITY ASSESSMENTS

1. Darshali A. Vyas et al., *Hidden in Plain Sight – Reconsidering the Use of Race Correction in Clinical Algorithms*, 383 The New England Journal of Medicine 874 (Aug. 27, 2020).
2. Joe Alper, Ronique Taffe, & Rose Marie Martinez, Examining the History, Consequences and Effects of Race-Based Clinical Algorithms on Health Equity, National Academies of Sciences. Engineering and Medicine 5 (2023).
3. Khiara M. Bridges, *Race in The Machine: Racial Disparities in Health and Medical AI*, 110 Va. L. Rev. 243, 286 (2024); *see also* Sonja Starr, *Statistical Discrimination*, 58 Harv. C.R.-C.L. L. Rev. 579, 636 (2023) (Noting that race norming or correction takes a racial disparity in a health indicator, (driven by other underlying racial disparities) and allows it to redefine what is 'normal for Black people."); *id.* (noting as an example, that with respect to respiratory impairments evaluated through race-corrected pulmonary tests from spirometry, "the medical foundation was always lacking" and "this reasoning overlooked many other reasons Black subjects might on average show reduced lung capacity such as environmental exposures during work or at home, 'inferior medical care [and] higher rates of infectious diseases,' nutritional differences, and the like."); *see generally* Vyas, et al., *Hidden in Plain Sight, supra* note 1, at 874–75 ("despite mounting evidence that race is not a proxy for genetic difference, it is has become embedded, somewhat insidiously within medical practice … Race adjustment 'is problematic because race is a social not a biological construct.'").
4. U.S. House Ways and Means Committee, Majority Staff Report, Fact Versus Fiction: Clinical Decision Support Tools and the (Mis)Use of Race 27 (Oct. 14, 2021).
5. Lundy Braun, Breathing Race into the Machine: The Surprising Career of the Spirometer from Plantation to Genetics (2014); *see* Meredith McCormack & David Kaminsky, *Beyond Diagnostics – Removing Race from Lung Function Test Interpretation*, 390 The New England Journal of Medicine 2122 (June 13, 2024); J.A. Diao et al., *Implications of Race Adjustment in Lung-Function Equations*, 390 The New England Journal of Medicine 2083, 2083 (June 13, 2024); Neil W. Schluger, *The Vanishing Rationale for the Race Adjustment in Pulmonary Function Test Interpretation*, 205 Am. J. Respiratory Critical Care Med. 612-(2022); Nicole Ramsey et al., *Deconstructing the Way We Use Pulmonary*

Function Test Race-Based Adjustments, 10 J. ALLERGY CLINICAL IMMUNOLOGY PRAC. 972 (2022).

6. Bessie A. Young, *Removal of Race from Estimation of Kidney Function*, 18 NATURE REV. NEPHROLOGY 201 (2022); Chi-yuan Hsu & Alan S. Go, *The Race Coefficient in Glomerular Filtration Rate-Estimating Equations and Its Removal*, 31 CURRENT OPINION IN NEPHROLOGY AND HYPERTENSION 527 (2022); Salman Ahmed et al., *Examining the Potential Impact of Race Multiplier Utilization in Estimated Glomerular Filtration Rate Calculation on African-American Care Outcomes*, 36 J. GEN. INTERNAL MED. 464, 466 (2020) (finding one-third of all Black patients with chronic kidney disease would be categorized with more severe disease if race norming were discontinued); Nwamaka D. Eneanya, et al., *Health Inequities and the Inappropriate Use of Race in Nephrology*, 18 NATURE REV. NEPHROLOGY 84 (2021); Cynthia Delgado et al., *Reassessing the Inclusion of Race in Diagnosing Kidney Diseases: An Interim Report from the NKF-ASN Task Force*, 32 J. AM. SOC'Y NEPHROLOGY 1305 (2021).
7. Michelle Fernandes et al., *Addressing Racial Inequities in Neuropsychological Assessment Requires International Prescriptive Standards, Not Demographically Adjusted Norms*, 18 NATURE REVIEWS: NEUROLOGY 377 (2022); Katherine L. Possin, Elena Tsoy, & Charles C. Windon, *Perils of Race-Based Norms in Cognitive Testing: The Case of Former NFL Players*, 78 JAMA NEUROL. 377, 377–78 (2021); NFL families seek to end "race-norming" in $1B settlement of brain injury claims, ABC News (May 14, 2021); Black NFL Players Call for End of Algorithm That Assumes Black Men Have Lower Cognitive Abilities, MKT. WATCH (May 14, 2021); Philip G. Gasquoine, *Race-Norming of Neuropsychological Tests*, 19 NEUROPSYCHOLOGY REV. 250 (2009); *see also* Michael L. Perlin, *"Your Corrupt Ways Had Finally Made You Blind": Prosecutorial Misconduct and the Use of "Ethnic Adjustments" in Death Penalty Cases of Defendants with Intellectual Disabilities*, 65 AM. U. L. REV. 1437 (2016).
8. *See*, e.g., Beza Merid & Vanessa Volpe, *Race Correction and Algorithmic Bias in Atrial Fibrillation Wearable Technologies*,7 HEALTH EQUITY 817 (2023); Vyas, et al., *Hidden in Plain Sight*, *supra* note 1, at 877 (noting that the American Heart Association's [AHA's] Heart Failure Risk Score algorithm, which predicts whether a patient who is admitted to the hospital is likely to die from heart failure and which clinicians use to guide referrals to cardiologists and allocation of healthcare resources, assigns non-Black patients three additional points, suggesting Black patients are at a lower risk of death. The AHA "does not provide a rationale for this adjustment" (citing Pamela Petersen et al., A *Validated Risk Score for In-Hospital Mortality in Patients with Heart Failure from the American Heart Association Get with the Guidelines Program*, 3 CIRCULATION: CARDIOVASCULAR QUALITY AND OUTCOMES 25–32 (2010)).
9. *See*, e.g., Sherri Ann M. Burnett-Bowie et al., *The American Society for Bone and Mineral Research Task Force on Clinical Algorithms for Fracture Risk Report*, 39 JOURNAL OF BONE AND MINERAL RESEARCH 517, 517 (Apr. 9, 2024) ("Using race or ethnicity when calculating disease risk may contribute to health disparities … While acknowledging the existence of racial and ethnic differences in fracture epidemiology, the Task Force determined that currently there is limited evidence to support the use of race and ethnicity–specific adjustments in US-FRAX."); *see also* Laura Yeckles, *Addressing Disparities in Osteoporosis Care and Outcomes for Black Americans*, OSTEOBOOST (Feb 18, 2025) ("Bias in Risk Assessment Tools: Many osteoporosis screening tools, such as the Fracture Risk Assessment Tool (FRAX), use race as a factor. However, these tools may underestimate the fracture risk for Black individuals, leading to fewer referrals for BMD [bone mineral density] testing and treatment.")

10. *See, e.g.*, Ayisha Buckley et al., *Racial and Ethnic Disparities among Women Undergoing a Trial of Labor after Cesarean Delivery: Performance of the VBAC Calculator with and without Patients' Ethnicity*, 29 REPROD. SCI. 2030 (2022).
11. Sonja Starr, *Statistical Discrimination*, 58 HARV. C.R.-C.L. L. REV. 579, 632 (2023) (emphasis added).
12. J.A. Diao et al., *Implications of Race Adjustment, supra* note 5, at 2083 (emphasis added); *see also* McCormack & Kaminsky, *Beyond Diagnostics, supra* note 5, at 2122 (The data sets, replacing race normed pulmonary equations with the race neutral GLI resulted in "Black persons classified as having restrictive disease and more severe [chronic obstructive pulmonary disease] and *more eligible for disability payments* and lung transportation.").
13. BRAUN, *supra* note 5, at 27–28.
14. *Id.* at 3–4.
15. Andrew Kouri et al., *Exploring the 175-year History of Spirometry and the Vital Lessons It Can Teach Us Today*, 30 EUR. RESPIR. REV. 1, 2 (2021).
16. BRAUN, *supra* note 5, at 28–29 (emphasis added).
17. Heidi L. Lujan & Stephen E. DiCarlo, *Science Reflects History as Society Influences Science: Brief History of "Race," "Race Correction," and the Spirometer*, 42 ADVANCES IN PHYSIOLOGICAL EDUC. 163, 164 (Feb. 9, 2018).
18. BRAUN, *supra* note 5, at xiii–xv.
19. *Id.* at xv.
20. *See*, e.g., Erin Texeira, Racial Basis for Asbestos Lawsuits? Owens Corning Seeks More Stringent Standard for Blacks, BALTIMORE SUN, (Mar. 25, 1999); Jim Fite & Paul Safchuck, *Will the Asbestos Companies Ever Learn*, BALTIMORE SUN (Mar. 27, 1999).
21. BRAUN, *supra* note 5, at xiv–xv; *see, e.g., Owens Corning Fails to Block Some Blacks from Asbestos Suit*, L.A. TIMES (Mar. 26, 1999).
22. Vyas, *Hidden in Plain Sight, supra* note 1, at 878.
23. JOE ALPER, *supra* note 2, at 14–15. There are multiple "spirometric measures of lung function, the most common being forced vital capacity (FVC), which refers to the volume of air expired after maximal inspiration, and forced expiratory volumes in one second (FEV1) which measure timed air flow." BRAUN, *supra* note 5, at 207, n.3. The SSA uses these measures in its criteria for automatic medical disability based on respiratory impairments at 20 C.F.R, Pt. 404, Subpt P., Appendix 1, Listing 3.00, et seq.
24. *Id.*
25. The name and other identifiers have been removed from this chart and PFTs for confidentiality purposes. The patient/disability claimant was a client of the author's free law school clinical program and was represented in the US District Court by third-year law students of the Rutgers Economic Justice and Public Benefits Clinic under the author's supervision.
26. The corresponding pulmonary function listing for children in the SSI children's program is at Listing 103.02(A), 20 C.F.R., Pt 404, Subpart P, Appendix 1.
27. The recent American Thoracic Society (ATS) Official Statement also points out that "State disability offices are known to use race-specific equations or adjustments in PFT interpretation" Niray R. Bhakta et al., *Race and Ethnicity in Pulmonary Function Test Interpretation: An Official American Thoracic Society Statement*, 207 AMERICAN JOURNAL OF RESPIRATORY AND CRITICAL CARE MEDICINE 978, 986 (Apr. 2023). PFTs are typically ordered by the state DDS in SSA disability cases and the state DDS evaluates the PFTs provided from whatever source in any event at the initial and reconsideration stages of SSA disability cases as described in Chapter 5. Although the ATS suggests that the SSA "only uses one PFT measure" in contrast to "the NHANES III race-specific equations," *id.* at 987, the only citation for that conclusion is to the SSA's listing 3.00 in 20 CFR, pt 404, and that listing regulation

does not mention any such restriction or otherwise support any implied conclusion of restrictions on the prevalent race-normed PFT practices. *See id.* at n. 95, p.994 (citing SSA's website reproducing that regulation). Indeed, the second PFT of the disability claimant in the sample chart from an actual recent (2021) SSA disability benefits appeal, supplied herein, states "NHANES III" on the test as well as "African" for the claimant. Moreover, unlike SSA's recent action in prospectively moving away from ordering or relying upon race-normed kidney function tests (eGFR) as explained in available SSA sub-regulatory guidance in POMS DI 24555.005.B.2 (Aug. 23, 2022) and discussed later, it has issued no similar guidance changing or otherwise describing its policy on respiratory impairments and/or any restrictions on the pervasive and well-established use of race-normed PFTs. *Cf.* POMS DI 34001.014 Respiratory Disorders (Oct. 7, 2016).

28. *See generally* Estimated Glomerular Filtration Rate (eGFR), National Kidney Foundation, (July 13, 2022), www.kidney.org/kidney-topics/estimated-glomerular-filtration-rate-egfr (describing eGFR and kidney function basics).
29. *See* Fernandino L. Vilson et al., *Removing Race from eGFR Calculations: Implications for Urologic Care*, 162 UROLOGY 42, 42–48 (Apr. 2022).
30. *Id.*
31. *Id.*
32. Juyhoun Han, Jennifer Tsai, & Rohan Khazanchi, *Medical Algorithms Lack Compassion: How Race-Based Medicine Impacted the Rights of Individuals Seeking Compassionate Release during COVID-19*, 26 STAN. TECH. L. REV. 49, 56 (2023) (quoting MDRH study authors, Andrew S. Levey, et al., *A More Accurate Method to Estimate Glomerular Filtration Rates from Serum Creatinine, A New Prediction Equation*, 130 ANNALS INTERNAL MED. 461, 464 (1999)).
33. ALPER, ET AL., NASEM REPORT *supra* note 2, at 12 (citation omitted).
34. *See* Jarvis Deberry, *Chris Rock Should Have Focused on Will Smith. But He Couldn't Help Himself*, MSNBC (Mar. 6, 2023).
35. Dorothy Roberts, *The Problem with Race-Based Medicine*, TEDMED Talk (Nov. 2015), www.youtube.com/watch?v=KxLMjn4WPBY
36. The corresponding kidney function listing for children in the SSI children's program is at Listing 103.02, 20 C.F.R., Pt 404, Subpart P, Appendix 1.
37. Social Security Administration, POMS DI 24555.005B.2 (Aug. 23, 2022) (emphasis in bold in original), https://secure.ssa.gov/poms.nsf/%20lnx/0424555005
38. Charles T. Hall, *Social Security Changed One of Its Listings But Kept It Secret*, SOCIAL SECURITY NEWS (June 21, 2022) (emphasis added), https://socsecnews.blogspot.com/search?q=kidney+function+race
39. *See* note 7 *supra* (and authorities collected therein). Chronic traumatic encephalopathy (CTE) is a progressive neurodegenerative disease caused by repeated head injuries, such as concussions and blows to the head. *See* Chronic Traumatic Encephalopathy (CTE), MAYO CLINIC, www.mayoclinic.org › syc-20370921
40. Katherine L. Possin, Elena Tsoy, & Charles C. Windon, *Perils of Race-Based Norms in Cognitive Testing: The Case of Former NFL Players*, 78 JAMA NEUROL. 377, 377 (2021).
41. *Id.*
42. Katherine L. Possin, Elena Tsoy, & Charles C. Windon, Perils of Race-Based Norms in Cognitive Testing: The Case of Former NFL Players, 78 JAMA NEUROL. 377, 377–378 (2021).
43. *Id.*
44. Darshali A. Vyas, Leo Eisenstein, & David Jones, *The Race Correction Debates – Progress, Tensions, and Future Directions*, 393 New England Journal of Medicine 1029, 1030 (Sept. 11, 2025).

45. Possin, *supra* note 42, at 377.
46. *Id.*
47. Starr, *supra* note 11, at 632. (emphasis added).
48. Vyas, et al., *The Race Correction Debates, supra* note 44, at 1030.
49. Vyas, et al., *Hidden in Plain Sight, supra* note 1, at 874.
50. *See* Vyas, et al., *The Race Correction Debates, supra* note 44, at 1032.
51. *See* Vyas, et al., *Hidden in Plain Sight,* (2020) *supra* note 1, at 874–82.
52. Darshali A. Vyas, Leo Eisenstein, & David Jones, *The Race Correction Debates – Progress, Tensions, and Future Directions,* 393 New England Journal of Medicine 1029, 1029 (Sept. 11, 2025).
53. *Id.*
54. *Id.*
55. Christina Amutah et al., *Misrepresenting Race – The Role of Medical Schools in Propagating Physician Bias,* 384 New Eng. J. Med. 872, 873–74 (2021); *see also* Bridges, *Race in the Machine,* at 251 ("most medical schools still approach race as a genetic fact instead of a social construction, with the result being that most physicians in the United States have not been disabused of the notion that people of color – black people, specifically – possess genes and genetic variations that make them get sicker and die earlier than their white counterparts.").
56. Amutah, *supra* note 55, at 875.
57. *See* Bridget Batch, *Confronting Race in Diagnosis: Medical Students Call for Reexamining How Kidney Function is Estimated,* [Association of American Medical Colleges], AAMCNews (Sept. 24, 2020) ("for 21 years, physicians have corrected for race in a formula that estimates kidney function. Students are increasingly questioning why, especially since kidney failure disproportionately impacts Black patients.").
58. Versha Pleasant, Alesha Kotian, Mayam Hammoud, & Rosalyn Maben-Feaster, *The Importance of Discussing the History of Racism in Medical Student Education,* 67 Clinical Obstetrics & Gynecology 499, 501 (Sept. 2024).
59. *Id.* A group of medical and public health students at University of California (UC) at Berkeley and at UC San Francisco, published a lengthy policy brief and report in 2020 seeking the abolition of biological race in medicine and medical education and explained their motivation for the report in the preamble:

    - In our textbooks, we are taught that race can serve as a risk factor for disease. Yet we know that race is a social construct, not a biological risk factor.
    - In clinical research, we are told that disparities in disease among Black and brown communities are due to culturally determined individual behaviors. Yet we know that structural barriers to food and stress-free lives, as well as targeted discrimination, prevent many people of color from achieving health and well-being.
    - In clinical practice, we are mentored by clinicians who blindly follow guidelines that instruct them to prescribe based on race rather than overall effectiveness. Yet we know that these guidelines are built on a deep history of biological racism and othering within medicine and health care.
    - We have found these scenarios to be commonplace and largely unchallenged throughout our medical education and training. Racist, outdated notions are taught in clinical education, solidified in research and perpetuated in practice. We are astounded, outraged, and driven to make a call to action.

    Noor Chadha, Bernadette Lim, Madeline Kane, & Brenley Rowland, Toward the Abolition of Biological Race in Medicine: Transforming

CLINICAL EDUCATION, RESEARCH AND PRACTICE. INSTITUTE FOR HEALING & JUSTICE IN MEDICINE 1 (2020).

60. Vyas, et al., *The Race Correction Debates, supra* note 44, at 1029.
61. *Id*. at 1030.
62. *Id*. at 1032; *see also* Cynthia Delgado et al., A *Unifying Approach for GFR Estimation: Recommendations of the NKF-ASN Task Force on Reassessing the Inclusion of Race in Diagnosing Kidney Disease*, 79 AMERICAN JOURNAL OF KIDNEY DISEASES 268, 269 ("The Task Force recommends immediate implementation of the Chronic Kidney Disease Epidemiology Collaboration creatinine equation refit without the race variable in all laboratories because the calculation does not include race, it included diversity in its development, its potential adverse consequences do not disproportionately affect any one group, and it is immediately available to all laboratories.").
63. Vyas, et al., *The Race Correction Debates, supra* note 44, at 1032; *see also* Starr, *supra* note 11, at 638 (positing in 2023 that because a race normed kidney function algorithm still "is used in countless labs throughout the country, the shift away from it will not be quick and will require 'sustained advocacy.'").
64. *Id*. at 1033; *see also* Niray R. Bhakta et al., *Race and Ethnicity in Pulmonary Function Test Interpretation: An Official American Thoracic Society Statement*, 207 AMERICAN JOURNAL OF RESPIRATORY AND CRITICAL CARE MEDICINE 978, 979 (Apr. 2023) (noting that "[c]urrent American Thoracic Society (ATS) standards promote the use of race and ethnicity-specific reference equations for pulmonary function test (PFT) interpretation" and recommending that "PFT laboratories should adopt a race-neutral approach to PFT interpretation.").
65. Vyas, et al., *The Race Correction Debates, supra* note 44, at 1033.
66. *Id*. at 1032–33.
67. Starr *supra* note 11, at 633 (citing and quoting POSITION STATEMENT ON THE USE OF RACE NEUROPSYCHOLOGICAL TEST NORMING AND PERFORMANCE PREDICTION, AMERICAN ACADEMY ON CLINICAL NEUROPSYCHOLOGY (Nov. 2021), https://theaacn.org/wp-content/uploads/2021/11/AACN-Position-Statement-on-Race-Norms.pdf
68. Vyas, et al., *The Race Correction Debates, supra* note 44, at 1032.
69. *Id*. at 1033.
70. Congressman Richard E. Neal, Ranking Member, U.S. House Ways and Means Committee. Press Release, *New Ways and Means Report Probes the Misuse of Race in Clinical Algorithms* (Oct. 14. 2021); *see* note 4 *supra* (summarizing the report's conclusions).
71. Letter from Senators Elizabeth Warren, Cory Booker Ron Wyden and Representative Barbara Lee to Gopal Khanna, Director, Agency for Healthcare Research and Quality, September 22, 2020. (on file with author).
72. *See* 89 Fed. Reg. 37701 (May 6, 2024).
73. 89 Fed. Reg. 87643-44 (May 6, 2024). An Artificial Intelligence Task Force of the National Academy of Social Insurance, recently cautioned against the use of algorithms powered by artificial intelligence "[i]n the case of evaluating applications for disability benefits [because] the range of potential areas of bias is extensive." TASK FORCE ON ARTIFICIAL INTELLIGENCE, EMERGING TECHNOLOGY AND DISABILITY BENEFITS, PHASE ONE REPORT, NATIONAL ACADEMY OF SOCIAL INSURANCE 8 (Apr. 2025). The report explained:

> AI Tools are informed by and learn from large data sets but these data sets can reflect underlying biases in the data, such as the sample used for the data set does not appropriately represent the entire population … Algorithms are built by humans. They are trained on data generated by humans. Humans discriminate, and so the algorithms they construct can do so as well. Understanding existing levels of

> discrimination – both implicit and explicit – based on race, gender, class and ability, is critical to understanding how AI may perpetuate bias.

Id.

74. *Id.* at 87644.
75. *See generally* Social Security Administration, *Disability Determination Process*, ssa.gov/disability/determination.htm ("The DDSs, which are fully funded by the Federal Government, are State agencies responsible for developing medical evidence and making the initial determination on whether or not a claimant is disabled or blind under the law.").
76. Students for Fair Admissions, Inc. v. President & Fellows of Harvard Coll., 600 U.S. 181, 206-07 (2023).
77. Starr, *supra* note 11, at 647; *see also* Ruquaiijah Yearby, *Transcript: Structural Racism, the Healthcare System and Health Justice*, 38 J.L. & HEALTH 21, 24 (2024) (arguing that "race-based medical standards … should be prohibited by law" namely "Title VI and the 14th Amendment's guaranty [of] equal treatment and access to health care," and "there are numerous examples of how race has been used as an explicit 'correction factor' to guide clinical decision-making in cardiology, cardiac surgery, nephrology, obstetrics, urology, oncology, endocrinology and pulmonology."); Han et al., *supra* note 32, at 75–76 (arguing that use of the race-normed eGFR for kidney impairment severity evaluation and resulting diminished opportunity for Black inmates to obtain compassionate release from prison, violates the equal protection clause).
78. Schweiker v. Hansen, 450 U.S. 785, 789 (1981).
79. *See* City of New York v. Heckler, 578 F. Supp. 1109, 1125 (E.D.N.Y. 1984), *aff'd*, City of New York v. Heckler, 742 F.2d 729 (2d Cir.), *aff'd sub. nom.*, Bowen v. City of New York, 476 U.S. 467 (1986). ("The Secretary's illegal policy has affected all class members who have been denied, or terminated from, benefits. As was conceded by defendants' own witness, administrative law judges routinely give great weight to the finding on residual functional capacity which is entered in the record by the state agency's internal review physician. Had the administrative law judges known that the assessment of residual functional capacity was not based on the doctor's professional opinion, the results in many cases might well have been different. The decisions denying benefits or terminating benefits must be reopened and determined by the Secretary using proper standards. The usual administrative appeal rights will follow. In the interim the Secretary will, from the date of this order, reinstate benefits of all class members until the claimant's eligibility is properly determined by the Secretary. No retroactive benefits will be awarded until the Secretary determines whether or not the initial denial was correct.").

CONCLUSION

1. Dr. Martin Luther King Jr., REMAINING AWAKE THROUGH A GREAT REVOLUTION. Speech given at the National Cathedral, Mar. 31, 1968. https://blog.library.si.edu/blog/2015/01/19/the-arc-of-the-moral-universe/

Index

Page numbers followed by "n" denote endnotes.

For EU product safety concerns, contact us at Calle de José Abascal, 56–1°,
28003 Madrid, Spain or eugpsr@cambridge.org.

www.ingramcontent.com/pod-product-compliance
Ingram Content Group UK Ltd.
Pitfield, Milton Keynes, MK11 3LW, UK
UKHW020840290926
15470UKWH00004B/1465

* 9 7 8 1 0 0 9 8 5 8 9 9 1 *